Strategic Litigation and Corporate Complicity in Crimes Under International Law

This book provides a comprehensive account of how non-state actors use international criminal law as a tool in the service of progressive political causes.

The critique that international criminal law and its institutions serve as an instrument in the hands of a few powerful states, and that its practice is characterized by double standards and selectivity, has received considerable attention. This book, however, focuses on an emerging practice of international criminal law that is informed by this critique. Using the framework of Third World Approaches to International Law, the book foregrounds the practice of non-state actors who navigate what critical scholars call a structurally biased legal system in order to achieve long-term political objectives. Innovatively, the book combines the concerns of Third World Approaches to International Law scholarship with strategic litigation that focuses on the accountability of corporations for their complicity in crimes under international law. Drawing on specific case studies, the book demonstrates that, while it is crucial to highlight the blind spots of the international criminal legal framework, it is also important to take into account the practice of non-state actors engaged in leveraging its emancipatory potential.

This original analysis of the implementation and legitimacy of international criminal law will be of interest to a wide range of scholars and activists working in relevant areas of law, politics, criminology, and international relations.

Kalika Mehta is a Postdoctoral Researcher at Humboldt University, Berlin.

Strategic Litigation and Corporate Complicity in Crimes Under International Law

A TWAIL Analysis

Kalika Mehta

Routledge
Taylor & Francis Group
a GlassHouse Book

First published 2024
by Routledge
4 Park Square, Milton Park, Abingdon, Oxon OX14 4RN

and by Routledge
605 Third Avenue, New York, NY 10158

Routledge is an imprint of the Taylor & Francis Group, an informa business

a GlassHouse book

British Library Cataloguing-in-Publication Data
A catalogue record for this book is available from the British Library

ISBN: 978-1-032-52064-3 (hbk)
ISBN: 978-1-032-52065-0 (pbk)
ISBN: 978-1-003-40504-7 (ebk)

DOI: 10.4324/9781003405047

Typeset in Sabon
by Deanta Global Publishing Services, Chennai, India

To my parents

Contents

List of Abbreviations

ATS	Alien Tort Statute
CCL No. 10	Control Council No. 10, Official Gazette of the Control Council for Germany No. 3, 31 January 1946, 50 et seq
CCR	Center for Constitutional Rights, New York
CELS	*Centro de Estudios Legales y Sociales,* Buenos Aires
CONADEP	*La Comisión Nacional Sobre la Desaparición de Personas* (National Commission on Disappeared Persons, Argentina)
ECCHR	European Center for Constitutional and Human Rights, Berlin
ECtHR	European Court of Human Rights
IACHR	Inter-American Commission on Human Rights
IACtHR	Inter-American Court of Human Rights
ICC	International Criminal Court
ICC Statute	Rome Statute of the International Criminal Court of 17 July 1998
ICJ	International Court of Justice
ICTR	International Criminal Tribunal for Rwanda
ICTY	International Criminal Tribunal for the former Yugoslavia
IECL	International Economic Criminal Law
ILC	International Law Commission
IMT	International Military Tribunal, Nuremberg
IMTFE	International Military Tribunal for the Far East, Tokyo
IS/ISIS	Islamic State or Islamic State of Iraq and Syria
MTJ	memory, truth, and justice
NGO	non-governmental organization
OTP	Office of the Prosecutor (International Criminal Court)
PMC	private military contractors
STL	Special Tribunal for Lebanon
TWAI(C)L	Third World Approaches to International Criminal Law
TWAIL	Third World Approaches to International Law
UNSC	United Nations Security Council

Acknowledgements

This book is based on my doctoral dissertation which was defended at the University of Hamburg, Germany, in September 2022. In this process, I have accumulated a series of debts of gratitude that I can only partially address here. First and foremost, I am immensely grateful to my supervisor Prof Dr Florian Jeßberger for his relentless encouragement and support. His guidance, a balanced combination of attention to detail and the bigger picture, has been a great source of learning and inspiration. I am thankful to Prof Dr Jochen Bung for his kind and positive second review of my dissertation. I am also grateful to Prof Dr Leonie Steinl for the early discussions that helped to narrow down two of the three key aspects of the book: strategic litigation and corporate accountability, followed by her consistent willingness to help throughout the process.

I would like to thank the following practitioners and experts who took time out of their busy schedules for an interview and provided crucial insights for this research: Katherine Gallagher (CCR), Shereef Akeel, Diego Morales (CELS), Tomás Ignacio Griffa (CELS), Prof Dr Gabriel Pereira, Claire Tixeire (ECCHR), and Cannelle Lavite (ECCHR). Also, many thanks to Mohammad for sharing his account and perspective on one of the cases. I am also very grateful to Andreas Schüller for his instrumental support at the beginning of this journey.

I would also like to thank the Directors of Albrecht Mendelssohn Bartholdy Graduate School of Law (AMBSL) for not only providing a well-structured space for this research but also for making this work financially possible. Many thanks to Christiane Andresen and Dr Ülkü Sezgi Sözen for all the administrative support at the university.

On a more personal note, I would like to thank Gretel Mejía Bonifazi and Avantika Tiwari for reviewing parts of the book. I am also grateful to Inga Schuchmann for her support on all the good and bad days of the writing phase. I am very thankful to Michael Eber for his patience and unceasing support in the last stages of the process. Gratitude is also due to Shelly Mittal, Abishek Choutagunta, Kelly Dhru, Nawaz Brohi, Alina Dinu, and Diksha Rai.

Finally, I am particularly thankful to the reviewers for their constructive suggestions that helped me improve the book. Many thanks to Colin Perrin and Naomi Round Cahalin at Routledge for making the publication of this book such a smooth process. Of course, all errors in style and substance remain my own.

Introduction

The words 'global justice', 'humanity', and 'international community' are recurring punctuations in a discussion on international criminal law which attributes individual responsibility for the most serious violations of international law. These universalist ideals proffered by international criminal law are frequently challenged for its unequal and selective application by governments and scholars alike. The implementation of international criminal law has been subject to multi-fold critiques, inter alia, on account of victor's justice,[1] double standards,[2] selectivity,[3] Eurocentricity,[4] and legitimacy deficits.[5] This has rightly led scholars to observe that the international criminal justice framework is built on structures of racial, imperial, economic, and gender-based domination and subordination. However, at the same time, a set of scholars also insist that public international law in general and international criminal law in particular can also be a platform to make counter-hegemonic claims. This book is situated precisely in the paradox of these convincing contradictory contentions.

1 Ronen Steinke, *The Politics of International Criminal Justice: German Perspectives from Nuremberg to The Hague* (Bloomsbury Publishing 2012); Florian Jeßberger, 'Die Krisen des Völkerstrafrechts' in *Festschrift für Gerhard Werle* (Mohr Siebeck 2022).

2 Makau Mutua, 'What Is TWAIL' (2000) 94 Proceedings of the Annual Meeting (American Society of International Law) 31.

3 Asad Kiyani, 'Group-Based Differentiation and Local Repression: The Custom and Curse of Selectivity' (2016) 14 Journal of International Criminal Justice 4, 939–957.

4 Obiora C. Okafor and Uchechukwu Ngwaba, 'The International Criminal Court as a "Transitional Justice" Mechanism in Africa: Some Critical Reflections' (2015) 9 International Journal of Transitional Justice 90; Kamari Clarke, *Fictions of Justice: The International Criminal Court and the Challenge of Legal Pluralism in Sub-Saharan Africa* (Cambridge University Press 2009).

5 Asad Kiyani, 'The Antinomies of Legitimacy: On the (Im-)possibility of a Legitimate International Criminal Court' (2015) African Journal of Legal Studies 8 (1–2); Mirjan Damaska, 'What Is the Point of International Criminal Justice' (2008) Chi-Kent Law Review 83: 329–368.

DOI: 10.4324/9781003405047-1

The practice of international criminal law is mainly driven by states,[6] if not only a few Western states, and its resulting problems have gained considerable attention in critical scholarship. Yet, this book is an attempt to underscore that a practice that is informed by these critiques is also parallelly brewing on the margins. The book enunciates this alternative practice of international criminal law where non-state actors navigate the structurally biased international legal system in furtherance of progressive social and political aims.

This enunciation takes place by way of an interaction between three distinct elements: first, the critique of international (criminal) law stemming from the scholarly movement of Third World Approaches to International Law (TWAIL); second, the accountability gap regarding corporate complicity in crimes under international law; third, the practice of strategic litigation that is informed by the first (TWAIL critique) and seeks to address the second (the accountability gap).

Throughout the book, the TWAIL scholarship[7] serves as an analytical framework for the underexamined practice of strategic litigation seeking accountability of corporations for their involvement in crimes under international law.

TWAIL is a body of work produced by a decentralized unorganized network of scholars countering the mainstream narrative of international law while interjecting it with the concerns of the Third World peoples. B.S. Chimni describes TWAIL as 'a loose network of Third World scholars who articulate a critique of the history, structure, and process of contemporary international law from the standpoint of Third World peoples, in particular its marginal and oppressed groups'.[8] It has evolved over time and as it stands now, TWAIL does not restrict itself to the binary of the colonizer state as the oppressor and the entire formerly colonized Third World as the subordinate. This scholarship also makes a distinction between the post-colonial Third World state and the Third World peoples, and it is the latter whose concerns drive the scholarly movement. The label of 'Third World' might appear a bit dated, but it is understood as a political grouping rather than an

6 See Gerry Simpson, *Law, War and Crime: War Crimes Trials and the Reinvention of International Law* (Polity Press 2007).

7 For a general discussion on TWAIL, see B. S. Chimni, 'The Past, Present and Future of International Law: A Critical Third World Approach' (2007) 8 Melbourne Journal of International Law 2, 499–515; Karin Mickelson, 'Taking Stock of TWAIL Histories'(2008) 10 International Community Law Review 4, 355–362; Obiora Okafor, 'Critical Third World Approaches to International Law (TWAIL): Theory, Methodology, or Both?' (2008) 10 International Community Law Review 4, 371–378; Antony Anghie, 'TWAIL: Past and Future' (2008) 10 International Communities Law Review 4, 479–481; James T. Gathii, 'TWAIL: A Brief History of Its Origins, Its Decentralized Network, and a Tentative Bibliography' (2011) 3 Trade, Law and Development 1, 26–64.

8 B. S. Chimni, *International Law and World Order: A Critique of Contemporary Approaches* (Cambridge University Press 2017) 15.

ostensibly 'objective demographic or economic coalition'[9] that attempts to make a 'common set of concerns heard'.[10]

Very broadly, TWAIL challenges the Eurocentricity of international law and argues that it is the handmaiden of colonialism and imperialism, and built on racial hierarchies and double standards.[11] Traditionally, the TWAIL scholarship gained ground as analytical critique but it has also taken up a reformist normative agenda overtime. TWAIL scholars critique the existing international legal order but at the same time insist on it being an instrument to strive towards a more equitable global order.

For the purposes of this book, the multifaceted nature of TWAIL scholarship and its overarching critiques of international law have been narrowed down to pinpoint some of its central concerns relevant to international criminal law. In the spirit of viewing international criminal law – a discipline that claims to protect the most marginalized – as an instrument to strive for change, this book enumerates four central concerns of Third World Approaches to International (Criminal) Law (TWAI(C)L). These four concerns are as follows: one, reform-oriented critique (that suggests a normative-activistic critical approach towards international criminal law and foregrounds the question of reform); two, relativizing universality (that emphasizes on pluralism and relative application of the so-called universal norms in various domestic jurisdictions); three, de-privileging the state (challenging the privilege of states as the sole law-making authority, particularly in so far as state practice forms an important element of customary international law); and four, addressing material inequality (addressing the power of international criminal law to maintain and advance unequal economic structures). These concerns form the foundation for the ensuing analysis of practice of strategic litigation.

Admittedly, TWAIL itself carries some blind spots[12] but for this book the critique arising from the broad rubric of TWAIL served as a coherent analytical framework for the practice of strategic litigation. With these identified TWAI(C)L concerns, the book adds to the expanding body of TWAIL scholarship engaging with international criminal law. While the other works

9 Sundhya Pahuja, 'A note on the use of 'Third World'' in *Decolonising International Law: Development, Economic Growth and the Politics of Universality* (Cambridge University Press 2011) 261–262; Vijay Prashad, *The Darker Nations: A Biography of the Short-lived Third World* (Leftword Books 2007).

10 Karin Mickelson, 'Rhetoric and Rage: Third World Voices in International Legal Discourse' (1998) 16 Wisconsin International Law Journal 353, 360 (hereinafter Mickelson, 'Rhetoric and Rage').

11 Makau Mutua, 'What Is TWAIL' (2000) 94 Proceedings of the Annual Meeting (American Society of International Law) 31.

12 See for example, Mickelson, 'Rhetoric and Rage' (n 10); Mohsen al Attar, 'TWAIL: A Paradox Within a Paradox' (2020) 22 International Community Law Review 163; Ishita Chakrabarty, and Guneet Kaur, 'Double Whammy: Targeted Minorities in South-Asian States' in Florian Jeßberger and others (eds), *International Criminal Law: A Counter-Hegemonic Project?* (TMC Asser Press 2022) 87–110.

mainly reflect on the institutions and conceptual aspects of international criminal law, this book brings to the fore novel actors in the practice of international law: non-governmental organizations pursuing strategic litigation.

Strategic litigation has become a catchphrase in the practice of international human rights and criminal law. Such frequent use of the label, however, implies a deceptively broad scope and diverts attention from a productive discussion on the politics of practising international law. Moreover, such characterization undercuts the sincere attempts that are being made to seek reforms and address structural problems within the legal framework.

This book conceptualizes the practice of strategic litigation as legal interventions that are made in pursuit of long-term structural goals. Where court victory is not an end in itself, or perhaps, not even one of the primary goals, these legal interventions are brought forth with an acute understanding of the flaws of the existing legal order. Strategic litigation is carried out in acknowledgement of the inherent defects of the international legal system and in the process, seeks to highlight, if not undermine, the structures that create and sustain them. This engagement of law is contextual and aware of the social, political, and economic realities of a given case of atrocity crimes. Strategic legal interventions are not made in pursuit of a disjointed idea of justice but are situated within the social movements that drive the cause.

As a starting point of the research that led to the concrete examples of strategic litigation discussed in this book, a wider net was cast on victim groups and non-governmental organizations who have brought legal interventions to secure accountability of corporations while explicitly invoking international criminal law. This ensured that these actors were at least, to a certain degree, familiar with one manifestation of selectivity in international criminal law, i.e. the lack of accountability for corporate conduct amounting to crimes under international law.

There is a clear gap in the law with respect to corporations and their complicity in crimes under international criminal law. This is despite the fact that corporations, in many cases, end up playing a significant role in large-scale violence and atrocity crimes either by enabling the perpetrator(s) or by aiding and abetting serious violations of international law. Yet international criminal law does not recognize the liability of corporations as perpetrators of crimes under international law. Corporations have never been prosecuted by an international court/tribunal for their involvement in core crimes such as war crimes, crimes against humanity, and genocide. The International Criminal Court (ICC) does not exercise jurisdiction over legal persons, including corporations, thereby resulting in an accountability gap.

However, individuals acting on behalf of the corporation may be held responsible for their conduct. But this narrow conception of responsibility leaves the institutions and complex structures that caused or enabled the violence outside the brackets of justice. The principle of individual criminal responsibility de-contextualizes large-scale violence, it creates an enemy and leaves the structures that enabled the enemy invisible. In principle, the individuals may be held accountable but the structures that sustained them tend to continue without any form of punishment, if not as their more resourceful and strengthened versions. Such impunity of enabling institutions risks continuation of similar structures of exploitation and violence, particularly in post-conflict or transitional justice contexts.[13]

In view of the current global economic order and the way in which transnational corporate groups are structured, a disregard for corporate accountability is another manifestation of geopolitical selectivity in international criminal law. It is not uncommon that operations of corporations headquartered in 'the West', while conducting businesses in the 'Third World', end up contributing to crimes under international law taking place in their host countries. In that case, an exclusive focus on direct perpetrators robs the situation of its complexity and nuance. This conception further feeds into the trope that such violence is a problem exclusive to the 'Third World' and the stakeholders from the 'the West' remain far removed from it.

This book relies on historical research to foreground the claim that this accountability gap in international criminal law vis-à-vis corporations exists not because of legal reasons but for reasons of political willingness and pragmatic considerations of few states.

At the same time, it must be acknowledged that the lack of international avenues to pursue corporate accountability has not automatically translated into absence of attempts to hold corporations accountable for crimes under international law. These attempts often manifest in the form of innovative transnational litigation before domestic courts which form the thematic focus of this book.

By pulling these three distinct unsettled and unsettling strands together–strategic litigation, corporate complicity in crimes under international law, and TWAIL–the book exemplifies that international criminal law is not only a site of domination and subordination but is also being employed as a platform for resistance and liberation. The discussion is substantiated by three detailed cases of how civil society organizations have sought corporate accountability for their complicity in large-scale human rights violations before domestic courts. As evident from the discussion on accountability gap, the decision to limit the case studies to domestic courts was not borne out of choice but compulsion to mirror the state of existing practice. In furtherance of this representative spirit, the book also adopts a broad notion of accountability that includes individual as well as collective liability sought through civil and criminal law proceedings in various domestic jurisdictions.

13 See generally Vasuki Nesiah, 'The Trials of History: Losing Justice in the Monstrous and the Banal' Law in Ruth Buchanan and Peer Zumbansen (eds), *Transition: Human Rights, Development and Transitional Justice* (Bloomsbury Publishing 2014) 289–308.

The analysis of strategic litigation practice is carried out through a qualitative multiple-case-study method. Three distinct case studies in the book serve to represent different kinds of cases initiated by strategic litigation organizations against corporations and corporate executives for their involvement in crimes under international law.

The case studies were selected after a preliminary enquiry of the universe of litigations which met the following criteria: initiated by non-state actors or victim groups; against corporations for serious violations of international law; directly or indirectly relying on international criminal law. This pilot case-mapping exercise produced a list of 38 such cases initiated between 2001 and 2022 before domestic courts (see Annexure for the full list). The case-mapping revealed that norms derived from international criminal law are being invoked before criminal courts and tribunals as well as in tort proceedings and before constitutional courts in different domestic jurisdictions. This list of cases was then indexed, labelled, and categorized based on the nature of alleged crimes, the jurisdiction where the litigation was brought, the countries where the crimes took place, and the organizations that initiated these litigations.

This larger universe of 38 litigations in 13 different jurisdictions revealed a trend that most cases could be evenly grouped into three broad categories: one, civil proceedings under the Alien Tort Statute in the United States; two, trials for business accountability held in a transitional justice context, mainly in Latin America; and three, extraterritorial prosecutions against corporations and their executives initiated in Europe. One case study was chosen from each of the three categories. The main aim of this selection process was for the chosen case studies to be representative of the their respective set of cases. This process required addressing substantive and practical questions such as analysing the representative nature of the cases as well as practical considerations such as access to documents and resources, status of the case, etc.

The three selected cases include the role of *Centro de Estudios Legales y Sociales* in corporate trials for historical crimes and particularly the case involving direct complicity of Ford Motors in crimes against humanity during the last military dictatorship (1976–1983) in Argentina; Center for Constitutional Rights and the case against CACI in the United States for war crimes committed in Iraq; and European Center for Constitutional and Human Rights and Sherpa focusing on the complicity of French cement company Lafarge in crimes against humanity committed in Syria. These three prototypes also ensured a broad representation of countries where these violations took place, jurisdictions where these litigations were pursued, organizations which led these litigations, and the ways in which corporations commit or contribute to crimes under international law.

Owing to the nature of questions around strategic litigation, this research would have been incomplete without primary research on the inner workings of strategic litigation organizations. As a result, expert interviews were conducted with practitioners and experts who have been closely involved with the aforementioned cases. The semi-structured interviews primarily dealt with questions concerning their strategy behind the choice of defendants, jurisdictions, legal frameworks, and practical challenges they faced in bringing these litigations. Overall, these interviews served a gap-filling purpose to provide access to information not available in secondary sources or to substantiate observations from legal briefs, judgments, and other primary and secondary sources. For each of the three case studies, two to three lawyers were interviewed who played a significant role in steering the litigations respectively in the United States, Argentina, and Germany/France. Owing to a combination of factors such as the global pandemic and wide geographical space covered in the research, all but two interviews were held virtually.

In terms of the structure of this book, it consists of seven chapters that are divided into three parts: Foundations (Part I), Case Studies (Part II), and Conclusions (Part III). Part I is further divided into three chapters dealing with disparate themes that collectively form the foundation for subsequent case studies. Chapter 1 discusses TWAIL's evolution and ambitions in the context of public international law. Then, it identifies four central concerns of a TWAIL interrogation and transposes these concerns to international criminal law to form the corpus of TWAI(C)L. Chapter 2 conceptualizes strategic litigation in the context of international criminal justice system. The chapter serves a twofold purpose: one, unpacking the meaning and implications of the frequently used catchphrase 'strategic litigation' and two, as a standard-setting framework for the case studies. As the last component of Part I, Chapter 3 traces the historical engagement of international criminal law with corporate accountability establishing the political nature of the debate surrounding accountability of corporations since the end of World War II. This chapter discusses the notion of accountability concerning corporate conduct as it pertains to this study while laying down the current status of international criminal law and corporate accountability.

Part II consists of three case studies that represent the practice of strategic litigation seeking corporate accountability for crimes under international law. Chapter 4, the first case study, deals with the practice of *Centro de Estudios Legales y Sociales* (CELS) Buenos Aires, Argentina, in a transitional justice context and particularly their attempts to address corporate complicity in crimes committed by the military dictatorship in Argentina. During that time, several industries and commercial sectors systematically contributed to the military repression in Argentina. Over a dozen of these national and multinational corporations are being investigated for their complicity. These trials concerning violations that were committed over 40 years ago are continuing to this day. The main focus of this chapter is a case against executives of Ford Motors which in 2018 resulted in their conviction for complicity in crimes against humanity. This case study is striking because throughout these four decades, lawyers and human rights defenders, including CELS, have consistently relied on international criminal law as an instrument to seek justice for past violations, thus laying the path to seek corporate accountability for historical violations. While focusing on the Ford case and CELS, the chapter also traces the journey of Argentinian transitional justice process '*memoria, verdad y justicia*' (memory, truth, and justice) and the implications of the often missing economic dimensions of large-scale violence.

Chapter 5 explores the employment of Alien Tort Statute (ATS) by the Center for Constitutional Rights (CCR), New York, to challenge privatization of war and seek accountability for war crimes committed by US private military contractors in Iraq. ATS is a jurisdictional provision that emanates from a 1789 statute which provides federal courts jurisdiction over violations of international law. The attempts to invoke the vocabulary of international criminal law in a tort law framework in the United States by CCR form the subject matter of this case study.

The chapter discusses how CCR has been strategically using international law to achieve broader political goals and then explores CCR's role in the revival of ATS. The case study zooms in on their ongoing case against CACI International Inc. and CACI Premier Technology while tracing pursuit of corporate accountability through ATS. In this case, CCR is representing Iraqi nationals who were subjected to torture, assault, cruel, inhumane, or degrading treatment and other war crimes while in detention at Abu Ghraib detention camp during the Iraq war. This lawsuit involving participation of US private military contractor in physical and mental abuse of detainees remains pending at the time this book was finalized. This case shows the implications of privatization of war and the resulting accountability gap for violations committed by private military security companies during an armed conflict. The journey of the case over the last decade is indicative of the obstacles in using a civil law framework against corporations for violations amounting to crimes under international law.

The final case study in Chapter 6 discusses similar interventions initiated in Europe. Lately, there has been an increasing reliance on criminal law to hold European corporations and their executives accountable for complicity in serious violations of international law committed in countries outside of Europe. In that vein, for the first time, a corporate entity is being charged with complicity in crimes against humanity in France for the conduct of its subsidiary outside of Europe. Criminal proceedings against the global cement leader, Lafarge Holcim, were initiated on the basis of complaints filed by two organizations: Berlin-based European Center for Constitutional and Human Rights (ECCHR) and Paris-based Sherpa. Under the French Criminal Code, a corporation can be prosecuted for their activities abroad provided one of its representatives is held liable for committing the crime. As a result, not only the top executives of this corporation but also the parent company itself has been indicted for complicity in crimes against humanity based on the conduct of its subsidiary in Syria.

Owing to the transnational nature of these proceedings and diverse skill sets required to bring actions in multiple jurisdictions, strategic litigation often involves several actors bringing collaborative legal interventions in pursuit of varied political objectives. To illustrate how strategic litigation works in this context, the case study focuses on ECCHR's involvement in extraterritorial prosecutions. The case against Lafarge exemplifies the ways in which corporations can be complicit in crimes under international law while conducting business in situations of armed conflict. The chapter also discusses the evidentiary and practical challenges particular to these legal interventions, for example, information asymmetry in business-related litigations, complex structure of corporate activity, and difficulties to establish linkages in extraterritorial litigations.

Finally, the common thread that binds these three tales is that these are non-state actors representing victims of crimes under international law, bringing litigation against corporations for their misconduct, and invoking international criminal law before domestic courts to achieve broader political objectives.

Part III of the book brings together the three case studies with the thematic and analytical framework set out in the earlier chapters. Chapter 7 serves a twofold purpose: it summarizes the main findings of the study and it discusses the implications of the practice of strategic litigation organizations as delineated in the case studies for the international criminal justice system at large.

The novelty of this book lies in two main aspects. Firstly, it applies TWAIL to international criminal law in general, referred to as Third World Approaches to International Criminal Law–TWAI(C)L, and then uses the concerns of TWAI(C)L to analyse the practice of strategic litigation in seeking accountability for corporate conduct amounting to crimes under international law. Secondly, based on a conceptualization of strategic litigation in the context of international criminal law, the book conducts a systematic analysis of this practice through three separate case studies.

The aim of the book is to push the critical discourse on international criminal law by highlighting the form(s) activism takes in the international criminal justice framework. The failures faced by these organizations in some ways confirm the claims of structural biases, but at the same time their rare successes hint at the emancipatory potential of international criminal law. In both cases, legal interventions initiated by non-state actors continue to impact the practice of international criminal law which deserves sustained scholarly attention on its own account. Wary of the fact that claims made in the book may be construed as a case of misplaced optimism in strategic litigation organizations or international criminal law, it must be clarified that this book does not make conclusive findings on this engagement between the two. The book is an invitation to a discussion on international criminal law that centres non-state actors, domestic courts, and its employment in furtherance of objectives other than those driven by the foreign policy of states.

As a final note, it is imperative to acknowledge that, somewhat paradoxically, the victims' perspective is not at the forefront in the case studies. The book also does not claim that these strategic legal interventions are necessarily victim-centred in every situation. This inconsistency, as demonstrated in the three case studies, is reflective of a central tension of the practice of strategic litigation that is driven by two goals that may not always align with each other: one, to challenge the underlying structures of a legal system and two, to meet the victims' idea of justice. This book is limited in so far as it is primarily concerned with the first goal.

References

Al-Attar M, 'TWAIL: A Paradox Within a Paradox' (2020) 22 International Community Law Review 163

Anghie A, 'TWAIL: Past and Future' (2008) 10 International Communities Law Review 4, 479–481

Chakrabarty I and Kaur G, 'Double Whammy: Targeted Minorities in South-Asian States' in Florian Jeßberger and others (eds), *International Criminal Law—A Counter-Hegemonic Project?* (TMC Asser Press 2022) 87–110

Chimni BS, 'The Past, Present and Future of International Law: A Critical Third World Approach' (2007) 8 Melbourne Journal of International Law 2, 499–515

Chimni BS, *International Law and World Order: A Critique of Contemporary Approaches* (Cambridge University Press 2017)

Clarke K, *Fictions of Justice: The International Criminal Court and the Challenge of Legal Pluralism in Sub-Saharan Africa* (Cambridge University Press 2009)

Damaska M, 'What Is the Point of International Criminal Justice' (2008) 83 Chi-Kent Law Review 329–368

Gathii JT, 'TWAIL: A Brief History of Its Origins, Its Decentralized Network, and a Tentative Bibliography' (2011) 3 Trade, Law and Development 1, 26–64

Jeßberger F, 'Die Krisen des Völkerstrafrechts' in Florian Jeßberger and others (eds), *Strafrecht and Systemunrecht: Festschrift für Gerhard Werle* (Mohr Siebeck 2022) 145–156

Kiyani A, 'Group-Based Differentiation and Local Repression: The Custom and Curse of Selectivity' (2016) 14 Journal of International Criminal Justice 4, 939–957

Kiyani A, 'The Antinomies of Legitimacy: On the (Im-)possibility of a Legitimate International Criminal Court' (2015) 8 African Journal of Legal Studies 1–2

Mickelson K, 'Rhetoric and Rage: Third World Voices in International Legal Discourse' (1998) 16 Wisconsin International Law Journal 353

Mickelson K, 'Taking Stock of TWAIL Histories' (2008) 10 International Community Law Review 4, 355–362

Mutua M, 'What Is TWAIL' (2000) 94 Proceedings of the Annual Meeting (American Society of International Law)

Nesiah V, 'The Trials of History: Losing Justice in the Monstrous and the Banal' in Ruth Buchanan and Peer Zumbansen (eds), *Transition: Human Rights, Development and Transitional Justice* (Bloomsbury Publishing 2014) 289–308

Okafor Obiora C and Ngwaba U, 'The International Criminal Court as a "Transitional Justice" Mechanism in Africa: Some Critical Reflections' (2015) 9 International Journal of Transitional Justice 90

Okafor Obiora C, 'Critical Third World Approaches to International Law (TWAIL): Theory, Methodology, or Both?' (2008) 10 International Community Law Review 4, 371–378

Simpson G, *Law, War and Crime: War Crimes Trials and the Reinvention of International Law* (Polity Press 2007)

Steinke R, *The Politics of International Criminal Justice: German Perspectives from Nuremberg to the Hague* (Bloomsbury Publishing 2012)

Part I

Foundations

Chapter 1

From TWAIL to TWAI(C)L

Third World Approaches to International Law (TWAIL) has been variably described as a movement, a methodology, a critique, an ideology, or an analytical tool.[1] In its essence, it is a multifaceted attempt by international legal scholars to critically engage with international law to highlight and address the colonial legacies in its structures. In other words, TWAIL is a scholarly movement against the domination of the Third World, entrenched in the structures and practice of international law.[2] Informed by the concerns of the Third World peoples, it goes a step further from critique and seeks reconstruction of international law to achieve a more just and inclusive international legal order. As a result, the questions of power, knowledge, colonial history, identity, and difference remain central to TWAIL.[3]

1 Obiora Chinedu Okafor, 'Critical Third World Approaches to International Law (TWAIL): Theory, Methodology, or Both?' (2008) 10 International Community Law Review 371 (hereinafter Okafor, 'Critical TWAIL: Theory, Methodology or Both'.)

2 Ironically, the birth of TWAIL has been attributed to an institution in the West. The birth of the label and a somewhat streamlined approach to international law took place at an academic conference dedicated to TWAIL in March 1997 at Harvard University. The conference was initiated and guided by a group of critical scholars consisting of Celestine Nyamu, Balakrishnan Rajagopal, Hani Sayed, Vasuki Nesiah, Elchi Nowrojee, Bhupinder Chimni, and James Thuo Gathii, who coined the name of the group as 'Third World Approaches to International Law' (TWAIL). This conference became the first of its kind where the TWAILers issued a vision statement that read in part: 'We are a network of scholars engaged in international legal studies, and particularly interested in the challenges and opportunities facing Third World peoples in the new world order. We understand the historical scope and agenda of the dominant voice of international law and scholarship as having participated in, and legitimated global processes of marginalization and domination that impact on the lives and struggles of Third World peoples'. Quote from James Thuo Gathii, 'Alternative and Critical: The Contributions of Research and Scholarship on Developing Countries to International Legal Theory' (2000) 41 Harvard International Law Journal 273 (hereafter Gathii, 'Alternative and Critical'); see James Thuo Gathii 'TWAIL: A Brief History of Its Origins, Its Decentralized Network, and a Tentative Bibliography' (2011) 3 Trade Law and Development 3, 28–29 (hereinafter Gathii, 'TWAIL: A Brief History').

3 See Antony Anghie, 'TWAIL: Past and Future' (2008) 10 International Community Law Review 4, 479.

DOI: 10.4324/9781003405047-3

This chapter begins with a discussion on TWAIL's evolution and ambitions in the context of public international law. The second section identifies four central concerns of a TWAIL interrogation and transposes these central concerns to international criminal law to form the corpus of Third World Approaches to International (Criminal) Law, abbreviated as TWAI(C)L. The chapter provides the analytical framework to examine the practice of strategic litigation in cases of corporate accountability for crimes under international law.

I. Unpacking TWAIL

One of the key texts on TWAIL entitled '*What Is TWAIL?*' by Makau Mutua strongly claims that the Third World views the regime of international law as 'illegitimate'.[4] According to him, the international legal system legitimizes, reproduces, and sustains the subordination of the Third World by the West.[5] Mutua traced back the origins of TWAIL concerns to anti-colonial movements, when the Third World perceived international law as a regime and discourse of domination and subordination.[6] He pointedly foregrounds the disconnect between anti-colonial aspirations and reality by acknowledging that the historical fight for freedom from European colonial rule was 'largely illusory' as the Third World continues to be politically, legally, and economically bonded to the former colonizers. For Mutua, TWAIL was simultaneously a proactive and reactive response to this condition of subordination and thus, was essentially a 'reconstructive movement' which seeks a new structure of international law.[7]

The contributions made by scholars such as Antony Anghie and B.S. Chimni in the early 21st century further streamlined TWAIL as a scholarly movement.[8] The questions they identified have continued to guide the research agenda of TWAIL scholars over the years. Painting in broad strokes,

4 Makau Mutua, 'What Is TWAIL?' (2000) 94 Proceedings of the ASIL Annual Meeting 31.
5 Ibid 31.
6 Ibid 36.
7 Ibid 41.
8 Antony Anghie, 'Time Present and Time Past: Globalization, International Financial Institutions, and the Third World Millennium Issue: Shaping the Parameters of International Law in the New Millennium' (1999) 32 New York University Journal of International Law and Politics 243; Antony Anghie and B.S. Chimni, 'Third World Approaches to International Law and Individual Responsibility in Internal Conflicts' (2003) 2 Chinese Journal of International Law 77 (hereinafter Anghie and Chimni, 'Individual Responsibility'); B.S. Chimni, 'Third World Approaches to International Law: A Manifesto' (2006) 8 International Community Law Review 3 (hereinafter Chimni, 'TWAIL Manifesto'); Antony Anghie, 'TWAIL: Past and Future' (2008) 10 International Community Law Review Volume 4; B.S. Chimni, *International Law and World Order: A Critique of Contemporary Approaches* (Cambridge University Press 2017).

they traced the development of TWAIL scholarship in two historical phases, distinguishing them by their dissimilar grounds of opposition and demands.

The first phase, referred to by them as TWAIL I, was rooted in the belief that the United Nations would usher in a phase of a just global order as opposed to the colonial international law which legitimized oppression.[9] The TWAIL discourse, in this phase, was focused on the nation-state and the principle of sovereignty, critiquing the use of international law by powerful nations to serve their own interests.[10] The scholars placed emphasis on the ability of Third World states to take an active part in international legal processes with the hope that they could engage as equals in the ever-expanding scope of modern international law.[11]

TWAIL II was an extension of the first phase in some respects and an absolute departure in others. The fundamental premise of colonization being instrumental in the formation of an unequal world remained constant across both phases. They were also 'united in their efforts to create a system of international law that acknowledged and furthered the interests of the people of the Third World'.[12] However, the second phase of scholarship also interrogates the violence and tensions vis-à-vis the post-colonial Third World nation-state and its peoples. TWAIL II scholars – from a more global and intersectional perspective – have challenged the Third World nation-state, its processes, and its resort to violence and authoritarianism.[13] These scholars also challenge the idea of sovereignty to the extent that it has enabled such violence by the post-colonial state against Third World peoples. TWAIL II scholarship is driven by the concerns of the people within the Third World, the workers, women, and other minorities, whose interests may not necessarily align with the post-colonial state. For example, they examine whether and how international human rights norms may be used to protect Third World peoples against the state and other international actors.[14] As a result, TWAIL II positions on, for example,

9 See R.P. Anand, *International Law and the Developing Countries* (Brill 1987); For a detailed study of the division between civilized and non-civilized states in nineteenth century international law, see Gerrit W Gong, *The Standard of 'Civilization' in International Society* (Clarendon 1984).

10 Anghie and Chimni, 'Individual Responsibility' (n 8) 80.

11 B.S. Chimni, 'Towards a Radical Third World Approach to Contemporary International Law' (2002) 5 International Center for Comparative Law and Politics Review 14, 15 (hereafter Chimni 'Towards a Radical TWAIL'); Madhav Khosla, 'The TWAIL Discourse: The Emergence of a New Phase' (2007) 9 International Community Law Review 291, 297 (hereafter Khosla, 'The TWAIL Discourse').

12 Antony Anghie, 'Rethinking International Law: A TWAIL Retrospective' (2003) 34 European Journal of International Law 1, 7–112, 8 (hereafter Anghie, 'A TWAIL Retrospective).

13 Makau Mutua, 'Why Redraw the Map of Africa: A Moral and Legal Inquiry' (1995) 16 Michigan Journal of International Law 13; Obiora Okafor, *Re-Defining Legitimate Statehood: International Law and State Fragmentation in Africa* (Martin Nijhoff 2000).

14 See Edward K. Quashigah and Obiora C. Okafor (eds), *Legitimate Governance in Africa: International and Domestic Legal Perspectives* (Kluwer Law International 1999).

how international human rights law differs from mainstream and critical northern views on human rights as well as from the views of Third World states themselves.[15] The scholars in the second phase also 'formulated an alternative account of the history of international law' that established imperialism as central to the identity and operations of the discipline.[16]

Such a dichotomy between TWAIL I and TWAIL II is simplistic and robs the complexity of arguments made by individual scholars.[17] This classification builds on the understanding that TWAIL is a body of work produced by a decentralized unorganized network of scholars countering the mainstream narrative of international law while interjecting it with the concerns of the Third World. The dichotomy does highlight key points of departure of the current TWAIL scholarship as well as the overall heterogeneity of the approach. The heterogeneity allows for a broad framework and thus, a decentralization of TWAIL. At the same time, the clearly delineated points of departure also allow the Third World scholars to move beyond the perspective of the post-colonial state and engage in a constructive dialogue over the limitations of international law.

As a counter-hegemonic and anti-hierarchical project, a non-coordinated plural treatment of TWAIL seems obvious and intuitive. Despite the lack of a unitary approach or perhaps because of it, the TWAIL project has managed to provide a unique institutionalized space where scholars and activists can simultaneously offer a critique and pursue a reformist agenda in the realm of international law. Before moving further to a discussion about its status and goals, however, it is imperative to unpack the terminology 'Third World' which has been a subject of conflict on its own account.

1. Terminology

A mere geographical determination of the term 'Third World' as a place is constricting and misleading.[18] In economic terms, some choose to group 'less developed', 'developing', or 'underdeveloped countries' as the Third World

15 Anghie and Chimni, 'Individual Responsibility' (n 8) 83.

16 Anghie, 'A TWAIL Retrospective' (n 12).

17 Anghie and Chimni, 'Individual Responsibility' (n 8) 87; see Ashish Nandy, 'The Other Within: The Strange Case of Radhabinod Pal's Judgment on Culpability' (1992) 23 New Literary History 45 (hereafter, Nandy 'The Other Within').

18 The term 'Third World' is credited originally to a French demographer Alfred Sauvy, who in 1952 in the pages of L'Observateur offered 'an evocative tripartite division of the planet into the First, Second and Third Worlds'. Sauvy explains of his own use of the expression 'Third World' that the Third World holds a position vis-à-vis the First and Second Worlds (that is, the industrialized capitalist and communist countries, respectively) comparable to that of the 'Third Estate' (the commoners) with respect to the First and Second estates (that is, the clergy and the nobility). That is, Sauvy's concept designated a political relation not a set demographic. See Marcin Wojciech Solarz, '"Third World": The 60th Anniversary of a Concept That Changed History' (2012) 33 Third World Quarterly 156.

as opposed to the developed and rich 'First World'.[19] Historically speaking, it denotes countries that have been under foreign rule at a point of time.[20] Contemporary post-colonial scholars, however, make a convincing case for the term Third World as a political grouping rather than an ostensibly 'objective demographic or economic coalition'.[21]

The common denominator across the Third World would be a shared history of colonialism combined with the lived experience of material conditions which are a legacy of the relationship between the colonized and the colonizer. This shared experience continues to be shaped by the evolving forces of neoliberal globalization in today's geopolitical situation.

Another important aspect of the label 'Third World' that needs unpacking is that 'there are multitudes of claims in various spaces that are both emancipatory and oppressive'.[22] Given the complexity of lived realities, there is a possibility of simultaneously having a North in the South, a South in the South, and a South in the North. This is a factor worth considering when resorting to labels and terminologies such as the Third World and Global South. In furtherance of this sensibility, TWAIL is a project reflective of the concerns and politics of the Third World peoples and not the Third World nation-states. Scholars such as Balakrishnan Rajagopal have interpreted the term Third World to also include non-state actors of various kinds, including social movements.[23]

2. *Advocacy or Analysis?*

As Obiora Okafor, another noted TWAIL-er acknowledges, 'approach' is a catchall term, describing 'method, procedure, modus operandi, way,

19 Karin Mickelson, 'Rhetoric and Rage: Third World Voices in International Legal Discourse' (1998) 16 Wisconsin International Law Journal 353, 356; Upendra Baxi, 'What May the "Third World" Expect from International Law?' (2006) 27 Third World Quarterly 713 (hereinafter Baxi, '"Third World" Expect from International Law?').

20 Khosla, 'The TWAIL Discourse' (n 11).

21 Sundhya Pahuja, 'A note on the use of 'Third World" in *Decolonising International Law: Development, Economic Growth and the Politics of Universality* (Cambridge University Press 2011) 261–262; Vijay Prashad, *The Darker Nations: A Biography of the Short-lived Third World* (Leftword Books 2007); Balakrishnan Rajagopal, 'Locating the Third World in Cultural Geography' (1998) Third World Legal Studies 1.

22 Sujith Xavier and others, 'Placing TWAIL Scholarship and Praxis: Introduction to the Special Issue of the Windsor Yearbook of Access to Justice' (2016) Windsor Yearbook of Access to Justice 33; Baxi, '"Third World" Expect from International Law?' (n 19) ; A Sajed, 'From the Third World to the Global South' (E-International Relations, 27 July 2020) <https://www.e-ir.info/2020/07/27/from-the-third-world-to-the-global-south/> accessed 19 December 2021.

23 Balakrishnan Rajagopal, 'Counter-hegemonic International Law: Rethinking Human Rights and Development as a Third World Strategy' (2006) 27 Third World Quarterly 5, 767–783 (hereinafter Rajagopal, 'Counter-hegemonic International Law')

technique, style, manner, [or] attitude'.[24] The ambiguity of the term combined with the decentralized scholarship produced under the TWAIL label raises pertinent questions on what TWAIL fundamentally seeks to achieve and how it should be perceived in the broader context of international legal scholarship.

Certainly, it would be an oversimplification to reduce TWAIL to merely a movement, ideology, or even a methodology.[25] Okafor argues that TWAIL offers both 'theories of, and methodologies for, analysing international law and institutions'.[26] Anghie and Chimni also lean towards classifying it as a methodology when they say TWAIL has become 'a distinctive way of thinking about what international law is and should be; they involve the formulation of a particular set of concerns and the analytical tools with which to explore them'.[27]

What makes matters complicated, however, is that TWAIL is a methodology with an explicit normative ambition.[28] It does not pose objectivity or neutrality in its engagement with international law. TWAIL scholars critique the existing international legal order but at the same time insist on it being an instrument to strive towards more equality, justice, and equity.[29] This duality manifests in the way TWAIL scholars unanimously ground their work in resistance against the status quo – the subjugation of the Third World peoples – while aspiring for a transformed plural alternative international legal order. For instance, the normative ambition of resistance to international law is apparent in Mutua's identification of the three basic objectives of TWAIL:

> The first is to understand, deconstruct, and unpack the uses of international law as a medium for the creation and perpetuation of a racialized hierarchy of international norms and institutions that subordinate non-Europeans to Europeans. Second, it seeks to construct and present an alternative normative legal edifice for international governance. Finally, TWAIL seeks through scholarship, policy, and politics to eradicate the conditions of underdevelopment in the Third World.[30]

Mohsen al Attar engages comprehensively with the two-dimensional analytic-normative nature of this scholarly enterprise and its place in international legal theory. While underscoring the activist, reformist, or guerrilla nature of the TWAIL project, he contends that it is a scholarly engagement

24 Okafor, 'Critical TWAIL: Theory, Methodology or Both' (n 1) 378.
25 Georges Abi-Saab, 'The Third World Intellectual in Praxis: Confrontation, Participation, or Operation behind Enemy Lines?' (2016) 37 Third World Quarterly 1957.
26 Okafor, 'Critical TWAIL: Theory, Methodology or Both' (n 1) 377.
27 Anghie and Chimni, 'Individual Responsibility' (n 8) 77.
28 See Mohsen al Attar, 'TWAIL: A Paradox within a Paradox' (2020) 22 International Community Law Review 163 (hereafter Attar, 'Paradox within a Paradox').
29 Antony Anghie, 'LatCrit and TWAIL' (2012) 42 California Western International Law Journal 311, 320.
30 Mutua, 'What is TWAIL?' (n 4) 31.

that is in fact a form of praxis.[31] For TWAIL scholars, 'intellectual work is an avenue through which radical political change is pursued'.[32] While some have challenged TWAIL for its biases and subjectivity,[33] TWAIL scholars insist that legal analysis cannot be detached from its political context.[34]

While the ambition to resist is unanimous across generations of TWAILers, their scholarship significantly differs on what the just international legal order they seek to achieve looks like and how it can be achieved. Some propose a reformist reconstruction of international law and others seek a radical overhaul of the whole system.[35] Gathii terms the former as integrationists who believed in the potential of the Third World's participation in international law to drive legal reform and the latter as nationalists who saw no hope for the Third World within the existing structure of international law and advocated radical restructuring instead.[36]

Therefore, united in fundamental opposition of the unjust global order, TWAIL is replete with internal contradictions, incoherencies, and disagreements on its content, strategy, and tactics. Nevertheless, at its core, using Mutua's words, TWAIL is 'antihierarchical, counterhegemonic, challenges universalism, and at the same time is coalitionary and open to other like-minded movements across the world'.[37]

To precisely lay down the core characteristics of a TWAIL enquiry in contemporary understanding: TWAIL is a scholarly critique with a political ambition that interrogates the relationship between international law and the conditions of the Third World, informed by the interests of the Third World peoples. The movement owes its diversity to multiple histories and manifold goals of transformation. As it stands now, it does not restrict itself to the binary of the colonizer state as the oppressor and the entire formerly colonized Third World as the subordinate. It analyses the structural factors on the axis of race, class, gender, etc. which perpetuate and sustain the power that is a legacy of colonialism and pervades state boundaries. Equally importantly, it combines this historical examination with the normative ambition of seeking transformation in the international legal order.

A TWAIL enquiry works with the understanding that in the era of globalization, complicated demographics, and complex structures of governance,

31 Attar, 'Paradox within a Paradox' (n 28) 188.

32 Ibid 196.

33 Tilmann Altwicker and Oliver Diggelmann, 'What Should Remain of the Critical Approaches to International Law: International Legal Theory as Critique' (2014) 24 Swiss Review of International & European Law 69, 75.

34 Mutua, 'What Is TWAIL' (n 4).

35 Mutua identifies a third splinter group which he calls 'minimalist assimilationists' – betrayers whose legacy must be rejected. Ibid 32.

36 James Gathii, 'International Law and Eurocentricity' (1998) 9 European Journal of International Law 184, 189

37 Mutua, 'What is TWAIL' (n 4) 32.

domination, and hegemony come in multilayered forms of international institutions and multinational corporations in addition to the powerful or authoritarian state. TWAIL sees its purpose in resistance to achieve a post-hegemonic international legal order. In doing that, it seeks to serve as an emancipatory project which views the use of international law as a vehicle for the protection of the interests of Third World peoples. It explicitly prioritizes the interests of Third World peoples over the decolonized Third World states. As a decentralized network of scholars engaging strategically with international law, defined by a commonality of concerns, it is an evolving work in progress.

II. Third World Approaches to International Criminal Law (TWAI(C)L)

Modern international criminal law, interestingly, is one sub-discipline that was conceived toprosecute crimes and oppression of colonization at Nuremberg and Tokyo. Yet, the overlapping goals of global justice do not exempt international criminal law from a TWAIL enquiry and critique.

Despite being served with the noble goal of guarding the conscience of humanity at large, the foundations of international criminal law are laid by power as well. One of the most popular statements from the Nuremberg trials testifies that such trials were 'one of the most significant tributes that power has ever paid to reason'.[38] It has already been argued, however, that these trials were convenient and self-serving attempts at the hands of then victorious and powerful states.[39]

The trials were critiqued as self-serving not merely for being a form of victor's justice against the defeated but also for conveniently leaving unaddressed the violations of the victors against their own colonies. Schabas voices this concern in explaining the distinct treatment of atrocities committed within international and internal armed conflicts as established by the Allied Powers, because the prospect of prosecuting 'crimes against humanity' for internal conflicts made the allied states 'uncomfortable with the ramifications that this might have with respect to treatment of their own minorities, not to mention their colonies'.[40]

In fact, one of the first TWAIL accounts can also be traced back to the bench of a post–World War II international tribunal, making the critique

38 On 21 November 1945, in his opening address, the American Robert Jackson, Public Prosecutor at the Nuremberg trial, recalls the historic importance of the trial of Nazi war criminals and lists the charges in detail. Robert Jackson, 'International Military Tribunal' (1945) The Department of State Bulletin 335, Vol. XIII, Publication 2432, US Government Printing Office, Washington, 850–860.

39 Ronen Steinke, *The Politics of International Criminal Justice: German Perspectives from Nuremberg to The Hague* (Bloomsbury London 2012) ch 1; See Florian Jeßberger, 'Die Krisen des Völkerstrafrechts' im *Festschrift für Gerhard Werle* (Mohr Siebeck 2022).

40 William Schabas, *An Introduction to the International Criminal Court* (5th edn, Cambridge University Press 2017) 35.

almost as old as modern international criminal law itself. Justice Radhabinod Pal at the International Military Tribunal for the Far East (1946–1948), in his 700-page dissenting judgment, sought to deconstruct the racial and colonial hierarchies within the structure of emergent international criminal law.[41] He exemplified the way racial hierarchies operated in the indictment of the Japanese on charges of waging an aggressive war and war crimes to justify his decision of acquittal of Japanese defendants.[42] Referring to colonial violence inflicted by the allied powers in Asia, Pal's dissenting judgment was a historically aware indictment on the motivations of the prosecuting states. In his view, anti-colonial justice took precedence over peace rather than peace taking precedence over justice.[43] A historical re-examination of international criminal law would establish that colonial encounters were essential to the formation and development of the sub-discipline.

Despite such early identification of the blind spots of the international criminal justice system, a comprehensive and explicit engagement of TWAIL and international criminal law has been minimal.[44] The few exceptions include the critique of individual criminal responsibility by Anghie and Chimni,[45] the Journal of International Criminal Justice (JICJ) symposium emphasizing the need of a TWAIL focus on ICL and related works by Kiyani, Xavier, and Reynolds,[46] and a chapter by Iyi who uses TWAIL as an analytic framework to expose the manifest contradictions in the construction of international criminal justice.[47]

41 Dissenting Judgment of Justice Pal, International Military Tribunal for the Far East (1948) <http://www.sdh-fact.com/CL02_1/65_S4.pdf> accessed 27 May 2020.

42 Ibid.

43 S. Kirsten Sellars, 'Imperfect Justice at Nuremberg and Tokyo', (2010) 21 European Journal of International Law 1100, 1096; Nandy 'The Other Within (n 15) 45; Mark Drumbl, 'Memorializing Dissent: Justice Pal in Tokyo' (2020) American Journal of International Law 114, 111–116; Sumedha Choudhary, 'Contextualising Radhabinod Pal's Dissenting Opinion in Contemporary International Criminal Law' (2021) 11 Asian Journal of International Law 223; Sujith Xavier, 'Locating and Situating Justice Pal: TWAIL, International Criminal Tribunals, and Judicial Powers' (2022) 12 Asian Journal of International Law 292 (hereinafter Xavier, 'Situating Justice Pal'); Rohini Sen and Rashmi Raman, 'Retelling Radha Binod Pal: The Outsider and The Native' in Frédéric Mégret and Immi Tallgren (eds), *The Dawn of a Discipline: International Criminal Justice and Its Early Exponents* (Cambridge University Press 2020).

44 See Michelle Burgis-Kasthala, 'Scholarship as Dialogue? TWAIL and the Politics of Methodology' (2016) 14 Journal of International Criminal Justice 4, 921– 937.

45 Anghie and Chimni, 'Individual Responsibility' (n 8) 77.

46 Asad Kiyani, John Reynolds, Sujith Xavier, 'Foreword' (2016) 14 Journal of International Criminal Justice 4, 915–920. Also see, Asad Kiyani, 'Third World Approaches to International Criminal Law' (2015) AJIL Unbound 109, 255–59; Xavier, 'Situating Justice Pal' (n 43).

47 John-Mark Iyi, 'Is International Criminal Justice the Handmaiden of the Contemporary Imperial Project? A TWAIL Perspective of Some Arenas of Contestations' in Florian Jeßberger and others (eds), *International Criminal Justice – A Counterhegemonic Project?* (Springer 2022) (hereinafter Jeßberger and others (eds), *Counterhegemonic Project?*)

Nevertheless, concerns shared by Third World scholars have found solidarity in the form of critical scholarship through scholars such as Steven Ratner,[48] Claire Nielsen,[49] Sara Kendall,[50] Sarah Nouwen,[51] Immi Tallgren,[52] and Richard Wilson[53] analysing the inconsistencies of the discipline.[54]

One common critique that binds these divergent critical perspectives together is 'selectivity' of international criminal law.[55] The selective application of the law against individuals from the Third World offers strong evidence to argue that it is a tool that exclusively targets and further marginalizes the oppressed and that it is an instrument in the hands of 'the West'. Rather than just tallying the numbers of African perpetrators filling the docks of the International Criminal Court (ICC) and of the situations pending investigation and preliminary examination with the Office of the Prosecutor (OTP) at the ICC,[56] TWAIL scholars make a more nuanced argument based on structural and operational selectivity that is distinguished from group-based selectivity.[57] As opposed to quantitative indicators for operational selectivity, group-based selectivity is determined if 'the likelihood of a perpetrator's prosecution – relative to other similarly – situated offenders – seems to depend on the group identity of the offender';[58] it is therefore a specific

48 Steven Ratner, 'The Schizophrenias of International Criminal Law' (1998) 33 Texas International Law Journal 237.

49 Claire Nielsen, 'From Nuremberg to The Hague: The Civilizing Mission of International Criminal Law', (2008) 14 Auckland University Law Review 81.

50 Sara Kendall, 'Donors Justice: Recasting International Criminal Accountability' (2011) 24 Leiden Journal of International Law 585.

51 Sara Kendall and Sarah Nouwen, 'Representational Practices at the International Criminal Court: The Gap between Juridified and Abstract Victimhood' (2013) 76 Law and Contemporary Problems 235.

52 Immi Tallgren, 'We Did It? The Vertigo of Law and Everyday Life at the Diplomatic Conference on the Establishment of the International Criminal Court' (1998) 12 Leiden Journal of International Law 683 (hereinafter Tallgren, 'We Did It?').

53 Richard A Wilson, *Writing History in International Criminal Trials* (Cambridge University Press 2011); Richard A Wilson, 'Through the Lens of International Criminal Law: Comprehending the African Context of Crimes at the International Criminal Court' (2011) 11 Studies in Ethnicity and Nationalism 106.

54 See Christine Schwöbel (ed), *Critical Approaches to International Criminal Law: An Introduction* (Routledge 2014); Dov Jacobs, 'Sitting on the Wall Looking in: Some Reflections on the Critique of International Criminal Law' (2015) 28 Leiden Journal of International Law 1.

55 Robert Cryer, *Prosecuting International Crimes: Selectivity and the International Criminal Law Regime* (Cambridge University Press 2005) 192 ('it is essentially impossible that selectivity does not occur') Timothy LH McCormack, 'Selective Reaction to Atrocity' (1996–97) 60 Albany Law Review 681.

56 Makau Mutua, 'Africans and the ICC: Hypocrisy, Impunity and Perversion' in Kamari M. Clarke and others (eds), *Africans and the ICC: Perceptions of Justice* (Cambridge University Press 2016) 47 – 60.

57 Asad Kiyani, 'Group-Based Differentiation and Local Repression: The Custom and Curse of Selectivity' (2016) 14 Journal of International Criminal Justice 4, 939 – 957.

58 Ibid 948.

subset of selectivity which takes the form of differentiating between parties to the conflict. Group-based selectivity in choosing perpetrators for prosecution in a given conflict situation challenges the non-discriminatory nature of these prosecutions and points to the fact that such selection contributes to maintaining the status quo of power relations, oppression, and marginalization in the international and domestic spheres.[59]

Beyond the institutions and their practice, substantive international criminal law also can be subjected to critique on the ground of bias reflected through misconduct it fails to criminalize. Each colonial encounter has stories of episodic atrocity crimes which could qualify as crimes under international law in the present understanding of the law. The absence of colonial crimes or colonialism per se as a crime with continuing legacy[60] points to a huge gap in the accountability discourse. Wolfgang Kaleck, in an anthology edited by himself along with Morten Bergsmo and Kyaw Yin Hlaing,[61] discusses the case of Nama and Herero genocide in modern-day Namibia during the German colonial rule.[62] Concerning colonial crimes, he alleges double standards on the part of the West: the inter-temporal rule of criminal law, the principle that only conduct that was criminal at the time of commission can be punished, was willingly ignored when it concerned European victims during World War II, but it became relevant when viewing episodes of atrocity crimes perpetrated by Europeans elsewhere.[63]

59 Sarah Nouwen, 'Legal Equality on Trial' (2012) 7 Netherlands Yearbook of International Law 151, 168.

60 As criminologists Marianne Nielsen and Linda M. Robyn state, colonialism is 'an ongoing process of invasion and oppression, a centuries-long crime, resulting in the destruction of lives, communities, cultures, human rights, and other grave social harms' in Marianne Nielsen and Linda M. Robyn, *Colonialism Is Crime* (Rutgers University Press 2019).

61 Not a TWAIL engagement per se, as the editors note that this anthology reflects how mainstream international lawyers relate to colonialism, colonial wrongs, and colonial grievances. This quote from the foreword explains: 'It is important that this issue not be left to 'specialists' only, but that mainstream lawyers – especially international criminal lawyers – become better informed and do not see this as an area reserved for historians, experts on Third World Approaches to International Law, or persons from former colonies'. Morten Bergsmo, Wolfgang Kaleck, Kyaw Yin Hlaing (eds), *Colonial Wrongs and Access to International Law* (TOAEP, 2020) ii (hereinafter, Bergsmo and others (eds), *Colonial Wrongs*).

62 In May 2021, the German foreign minister declared that a 'reconciliation agreement' had been reached between Namibia and Germany concerning crimes committed during German colonial rule. The fact that negotiations on historical accountability even took place speaks volumes on the persistence and dedication of descendants of the victims of Nama and Herero communities to seek justice. Following a process fraught with serious irregularities such as absence of important stakeholders, the German government acknowledged that the violations committed between 1904 and 1908 against the Nama and Herero communities amounted to what would be 'from today's perspective – a genocide'. See statement from German Federal Foreign Office <https://www.auswaertiges-amt.de/en/newsroom/news/-/2463598 accessed 20 December 2021.

63 Wolfgang Kaleck, 'On Double Standards: An Emerging European Custom on Accountability for Colonial Crimes' in Bergsmo and others (eds), *Colonial Wrongs* (n 61) 15.

These contributions, albeit preliminary in their engagement with international criminal law, have been setting the course of future research agenda from their respective perspectives.

At this stage, emphasis must be placed on the distinction between international criminal justice as a project – an aggregate of consistent attempts made by the international community to prosecute grave human rights violations, international criminal law – the norms and doctrines forming a sub-discipline of public international law in general, and the international institutions such as the ad hoc tribunals and the ICC as the primary sites where international criminal law comes into operation. Although inextricably linked and instrumental to each other, the fallacies of one being transposed to reject the other seem unjustified. The limitations of the ad hoc tribunals and the ICC get stretched in making the argument that international criminal law is a failing sub-discipline of public international law and international criminal justice is an unrealistically ambitious project.[64] Inefficiency, selectivity and inequality in representation, inter alia, in the operation of the ICC get cited in misdirected challenges of the legitimacy of international criminal justice as a project. However, a critique of the institutions in combination with a constructive account of reforms would rather strengthen the promise in international criminal justice than flag its failure. Such a paradoxical approach between reform and resistance has been inherent in the works of most TWAIL scholars across phases.

Given the broad scope of TWAIL, it is important to pinpoint some of its key aspects which would be relevant to international criminal law. While mapping out the central concerns of a multifaceted scholarship as TWAIL is prone to oversimplification, doing so serves a twofold purpose: one, to generally streamline TWAIL engagement with international criminal law; two, to operate as the analytical framework for the practice of strategic litigation in so far as it engages with corporate accountability.

III. TWAI(C)L's Key Concerns

1. Reform-oriented Critique

TWAIL scholars have been pointing out the inherently imperial or hegemonic nature of international law in general. There are contrasting approaches, however, to the question: what would be the ideal response of the postcolonial? One end of the spectrum suggests that the imperial quality of the international law project is exclusionary; therefore, the oppressed should

64 Mirjan Damaska, 'What Is the Point of International Criminal Justice' (2008) 83 Chi-Kent Law Review, 329–368; Alfred Rubin, 'Challenging the Conventional Wisdom: Another View of the International Criminal Court' (1999) Journal of International Affairs, 783–794.

not even engage with the legal system and disassociate altogether.[65] Another more common approach suggests an understanding of the international legal project as bearing a 'dual' quality which has a hegemonic structure but simultaneously provides spaces for counter-hegemonic engagement with its norms and principles.[66] In other words, this reform-oriented approach seeks to challenge the established power dynamics but not to dismiss the emancipatory potential of the international legal order, instead to pose those challenges *within* the international criminal justice system so as to advance the interests of the Third World peoples.

This normative ambition to engage in the reconstruction of the international criminal justice system is as essential as the critique of substantive international criminal law and its institutions. Despite all its structural biases, the importance of the vocabulary of international criminal law in the existing world order cannot be dismissed. In light of the significance of law as a medium to allow contestation, harsh critiques such as perpetuation of power structures, impunity at large of the powerful, and lack of enforceability do not warrant an all-out boycott but rather a re-engagement to achieve a more just legal order.

Responses to international criminal law and its institutions by Third World governments and Third World peoples reflect that the two sides of the project – oppressive and emancipatory – coexist without necessarily displacing each other. States such as India[67] and China[68] choosing to not sign the ICC Statute was a sign of cynicism that the ICC will become yet another unwarranted tool for the West to intervene in their internal matters. Various governments from the African continent threatened to withdraw[69] after joining, arguably in response to frustration and disappointment in the capacity of international law (or institutions) to deliver on its universalist promises.

65 For a radical rejection of any emancipatory value of international law, see China Mieville, *Between Equal Rights: A Marxist Theory of International Law* (Brill 2005); China Mieville, 'The Commodity-Form Theory of International Law: An Introduction' (2004) 17 Leiden Journal of International Law 2, 271.

66 B.S. Chimni, 'TWAIL Manifesto' (n 8); Balakrishnan Rajagopal, 'International Law and Social Movements: Challenges of Theorizing Resistance' (2002) 41 Columbia Journal of Transnational Law 397; Antony Anghie, *Imperialism, Sovereignty and the Making of International Law* (Vol 37, Cambridge University Press 2007) (hereinafter Anghie, *Sovereignty*) 316.

67 Devasheesh Bais, 'India and the International Criminal Court' (2016) FICHL Policy Brief Series No. 54 <https://www.toaep.org/pbs-pdf/54-bais> accessed 21 December 2021; Suzannah Linton, 'India and China Before, At, and After Rome' (2018) 6 Journal of International Criminal Justice 2, 265–294.

68 Lu Jianping and Wang Zhixiang, 'China's Attitude Towards the ICC' (2005) 3 Journal of International Criminal Justice 608; Dan Zhu, 'China, Crimes Against Humanity and the International Criminal Court' (2018) 16 Journal of International Criminal Justice 1021.

69 Manisuli Ssenyonjo, 'State Withdrawal Notifications from the Rome Statute of the International Criminal Court: South Africa, Burundi and the Gambia' (2018) 29 Criminal Law Forum, 63–119; Kamari M. Clarke, Abel S. Knottnerus and Eefje De Volder (eds). *Africa and the ICC* (Cambridge University Press 2016); Gerhard Werle, Lovell Fernandez and Moritz Vormbaum, *Africa and the International Criminal Court* (TMC Asser Press 2014) 303.

Contrary to the state stance, the Third World peoples have consistently turned to the ICC with the hope of protection and accountability for atrocities and violations committed by the oppressor of varied kinds. A large number of communications filed under Article 15 of the ICC Statute from or on behalf of victims,[70] inter alia, in Cambodia, the Philippines, Palestine, Myanmar-Bangladesh, Colombia, and Nigeria requesting action serves as an indicator of victims' and their representatives' faith in an international court as an additional venue to seek justice.[71] Even if one may not perceive this as an unreserved reflection of their belief in the ICC, it is certainly an indicator of how the vocabulary of international criminal justice resonates, supports, and strengthens their status and demands. International criminal justice has permeated the debates in political discourse, becoming an increasingly important indicator of collective justice.[72]

Scholars have responded to this disappointment in ways other than cynicism and absolute withdrawal. Their responses have been a combination of frustration and hope where a systematic process of resistance to the structural inequalities within the international criminal justice project is accompanied with the continuous claim for reform.[73] Chimni has argued that this tendency of TWAIL scholars to remain within the realm of international law is an outcome of fear, for he alleges it would be dangerous to leave a powerful arena and look for another language in which to speak,[74] to which Pahuja and Eslava respond that if fear is one dimension of this position, the other would be hope or faith in the transformative potential of international law.[75]

70 Few examples of communications under Article 15 of the Rome Statute: On situation in Cambodia <https://www.fidh.org/IMG/pdf/executive_summary-2.pdf> accessed 21 December 2021; Colombia <https://www.ecchr.eu/fileadmin/Juristische_Dokumente/Executive_Summary_ECCHRSismaCAJAR_ICCCommunicationVSXinColombia_EN.pdf> accessed 21 December 2021; Myanmar <https://www.legalactionworldwide.org/accountability-rule-of-law/law-icc-victim-submission-for-rohingya-clients-following-nug-declaration/> accessed 21 December 2021.

71 Leila Ullrich, 'Beyond the "Global–Local Divide": Local Intermediaries, Victims and the Justice Contestations of the International Criminal Court' (2016) 14 Journal of International Criminal Justice 543; Carolyn Hoyle and Leila Ullrich, 'New Court, New Justice? The Evolution of "Justice for Victims" at Domestic Courts and at the International Criminal Court' (2014) 12 Journal of International Criminal Justice 681; Karolina Aksamitowska, The Counter-Hegemonic Turn to 'Entrepreneurial Justice'in International Criminal Investigations and Prosecutions in Syria and Eastern Ukraine' in Jeßberger and others, *Counterhegemonic Project?* (n 47).

72 Sarah Nouwen and Wouter Werner, 'Monopolizing Global Justice: International Criminal Law as Challenge to Human Diversity' (2015) 13 Journal of International Criminal Justice 157, 160–2.

73 Luis Eslava and Sundhya Pahuja, 'Between Resistance and Reform: TWAIL and the Universality of International Law Special Issue: Third World Approaches to International Law' (2011) 3 Trade, Law and Development 116 (hereinafter Eslava and Pahuja, 'Resistance and Reform').

74 Chimni, 'TWAIL Manifesto' (n 8).

75 Eslava and Pahuja, 'Resistance and Reform' (n 73) 117.

Balakrishnan Rajagopal reconciles between the two seemingly conflicting sides and acknowledges the hegemonic Western discourse of modern human rights but recognizes that the hegemonic and counter-hegemonic capacities of human rights can coexist.[76]

The book is an attempt to extend this reasoning to international criminal law. Through this book, the author contends that while it is important to critique the discipline and the practice that sustains domination, it must be engaged with not out of fear but driven by the courage to resist. Particularly, from the perspective of Third World peoples, it is imperative to explore a practice that is informed by the critique of the discipline and yet paves the path to leverage the emancipatory potential of the law, thus offering a reform-based critique.

2. *Relativizing the Universal*

In a TWAIL quest for a post-hegemonic just global order, the emphasis on pluralism is crucial. It is a quest for a world that stands on 'the moral equivalency of cultures and peoples'[77] as opposed to the assumed sovereign equivalency of modern states.[78] It is underlined by a 'recognition of multiple identities, heterogeneity, and the rejection of universalist modes of reasoning'.[79] In seeking space for acknowledgement and recognition for the under-represented sections of humanity, a classic TWAIL work would challenge the universalist claims of international law.

Universal justice is the concentrated version of the grand narrative of the human rights enterprise. The discourse on the modern human rights corpus has been famously presented by Mutua in the prism of 'savages, victims, and saviors';[80] 'savagery' being supposedly inherent in the cultural foundations of certain societies, where the state only acts as the neutral and passive instrument of these 'savage' foundations.[81] 'Victimhood' is attributed to a powerless and helpless innocent whose naturalist attributes have been negated by the primitive actions of the state or its cultural foundations.[82] Finally, the 'saviour' is the good angel who protects, vindicates, civilizes, and safeguards the victim from savagery.[83] Mutua argues that such a narrative tends to paint a unilateral picture of justice where one culture is deemed as the ideal framework and gives way to the process of 'othering' of the rest.

76 Rajagopal, 'Counter-Hegemonic International Law' (n 23).
77 Mutua, 'What Is TWAIL?' (n 4) 36.
78 Anghie, *Sovereignty* (n 65).
79 Gathii, 'TWAIL: A Brief History' (n 2) 26.
80 Makau Mutua, 'Savages, Victims, and Saviors: The Metaphor of Human Rights' (2001) Harvard International Law Journal 42, 201.
81 Ibid 202.
82 Ibid 203.
83 Ibid 204.

International criminal law, relying on words such as 'humanity' and 'international community as a whole',[84] offers similar universalist claims without giving due regard to questions such as who constitutes this community and which values and norms are being attributed to the entirety of mankind.[85]

For instance, the first sentence of the ICC Statute proclaims that it is 'conscious that all peoples are united by common bonds, their cultures pieced together in a shared heritage, and concerned that this delicate mosaic may be shattered at any time'.[86] The Rome Conference, attended by all UN member states and numerous NGOs, was chasing the goal of conceiving a universal institution which would act beyond the special interests of select states. The multilateral genesis of the Statute has been relied upon to establish the lack of preference of one legal culture over another. The ICC may be considered as an improvement in the democratic and participatory aspect of international law-making as opposed to the ICTY and ICTR.[87] Regardless, a discussion of the genuineness of this consensus continues to be desirable and inevitable.[88] How much space has the 'other' been able to claim in the interaction that led to the consensus?

The universal element of the international criminal justice project manifests itself in the form of individual criminal responsibility for core crimes that trigger special concern of the international community as a whole and gives rise to unique jurisdictional consequences.[89] The category of universally binding international criminal legal norms also includes doctrines governing forms of liability for commanders and determining the illegality of superior orders operating in the specific contexts of mass criminality,[90] to the extent that even third states without any direct connection to the crimes can

84 Preamble to Rome Statute of the International Criminal Court underlines, 'it is the duty of every State to exercise its criminal jurisdiction over those responsible for' 'the most serious crimes of concern to the international community as a whole must not go unpunished', see Gerhard Werle and Florian Jeßberger, *Principles of International Criminal Law* (4th edn, Oxford University Press 2020) 36 ff.

85 Tallgren, 'We Did It?' (n 52) 683.

86 Preamble, ICC Statute.

87 Anghie and Chimni, 'Individual Responsibility' (n 8) 95.

88 The ICC Statute per se can be challenged on many accounts from a TWAIL perspective such as not outlawing nuclear weapons, excessive powers to the Security Council, and missing colonial crimes, etc.

89 Kamari M Clarke, *Fictions of Justice: The International Criminal Court and the Challenge of Legal Pluralism in Sub-Saharan Africa* (Cambridge University Press 2009); AKA Greenawalt, 'The Pluralism of International Criminal Law' (2011) 86 Indiana Law Journal 1063 (hereinafter Greenwalt, 'Pluralism').

90 See London Charter, Article 8 (superior orders); Allied Control Council Law No. 10, Article II(4)(b), Dec. 20, 1945 (superior orders); Protocol Additional to the Geneva Conventions of 12 August 1949 and Relating to the Protections of Victims of International Armed Conflicts (Protocol I), Article 87, December 12, 1977 (duty of commanders); ICTY Statute, Article 7(3) (command responsibility); Article 7(4) (superior orders); ICTR Stature, Article 6(3) (command responsibility); Article 6(4) (superior orders).

potentially initiate prosecutions against the perpetrators of core crimes under the principle of 'universality'.

In that regard, this study focuses on domestic application of the ostensibly universal principles as a means to relativize the law and accommodate plurality. It is in this space where the legitimacy of the universal claim to duty of conferring a sense of justice to the population affected by atrocities is tested.[91] Uniformity of criminal law norms still ends up giving way to discretion in matters such as sentencing practices, etc.[92] reflecting varying degrees of retributive and utilitarian considerations in different contexts. Beyond the core criminal offences, the law changes its character in the forum it is applied: the domestic court, international tribunals, or hybrid tribunals.

The complementarity framework in the ICC Statute explicitly gives way to genuine investigations and prosecutions even where substantive criminal law may not mirror the ICC Statute precisely.[93] The language of Article 17 has been criticized for being imperialist; however, the practice, provided unwillingness is not confused with inability, promises a potential for different avenues for delivering justice.[94] When it comes to the international tribunals, certainly they are bound by their statutory framework; however, when a given aspect is unclear, the Court may resort to those principles of national laws which are not inconsistent with the Statute.[95] The significance of this provision depends on the Court's interpretative approach.[96] A clear example of the relative practice of these universalized norms is their application by hybrid tribunals, for

91 Robert Cryer and others, *An Introduction to International Criminal Law and Procedure* (Cambridge University Press 2007) 91–92.

92 In search of a uniform sentencing framework, see Jens David Ohlin, 'Towards a Unique Theory of International Criminal and the Potential Sentencing' in G Sluiter and S Vasiliev (eds), *International Criminal Procedure: Towards a Coherent Body of Law* (CMILP 2009) 373; William Schabas, 'Sentencing By International Tribunals: A Human Rights Approach' (1996) 462 Duke Journal of Comparative and International Law 461; Robert D. Sloane, 'The Expressive Capacity Of International Punishment: The Limits Of The National Law Analogy of International Criminal Law' (2007) 43 Stanford Journal of International Law 39; Ida L. Bostian, 'Cultural Relativism in International War Crimes Prosecutions: The International Criminal Tribunal for Rwanda' (2005) ILSA Journal International & Comparative Law 12.

93 William Burke-White, 'Proactive Complementarity: The International Criminal Court and National Courts in the Rome System of International Justice' (2008) 49 Harvard International Law Journal 53.

94 Frederick Cowell, 'Inherent Imperialism: Understanding the Legal Roots of Anti-Imperialist Criticism of the International Criminal Court' (2017) 15 Journal of International Criminal Justice 4, 667–687.

95 Article 21, the ICC Statute: '[G]eneral principles of law derived by the Court from national laws of legal systems of the world *including, as appropriate, the national laws of States that would normally exercise jurisdiction over the crime,* provided that those principles are not inconsistent with this Statute and with international law and internationally recognized norms and standards'.

96 Greenwalt, 'Pluralism' (n 89) 1128.

example, the Special Tribunal for Lebanon's prosecution of corporations[97] and the crime of terrorism.[98]

Therefore, the debate between the universal and relative loses some of its significance when international criminal law is being practiced before domestic courts. Instead, the important question is what kind of universality is to be embraced and what kind of universality should be resisted to maintain the emancipatory potential of the international criminal justice project.[99]

Situated within the duality of resistance and engagement, reaching towards a semblance of an 'open' universality, this book takes on the invitation to give TWAIL scholarship a methodological push to revisit and engage with international law not as a normative or ideological project but as a set of concrete practices that express themselves in the material world.[100] In order to contest the inadequacies of international criminal law and to interrogate its true emancipatory potential, this book delves into a study of a divergent praxis of universal ideals. Outside the radius of the international criminal courts and tribunals and the United Nations Security Council, there are subjects which are engaging and re-engaging with international criminal law to give it a more inclusive identity. The attempt is to engage with the everyday life of international criminal law and, therefore, to some extent, examine the traditional façade in which it is represented and understood to be practised: as the law of exceptional, state-centric actions, reflective of and dependent on geopolitical power dynamics.

Thus, it may be of strategic value to view the normative universal element of international criminal law as a potential influence on domestic frameworks, but it is equally important to evaluate how the local understanding of international criminal justice is informing its practice and, consequently, influencing its imperial character, if at all. In other words, it is to emphasize the importance of extra-institutional forms of practising international criminal law in determining the 'successes' or 'failures' of the institutional forms.[101] These non-institutional spaces constitute resistance that remains beyond the boundaries of normative legal discourse.

97 Al Akhbar Beirut SAL [2015] STL, Case No. STL-14-06/PT/AP/AR126.1 and New TV SAL [2014] STL, Case No. STL-14-05/PT/AP/AR126.1.

98 Cécile Aptel, 'Some Innovations in the Statute of the Special Tribunal for Lebanon' (2007) 5 Journal of International Criminal Justice 5, 1107–1124.

99 David Fidler, 'Revolt Against or From Within the West? TWAIL, the Developing World, and the Future Direction of International Law' (2003) 2 Chinese Journal of International Law 29 (hereinafter Fidler, 'Revolt Against or From Within); Mutua, 'What Is TWAIL?' (n 4); Antony Anghie, 'Finding the Peripheries: Sovereignty and Colonialism in Nineteenth-Century International Law' (1999) 40 Harvard International Law Journal 1.

100 Eslava and Pahuja, 'Resistance and Reform' (n 73) 108; Linda Zerilli, 'This Universalism which Is Not One' (1998) 28 Diacritics 2.

101 See Claus Offe, 'New Social Movements: Challenging the Boundaries of Institutional Politics' (1985) 52 Social Research 817 (1985); Balakrishnan Rajagopal, 'From Resistance

A study of everyday practice of international criminal law is a departure from traditional international criminal law scholarship as it does not view the discipline in terms of a restricted body of norms. In addition to that, moving beyond the traditional theoretical critique of international law, the book locates actors and ways of resistance against the oppression of international legal project at local sites. The book foregrounds transnational organizations engaging in strategic litigation of international criminal law as a challenge to the predominant notions of spatial boundaries in which international criminal law is elaborated and practised.

3. De-privileging the State

Concerning substantive international law, its formation and implementation continue to be an exclusive prerogative of the states. Customary norms constitute the applicable law of international and internationalized criminal courts/tribunals.[102] States hold not only a significant influence on how international criminal law is practised but also their practice impacts the formation of law and legal norms.[103]

TWAIL scholars argue that customary international law (CIL) per se is an essentially undemocratic source of international law. The democratic deficit flows from, among other things, the absence of availability of state practice of Third World states, the paucity of writings of its publicists, the lack of adequate weight given to qualifying resolutions of international organizations, and 'the nonrecognition of the practices of global civil society'.[104] Joycelin Chinwe Okubuiro has also argued that customary international law is not only hegemonic in its form (in that it has a bias towards centralized power structures modelled on the Westphalian state), but also in its substance (in that it is more likely for the powerful states to influence the making of customary norms).[105]

to Renewal: The Third World, Social Movements, and the Expansion of International Institutions Symposium: International Law and the Developing World: A Millennial Analysis' (2000) 41 Harvard International Law Journal 529; Balakrishnan Rajagopal, *International Law from Below: Development, Social Movements and Third World Resistance* (Cambridge University Press 2003)

102 Yudan Tan, 'The Identification of Customary Rules in International Criminal Law' (2018) 34 Utrecht Journal of International & European Law 92.

103 Harmen van der Wilt, 'State Practice as Element of Customary International Law: A White Knight in International Criminal Law?' (2019) 20 International Criminal Law Review 5, 785.

104 Bhupinder Singh Chimni, 'Customary International Law: A Third World Perspective' (2018) 112 American Journal of International Law 1, 46 (hereinafter Chimni, 'Customary International Law').

105 J.C. Okubuiro, 'Application of Hegemony to Customary International Law: An African Perspective' (2018) 7 Global Journal of Comparative Law 2, 232–271 (hereinafter

To address this deficit, B.S. Chimni advocates for a postmodern doctrine of customary international law that distinguishes between *opinio juris* as a constituent element of customary international law and *opinio juris communis* representing universal conscience in order to inject progressive content into the international legal order.[106]

Opinio Juris communis is a concept most recently elaborated by Judge Cançado Trindade in his dissenting opinion in the *Marshall Islands v. India* case before the International Court of Justice.[107] In his view, 'it is the universal juridical conscience that is the ultimate material source of international law'.[108] This conscience is 'no longer only of nations and peoples – sustained in the past by the historical school – but of the international community as a whole, heading towards the universalization of international law'.[109]

Chimni argues that the distinction between *opinio juris* and *opinio juris communis* must be reframed and reconfigured to decolonize it. Decolonization of this element making up a customary norm would be to include the practices of both international organizations and global civil society, if these norms are to serve the purpose of facilitating a post-hegemonic global order.[110] Moreover, restructuring the international customary process that takes into account activities of non-state actors will provide an inclusive system for wider participation.[111]

Particularly with respect to international criminal law, a study of global civil society actors would also reflect the potential of international criminal justice in challenging hegemony. The reliance on terms such as 'humanity' and 'conscience of the international community' makes it imperative that when international crimes are being questioned in a context, the actors immediately affected by them are important stakeholders in the accountability process to inform these broad notions. In order to give any meaning to the international criminal justice processes, it is crucial that their context-specific understanding of justice and accountability are as much the driving factors

---

Okubuiro, 'Customary International Law').

106 Chimni, 'Customary International Law' (n 104) 6.

107 Dissenting Judgment of Judge Cançado Trindade in *Marshall Islands v. India* [2016] ICJ.

108 Ibid 114. He further elaborates on this in A. Cançado Trindade, '*International Law for Humankind: Towards a New Jus Gentium*' (2nd edn, Nijhoff/The Hague Academy of International Law 2013) 139–161.

109 Ibid 181.

110 Chimni, 'Customary International Law' (n 104) 41; Vasuki Nesiah, 'Decolonial CIL: TWAIL, Feminism, and an Insurgent Jurisprudence' (2018) 112 AJIL 313, 316; Parfitt, 'The Spectre of Sources' (2014) 25 European Journal of International Law 297; Matilda Arvidsson and Miriam Bak McKenna, The Turn to History in International Law and the Sources Doctrine: Critical Approaches and Methodological Imaginaries (2020) 33 Leiden Journal of International Law 1, 37–56.

111 Okubuiro, 'Customary International Law' (n 105).

of the process as the declared principles of the states in the form of treaties and statutes.

The discipline's exclusive dependence on states for its practice makes it essentially unable to transcend great power accommodation and to involve the Global South in the shaping of international law. In that vein, the subjects of this book are transnational strategic litigation organizations, a small fraction in the sea of non-governmental organizations, who are practising international criminal law strategically to pursue broader objectives.[112] Their practice and their influence pose, albeit only a small, challenge to the exclusive role of states in the development and implementation of international criminal law.

These global civil society actors approach international criminal law recognizing that it serves as an instrument of hegemony but at the same time offers the signposts of and for a struggle against that hegemony. In doing that, such actors end up making the practice of international criminal law more inclusive and representative.

The focus on a 'global' or 'transnational' civil society as opposed to 'local' draws on another classic debate in TWAIL scholarship – the choice between a revolt against the West or a revolt from within the West.[113] With the globalized nature of atrocities and the transnational character of the perpetrators, it has become essentially impossible to envision a successful geographically confined movement to counter these injustices. Therefore, the coalition of like-minded critical movements across the divides of the First and Third World seem not only promising but also essential to combat powerlessness and the victimization of the Third World as well as marginalized communities in the West.[114]

Such transnational non-state actors can potentially transcend the difference between the First and Third Worlds in pushing for accountability of international crimes, articulating demands for justice in a framework best addressed to their needs. They are not reflective of the interests of a post-colonial Third World state, instead of the Third World peoples who may have no recourse to justice, at times, against the tyranny of their own state.

A study of their practice serves a dual function in the analysis of international criminal law: firstly, owing to its current nascent stage of development, an evaluation of their practice in the determination of customary rules offers to make the substantive international criminal law more democratic.

112 For an overview of the various kinds of roles strategic litigation organizations are playing in the practice of international criminal justice, see Florian Jeßberger and Leonie Steinl, 'Strategic Litigation in International Criminal Justice: Facilitating a View from Within' (2022) 20 Journal of International Criminal Justice 2, 379 – 401.

113 See Fidler, 'Revolt Against or From Within' (n 99).

114 Mutua, 'What Is TWAIL?' (n 4) 38.

Secondly, their groundedness (as opposed to state-driven procedures) offers an insight into the design of the procedures which can be adapted to address the needs and demands of those most directly affected.

4. *Addressing Material Inequality*

Another fundamental TWAIL preoccupation has been to unpack the ways in which international legal doctrines contribute to the dominance of certain states by favouring their interests in maintaining an unjust international economic order.[115] International law may not be the only factor advancing material inequality in the global order; nevertheless, it still offers the cloak for exploitative commercial expansion without proportionate consequences. As Anghie delineates the colonial origins of international law, he traces its conception to the conflict arising from the European conquest of the resources belonging to Indigenous peoples.[116] Many legal doctrines have furthered colonial economic interventions such as the doctrine of discovery, *terra nullius*, the mandate system after World War I, and trusteeship after World War II, contributing to the injustices of the current economic order.[117] The beneficiaries of such expansion and favours remain former colonizers as the headquarters of giant transnational corporations. The invisibility of the colonial legacy within contemporary international legal doctrines facilitates the continued structural embeddedness of these unequal relations. European privilege is maintained through various seemingly 'neutral' laws that deny alternative ways of economic or political distribution.[118] Therefore, the

115 See Anghie, *Sovereignty* (n 66); Sandhya Pahuja, *Decolonising International Law: Development, Growth, and the Politics of Universality* (Cambridge University Press 2011); B.S. Chimni, 'Capitalism, Imperialism, and International Law in the Twenty-First Century' (2012) 14 Oregon Review of International Law 17; Kwame Nkrumah, *Neo-Colonialism: The Last Stage of Imperialism* (Thomas Nelson & Sons 1965).

116 Based on the moral justifications offered by Vitoria, a leading Jesuit theologian of 16th century, on the Spanish conquests in Latin America. These justifications were also mirrored in the writing of Hugo Grotius in the following century when confronted with Dutch acquisitions – constituting the foundations of international law. Anghie, *Sovereignty* (n 66) 13–31; see R Hernandez, 'The Internationalization of Francisco de Vitoria and Domingo de Soto' (1991) 15 Fordham International Law Journal 1031.

117 John Linarelli, Margot E Salomon, and Muthucumaraswamy Sornarajah, *The Misery of International Law: Confrontations with Injustice in the Global Economy* (Oxford University Press 2018) 84–87 (hereinafter Linarelli and others, *Misery of International Law*).

118 See James T. Gathii, 'Third World Approaches to International Economic Governance' in Richard Falk, Balakrishnan Rajagopal and Jacqueline Stevens (eds), *International Law and the Third World: Reshaping Justice* (Routledge 2008) 255; Obiora Okafor, 'Newness, Imperialism, and International Legal Reform In Our Time: A TWAIL Perspective' (2005) 43 Osgoode Hall Law Journal 171; Balakrishnan Rajagopal, 'International Law and the

liberal ideology prevalent in international law that draws formal distinctions between the law, the market, and politics is contested by TWAIL scholars.[119]

The 1960s and 1970s witnessed a sustained, yet unsuccessful, attempt by formerly colonized peoples seeking to bring a new world order to ensure that the resources found in their lands are not exploited to the benefit of others. Even when these states became formally independent, their economies were controlled by the multinational companies established during colonial times, for instance, the tea plantations in Sri Lanka and oil in Nigeria.[120] As a response to this continued economic dependence came 'New International Economic Order' – a set of normative prescriptions by Third World states expressed through various UN instruments.[121] These prescriptions aspiring for economic self-determination did not seek to dismantle the existing economic structures, in fact, they were informed by market-oriented logic. Some of their ideas included a redistributive agenda to remedy centuries of colonial deprivations, granting of aid by rich nations to the Third World as an obligation, transfer of technology to developing countries, permanent sovereignty over natural resources, and regulation and supervision of the transnational corporations by the host states.[122] However, the resolutions were dismissed by 'the West' on political and legal grounds.[123] The geopolitical developments of the next two decades ensured that these proposals were forgotten.[124] As a result, the legacy of economic exploitation of Third World peoples for the

Development Encounter: Violence and Resistance at the Margins' (1999) Proceedings of the 93rd Annual Meeting of the American Society of International Law 16, 20–21, 25.

119 James T. Gathii, 'Neoliberalism, Colonialism, and International Governance: Decentring the International Law of Governmental Legitimacy' (2000) 98 Michigan Law Review 1996, 2025; Antony Anghie, 'Colonialism and the Birth of International Institutions: Sovereignty, Economy and the Mandate System of the League of Nations' (2001) 34 NYU Journal of International Law & Politics 513; for the critique that TWAIL scholarship is not radical enough on this account, see John D Haskell, 'Trail-ing TWAIL: Arguments and Blind Spots in Third World Approaches to International Law' (2014) 27 Canadian Journal of Law & Jurisprudence 2, 383–414.

120 Ibid 90.

121 Key documents include the Declaration of Bandung Conference, 1955; Resolution on Permanent Sovereignty over Natural Resources GA Resolution 1803 (XVII) 14 Dec. 1962; common Article 1(2) of the International Covenant on Civil and Political Rights (1966) and the International Covenant on Economic, Social and Cultural Rights (1966); finally leading to the Resolution on the Establishment of a New International Economic Order was passed at the Sixth Special Session of the General Assembly on 1 May 1974.

122 Declaration on the Establishment of a New International Economic Order (1 May 1974) A/Res/5-6/3201.

123 See Giorgio Sacerdoti, 'New International Economic Order (NIEO)', Max Planck Encyclopaedia of Public International Law (June 2014); Kamal Hossein (ed), *Legal Aspects of the New International Economic Order* (Francis Pinter 1980).

124 For a succinct history of the entire NIEO proposal, see Linarelli and others, *Misery of International Law* (n 117) ch 3.

favour and benefit of the economic elite of the richer nations continues and manifests itself in different forms.

The central concern of addressing material inequality through international law is the thematic focus of this study as it pertains to the international criminal justice system. The book concerns itself largely with the accountability of corporations for their contribution to and involvement in crimes under international law. ICC's lack of jurisdiction over corporations and consequent disregard of the context in which violence takes place strengthens the critique that

> violence has been displaced in part from the first to the Third World by a number of international practices which have resulted in the South's subjection to a range of unsustainable economic and social policies policed by international financial and trade institutions that enrich and favour the North.[125]

This strand of criticism goes beyond the classic critique of selective enforcement of international criminal law.[126] Even in situations which receive consideration by international courts and where prosecution of atrocity crimes ends up taking place, the selection of perpetrators focuses solely on the local conditions of violence implicitly suggesting that violence is endogenous to the Third World and renders invisible the external actors and factors driving the conflict.[127] Such perpetuation of impunity for multinational corporations presents an incomplete and misleading narrative of atrocity crimes and the context in which they take place.

This underlining of external factors is not intended to be an alibi or justification for various unfortunate reasons driving the conflict in the Third World. It is to only highlight that these clashes are not only remnants of reckless colonial policies of the past, but also transnational business actors, primarily headquartered in the West, continue to play a significant role in sustaining and fuelling these conflicts.[128] The fact that these actors, for whatever substantive legal or policy reasons, are not being called to accountability further points to the systemic bias contrary to the claims of universality made by international criminal law.

125 Anghie, Chimni, 'Individual Responsibility' (n 8) 196.

126 See Res Schuerch, *The International Criminal Court at the Mercy of Powerful States* (Springer 2017) 978–94.

127 See Anghie, Chimni, 'Individual Responsibility' (n 8) 195–200; Joanna Kyriakakis, 'Corporations Before International Criminal Courts: Implications for the International Criminal Justice Project' (2017) 30 Leiden Journal of International Law 221, 227 (hereinafter Kyriakakis, 'Corporations Before International Criminal Courts').

128 See Eberechi Ifeonu, *Armed Conflict in Africa and Western Complicity: A Disincentive for African Union's Cooperation with the ICC* (The Africa Law Institute 2009).

The purpose of the argument is also to not pose prosecution of corporations as a comprehensive solution to the structural biases within the international criminal law and enforcement procedures. The emphasis on prosecutions of corporations is instructive on how international accountability practices could acknowledge and respond to the in-egalitarian global economic order underlying atrocity crimes. Multiple conflict studies point to a relationship between global economic structures and conflicts as illustrative of North–South relations.[129] An attempt at attributing responsibility for atrocity crimes should also include the role that international actors play in promoting, facilitating, and escalating the situation. Such prosecutions will not only further the expressivist goals of the international criminal justice project in the eyes of those witnessing these trials across the globe but they will also potentially draw the behaviour of global corporations into the normative order constructed by international criminal justice.[130]

The scope of the argument is not only restricted to the inclusion of corporate complicity in crimes under international law but also to emphasize the need to prosecute and charge multinational corporations as entities to mark a departure from the singular idea of individual criminal responsibility. It questions whether individual responsibility alone can appropriately address the instrumental role such entities play in the context of large-scale violations. Such modes of responsibility lead to individualization of conflict, simplifying the context which then gets robbed of its systematic nature of the violations, complexity, and nuance. A due acknowledgement of corporate responsibility in a given conflict not only brings more context to the conventional linear narrative of direct violence but also makes the conflict less local, less indigenous, less specifically a problem of the 'uncivilized' Third World.

IV. Conclusion

Critical scholarship under the broad moniker of TWAIL shares a dual relationship with international law, i.e. it treats it as a subject of critique and as an instrument to strive for justice. This chapter pinpoints four key concerns of the TWAIL scholarship in so far that they are applicable to international criminal law: offering reform-oriented critique, relativizing the universal, de-privileging the state, and addressing material inequality. These central concerns will be the foundation for the subsequent analysis of strategic litigation seeking corporate accountability within international criminal law. While doing that, the author also attempts to fill a gap in TWAIL scholarship

129 Ibid; Abdallah Bujra, 'African Conflicts: Their Causes and Their Political and Social Environment' (2002) Development Policy Management Forum.

130 Kyriakakis, 'Corporations Before International Criminal Courts' (n 127) 231.

by employing its arguments on concrete case studies that attest TWAIL's assertions.

References

Abi-Saab G, 'The Third World Intellectual in Praxis: Confrontation, Participation, or Operation behind Enemy Lines?' (2016) 37 Third World Quarterly 1957

Aksamitowska K, 'The Counter-Hegemonic Turn to "Entrepreneurial Justice" in International Criminal Investigations and Prosecutions in Syria and Eastern Ukraine' in Jeßberger and others (eds), *International Criminal Justice – A Counterhegemonic Project?* (Springer 2022)

Al Attar M, 'TWAIL: A Paradox within a Paradox' (2020) 22 International Community Law Review 163

Altwicker T and Diggelmann O, 'What Should Remain of the Critical Approaches to International Law: International Legal Theory as Critique' (2014) 24 Swiss Review International & European Law 69

Anand RP, *International Law and the Developing Countries* (Brill 1987)

Anghie A and Chimni BS, 'Third World Approaches to International Law and Individual Responsibility in Internal Conflicts' (2003) 2 Chinese Journal of International Law 77

Anghie A, 'Colonialism and the Birth of International Institutions: Sovereignty, Economy and the Mandate System of the League of Nations' (2001) 34 NYU Journal of International Law & Politics 513

Anghie A, 'LatCrit and TWAIL' (2012) 42 California Western International Law Journal 311

Anghie A, 'Time Present and Time Past: Globalization, International Financial Institutions, and the Third World Millenium Issue: Shaping the Parameters of International Law in the New Millennium' (1999) 32 New York University Journal of International Law and Politics 243

Anghie A, 'TWAIL: Past and Future' (2008) 10 International Community Law Review 4

Anghie A, 'Finding the Peripheries: Sovereignty and Colonialism in Nineteenth-Century International Law' (1999) 40 Harvard International Law Journal 1

Angie A, 'TWAIL: Past and Future' (2008) 10 International Community Law Review 4, 479

Aptel C, 'Some Innovations in the Statute of the Special Tribunal for Lebanon' (2007) 5 Journal of International Criminal Justice 5, 1107–1124

Arvidsson M and McKenna MB, 'The Turn to History in International Law and the Sources Doctrine: Critical Approaches and Methodological Imaginaries' (2020) 33 Leiden Journal of International Law 1, 37–56

Bais D, 'India and the International Criminal Court' (2016) FICHL Policy Brief Series No. 54 <https://www.toaep.org/pbs-pdf/54-bais> accessed 21 December 2021

Baxi U, 'What May the "Third World" Expect from International Law?' (2006) 27 Third World Quarterly 713

Bergsmo M, Kaleck W, Hlaing K (eds), *Colonial Wrongs and Access to International Law* (TOAEP 2020)

Bostian I, 'Cultural Relativism in International War Crimes Prosecutions: The International Criminal Tribunal for Rwanda' (2005) ILSA Journal International & Comparative Law 12

Burgis-Kasthala M, 'Scholarship as Dialogue? TWAIL and the Politics of Methodology' (2016) 14 Journal of International Criminal Justice 4, 921–937

Burke-White W, 'Proactive Complementarity: The International Criminal Court and National Courts in the Rome System of International Justice' (2008) 49 Harvard International Law Journal 53

Chimni BS, 'Capitalism, Imperialism, and International Law in the Twenty-First Century' (2012) 14 Oregon Review of International Law 17

Chimni BS, 'Customary International Law: A Third World Perspective' (2018) 112 American Journal of International Law 1, 46

Chimni BS, 'Third World Approaches to International Law: A Manifesto' (2006) 8 International Community Law Review 3

Chimni BS, 'Towards a Radical Third World Approach to Contemporary International Law' (2002) 5 International Center for Comparative Law and Politics Review 14

Chimni BS, *International Law and World Order: A Critique of Contemporary Approaches* (Cambridge University Press 2017)

Choudhary S, 'Contextualising Radhabinod Pal's Dissenting Opinion in Contemporary International Criminal Law' (2021) 11 Asian Journal of International Law 223

Clarke KM, *Fictions of Justice: The International Criminal Court and the Challenge of Legal Pluralism in Sub-Saharan Africa* (Cambridge University Press 2009)

Clarke KM, Knottnerus AS and De Volder E (eds), *Africa and the ICC* (Cambridge University Press 2016)

Cowell F, 'Inherent Imperialism: Understanding the Legal Roots of Anti-Imperialist Criticism of the International Criminal Court' (2017) 15 Journal of International Criminal Justice 4

Cryer R and others, *An Introduction to International Criminal Law and Procedure* (Cambridge University Press 2007)

Cryer R, *Prosecuting International Crimes: Selectivity and the International Criminal Law Regime* (Cambridge University Press 2005)

Damaska M, 'What Is the Point of International Criminal Justice' (2008) 83 Chi-Kent Law Review 329–368

Drumbl M, 'Memorializing Dissent: Justice Pal in Tokyo' (2020) 114 American Journal of International Law 11

Eslava L and Pahuja S, 'Between Resistance and Reform: TWAIL and the Universality of International Law Special Issue: Third World Approaches to International Law' (2011) 3 Trade, Law and Development 116

Fidler D, 'Revolt Against or from Within the West? TWAIL, the Developing World, and the Future Direction of International Law' (2003) 2 Chinese Journal of International Law 29

Gathii JT, 'Alternative and Critical: The Contributions of Research and Scholarship on Developing Countries to International Legal Theory' (2000) 41 Harvard International Law Journal 273

Gathii JT, 'International Law and Eurocentricity' (1998) 9 European Journal of International Law 184

Gathii JT, 'Neoliberalism, Colonialism, and International Governance: Decentering the International Law of Governmental Legitimacy' (2000) 98 Michigan Law Review 1996, 2025

Gathii JT, 'Third World Approaches to International Economic Governance' in Richard Falk, Balakrishnan Rajagopal and Jacqueline Stevens (eds), *International Law and the Third World: Reshaping Justice* (Routledge Press 2008) 255–268

Gathii JT, 'TWAIL: A Brief History of Its Origins, Its Decentralized Network, and a Tentative Bibliography' (2011) 3 Trade Law and Development 28–29

Gong G, *The Standard of "Civilization" in International Society* (Clarendon 1984)

Greenawalt AKA, 'The Pluralism of International Criminal Law' (2011) 86 Indiana Law Journal 1063

Haskell JD, 'Trail-ing TWAIL: Arguments and Blind Spots in Third World Approaches to International Law' (2014) 27 Canadian Journal of Law & Jurisprudence 2, 383–414.

Hernandez R, 'The Internationalization of Francisco de Vitoria and Domingo de Soto' (1991) 15 Fordham International Law Journal 1031

Hossein K (ed), *Legal Aspects of the New International Economic Order* (Francis Pinter 1980)

Hoyle C and Ullrich L, 'New Court, New Justice? The Evolution of "Justice for Victims" at Domestic Courts and at the International Criminal Court' (2014) 12 Journal of International Criminal Justice 681

Ifeonu E, *Armed Conflict in Africa and Western Complicity: A disincentive for African Union's Cooperation with the ICC* (The Africa Law Institute 2009)

Iyi JM, 'Is International Criminal Justice the Handmaiden of the Contemporary Imperial Project? A TWAIL Perspective of Some Arenas of Contestations' in Florian Jeßberger and others (eds), *International Criminal Justice – A Counterhegemonic Project?* (Springer 2022)

Jacobs D, 'Sitting on the Wall Looking in: Some Reflections on the Critique of International Criminal Law' (2015) 28 Leiden Journal of International Law 1

Jeßberger F, 'Die Krisen des Völkerstrafrechts' im *Festschrift für Gerhard Werle* (Mohr Siebeck 2022)

Jianping J and Zhixiang W, 'China's Attitude Towards the ICC' (2005) 3 Journal of International Criminal Justice 608

Justice Pal, International Military Tribunal for the Far East (1948) <http://www.sdh-fact.com/CL02_1/65_S4.pdf> accessed 27 May 2020

Kendall S and Nouwen S, 'Representational Practices at the International Criminal Court: The Gap between Juridified and Abstract Victimhood' (2013) 76 Law and Contemporary Problems 235

Kendall S, 'Donors Justice: Recasting International Criminal Accountability' (2011) 24 Leiden Journal of International Law 585

Khosla M, 'The TWAIL Discourse: The Emergence of a New Phase' (2007) 9 International Community Law Review 291

Kiyani A, 'Third World Approaches to International Criminal Law' (2015) 109 AJIL Unbound 255–259

Kiyani A, 'Group-Based Differentiation and Local Repression: The Custom and Curse of Selectivity' (2016) 14 Journal of International Criminal Justice 4, 939–957

Kiyani A, Reynolds J, and Xavier S, 'Foreword' (2016) 14 Journal of International Criminal Justice 4, 915–920

Kyriakakis J, 'Corporations before International Criminal Courts: Implications for the International Criminal Justice Project' (2017) 30 Leiden Journal of International Law 221

Linarelli J, Salomon M and Sornarajah M, *The Misery of International Law: Confrontations with Injustice in the Global Economy* (Oxford University Press 2018)

Linton S, 'India and China Before, At, and After Rome' (2018) 6 Journal of International Criminal Justice 2, 265–294

McCormack TLH, 'Selective Reaction to Atrocity' (1996–97) 60 Albany Law Review 681

Mickelson K, 'Rhetoric and Rage: Third World Voices in International Legal Discourse' (1998) 16 Wisconsin International Law Journal 353

Mieville C, 'The Commodity-Form Theory of International Law: An Introduction' (2004) 17 (2) Leiden Journal of International Law 271

Mieville C, *Between Equal Rights: A Marxist Theory of International Law* (Brill 2005)

Mutua M, 'Africans and the ICC: Hypocrisy, Impunity and Perversion' in Clarke and others (eds), *Africans and the ICC: Perceptions of Justice* (Cambridge University Press 2016)

Mutua M, 'Savages, Victims, and Saviors: The Metaphor of Human Rights' (2001) 42 Harvard International Law Journal 201

Mutua M, 'What Is TWAIL?' (2000) 94 Proceedings of the ASIL Annual Meeting 31

Mutua M, 'Why Redraw the Map of Africa: A Moral and Legal Inquiry' (1995) 16 Michigan Journal of International Law 1113

Nandy A, 'The Other Within: The Strange Case of Radhabinod Pal's Judgment on Culpability' (1992) 23 New Literary History 45

Nesiah V, 'Decolonial CIL: TWAIL, Feminism, and an Insurgent Jurisprudence' (2018) 112 American Journal of International Law 313

Nielsen C, 'From Nuremberg to the Hague: The Civilizing Mission of International Criminal Law' (2008) 14 Auckland University Law Review 81

Nielsen M and Robyn LM, *Colonialism Is Crime* (Rutgers University Press 2019)

Nkrumah K, *NeoColonialism: The Last Stage of Imperialism* (Thomas Nelson & Sons 1965)

Nouwen S and Werner W, 'Monopolizing Global Justice: International Criminal Law as Challenge to Human Diversity' (2015) 13 Journal of International Criminal Justice 157, 160–162

Nouwen S, 'Legal Equality on Trial' (2012) 7 Netherlands Yearbook of International Law 151, 168

Offe C, 'New Social Movements: Challenging the Boundaries of Institutional Politics' (1985) 52 Social Research 817

Ohlin JD, 'Towards a Unique Theory of International Criminal and the Potential Sentencing' in G Sluiter and S Vasiliev (eds), *International Criminal Procedure: Towards a Coherent Body of Law* (CMILP 2009) 373– 404

Okafor O, 'Critical Third World Approaches to International Law (TWAIL): Theory, Methodology, or Both?' (2008) 10 International Community Law Review 371

Okafor O, 'Newness, Imperialism, and International Legal Reform in Our Time: A TWAIL Perspective' (2005) 43 Osgoode Hall Law Journal 171
Okafor O, *Re-Defining Legitimate Statehood: International Law and State Fragmentation in Africa* (Martin Nijhoff 2000)
Pahuja S, *Decolonising International Law: Development, Economic Growth and the Politics of Universality* (Cambridge University Press 2011)
Parfitt, 'The Spectre of Sources' (2014) 25 European Journal of International Law 297
Prashad V, *The Darker Nations: A Biography of the Short-lived Third World* (Leftword Books 2007)
Quashigah E and Okafor O (eds), *Legitimate Governance in Africa: International and Domestic Legal Perspectives* (Kluwer Law International 1999)
Rajagopal B, 'Counter-Hegemonic International Law: Rethinking Human Rights and Development as a Third World Strategy' (2006) 27 Third World Quarterly 5, 767–783
Rajagopal B, 'From Resistance to Renewal: The Third World, Social Movements, and the Expansion of International Institutions Symposium: International Law and the Developing World: A Millennial Analysis' (2000) 41 Harvard International Law Journal 529
Rajagopal B, 'International Law and Social Movements: Challenges of Theorizing Resistance' (2002) 41 Columbia Journal of Transnational Law 397
Rajagopal B, 'International Law and the Development Encounter: Violence and Resistance at the Margins' (1999) Proceedings of the 93rd Annual Meeting of the American Society of International Law 16
Rajagopal B, 'Locating the Third World in Cultural Geography' (1998) Third World Legal Studies 1
Rajagopal B, *International Law from Below: Development, Social Movements and Third World Resistance* (Cambridge University Press 2003)
Ratner S, 'The Schizophrenias of International Criminal Law' (1998) 33 Texas International Law Journal 237
Rubin A, 'Challenging the Conventional Wisdom: Another View of the International Criminal Court' (1999) Journal of International Affairs, 783–794
Sacerdoti G, 'New International Economic Order (NIEO)' in R. Wolfrun (ed)) *Max Planck Encyclopaedia of Public International Law* (OUP 2015)
Sajed A, 'From the Third World to the Global South' (*E-International Relations*, 27 July 2020) <https://www.e-ir.info/2020/07/27/from-the-third-world-to-the-global-south/> accessed 19 December 2021
Schabas W, 'Sentencing by International Tribunals: A Human Rights Approach' (1996) 462 Duke Journal of Comparative and International Law 461
Schabas W, *An Introduction to the International Criminal Court* (5th edn, Cambridge University Press 2017)
Schuerch R, *The International Criminal Court at the Mercy of Powerful States* (Springer 2017)
Schwöbel C (ed), *Critical Approaches to International Criminal Law: An Introduction* (Routledge 2014)
Sellars SK, 'Imperfect Justice at Nuremberg and Tokyo' (2010) 21 European Journal of International Law 1100

Sen R and Raman R, 'Retelling Radha Binod Pal: The Outsider and The Native' in Frédéric Mégret and Immi Tallgren (eds), *The Dawn of a Discipline: International Criminal Justice and Its Early Exponents* (Cambridge University Press 2020) 230–259

Sloane RD, 'The Expressive Capacity of International Punishment: The Limits of the National Law Analogy of International Criminal Law' (2007) 43 Stanford Journal of International Law 39

Solarz M, '"Third World": The 60th Anniversary of a Concept That Changed History' (2012) 33 Third World Quarterly 156

Ssenyonjo M, 'State Withdrawal Notifications from the Rome Statute of the International Criminal Court: South Africa, Burundi and the Gambia' (2018) 29 Criminal Law Forum 63–119

Steinke R, *The Politics of International Criminal Justice: German Perspectives from Nuremberg to The Hague* (Bloomsbury London 2012)

Tallgren I, 'We Did It? The Vertigo of Law and Everyday Life at the Diplomatic Conference on the Establishment of the International Criminal Court' (1998) 12 Leiden Journal of International Law 683

Tan Y, 'The Identification of Customary Rules in International Criminal Law' (2018) 34 Utrecht Journal of International & European Law 92

Trindade AC, *International Law for Humankind – Towards a New Jus Gentium* (2nd edn, Nijhoff/The Hague Academy of International Law 2013)

Ullrich L, 'Beyond the "Global–Local Divide": Local Intermediaries, Victims and the Justice Contestations of the International Criminal Court' (2016) 14 Journal of International Criminal Justice 543

Van der Wilt H, 'State Practice as Element of Customary International Law: A White Knight in International Criminal Law?' (2019) 20 International Criminal Law Review 5, 785

Werle G, Fernandez L and Vormbaum M, *Africa and the International Criminal Court* (TMC Asser Press 2014)

Wilson RA, 'Gangster's Paradise? Framing Crime in Sub-Saharan Africa' (2013) 4 Humanity 449

Wilson RA, 'Through the Lens of International Criminal Law: Comprehending the African Context of Crimes at the International Criminal Court' (2011) 11 Studies in Ethnicity and Nationalism 106

Wilson RA, *Writing History in International Criminal Trials* (Cambridge University Press 2011)

Xavier S and others, 'Placing TWAIL Scholarship and Praxis: Introduction to the Special Issue of the Windsor Yearbook of Access to Justice' (2016) Windsor Yearbook of Access to Justice 33

Xavier S, 'Locating and Situating Justice Pal: TWAIL, International Criminal Tribunals, and Judicial Powers' (2022) 12 Asian Journal of International Law 292

Zerilli L, 'This Universalism Which Is Not One' (1998) 28 Diacritics 2

Zhu D, 'China, Crimes Against Humanity and the International Criminal Court' (2018) 16 Journal of International Criminal Justice 1021

Chapter 2

Conceptualizing Strategic Litigation

Strategic litigation has become a buzzword in international legal practice. Unlike other similar terms such as 'public interest litigation', 'social cause lawyering', or 'cause lawyering' which hold traction in distinct domestic jurisdictions, the ambiguity and versatility of the term 'strategic litigation' makes it susceptible to overuse across actors with varied specializations. From human rights defenders and non-governmental organizations to law firms and corporations, the appeal of branding their engagement with law as 'strategic' seems inescapable. With non-state organizations increasingly resorting to the international criminal legal framework, there are several actors in the field who claim the label of 'strategic litigation' while practising international criminal law as well. Particularly with a state-driven and rapidly evolving discipline such as international criminal law, international lawyers' attraction to call every intervention within the realm of international criminal justice strategic litigation is evident and even understandable to an extent. But at the same time, since the term is so overworked, the actors feel compelled to clarify and distinguish themselves from the others while still claiming their stakes on the label.[1]

To match the overemployment of the term strategic litigation by practitioners, there has been a considerable amount of scholarship analysing these interventions.[2] However, most scholarly works have also accepted the term

1 For an overview of how non-governmental organizations are navigating the practice of international criminal law, see Florian Jeßberger and Leonie Steinl, 'Strategic Litigation in International Criminal Justice: Facilitating a View from Within' (2022) Journal of International Criminal Justice 20 (2), 379–401 (hereinafter Jeßberger and Steinl, 'Strategic Litigation: A View from Within').

2 Andreas Fischer-Lescano, 'From Strategic Litigation to Juridical Action' in Miriam Saage-Maaß and others (eds), *Transnational Legal Activism in Global Value Chains: The Ali Enterprises Factory Fire and the Struggle for Justice* (Springer 2021) 299–312; Kjersti Lohne, *Advocates of Humanity: Human Rights NGOs in International Criminal Justice* (Oxford University Press 2019); Helen Duffy, *Strategic Human Rights Litigation: Understanding and Maximising Impact* (Hart Publishing 2018); Gesine Fuchs, 'Strategic Litigation for Gender

DOI: 10.4324/9781003405047-4

rather uncritically. Such frequent and unreflective use of the term makes the label misleading in many ways. It makes the label seem much broader in scope than it actually is. More importantly, the political characterization of legal interventions for pragmatic purposes has implications for the legitimacy of the institutions and the discipline at large. An ambiguous umbrella term diverts attention from a productive discussion on the politics of engaging with public international law and international criminal law in particular. Such characterization undermines sincere attempts to seek reforms and address structural problems within the legal framework.

Therefore, this chapter conceptualizes the label of strategic litigation. Borrowing from Rob Knox's brilliant contribution, it begins with a discussion on the semantics of the term 'strategic' in strategic litigation before analysing whether it is being appropriately used and what practice would, in fact, qualify as strategic litigation. The purpose is not to build constrained boundaries with a strict definition of strategic litigation. Instead, the underlying objective is to identify and describe key constituent elements of strategic litigation as a concept which will form the basis of subsequent practice analysis.

I. 'Strategy' in Strategic Litigation

Rob Knox offers an insightful account for contemporary critical scholarship attempting to intervene in international politics. His meticulous distinction between strategy and tactics reflecting on the politics of leftist or critical international lawyers serves as a valuable starting point in this discussion.[3] Knox

Equality in the Workplace and Legal Opportunity Structures in Four European Countries' (2013) 28 Canadian Journal of Law and Society / La Revue Canadienne Droit et Société 189; Ezequiel A González-Ocantos, *Shifting Legal Visions: Judicial Change and Human Rights Trials in Latin America* (Cambridge University Press 2016) ch 2; J. Goldschmidt, 'Strategic Litigation by Equality Bodies and National Human Rights Institutions to Promote Equality' in Yves Haeck and others, *The Realisation of Human Rights: When Theory Meets Practice* (Equinet 2014); Aidan O'Neill, 'Strategic Litigation before the European Courts' (2015) 16 ERA Forum 495; Alexander Graser and Christian Helmrich (eds), *Strategic Litigation: Begriff und Praxis* (Nomos 2019); Catherine Corey Barber, 'Tackling the Evaluation Challenge in Human Rights: Assessing the Impact of Strategic Litigation Organisations' (2012) 16 The International Journal of Human Rights 411; Ole Solvang, 'Chechnya and the European Court of Human Rights: The Merits of Strategic Litigation' (2008) 19 Security and Human Rights 208; Freek Van der Vet, *Finding Justice at the European Court of Human Rights : The Dynamics of Strategic Litigation and Human Rights Defense in the Russian Federation* (Doctoral Dissertation, University of Helsinki 2014); Sandra Carvalho and Eduardo Baker, 'Strategic Litigation Experiences in the Inter-American Human Rights System Human Rights in Motion: Tools: Essay' (2014) 20 International Journal on Human Rights 449.

3 Robert Knox, 'Strategy and Tactics' (2010) 21 Finnish Yearbook of International Law 193–229 (hereinafter, Knox 'Strategy and Tactics'); Karl von Clausewitz, *War Politics and Power* (Chicago 1965) 171.

points out that the business terminology of 'strategy' had in fact percolated to politics through military theorists. Military jargon traditionally distinguished between strategy as the plan to win a *long-term war* and tactics as methods employed to win an individual *immediate battle*.[4] In a political context, it would mean that strategy concerns itself with achieving long-term objectives, whereas tactics take care of immediate effect. Importantly, however, strategy and tactics are interrelated, as tactics can be employed with a view to have long-term strategic consequences.

Therefore, according to Knox, two key aspects which would qualify a political intervention as strategic are the temporal and structural nature of the objective.[5] The temporal aspect alone, in this case, does not automatically translate anything long-term as strategic. It reflects far-sightedness, that which is beyond the immediate. In a politico-legal sense, it is to evaluate the impact of any legal intervention on the issues involved in the long term. Naturally, then, far-sightedness is measured against the trajectory of the political or social issues. In other words, the long-term nature of an intervention essentially depends on the nature of the goal. In the battlefield metaphor, the far-sightedness would depend on what is the *war* that is being fought. To clarify this in the context of the use of international (criminal) law, if the approach is far-sighted, i.e., goes beyond the specific prosecution/conviction/legal victory to contribute towards achieving a structural objective, it would satisfy the temporal aspect of a strategic approach.

The second, more defining element of a strategy is 'the objective'.[6] What is the war that is being fought? In the political sphere, arguably, the strategic objective of any intervention would be determined by the positionality of the actors. From a Marxist political economy point of view, if the intervention does not aim towards the goal of capturing the modes of production and overturning them, it would not be a strategic intervention. From a post-colonial perspective, if the objective is not to challenge the basic structure of imperialism, then the intermediary tactical measures and the overall approach may not be qualified as strategic.[7] By that logic, anything that does not aim to dismantle capitalism or imperialism is not strategic from their respective vantage points.

When it comes to an organization's or lawyer's engagement with international criminal law, what would qualify as a strategic engagement with law depends on what is the overarching goal of such engagement. There is abundant critical scholarship on international criminal law which may serve as a guide to mark the battlefield for the practitioner who seeks critical

4 Ibid 197–8.
5 Ibid 198.
6 Ibid 198, 204.
7 Ibid.

engagement. With the boundaries of the structure and its critique carefully delineated in theory, they can potentially serve as a parameter to evaluate whether the objectives of practitioners claiming to be strategic qualify as such or not.

The liberal understanding of the law argues that international criminal law while regulating individual responsibility for well-defined crimes under international law, protects 'peace, security, and [the] well-being of the world' as fundamental values of the 'international community'.[8] The prosecutors, states, and non-governmental organizations that promote such practice of international criminal law with a view to protecting the peace, security, and well-being of the world fall squarely into the liberal legal understanding of the term. A prosecutorial claim of 'strategically' choosing to go after one defendant over another, choosing one charge over the other is not actually a strategic engagement with the law but merely a clever use of legal framework. Such practice works to enhance the implementation of the law and aims at maintaining and upholding the status quo. The choices made in such engagement with the law are at best tactical, not strategic.

An example of such a use of the term in the context of international human rights law could help clarify this logic further. Equinet, the European Network of Equality Bodies (public institutions fighting discrimination at the national level), issued a handbook on strategic litigation in 2017 as an explainer meant for its member institutions.[9] The report lays down the possible objectives of strategic litigation as the following:

> To clarify or establish a point of law / the meaning of a particular legal provision; to effect a change in the law; to obtain judicial clarity on the application of equality and non-discrimination law; to establish that non-discrimination law covers or does not cover a particular situation; to highlight a serious issue such as a policy or practice which has a negative effect on many people, as part of a wider campaign for legal and social change; to ensure that non-discrimination law is upheld; to overturn

8 Cassese described the objective of international criminal law (in line with the Preamble of the Rome Statute) as 'protecting society against the most harmful transgressions of legal standards of behaviour perpetrated by individuals' in Antonio Cassese, *International Criminal Law* (3rd edn, Oxford University Press 2008); Gerhard Werle and Florian Jeßberger, *Principles of International Criminal Law* (4th edn, Oxford University Press 2020); Robert Cryer and others, *An Introduction to International Criminal Law and Procedure* (Cambridge University Press 2010); M. Cherif Bassiouni, 'The Philosophy and Policy of International Criminal Justice' in L.C. Vohrah, Fausto Pocar, Yvonne Featherstone (eds) *Man's Inhumanity to Man* (Kluwer International 2003) 65.

9 Equinet, European Network of Equality Bodies, *Strategic Litigation – A Handbook* (Equinet 2017) <https://www.archive.equineteurope.org/IMG/pdf/equinet-handbook_strategic-litigation_def_web.pdf> accessed 3 January 2022.

'bad' case law; to establish legal precedent, enabling others to enforce their rights more confidently.[10]

In this understanding, any intervention that seeks to promote better and enhanced implementation of human rights law would automatically become strategic litigation. It promotes the liberal understanding of international law and human rights as the determinate body of rules which reflect and protect all interests equally. If there are some blind spots that could be addressed by making a sound legal argument before the court, the law would stand corrected with the rule of law enforced as it is intended. In that case any lawyer would choose the most promising path, the most promising tactics, to achieve a courtroom victory and intended goals. Basically, this logic results in the overuse of the term, where actors are tempted to label every choice in litigation as strategic litigation.

With respect to prosecution of egregious human rights violations amounting to crimes under international law, this liberal understanding of the criminal framework has been challenged comprehensively within scholarship. Critical scholars do not buy into the idea of fundamental protection of peace and security of mankind and international criminal law being a pure force for good.[11] Regardless of the theoretical traditions which inform the perspective of critical scholars, their central argument is that international criminal

10 Ibid 9.

11 Christine Schwöbel, *Critical Approaches to International Criminal Law: An Introduction* (Routledge 2014) (hereinafter Schwöbel, *Critical Approaches*); Grietje Baars, '"It's Not Me, It's the Corporation": The Value of Corporate Accountability in the Global Political Economy' (2016) 4 *London Review of International Law* 127 (hereinafter Baars, 'It's Not Me, It's the Corporation'); Antony Anghie, *Imperialism, Sovereignty and the Making of International Law* (Vol 37, Cambridge University Press 2007) (hereinafter Anghie, *Sovereignty*); Evelyne Asaala, 'Rule of Law or Realpolitik? The Role of the United Nations Security Council in the International Criminal Court Processes in Africa' (2017) 17 African Human Rights Law Journal 265; B.S. Chimni, 'Customary International Law: A Third World Perspective' (2018) 112 American Journal of International Law 1, 46; James Gathii, 'International Law and Eurocentricity' (1998) 9 European Journal of International Law 184; Balakrishnan Rajagopal, 'From Resistance to Renewal: The Third World, Social Movements, and the Expansion of International Institutions Symposium: International Law and the Developing World: A Millennial Analysis' (2000) 41 Harvard International Law Journal 529; Martti Koskenniemi, *From Apology to Utopia: The Structure of International Legal Argument* (Cambridge University Press 2005) 67; Martti Koskenniemi, 'Between Impunity and Show Trials' (2002) Max Planck Yearbook of United Nations Law 6, 1; John Dugard, 'Palestine and the International Criminal Court' (2013) 11(3) Journal of International Criminal Justice 563; for a discussion on the African states' concerns about an anti-African bias of the ICC, see Charles Jalloh and Ilias Bantekas (eds), *The International Criminal Court and Africa* (2017); Sergey Vasiliev, 'The Crises and Critiques of International Criminal Justice' in Kevin Jon Heller and others (eds), *The Oxford Handbook of International Criminal Law* (Oxford University Press 2020).

law is indeterminate and vulnerable to political influences, and that the law and legal institutions are structurally biased towards certain choices and outcomes, which are perceived to be exploitative for the marginalized. Among themselves, the critical scholars may disagree on the ways and extent of marginalization that is furthered by the international criminal justice system; however, all of them do agree on one thing: international criminal law is a political instrument and its practice requires making highly political choices. Then, if the international criminal justice system is a political mechanism and the critique argues that it is biased in a manner that it enables and perpetuates structures of domination and exploitation, what does it mean to engage strategically with international criminal law?

While acknowledging its structural biases, one might even ask if there is any possibility to engage with international criminal law without running the risk of reinforcing subordination on the basis of race, class, gender, or colony? In that sense, even successful prosecutions and convictions of perpetrators of the most egregious of violations would also essentially legitimize the system and perpetuate domination.[12]

Let us take the initiation of the preliminary examination in the situation of the United Kingdom–Iraq by the Office of the Prosecutor (OTP) as an example. The preliminary examination was opened on the basis of alleged crimes committed by members of the UK armed forces in the context of the Iraq war and occupation from 2003 to 2008, including murder, torture, and other forms of ill-treatment. The first Article 15 communications concerning the situation were filed in 2004 before the then newly established court and its Prosecutor. The OTP swiftly closed the preliminary examination in 2006, arguing that the gravity threshold had not been reached due to the low number of cases. In 2014, the European Center for Constitutional and Human Rights, Berlin (ECCHR) and Public Interest Lawyers, London, together filed a new Article 15 communication including more testimonies and cases, which led to the reopening of the situation within months.[13] In 2017, the OTP acknowledged that there was a reasonable basis to believe that war crimes had been committed by UK troops in Iraq. This was the first time a Western state was being investigated by the ICC. But in 2020 the OTP closed the investigations yet again and felt compelled to issue an extraordinary 184-page long report citing their reasons to do so.[14]

12 Grietje Baars, 'Making ICL History: On the Need to Move Beyond Prefab Critiques of ICL' in Schwöbel (ed), *Critical Approaches* (n 11) 196–218; Grietje Baars, *The Corporation, Law and Capitalism: A Radical Perspective on the Role of Law in the Global Political Economy* (Brill 2019).

13 ICC Situation in Iraq/UK <https://www.icc-cpi.int/iraq> accessed 3 January 2022.

14 ICC Situation in Iraq/UK – OTP Final Report (2020) <https://www.icc-cpi.int/itemsDocuments/201209-otp-final-report-iraq-uk-eng.pdf> accessed 3 January 2022.

Since its inception, until 2019 when OTP requested initiation of an investigation against the conduct of US soldiers in Afghanistan, the preliminary examination against the UK was the only active proceeding against a state from the 'Global North' or a veto-holding member of the UNSC. For every critique of ICC's double standards and anti-Africa bias, the opening of an examination against the UK on account of submissions made by non-governmental organizations served as a strong counter. The fact that the investigation was closed citing unsatisfactory reasons, giving a pass to the UK's questionable attempts to shield their high-ranking civilian and military officers, was not surprising.[15] But the existence of these proceedings, for some time, ended up contributing to some extent in the enhancement of ICC's legitimacy as a neutral institution which could potentially transcend the politics of the states and UNSC.

Scholars practising international human rights and humanitarian law have identified this as an existential dilemma for themselves. This question has been omnipresent in grasping the relationship between law and critical politics: *reform or revolution?*

In the political-legal realm, the international lawyer could aim at reconfiguring the terms of the legal framework as their strategic aim; seek to overturn the logic of law-making; or entirely abandon the legal project. The axes of this discussion, however, are different for praxis and the legal theoretical critique. Where theoretical positions allow us to reframe the legal debate entirely, the practitioner, even when informed by a certain set of values, is inherently limited in their engagement with the law. In engaging with international law on the terms set according to the interests of (a limited number of) states, one always runs the risk of legitimizing the broad structures, i.e. the hegemony and the concentration of power. Therefore, from a truly critical legal perspective, the use of law and litigation to advance the interests of the exploited can never be strategic.[16] According to this view, it is tactical at its best if it highlights the oppression of the structures, and enabling at its worst as it ends up legitimizing the existing power structures and perpetuating subordination. Is abandonment of law the only option for the critical practitioner?

15 See Andreas Schüller, 'The ICC, British War Crimes in Iraq and a Very British Tradition' (2020) Opinio Juris <http://opiniojuris.org/2020/12/11/the-icc-british-war-crimes-in-iraq-and-a-very-british-tradition/> accessed 3 January 2022; Kevin Jon Heller, 'The Nine Words that (Wrongly) Doomed the Iraq Investigation' (2020) Opinio Juris <https://opiniojuris.org/2020/12/10/the-nine-words-that-wrongly-doomed-the-iraq-investigation/> accessed 3 January 2022.

16 See Michael Sfard, 'The Price of Internal Legal Opposition to Human Rights Abuses' (2009) 1 Journal of Human Rights Practice 37 (hereinafter Sfard, 'Price of Internal Legal Opposition'); David Kennedy 'International Human Rights Movement: Part of the Problem?' (2002) 15 Harvard Human Rights Journal 101–125.

Making a case for the emancipatory potential of the international legal order, TWAIL scholars such as B.S. Chimni, Balakrishnan Rajagopal, and Antony Anghie have explicitly argued for a continuous engagement with the law, regardless of the structural biases of the international legal framework.[17] The following is an excerpt of Anghie's reasoning:

> At the very least, I believe that the Third World cannot abandon international law because law now plays such a vital role in the public realm and in the interpretation of virtually all international events. It is through the vocabulary of international law, concepts of 'self-defence', 'human rights' and 'humanitarian intervention' that issues of cause, responsibility, and fault are being discussed and analysed, and interpretations of these doctrines which reproduce imperial relations must be contested.[18]

Realizing the importance of the mere vocabulary and narrative of international criminal law in the global order today, a total 'revolution' or abandonment of the framework is not an option for the critical practitioner.[19] Returning to the war metaphor, the battlefield within which an international criminal lawyer finds themselves is that they have to engage with the law despite acknowledging that this choice to employ international criminal law for any social or political goal is an act of legitimizing the liberal framework and its structural biases.

With that as the baseline, one arrives at a conclusive point to be able to answer the question: what is a strategic engagement with international (criminal) law?

Strategic litigation highlights the structural biases of the system and works towards countering those structural biases. It is a praxis that is not disjointed from but informed by the theoretical critiques of the legal framework. A strategic legal intervention that purely aims at highlighting the inadequacies and biases of the system would also be working towards a strategic objective. Strategic litigation would resort to international criminal law for the purposes of supporting, defending, and protecting those who seek to challenge the patterns of exploitation and subordination. A strategic international lawyer

17 B.S. Chimni, 'Third World Approaches to International Law: A Manifesto' (2006) 8 International Community Law Review 3; Balakrishnan Rajagopal, 'International Law and Social Movements: Challenges of Theorizing Resistance' (2002) 41 Columbia Journal of Transnational Law 397; Anghie, *Sovereignty* (n 11) 316.

18 Anghie, *Sovereignty* (n 11) 318.

19 On leveraging transformative potential of international law through the language of universal justice, also see Martti Koskenniemi, 'What should international lawyers learn from Karl Marx?' (2004) 17 Leiden Journal of International Law 2, 229–246; Barrie Sander, 'The Expressive Turn of International Criminal Justice: A Field in Search of Meaning' (2019) 32 Leiden Journal of International Law, 851–872.

uses the international criminal justice system to bridge the gap between the lawmakers and those most affected by it. A practice of strategic litigation would use tactics that contribute to building a long-term sustainable movement where the marginalized can define the terms in which the law is being enforced and practised. For strategic litigation, a complaint, an arrest warrant, a trial, or a conviction are mere tactics that serve to achieve the two strategic objectives: highlighting structural biases of the system *and* countering them. Therefore, strategic litigation, essentially, is a tactical use of international law in furtherance of a strategic objective.

In doing that, the critical practitioner speaks to the counter-hegemonic potential of international law. A strategic approach is as much about creatively using the legal arguments as it is about achieving the long-term emancipatory goals. The objectives move beyond the improvement and expansion of legal institutions, but address the inclusions and exclusions created through these institutions. Sometimes, it may take the form of an isolated action such as filing a *habeas corpus* petition on behalf of a Guantanamo detainee with the intention to publicize the illegalities of the war on terror.[20] At other times, it takes the shape of a series of actions brought before various courts in different jurisdictions to highlight the systematic nature of the crimes involved. For instance, the complicity of multinational corporations in the crimes committed by the military dictatorship in Argentina was challenged in the home jurisdictions of these corporations such as the United States and Germany, as well as in Argentina using whatever legal tools were available to challenge this conduct.[21]

Given the complexity of relations at play, there cannot be rigid indicators or milestones setting forth a straightforward definition to determine if any engagement with international criminal law is strategic. It is difficult to measure the effectiveness of a particular legal argument towards its strategic goal. Therefore, in an exercise of broad classification of whether a given approach can be characterized as strategic, the following two key constituents could serve an indicative purpose: combining the legal with extra-legal and choosing reform over repair.

II. Combining the Legal with the Extra-legal

A strategic legal intervention while realizing the central importance of the legal framework also does not lose sight of the extra-legal. Strategic litigation consciously uses the vocabulary of international criminal law to lend weight to political action outside the courtroom. The social, political, and legal aspects of any intervention complement each other without working

20 See Chapter 5.
21 See Chapter 4.

in isolating binaries.[22] The permeation could work both ways: the lawyer may seek the activist, or the activist could reach out to the lawyer to amplify the movement with a coherent strategic aim. History offers many examples where the law has been used to dismantle oppressive structures.[23] Social movements literature provides comprehensive arguments emphasizing on the importance of extra-institutional forms of mobilization which determine the 'success' or 'failure' of institutional forms.[24]

The use of law to build political movements has taken different shapes and forms. Jules Lobel, a human rights lawyer, and former President of the New York-based organization Centre for Constitutional Rights (CCR), reflects on the alternative use of law and courts in a democratic society. He sees the courts as a forum for protest.[25] Such use of courts, naturally, works with a reduced emphasis on winning, and a lesser role of the judge where the litigator is using the courtroom struggle to build a political movement. In that case, winning becomes ancillary in the use of a courtroom viewed alongside social and extra-legal activism. The final aim may be to promote a political goal, but the terminology of 'international crimes', as Katherine Gallagher, another lawyer from the same organization noted, helps in calling the conduct what it is.[26]

To illustrate this approach, Megan Fairlie has called one of CCR's classic uses of the court for non-court advances a 'strategic communication' before the ICC.[27] A communication under Article 15 of the ICC Statute was filed by

22 Jules Lobel, 'Courts as Forums for Protest' (2004) 52 UCLA Law Review 477 (hereinafter Lobel, 'Courts for Protest'); Wolfgang Kaleck, 'From Pinochet to Rumsfeld: Universal Jurisdiction in Europe 1998–2008' (2009) 30 Michigan Journal of International Law 927, 976–77; Jules Lobel, *Success Without Victory: Lost Legal Battles and the Long Road to Justice in America* (NYU Press 2006); Helen Duffy, *Strategic Human Rights Litigation* (n 2) 4.

23 One such example of using the structure to critique the structure can be derived from the political movement against British colonialism in India. The Hindustan Socialist Republican Association (HSRA) in the late 1920s decided to change their tactics from isolated attempts to mobilizing the masses for all-out revolution. Two of the activists, Bhagat Singh and B.K. Dutt, were asked to intentionally commit a crime so that they would be arrested and tried by the British government. Their sole objective was to use the trial court as a forum for mobilization to publicize their movement. Bipan Chandra and others, *India's Struggle for Independence* (Penguin UK 2016).

24 Rajagopal, 'From Resistance to Renewal' (n 10) 235; see Neil Smelser, *Theory of Collective Behavior* (Free Press 1962); Marc Schneiberg and Michael Lounsbury, 'Social Movements and Institutional Analysis' (2008) *The Handbook Of Organizational Institutionalism* 648, 670; David West, *Social Movements in Global Politics* (Polity 2013).

25 Lobel, 'Courts for Protest' (n 22) 477.

26 Interview with Katherine Gallagher, Senior Staff Attorney, CCR (online, 18 March 2021).

27 Megan Fairlie, 'The Hidden Costs of Strategic Communications for the International Criminal Court' (2016) 51 Texas International Law Journal 281.

CCR on behalf of SNAP (Survivors' Network of those Abused by Priests)[28] before the OTP to request opening a preliminary examination against high-level Vatican officials for rape and sexual violence, and torture amounting to crimes against humanity.[29] Even at the time of filing this communication, the likelihood of such an investigation ever being initiated by the ICC Prosecutor was at best minimal. Nevertheless, the communication became a hook to gather significant media attention towards this Vatican-targeted campaign which then enhanced worldwide awareness of the exploitation of the most vulnerable within the Catholic Church's structures,[30] finally followed by the resignation of Pope Benedict XVI.[31]

This use of legal interventions as complementary to the extra-legal interventions is fundamentally different from the traditional relationship of using the law to achieve political aims by way of legal reforms.[32] Strategic litigation reverses the relationship between law and politics, where legal reform is not the end goal but a significant starting point to inspire political action. It looks at the legal struggle as a part of a broader political campaign, not the engine of change itself.[33] Realizing the central importance of legal vocabulary and interventions but at the same time not seeing law as an end exponentially reduces the importance of a courtroom victory.

28 SNAP claims to be the largest, oldest, and most active support group for women and men wounded by religious and institutional authorities (priests, ministers, bishops, deacons, nuns, coaches, teachers, and others) <https://www.snapnetwork.org/> accessed 14 June 2021.

29 Communication filed by CCR to the ICC (2011) <https://ccrjustice.org/sites/default/files/assets/Survivors%20Network%20Art%20%2015%20Communication%20to%20ICC%20OTP%20(3).pdf> accessed 14 June 2021.

30 The communication was followed by provocative news headlines such as Karen McVeigh, 'Pope accused of crimes against humanity by victims of sex abuse' (The Guardian, September 2011) <https://www.theguardian.com/world/2011/sep/13/pope-crimes-humanity-victims-abuse accessed 15 June 2021>; 'Pope Sued for Alleged Crimes Against Humanity' (Voice of America, September 2011) <https://www.voanews.com/a/pope-sued-for-alleged-crimes-against-humanity-129731318/170867.html> accessed 15 June 2021.

31 Karen McVeigh, 'Pope Benedict Resigns: Sex Abuse Survivors Hope Move Eases Prosecution' (*The Guardian*, February 2013) <http://www.guardian.uk/world/2014/feb/11/poperesigns-sex- abuse-survivors> accessed 14 June 2021; Russell Goldman, 'Pope Benedict's Legacy Marred by Sex Abuse Scandal' (ABC News, February 2013) <https://abcnews.go.com/Blotter/pope-benedicts-legacy-marred-sex-abuse-scandal/story?id=18466726> accessed 15 June 2021.

32 Lobel, 'Courts for Protest' (n 22); Orly Lobel, 'The Paradox of Extralegal Activism: Critical Legal Consciousness and Transformative Politics' (2006) 120 Harvard Law Review 937.

33 Douglas NeJaime, 'Winning through Losing' (2010) 96 Iowa Law Review 941; Ben Depoorter, 'The Upside of Losing' (2013) 113 Columbia Law Review, 817–862.

III. Choosing Reform over Repair

The distinguishing feature of strategic litigation is that the choice reflects the objective of challenging the status quo in a way that helps reform the system. If interventions are made in vain, with the effort of repairing the existing legal system being without any social and political implications, then those interventions are mere tactics to preserve the order as it is. For instance, some scholars would argue that exceptional international trials of corporations in fact provide the economic elite the opportunity to claim legitimacy, and as a result, they end up repairing the imperialist or capitalist structures.[34]

As highlighted in the discussion above, any engagement with the law as a tool to achieve political aims is fraught with predicaments. These dilemmas speak to a complex world of ambiguities, trade-offs, tensions, internal debates, and 'roads not taken', which forms much of the practice of international criminal law.[35] The act of conscientious choosing does not end in choosing a goal and the means of international criminal law. The dilemmas persist in choosing a particular jurisdiction over the other, in choosing the defendant that most adequately reflects the criminality of the system, in choosing the partners with whom to collaborate, in choosing the legal arguments, and most important of all, in choosing the victims to support and represent. In all these choices, the possibility of reinforcing exploitative social and political structures looms large. If these practices keep reinforcing the imperialist tendencies while branding themselves as strategic litigation, they risk doing a disservice to the cause.

For instance, on collaborations, a strategic choice would be one that addresses the critique of inequality perpetuated by the international legal order. From a TWAIL perspective, a critical practice of international law would build itself on partnerships that transcend the borders of nation-states where Third World peoples located across the geographical 'Global North' and 'Global South' can collectively work towards building a sustained movement. Conscientious collaborations would reflect a synergy between grassroots organizations closely connected to the marginalized and those intervening in global politics. The legal interventions of practitioners in London, Berlin, Geneva, or New York, in that sense, would be primarily driven by a notion of justice most meaningful to the people directly affected by egregious violations of human rights. These collaborations would essentially reflect on the existing social and political relationships and work actively towards reconfiguring these relationships.

34 Baars, 'It's Not Me, It's the Corporation' (n 11) 127–163; Sfard, 'Price of Internal Legal Opposition' (n 16).

35 Ron Dudai, 'Introduction - Rights Choices: Dilemmas of Human Rights Practice' (2014) 6 Journal of Human Rights Practice 389–398.

Another such choice which has the potential to reflect this understanding of an imbalance of power and work towards tilting the scales is the choice of a case. For instance, when one of the goals is to challenge the perils of capitalism, a strategic approach would be to take up emblematic cases against multinational corporations which highlight the ways in which the criminal legal system is inadequate to capture violence inflicted indirectly by economic structures.

On choosing a victim, a more intricate, transcendental, or radical critique could be made regarding the construction of the 'ideal victim' which then reproduces the 'savage, victim, saviour' relations within international criminal justice system.[36] Christine Schwöbel-Patel alleges international criminal justice as a brand has created and reinforced a stereotypical notion of the 'ideal' victim: (i) weakness and vulnerability; (ii) dependency, and (iii) grotesqueness.[37] In this context, a practice that is not disjointed from the broader critique would at least allow the victims to speak for themselves and try not to reproduce the feminized, infantilized, and racialized stereotypes. In a strategic legal intervention, victims will have the space to assert their agency, perhaps, as a part of a larger movement.

IV. Conclusion

To sum up, this section attempts to clarify the underpinnings of the frequently used (and misused) terminology of strategic litigation, particularly in the context of international criminal justice. Firstly, the use of the term strategic underlines the political characterization of the legal intervention. Borrowing from the traditional semantics of the term and strategy, as distinguished from tactics, it is emphasized that strategic litigation is primarily a qualification of the objective and not the methods. It is a tactical approach to use international law in furtherance of a strategic objective. Two key aspects which qualify as a political-legal intervention as strategic are temporal and structural. Whereas the temporal aspect reflects far-sightedness beyond an immediate case, the structural aspect speaks to the social–political relations which create and sustain the system.

The critical practitioner in choosing to engage with international criminal law to seek strategic objectives works with the basic understanding of the

36 See Karen Engle, 'Feminism and Its (Dis)Contents: Criminalizing Wartime Rape in Bosnia and Herzegovina' (2005) 99 American Journal of International Law 778; Leila Ullrich, 'Beyond the "Global–Local Divide" Local Intermediaries, Victims and the Justice Contestations of the International Criminal Court' (2016) 14 Journal of International Criminal Justice 543.

37 Christine Schwöbel-Patel, 'The "Ideal" Victim of International Criminal Law' (2018) 29 European Journal of International Law 703; Christine Schwöbel-Patel, *Marketing Global Justice: The Political Economy of International Criminal Law* (Oxford University Press 2021).

structural biases of the legal system. However, realizing the central importance of the framework within international politics, they continue to employ international criminal law for strategic objectives such as to highlight the inadequacies of the system; to defend, promote, or support those who do; to challenge double standards; or bridge the gap between lawmakers/enforcers and the ones most affected by atrocity crimes.

Strategic litigation is an approach towards using the law in a manner that is not disjointed from the overall critique of the system. In doing that, the critical legal practitioner employs the legal with the extra-legal and chooses reform of the system over a status quo preserving exercise of repair. Combining the legal and the extra-legal essentially means using law and courtrooms as a tactic along with other methods and ways to achieve political aims beyond a courtroom victory or a legislative reform. The practice that chooses reforms over a mere repair service proactively makes choices which counter the existing relations of domination and subordination while picking cases, collaboration partners, defendants, as well as the victims.

For the purposes of this book, however, this practice carried out by non-governmental organizations is being examined for their role as democratizing agents within the international criminal justice system. Within the thematic framework of corporate responsibility, the three case studies will analyse how transnational civil society organizations which engage in strategic litigation serve as norm entrepreneurs. They have expanded the practice of international criminal law in domestic courts while trying to fill accountability gaps left because of reasons such as political unwillingness.

A note of caution is in order, however. Strategic legal interventions in international criminal law continue to be a tool in the hands of very few highly specialized lawyers mostly with their bases in political capitals across the West.[38] This practice, as a form of activism within the international criminal justice system, needs to be analysed without the extravagant claims of humanity, inclusiveness, and true representation of victims' interests. But what needs to be considered is that these professionals with recognized expertise and competence backed by progressive values and relevant knowledge of the discipline have been transplanting norms horizontally (from one domestic jurisdiction to the other) and vertically (from international law to domestic law) while seeking social and political change.

Finally, the underlying purpose of placing focus on these entities is that their practice highlights the possibilities to transcend some of the main critiques against the legal framework. Despite its elitism, political biases, and West-centredness, it offers a credible alternative discourse on the practice of international criminal law. This conceptualization offers the counterpoint to mainstream international criminal law practice in three ways: one, it decentres

38 See Jeßberger and Steinl, 'Strategic Litigation: A View from Within' (n 1).

the discourse from the state to the peoples; two, it explores perceptions of international criminal law in local and domestic contexts; three, it presents an alternative way of using the law in the service of social and political movements.

References

Asaala E, 'Rule of Law or Realpolitik? The Role of the United Nations Security Council in the International Criminal Court Processes in Africa' (2017) 17 African Human Rights Law Journal 265

Baars G, '"It's Not Me, It's the Corporation": The Value of Corporate Accountability in the Global Political Economy' (2016) 4 London Review of International Law 127

Baars G, 'Making ICL History: On the Need to Move Beyond Prefab Critiques of ICL' in Schwöbel (ed), *Critical Approaches to International Criminal Law* (Routledge 2014) 196–218

Baars G, *The Corporation, Law and Capitalism: A Radical Perspective on the Role of Law in the Global Political Economy* (Brill 2019)

Bassiouni MC, 'The Philosophy and Policy of International Criminal Justice' in LC Vohrah, Fausto Pocar and Yvonne Featherstone (eds), *Man's Inhumanity to Man* (Kluwer International 2003) 65–126

Barber CC, 'Tackling the Evaluation Challenge in Human Rights: Assessing the Impact of Strategic Litigation Organisations' (2012) 16 The International Journal of Human Rights 411

Carvalho S and Baker E, 'Strategic Litigation Experiences in the Inter-American Human Rights System Human Rights in Motion: Tools: Essay' (2014) 20 International Journal on Human Rights 4

Cassese A, *International Criminal Law* (3rd edn, Oxford University Press 2008)

Chandra B and others, *India's Struggle for Independence* (Penguin 2016)

Communication filed by CCR to the ICC (2011) <https://ccrjustice.org/sites/default/files/assets/Survivors%20Network%20Art%20%2015%20Communication%20to%20ICC%20OTP%20(3).pdf> accessed 14 June 2021

Cryer R and others, *An Introduction to International Criminal Law and Procedure* (Cambridge University Press 2010)

Depoorter B, 'The Upside of Losing' (2013) 113 Columbia Law Review 817–862

Dudai R, 'Introduction—Rights Choices: Dilemmas of Human Rights Practice' (2014) 6 Journal of Human Rights Practice 389–398

Duffy H, *Strategic Human Rights Litigation: Understanding and Maximising Impact* (Hart Publishing 2018)

Dugard J, 'Palestine and the International Criminal Court' (2013) 11 Journal of International Criminal Justice 3, 563

Engle K, 'Feminism and Its (Dis)Contents: Criminalizing Wartime Rape in Bosnia and Herzegovina' (2005) 99 American Journal of International Law 778

Equinet, *European Network of Equality Bodies, Strategic Litigation – A Handbook* (Equinet 2017) <https://www.archive.equineteurope.org/IMG/pdf/equinet-handbook_strategic-litigation_def_web.pdf> accessed 3 January 2022

Fairlie M, 'The Hidden Costs of Strategic Communications for the International Criminal Court' (2016) 51 Texas International Law Journal 281

Fischer-Lescano A, 'From Strategic Litigation to Juridical Action' in Miriam Saage-Maaß and others (eds), *Transnational Legal Activism in Global Value Chains: The Ali Enterprises Factory Fire and the Struggle for Justice* (Springer International Publishing 2021) 299–312

Gathii J, 'International Law and Eurocentricity' (1998) 9 European Journal of International Law 184

Graser A and Helmrich C (eds), *Strategic Litigation: Begriff und Praxis* (Nomos 2019)

Goldman R, 'Pope Benedict's Legacy Marred by Sex Abuse Scandal' (ABC News, February 2013) <https://abcnews.go.com/Blotter/pope-benedicts-legacy-marred-sex-abuse-scandal/story?id=18466726> accessed 15 June 2021

Goldschmidt J, 'Strategic Litigation by Equality Bodies and National Human Rights Institutions to Promote Equality' in Haeck and others (eds), *The Realisation of Human Rights: When Theory Meets Practice* (Equinet 2014) 461–474

González-Ocantos EA, *Shifting Legal Visions: Judicial Change and Human Rights Trials in Latin America* (Cambridge University Press 2016) 27

Heller KJ, 'The Nine Words that (Wrongly) Doomed the Iraq Investigation' (2020) Opinio Juris <https://opiniojuris.org/2020/12/10/the-nine-words-that-wrongly-doomed-the-iraq-investigation/> accessed 3 January 2022

ICC Situation in Iraq/UK – OTP Final Report (2020) <https://www.icc-cpi.int/itemsDocuments/201209-otp-final-report-iraq-uk-eng.pdf> accessed 3 January 2022

Jalloh C and Bantekas I (eds), *The International Criminal Court and Africa* (Oxford University Press 2017)

Jeßberger F and Steinl L, 'Strategic Litigation in International Criminal Justice: Facilitating a View from Within' (2022) 20 (2) Journal of International Criminal Justice 379–401

Knox R, 'Strategy and Tactics' 21 Finnish Yearbook of International Law 193–229

Koskenniemi M, 'Between Impunity and Show Trials' (2002) 6 Max Planck Yearbook of United Nations Law 1, 1–32

Koskenniemi M, *From Apology to Utopia: The Structure of International Legal Argument* (Cambridge University Press 2005)

Lobel O, 'The Paradox of Extralegal Activism: Critical Legal Consciousness and Transformative Politics' (2006) 120 Harvard Law Review 937

Lohne K, *Advocates of Humanity: Human Rights NGOs in International Criminal Justice* (Oxford University Press 2019)

McVeigh K, 'Pope Accused of Crimes Against Humanity by Victims of Sex Abuse' (The Guardian, September 2011) <https://www.theguardian.com/world/2011/sep/13/pope-crimes-humanity-victims-abuse> accessed 15 June 2021

NeJaime D, 'Winning Through Losing' (2010) 96 Iowa Law Review 941

O'Neill A, 'Strategic Litigation before the European Courts' (2015) 16 ERA Forum 495

Rajagopal B, 'From Resistance to Renewal: The Third World, Social Movements, and the Expansion of International Institutions Symposium: International Law and the Developing World: A Millennial Analysis' (2000) 41 Harvard International Law Journal 529

Rajagopal B 'International Law and Social Movements: Challenges of Theorizing Resistance' (2002) 41 Columbia Journal of Transnational Law 397

Schüller A, 'The ICC, British War Crimes in Iraq and a Very British Tradition' (2020) Opinio Juris <http://opiniojuris.org/2020/12/11/the-icc-british-war-crimes-in-iraq-and-a-very-british-tradition/> accessed 3 January 2020

Schwöbel-Patel C, 'The "Ideal" Victim of International Criminal Law' (2018) 29 European Journal of International Law 703

Sfard M, 'The Price of Internal Legal Opposition to Human Rights Abuses' (2009) 1 Journal of Human Rights Practice 37

Solvang O, 'Chechnya and the European Court of Human Rights: The Merits of Strategic Litigation' (2008) 19 Security and Human Rights 208

Ullrich L, 'Beyond the "Global–Local Divide" Local Intermediaries, Victims and the Justice Contestations of the International Criminal Court' (2016) 14 Journal of International Criminal Justice 543

Van der Vet F, *Finding Justice at the European Court of Human Rights: The Dynamics of Strategic Litigation and Human Rights Defense in the Russian Federation* (Doctoral Dissertation, University of Helsinki 2014)

Vasiliev S, 'The Crises and Critiques of International Criminal Justice' in Kevin Jon Heller and others (eds), *The Oxford Handbook of International Criminal Law* (Oxford University Press 2020) 626–651

Chapter 3

Corporate Accountability and International Criminal Law

Diffused structures of multinational corporations may be novel, but their involvement in large-scale human rights violations is well documented since the conception of the 'settler corporation'. One of these settler corporations, the English East India Company, a corporate body chartered in 1600, has been described as 'the CIA, the NSA, and the biggest, baddest multinational corporation on earth' wrapped into one corporation.[1] Other similar entities such as the Dutch East India Company and Hudson's Bay Company were also engaged in the dual roles of trade and administration of Canada, Indonesia, and parts of Africa. They were creatures of domestic law used by the home state as agents of economic exploitation of the colonial territories.[2] These corporations were not mere merchants minding their own business, instead their conduct oscillated between trade and governance, often leading to their involvement in mass atrocities and massacres amounting to genocide and crimes against humanity *avant la lettre* in the 1700s.[3] These business entities are credited to be the direct ancestors of the modern transnational corporate groups.[4] In the contemporary global economic order, the form of

1 Phillip Stern, 'The English East India Company and the Modern Corporation: Legacies, Lessons, and Limitations' (2015) Seattle UL Rev. 39, 423; Nick Robins, *The Corporation that Changed the World: How the East India Company shaped the Modern Multinational* (Pluto Press 2012).

2 Steven R Ratner, 'Corporations and Human Rights: A Theory of Legal Responsibility' (2001) 111 The Yale Law Journal 443, 452–459 (hereinafter Ratner, 'Corporations and HR').

3 Wim Huisman, Annika van Baar, and Madelijne Gorsira, 'Corporations and Transnational Crime' in Gerben Bruinsma (ed), *Histories of Transnational Crime* (Springer 2015); Nick Robins, 'Loot: In Search of the East India Company, the World's First Transnational Corporation' (2002) 14 Environment and Urbanization 79; Michael J Kelly, *Prosecuting Corporations for Genocide* (Oxford University Press 2016) 17–26.

4 For a conceptualization of transnational corporate group in context of international criminal law that draws upon investment and corporate laws, see Marie Kuntz, *Conceptualizing Transnational Corporate Groups for International Criminal Law* (Nomos Verlagsgesellschaft

DOI: 10.4324/9781003405047-5

transnational corporate groups might have changed, but the operations of multinational corporations in the formerly colonized nations continue to raise human rights concerns.[5] Examples include a subsidiary of a French bank providing banking services to a dictatorial government in Sudan;[6] a Dutch company supporting construction of the security barriers between Israel and Palestine;[7] German and French companies selling surveillance technologies

mbH & CoKG 2017) (hereinafter Kuntz, *Conceptualizing Corporate Groups)*. This book relies on Kuntz' conceptualization of corporations to discuss corporate responsibility under international criminal law: 'A transnational corporate group can be seen as an economic entity if it consists of a unitary organization of personal, tangible and intangible elements, which pursue a specific economic aim on a long-term basis. This will be the case if (1) the parent has the power to control its subsidiaries and (2) it also exercised this power. The parent has the power to control if it either owns a majority of the shareholdings in the subsidiary with the corresponding voting rights or if it holds specific voting or similar rights that allow the parent to at least veto the subsidiary's essential decisions. The parent actually exercises its control if it either influences the subsidiary's day-to-day business or if it exercises strategic control over the essential decisions, such as those that concern the budget, business plan, appointment of senior managers or major investments. An integrated business strategy, personnel links, a unified corporate group appearance including a common corporate culture and, to a lesser extent, reporting obligations all indicate the actual exercise of parental control'. Kuntz, *Conceptualizing Corporate Groups,* 337.

5 See Wolfgang Kaleck and Miriam Saage-Maaß, 'Corporate Accountability for Human Rights Violations Amounting to International Crimes' (2010) 6 Journal of International Criminal Justice 699, 703 (hereinafter, Kaleck and Saage-Maaß, 'Corporate Accountability'); Florian Jeßberger, Corporate Involvement in Slavery and Criminal Responsibility under International Law'(2016) 14 Journal of International Criminal Justice 2, 327–34.

6 FIDH, 'Sudanese victims ask French judges to investigate BNP Paribas' role in atrocities' (26 September 2019) <https://www.fidh.org/en/region/Africa/sudan/sudanese-victims-ask-french-judges-to-investigate-bnp-paribas-role-in> accessed 21 February 2022; 'France opens probe into BNP Paribas over its role in Sudan' (Reuters, 24 September 2020) <https://www.reuters.com/article/us-france-bnp-paribas-probe-sudan-idUSKCN26F37Q> accessed 21 February 2022; also see Annexure.

7 See Al Haq Complaint: Report of War Crimes and Crimes against Humanity by Rival, a Dutch corporation, the Netherlands for its participation in constructing the wall between Israel and Palestine that was deemed illegal by the International Court of Justice (ICJ) in 2004. In May 2013, the Dutch Public Prosecutor dismissed the case < https://www.alhaq.org/cached_uploads/download/alhaq_files/images/stories/PDF/accoutability-files/Complaint%20-%20English.pdf> accessed 21 February 2022.

to the repressive governments in Turkey,[8] Syria,[9] and Libya;[10] a Dutch corporation colluding with the Nigerian government in arresting and executing activists and human rights defenders;[11] German and Italian companies selling arms to countries with active conflicts or to groups/states reportedly committing war crimes in Colombia,[12] Yemen;[13] or a Swedish company forming a consortium with local actors in Sudan contributing to thousands of deaths and forced displacements of the local population.[14]

8 The Munich-based companies FinFisher GmbH, FinFisher Labs GmbH and Elaman GmbH are accused of selling FinSpy software to Turkey without the German government's permission. The prosecutor's office in Munich has opened investigations into the case. In October 2020, it carried out a search in FinFisher's offices. For more details, see <https://www.ecchr.eu/en/case/german-prosecutor-launches-investigation-of-german-companies-for-allegedly-selling-spyware-for-turkish-authorities/> accessed 21 February 2022; also see Annexure.

9 Qosmos, a French technology company, is being investigated for acting as an 'assisted witness' in alleged torture in Syria. Allegedly, Qosmos supplied the Syrian government with Deep Packet Inspection (DPI) software to track, torture, and execute dissidents. Fatima Hansia, 'French Tribunal Investigates Qosmos Over Surveillance Software Use In Syria' (Corpwatch, 21 July 2015) <https://www.corpwatch.org/article/french-tribunal-investigates-qosmos-over-surveillance-software-use-syria> accessed 21 February 2022; also see Annexure.

10 In June 2021, four executives of Amesys and Nexa Technologies were indicted by investigating judges of the crimes against humanity and war crimes unit of the Paris Judicial Court for complicity in torture in the Libyan portion of the investigation and complicity in torture and enforced disappearance in the Egyptian portion. See 'Surveillance & torture in Egypt & Libya: Amesys and Nexa Technologies executives indicted' (BHRRC, 22 June 2021) <https://www.business-humanrights.org/de/neuste-meldungen/surveillance-and-torture-in-egypt-libya-amesys-and-nexa-technologies-executives-indicted/> accessed 21 February 2022; see Annexure.

11 In the 1990s, the Nigerian government carried out a horrific crackdown on protesters against pollution caused by oil giant Shell in the Ogoniland region. It culminated in the execution of writer and activist Ken Saro-Wiwa and eight other men, known collectively as the Ogoni Nine. See Amnesty International, 'Shell: A criminal enterprise?' (18 May 2020) <https://www.amnesty.org.uk/shell-criminal-enterprise> accessed 21 February 2022.

12 'Sig Sauer: German gun maker execs strike court deal over illegal sales' (DW, 03 April 2019) <https://www.dw.com/en/sig-sauer-german-gun-maker-execs-strike-court-deal-over-illegal-sales/a-48189995> accessed 21 February 2022.

13 Criminal investigations are ongoing against managers of RWM Italia SpA, a German arms manufacturer Rheinmetall AG's Italian subsidiary, and senior officials of Italy's National Authority for the Export of Armament (UAMA) for their role in a deadly Saudi/United Arab Emirates-led military coalition airstrike in Deir Al-Ḥajārī in northwest Yemen. For more details, see 'European responsibility for war crimes in Yemen' (ECCHR) <https://www.ecchr.eu/en/case/european-responsibility-for-war-crimes-in-yemen/> accessed 21 February 2022; see Annexure.

14 The Swedish government has authorized the Swedish Prosecution Authority to proceed to prosecution against two corporate directors of the Swedish oil company Lundin Oil and Lundin Petroleum, in Sudan (now South Sudan) for aiding and abetting gross crimes against international law. See 'Sweden authorises indictment of Lundin Oil executives over alleged complicity in war crimes in So. Sudan; co. denies allegation' (BHRRC, 18 October 2018)

The long history of corporate involvement in crimes under international law does not, however, match the practice of holding corporations accountable under international criminal law. Corporations have never been prosecuted by an international court/tribunal for their involvement in core crimes such as war crimes, crimes against humanity, and genocide. In fact, the ICC does not even have jurisdiction over legal persons, including corporations.[15] This gap in accountability of corporations for their complicity crimes under international law is a result of a combination of normative as well as political obstacles. [16]

Substantively, the question of corporate accountability under international criminal law faces two fundamental yet distinct issues: one, criminal accountability of corporations as legal entities, in other words, corporate criminality; and two, attribution of responsibility for international crimes committed through economic conduct in complex corporate structures. Both of these issues have been dealt with extensively by international criminal legal scholarship.[17]

<https://www.business-humanrights.org/en/latest-news/sweden-authorises-indictment-of-lundin-oil-executives-over-alleged-complicity-in-war-crimes-in-so-sudan-co-denies-allegations/> accessed 21 February 2022; see Annexure.

15 Article 25 (1), ICC Statute; Article 6 ICTY Statute; Article 5 ICTR Statute. The Statutes of the Special Court of Sierra Leone and the Special Tribunal for Lebanon do not explicitly refer to 'natural' persons, instead mention 'individual criminal responsibility', see Article 6, section 5 SCSL Statute and article 3(1) STL Statute.

16 Kaleck and Saage-Maaß, 'Corporate Accountability' (n 5).

17 Forian Jeßberger, Julia Geneuss (eds), 'Transnational Business and International Criminal Law', (2010) Special Issue, Journal of International Criminal Justice, 8; Florian Jeßberger, Wolfgang Kaleck, Tobias Singelnstein (eds), *Wirtschaftsvölkerstrafrecht* (Nomos Verlag 2015) (hereinafter Jeßberger, Kaleck, Singelnstein (eds), *Wirtschaftsvölkerstrafrecht)*; Kai Ambos, *Wirtschaftsvölkerstrafrecht:Grundlagen der Völkerstrafrechtlichen Verantwortlichkeit von Unternehmen'* (Dunker and Humblot 2018); Richard Soyer 'Unternehmensstrafrecht, Schutz von Menschenrechten und Strafzwecktheorien' in Kert, Lehner (eds) *Vielfalt des Strafrechts im Internationalen Kontext* (Festschrift für Frank Höpfel zum 65. Geburtstag 2018) 113, 125; International Commission of Jurists (ICJ), *Corporate Complicity & Legal Accountability* (Vol. II, Criminal Law and International Crimes 2008) (hereinafter ICJ, Corporate Complicity); Alex Batesmith, 'Corporate Criminal Responsibility for War Crimes and Other Violations of International Humanitarian Law: The Impact of Business and Human Rights Movement' in Harvey, Summers, White (eds), *Contemporary Challenges to the Laws of War: Essays in Honour of Professor Peter Rowe* (Cambridge University Press 2014); Caroline Kaeb, 'The Shifting Sands of Corporate Liability under International Criminal Law' 49, 351 (Demands for corporate accountability have risen significantly over the last decades) (hereinafter Kaeb, 'Shifting Sands'); Franziska Oehm, 'Grundlagen der strafrechtlichen Verantwortlichkeit von wirtschaftlichen Akteuren für Menschenrechtsverletzungen' in Markus Krajewski, Franziska Oehm and Miriam Saage-Maaß (eds), *Zivil-und strafrechtliche Unternehmensverantwortung für Menschenrechtsverletzungen* (Springer 2018), 182; Ronald Slye, 'Corporations, Veils, and International Criminal Liability' (2008) 33 Brook Journal of International Law 955, 21 (hereinafter Slye, 'Corporations, Veils') ; Joanna Kyriakakis, 'Prosecuting Corporations for

With regard to the first problem of culpability of corporations as entities, despite the fact that the ICC does not exercise personal jurisdiction over corporations, there is an emerging consensus that a general principle of international law already exists on liability of legal persons for serious violations of international law.[18]

Concerning the second question, international economic criminal law (IECL) discusses the conduct of companies *and* their persons in-charge resulting in crimes under international law.[19] IECL's focus on corporations to hold them accountable[20] under international criminal law is based on the premise that committing large-scale political crimes is usually only possible with vast organizational and financial resources, often provided by economic actors. Given the context of a globalized economy, the decisions to contribute such financial and organization resources, increasingly dispersed across borders, are being made through complex structures. The question of attributing responsibility in corporate structures remains pressing while holding corporations accountable for their complicity in crimes under international law.[21]

International Crimes: The Role for Domestic Criminal Law' in Larry May and Zachary Hoskins (eds), *International Criminal Law and Philosophy* (Cambridge University Press 2010) 108–137 (hereinafter Kyriakakis, 'Prosecuting Corporations'); Sara Sun Beale, 'A Response to the Critics of Corporate Criminal Liability' (2009) 46 American Criminal Law Review 1481; Desislava Stoichkova, *Towards Corporate Liability in International Criminal Law* (Intersentia 2010) (hereinafter Stoichkova, *Towards Corporate Liability*).

18 Jendrik Adam argues that a general principle under international law on corporate accountability for serious human rights violations already exists and develops a criminality model that is based in particular on attribution theory which can be integrated into the Rome Statute. See Jendrik Adam, *Die Strafbarkeit Juristischer Personen im Völkerstrafrecht* (Nomos Verlag 2015) (hereinafter Adam, *Strafbarkeit Juristischer Personen*). Also, Special Tribunal for Lebanon (STL) decided in two cases that it has criminal jurisdiction over corporations (however, both the cases were involving offence of contempt) *Al Akbar Beirut SAL* (Case no. STL-14-05.) and *New TV SAL* (Case no. STL-14-06.); Nadia Bernaz, 'Corporate Criminal Liability under International Law: the New TV SAL and Akhbar Beirut SAL cases at the Special Tribunal for Lebanon' (2015) 13 Journal of International Criminal Justice 2, 313–330; Florian Jeßberger, 'Zur Einführung' in Jeßberger, Kaleck, and Singelnstein (eds), *Wirtschaftsvölkerstrafrecht*) (n 17)13; Zhifeng Jiang, 'International Criminal Responsibility of the Corporate Entity for Complicity in International Crimes: A Policy and Legal Case' (2020) 5 Cambridge Law Review 12.

19 Florian Jeßberger, 'Zur Einführung' in Jeßberger, Kaleck, and Singelnstein (eds), *Wirtschaftsvölkerstrafrecht)* (n 17); Kai Ambos, 'International Economic Criminal Law' (2018) 29 Criminal Law Forum 4, 500 (hereinafter Ambos, 'IECL').

20 Jochen Bung, 'Nauckes Narrative – politisches Wirtschaftstrafrecht statt Wirtschaftsvo¨lkerstrafrecht?' in Jeßberger, Kaleck, and Singelnstein (eds), *Wirtschaftsvölkerstrafrecht* (n 17) 129, 131.

21 For an overview on (German) criminal law and problems in attribution of responsibility, see I. Zerbes, 'Globales Wirtschaftshandeln als Gegenstand des Straf- und Strafverfahrensrechts. Eine Bestandsaufnahme' in Jeßberger, Kaleck, and Singelnstein (eds), *Wirtschaftsvölkerstrafrecht* (n 17) 205–240.

Thus, IECL's primary concern is to determine under what conditions and to what extent economic actors may be criminalized under international criminal law for their involvement in crimes under international law.[22]

The chapter begins with a discussion on the missed opportunities during the Nuremberg trials on the question of corporate accountability, therefore failing to establish a strong foundation of IECL for political reasons. The second section briefly addresses the current status of international criminal law concerning culpability of corporations as legal persons. The third section deals with the key question of attributing responsibility for corporate conduct under international criminal law. Finally, the concluding section clarifies the broad notion of accountability adopted for the purposes of this book. Overall, this chapter serves as the thematic foundation for the case studies discussed in Part II.

I. The Legacy of Nuremberg Trials

The only time an international tribunal even remotely engaged with the possibility of prosecuting corporate executives to capture the economic aspects of atrocity crimes was at the International Military Tribunal (IMT), Nuremberg. In the end, however, senior corporate officials were convicted only in the zonal trials held by Allied Powers individually and the judgments left a confused legacy of '[c]rimes against international law are committed by men, not by abstract entities' while holding individuals accountable for their complicity in international crimes through corporate conduct.[23]

22 Stefan Kirsch, *Völkerstrafrechtliche Risiken unternehmerischer Tätigkeit* (Neue Zeitschrift für Wirtschafts, Steuer- und Unternehmensstrafrecht 2014) 212.

23 *Trial of Carl Krauch and Twenty-Two Others* [1948] (United States Military Tribunal, Nuremberg, 14 August 1947–29 July 1948, Law Reports of Trials of war Criminals (UNWCC), Volume X, London) (hereinafter IG Farben Trial). It is disputed whether these judgments can be relied on to build a case on collective corporate responsibility (as opposed to just individual criminal responsibility). Andrew Clapham and Steven Ratner claim these judgments as discreet acknowledgement of the principle of collective corporate responsibility for crimes under international law. On the contrary, scholars such as Van der Wilt read Nuremberg judgments, particularly Farben, as the most outspoken rejection of the principle of corporate responsibility. Nonetheless, what can certainly be agreed upon, as Florian Jeßberger observes relying on the political and historical context of the judgments, that these trials did at least highlight the responsibility of industry and business through international criminal law and holds value for laying down the foundation for individual criminal responsibility for business activity. See Andrew Clapham, 'The Question of Jurisdiction Under International Criminal Law Over Legal Persons: Lessons from the Rome Conference on an International Criminal Court', in MT Kamminga and S Zia-Zarifi (eds), *Liability of Multinational Corporations Under International Law* (Kluwer International 2000) 139–195 (hereinafter Clapham, 'Lessons from Rome'); Ratner, 'Corporations and HR' (n 2) 478; Harmen van der Wilt, 'Corporate Criminal Responsibility for International Crimes: Exploring the Possibilities' (2013) 12 Chinese Journal of International Law 1, 43–77; Florian

Corporate defendants were not tried before the IMT but taken up by the Allied Powers in their unilateral zonal trials that followed the international trial. The US Military Tribunals held 12 subsequent trials in Nuremberg, which included members of the top management of corporations such as IG Farben, Krupp, and Flick for their role in the war effort of the Third Reich. The French and the British also held trials against corporate leaders for their involvement in crimes committed by Germany during World War II. The fact that corporate responsibility was missing in the international trial was not because it was not a part of their initial plan, but because of political and practical barriers that emerged during the international trial. A closer look at the factors that influenced the 'industrialist trials' in Nuremberg is an origin story that speaks of the vested interests of the Allied Powers and their legacy on current standards of international law.

1. *The Missing International Trial*

The role of businesses in the German war effort had been no secret, even during the war including forcible population transfers for slave labour, the development of efficient ovens for use in crematoria, distribution of Zyklon B used at chambers such as Auschwitz,[24] and financial support to the regime for the war effort and deriving consistent profits from it all through the 1930s.[25] Legal historian Jonathan Bush, in his decade-long study, assessed an understated aspect of the Nuremberg trials: the time in the lead up to the trials, where those who planned the most influential war crimes trials explored multiple possibilities of holding giant industrial companies liable and why they decided against it.[26]

Jeßberger, 'On the Origins of Individual Criminal Responsibility under International Law for Business Activity: IG Farben on Trial' (2010) 8 Journal of International Criminal Justice 3, 783–802 (hereinafter Jeßberger 'Origins of individual criminal responsibility'); J Kolieb, 'Through the Looking-Glass: Nuremberg's Confusing Legacy on Corporate Accountability under International Law Academy on Human Rights and Humanitarian Law: Articles and Essays on Transitional Justice, International Human Rights, and Humanitarian Law' (2016) 32 American University International Law Review [i].

24 In *re Tesch & Others* [1946] British Military Court, 1 UN WCC, Law Reports of Trials of War Criminals 93 (hereinafter *the Zyklon B case*).

25 Annika van Baar, 'Corporate involvement in the Holocaust and other Nazi crimes' in JG van Erp and others (eds) *The Routledge Handbook of White-collar and Corporate Crime in Europe* (Routledge 2015) 155–172; VR Berghahn 'Writing the History of Business in the Third Reich: Past Achievements and Future Directions', in Francis Nicosia, Jonathan Huener (eds), *Business and Industry in Nazi Germany* (Bergahn Books 2004) 129–48.

26 Jonathan A Bush, 'The Prehistory of Corporations and Conspiracy in International Criminal Law: What Nuremberg Really Said Essay' (2009) 109 Columbia Law Review 1094 (hereinafter Bush, 'Prehistory of Corporations'); another interesting historical account is offered in Grietje Baars, 'Capitalism's Victor's Justice? The Hidden Stories behind the Prosecution of

In setting the tone of the Nuremberg Trials, Justice Robert Jackson (the US Chief Prosecutor) declared:

> Whom will we accuse and put to their defence? We will accuse a large number of individuals and officials who were in authority in the government, in the military establishment, including the General Staff, and in the financial, industrial, and economic life in Germany who by all civilized standards are provable to be common criminals.[27]

The 'economic case' was going to be key in presenting the grand totality of the historical narrative of the war through the IMT trial. After gathering substantial evidence to build a case against the industrialists, prosecutorial chiefs of all four teams of the Allied Powers readily and unanimously agreed to include the chief of Krupp as the only representative industrialist in the list of 24 defendants for the first international trial.[28] He was to be indicted for the common charge of conspiracy and on all three substantial charges of war crimes, crimes against humanity, and genocide.[29]

However, it was later discovered that the four teams were thinking of different Krupp chiefs all this time. British, French, and Soviet prosecutors intended to indict Gustav Krupp, who led the firm in the 1930s as it helped arm the regime for aggression in the wake of stronger evidence against him, while Jackson was thinking of Alfried Krupp (Gustav's son), who took control of the corporation 1943 onwards, the years when the firm deployed tens of thousands of slave labourers under inhumane conditions.[30]

The cover-up for this miscommunication led to a hasty decision on including the father, Gustav Krupp, in the list, overlooking the formal process of medical examination of the accused person. When the indictment was finally served on Krupp, he was reported to be unable to stand the trial owing to his old age and state of health. The court rejected Jackson's subsequent plea to

Industrialists Post-WWII' in Kevin Heller and Gerry Simpson (eds), *The Hidden Histories of War Crimes Trials* (Oxford University Press 2013).

27 Robert H Jackson, *Report to the President of the United States* (Vol 12, State Bulletin 1945) 1074.

28 The perpetrators were charged individually and as members of any of the groups or organizations named in the indictment.

29 Bush, 'Prehistory of Corporations' (n 26) 1110.

30 Bush, 'Prehistory of Corporations' (n 26) 1111. Other works (primarily British and European authors) refer that the misunderstanding was the other way round: Jackson had been arguing for Gustav, whereas Shawcross and others were thinking of Alfried. See Donald Bloxham, '"The Trial That Never Was": Why There Was No Second International Trial of Major War Criminals at Nuremberg' (2002) 87 History 285, 41 (hereinafter Bloxham, 'The Trial That Never Was').

replace the father with the son,[31] citing the UK's ground of objection that this will cause further delay in the beginning of the trial, and hence suspended the trial against Krupp entity's conduct altogether.[32]

The inclusion of Krupp before the IMT and the prosecution of a corporate leader by an international tribunal would have established that the economic aspects of systematic violence were to be a mandatory part in any exercise of international criminal justice.

To make up for the absurd series of events, the French and British prosecutors resolved that Alfried Krupp and other businessmen will be brought to trial before IMT in the second international trial which will be held only for the businessmen.[33] However, by the spring of 1946, the British and Americans had grown ambivalent of this resolve to conduct the follow-up trials and not just for reasons of difficulty in trying corporate conduct. A major factor for consideration was the policy towards German businesses that were now at the mercy of Allied Powers. Jonathan Bush argues that with many other considerations at play, the decision on whether to conduct an international trial of the industrialists depended on reasons that went beyond dispassionate legal claims on whether to try IG Farben as a corporate entity or its heads on the basis of individual criminal responsibility.[34]

By late 1946, the US economic planners had arrived at this consensus that Allied reparations commitments required a functioning German economy. Hence, German reconstruction was to be made a priority.[35] Most planners had concluded that political and economic stability could only be achieved

31 *Trial of the Major War Criminals before the International Military Tribunal* (1945–46), Answer of the United States Prosecution to the Motion on Behalf of Defendant Gustav Krupp Von Bohlen (IMT Nuremberg, Vol 1, 1947) 134 (The United States respectfully submits that no greater disservice to the future peace of the world could be done than to excuse the entire Krupp family and the armament enterprise from this trial in which aggressive war-making is sought to be condemned. The 'interests of justice' cannot be determined without taking into account justice to the men of four generations whose lives have been taken or menaced by Krupp munitions and Krupp armament, and those of the future who can feel no safety if such persons as this escape all condemnation in proceedings such as this.)

32 See Telford Taylor, *The Anatomy of the Nuremberg Trials: A Personal Memoir* (Knopf 1992) 89–94 (describing Krupp indictment fiasco); Bush, 'Prehistory of Corporations' (n 26) 1112.

33 As the first trial was underway, representatives from the Allied Powers signed Control Council Law No. 10, a definitive agreement concerning future trials of additional major defendants. The law authorized both multilateral trials similar to the one taking place in Nuremberg before the IMT and other additional unilateral trials in any of the four occupation zones by one or more of the major allies.

34 Bush, 'Prehistory of Corporations' (n 26) 1117–1123.

35 According to Josiaah Dubois (US State Attorney who heads the Farben trial later), at the Potsdam Conference, a confidential memo was being circulated among the US delegation which clearly mentioned 'That our goal should be our goal should be rebuilding a strong Germany as a buffer against Communism', Oral History Interview with Josiah E. Dubois,

with the participation of German industry run by the same managers, regardless of their culpability in the horrific crimes.[36]

By the end of the first IMT trial, Jackson and the US prosecutorial camp were convinced that zonal trials as opposed to multinational trials were the best way forward.[37] Given Jackson's unique mandate and role in steering the Nuremberg proceedings, his opinions and convictions were a vital element in setting the course. In his report to the president, he recalled the Krupp incident to substantiate his scepticism about another international proceeding:

> [I]f they (the Soviet, French, and British) were unwilling to take the additional time necessary to try industrialists in this case, it does not create an obligation on the United States to assume the burdens of a second international trial.[38]

The British Foreign Office was even more reluctant for a second lengthy trial, which they feared would be anticlimactic and would detract attention from the achievements of the first, for which they had little enthusiasm in the first place.[39] Despite the French being enthusiastic for a multinational action against business leaders, the option of zonal trials preceded over the plan of the second IMT trial. The international trial of the industrialists became a collateral damage to the change of policy towards Germany.[40] In some ways,

Jr by Richard D. McKinzie (Trumann Library Museum 29 June 1973) available online at < www.trumanlibrary.gov/library/oral-histories/duboisje> accessed 30 January 2022.

36 Bush, 'Prehistory of Corporations' (n 26) 1121.

37 Robert Jackson to the President on American Participation in Future International Trials of Nazi War Criminals (May 13, 1946), reprinted in Telford Taylor, Final Report to the Secretary of the Army on the Nuremberg War Crimes Trials Under Control Council Law No. 10 (1949) 276, 277 (hereinafter Taylor Report).

38 Bush cites private exchanges between representatives which hint at Jackson's disgust and unwillingness to work with the Soviets, and also perhaps the senior French prosecutor, Charles Dubost, who he felt was a Communist. Bush, 'Prehistory of Corporations' (n 26) 1127. Furthermore, the rule of rotational presidency of the IMT would have meant that either the Soviet or the French Prosecutor would have been elevated to the position. Bloxham, 'The Trial That Never Was' (n 30) 51. British Foreign Secretary Orme Sargeant feared that such a second trial would become a 'battle between capitalism and communism' and that '[t]he Russians might exploit the proceedings to discuss irrelevancies such as [the British] attitude to German rearmament'. See Donald Bloxham, 'Defeat, Due Process, and Denial: War Crimes Trials and Nationalist Revisionism in Comparative Perspective' in J Macleod (ed), *Defeat and Memory: Cultural Histories of Military Defeat in the Modern Era* (Springer 2008) 149.

39 Bloxham, 'The Trial That Never Was' (n 30).

40 First public acknowledgement of the change in policy can be traced to 6 September 1946, in an address entitled Restatement of Policy on Germany given in Stuttgart by US Secretary of State, Jimmy Byrnes available online at <https://usa.usembassy.de/etexts/ga4-460906.htm> accessed 31 January 2022.

this was also a reflection of ideological and political differences amongst the representatives of the Allied Powers, who were to define the ensuing Cold War.

The absence of international trial did not mean absolute impunity for 'the generals in grey suits'[41] who contributed in varying degrees to the German war effort. The zonal trials were held as per the Control Council Law No. 10 of 20 December 1945,[42] which authorized each of the four German Occupation Zone Commanders to arrest the suspected war criminals and to establish 'appropriate tribunals' for their trials.[43] The law laid down the applicable substantive crimes (crimes against peace, war crimes, and crimes against humanity), and determined the modes of criminal responsibility and consequent sanctions.

The British Military Tribunal prosecuted the owner and two employees of corporations Tesch and Stabenow for selling the toxic Zyklon B gas for distribution in concentration camps in Germany. They were convicted for committing war crimes as the tribunal held international humanitarian law to be applicable not only to combatants and state authorities but also to 'anyone who was in a position to assist in their violation'.[44] In the absence of direct evidence corroborating shared intent, the tribunal held the *mens rea* standard to be 'knowledge or foreseeable knowledge' of the use of Zyklon B by the Nazis, which was derived from the person's position in the corporation.[45]

In 1948, the French Military Tribunal prosecuted the directors of the iron and steel Röchling Company for crimes against peace and war crimes. The tribunal convicted them on a similar basis for having the knowledge of the inhuman working conditions in their plants and actively seeking slave labour from the Third Reich.[46]

Owing to extensive documentation, explicit underlying legal policy, and prosecutorial rigor, subsequent trials by the US Military Tribunal at Nuremberg (in the same IMT Nuremberg courtroom) have caught more attention than others in scholarship and otherwise. These trials have been subject to a renewed interest, particularly, in international criminal law

41 Josiah E DuBois, *Generals in Grey Suits: The Directors of the 'IG Farben' Cartel, their Conspiracy and Trial at Nuremberg* (The Bodley Head 1953).

42 Control Council No. 10, Official Gazette of the Control Council for Germany No. 3, 31 January 1945, 50 (hereinafter CCL No. 10).

43 Article II, CCL No. 10: Punishment of Persons Guilty of War Crimes, Crimes Against Peace and Against Humanity.

44 *The Zyklon B case* (n 24) 103.

45 Ibid 101.

46 Hersch Lauterpacht (ed), *Annual Digest and Reports of Public International Law Cases – 1948* (Butterworth & Co. 1953) 411.

scholarship.[47] They represent the first attempt to hold individuals accountable for their business activity under international criminal law.[48] Perhaps an additional, implicit finding was that corporations (for which the individual businessmen worked) were collectively responsible for war crimes.[49]

As much as the trials indicate a step in the direction of corporate responsibility, they also represent a squandered opportunity to lay down the foundations of IECL. For reasons which were not purely legal and substantive, the courts remained short of trying corporations as anentity.

The next section discusses three alternatives that were presented before the US prosecutorial team to capture corporate criminality and their reasons for choosing individual criminal responsibility over the other proposals. The aim of the following discussion is not to comment on the debate between corporate criminal responsibility and individual criminal responsibility. However, the underlying idea is to argue that the current state of the norm and absence of practice concerning economic actors is not so much for legal or substantive problems such as difficulties in attributing conduct within a corporate structure, but instead for policy-based choices made by 'the West'.

2. Alternative Proposals for Corporate Responsibility at Nuremberg

The US Military Tribunal[50] held 12 trials between October 1946 and June 1949. Out of the 12, three were against industrialists from Flick, Krupp, and IG Farben. The official basis for the selection of these cases was

> to determine, in the light of the best available information, where the deepest individual responsibility lay for the manifold crimes committed under the aegis of the Third Reich. ... It was necessary to scrutinize the conduct of leaders in all occupations, and to let the chips fall where they might.[51]

47 See KR Jacobson, 'Doing Business with the Devil: The Challenges of Prosecuting Corporate Officials whose Business Transactions Facilitate War Crimes and Crimes Against Humanity' (2005) Air Force Law Review 56, 167; Gwynne Skinner, 'Nuremberg's Legacy Continues: The Nuremberg Trials' Influence on Human Rights Litigation in US Courts under the Alien Tort Statute' (2008) Albany Law Review 71, 321.

48 See Jeßberger 'Origins of Individual Criminal Responsibility' (n 23) 783–802.

49 Clapham, 'Lessons from Rome' (n 23) 140; Ambos, 'IECL' (n 19) 506.

50 Established by the US Military Governor pursuant to Military Government Ordinance No. 7 of 18 October 1946.

51 Preliminary Report to the Secretary of the Army by the Chief of Counsel for War Crimes (12 May 1948) 2–3 as quoted in Appendix to the Taylor Report (n 37) at 278.

As indicated earlier, the law recognized four categories of crimes: crimes against peace, war crimes, crimes against humanity, and membership in categories of a criminal group or organization.[52] In one of the interviews, Dubois, the main prosecutor in the industrialist trial against IG Farben, narrates that even before he came to Nuremberg, he was instructed by the US War Department to ensure that there will be no aggressive war charge against the industrialists.[53] The 'conciliatory moderate' outcome of the trials reflects the dilemma of holding prospective economic partners accountable for their past deeds.[54]

One of the first proposals was to use the theory of conspiracy liability, modelled after the first IMT indictment. It was suggested by Drexel Sprecher, who was a senior on both Jackson's, and his successor's (Taylor) team of prosecutors, to try the corporations acting as co-conspirators in the plan which would then allow prosecution of members involved.[55] According to the CCL No. 10, however, the organizations which would be considered criminal were those which were declared as such by the IMT under the London Charter. Since this was June 1946 already and the London Charter was going to expire on August 8, 1946, time was running out. Any attempt to prolong it would have required cooperation from the other three reluctant allies.[56]

The primary advantage of using a conspiracy model would have been a lower evidentiary threshold where multiple defendants could be tried on substantive charges without having to prove every fact and detail of commission of these crimes for each defendant individually. There were two major

52 Control Council Law10, Article II '1. Each of the following acts is recognized as a crime: (a) Crimes against Peace: Initiation of invasions of other countries and wars of aggression in violation of international laws and treaties, including but not limited to planning, preparation, initiation or waging a war of aggression, or a war of violation of international treaties, agreements or assurances, or participation in a common plan or conspiracy for the accomplishment of any of the foregoing. (b) War Crimes: Atrocities or offenses against persons or property constituting violations of the laws or customs of war, including, but not limited to, murder, ill treatment, or deportation to slave labour or for any other purpose, of civilian population from occupied territory, murder, or ill treatment of prisoners of war or persons on the seas, killing of hostages, plunder of public or private property, wanton destruction of cities, towns or villages, or devastation not justified by military necessity. (c) Crimes against Humanity: Atrocities and offenses, including, but not limited to, murder, extermination, enslavement, deportation, imprisonment, torture, rape, or other inhumane acts committed against any civilian population, or persecutions on political, racial, or religious grounds whether or not in violation of the domestic laws of the country where perpetrated. (d) Membership in categories of a criminal group or organization declared criminal by the International Military Tribunal'.

53 Despite this warning, two out of three industrialists' cases were charged with crimes against peace for initiating, panning, preparing for an aggressive war.

54 See Taylor Report (n 37) 305–6.

55 Bush, 'Prehistory of Corporations' (n 26) 1147.

56 Ibid 1148.

hurdles in this case: first, this model of conspiracy was not only novel for German law, but also unfamiliar for Soviet and French lawyers. Second, the hurriedly drafted definitions of the London Charter led to confusion about whether conspiracy charges applied only to crimes against peace or included war crimes and crimes against humanity as well.[57]

The second alternative theory was proposed by a leftist New York attorney, Abraham Pomerantz,[58] to try IG Farben and Krupp as 'corporate entities'.[59] By charging these corporations as entities, he was aiming at efficient and easier evidence-gathering, ridding the prosecution of the requirement to prove an actual agreement between the members that would have been a *sine qua non* for a conspiracy charge. Moreover, this would have laid a 'legal and moral foundation for the expropriation of all or any part of these properties'.[60] According to him, this would have also 'demonstrated to the German people the real powers behind Hitler and NSDAP [*Nationalsozialistische Deutsche Arbeiterpartei*]'.[61]

His model satisfied the common law tests for liability, already applicable in the United States and the United Kingdom, where the acts need to be within the scope of the defendants' business, carried out by employees or officers on orders of a 'superior agent'.[62] To the absence of an explicit norm on corporate responsibility, Pomerantz argued that there was neither anything explicitly precluding nor denying corporate liability.[63] Jonathan Bush claims that no record exists of how and why this proposal was rejected by Taylor.[64] But one of his colleagues, Drexel Sprecher, seems to have offered the following non-legal and rather practical pleas against it: confusion of issues at trial would have likely unclear coverage from the press and that public opinion will not tolerate a confused case, or one lengthy case would mean no further cases.[65]

57 London Charter Article 6, Bush, 'Prehistory of Corporations' (n 26) 1139.

58 He was brought in initially as the 'big-picture strategist' but later resigned by December 1946 arguably for protesting the US policy of depriving the Nuremberg Trials of resources, for refusing to cooperate with the Allies (especially the Soviets). Bush, 'Prehistory of Corporations' (n 26) text for note 278, 1171–72.

59 AL Pomerantz, *Feasibility and Propriety of Indicting IG Farben and Krupp as Corporate Entities* (27 August 1946); Bush, 'Prehistory of Corporations' (n 26) 1150.

60 Ibid.

61 Ibid.

62 *United States v. Dotterweich* [1943] 320 US 277, 281–82 (discussing corporate criminal liability under Food and Drug Act); *re Agent Orange Prod. Liab. Litig.* [2005] 373 F. Supp. 2d 7, 57 (EDNY); *Rex v ICR Haulage* [1944] 1 KB 551, 559 (allowing corporate liability); *Dir. Pub. Prosecutions v Kent and Sussex Contractors* [1944] 1 KB 146, 159 (also allowing corporate liability).

63 Bush, 'Prehistory of Corporations' (n 26) 1155.

64 Ibid 1156.

65 Ibid 1157.

A third alternative came from Slovak-born, US-raised prosecutor Leo Drachsler. He proposed an 'institutional approach' which could have addressed the fact that German industrialists had served as the 'third pillar' of the regime along with the Nazi Party-controlled government and the military, and that in important ways this third pillar was 'a single organization', 'a single entity'.[66] In that vein, they were to be considered as 'quasi-public' institutions. This proposal had elements of both Sprecher and Pomerantz: the doctrinal basis of the indictment and charges of conspiracy, viewing the industrialists' associations as a vehicle through which they contributed to the criminal conspiracy.[67] As for the responses to this proposal, available records suggest vague hints of concern about the press and broader public hostility.[68]

By holding individual perpetrators liable for international crimes for their complicity through economic action, the industrialists' trials highlighted the significance of economic activity in atrocity crimes. Nuremberg trials left a legacy of omissions leading to significant consequences in the context of international economic criminal law. Firstly, a quadripartite trial against corporations or even individuals behind them would have laid the foundation of including economic drivers of the conflict as an integral part of the criminal enterprise. Secondly, the possibility of having entities like IG Farben and others to be declared illegal under the London Charter could have established a precedent for culpability of corporations.[69] The idea of criminal responsibility of corporations as independent entities was not rejected for being legally unsound but skipped by the prosecutors for practical and political reasons. The cases that were tried by the Allied Powers independently leave a fragmented and inconsistent standard to attribute criminal responsibility to corporate leaders.

To sum up, the Nuremberg trials tell a story of squandered opportunity to lay down a strong foundation of international economic criminal law. The discussion is instructive in two main ways: exclusion of the economic aspects of systematic large-scale crimes from the mandate of international criminal justice, and the reasons that led to the preference of individual responsibility vis-à-vis collective criminality of corporations.

66 Ibid 1158.

67 Ibid 1159.

68 Ibid 1160.

69 See Kim Christian Priemel, 'Mehr Exempel als Modell. Die Nürnberger Prozesse gegen deutsche Industrielle und die Ursprünge des Wirtschaftsvölkerstrafrechts' in Jeßberger, Kaleck, and Singelnstein (eds), *Wirtschaftsvölkerstrafrecht* (n 17).

II. Corporate Criminality under International Criminal Law

The framing of the Nuremberg model's preference of individual responsibility over collective corporate liability as a 'missed opportunity' indicates that somehow bringing corporations as abstract entities within the ambit of international criminal law is desirable and valuable.[70]

One of the key objectives to advocate corporate criminality in the context of atrocity crimes is to highlight the economic and political structures that cause and sustain large-scale violence.[71] The principle of individual criminal responsibility de-contextualizes large-scale violence. It creates an enemy and leaves the structures that enabled the enemy invisible. While the individuals may be held accountable, the structures that sustained them tend to continue without any form of reprimand.[72] This view recognizes that the blameworthiness of the behaviour of corporations may exceed the responsibility of individuals and places the emphasis on the responsibility of a corporation as an autonomous agent.[73]

TWAIL scholars have also pointed to how 'violence has been displaced in part from the First to the Third World' by the international economic order.[74] The modern transnational corporate groups, often headquartered in the West, stand to profit from the violence or be complicit directly or indirectly through their subsidiaries.[75] As a result, accountability practices where individual responsibility does not take into account the wider geo-political

70 See James Stewart, 'The Turn to Corporate Criminal Liability for International Crimes: Transcending the Alien Tort Statute' (2014) 47 New York University Journal of International Law and Politics, 121–206; Kyriakakis, 'Prosecuting Corporations' (n 17) 108–137.

71 See Wolfgang Naucke, *Der Begriff der politischen Wirtschaftsstraftat – Eine Annäherung* (Vol 33, LIT Verlag 2012); Florian Jeßberger, 'Zur Einführung' in Jeßberger, Kaleck, and Singelnstein (eds), *Wirtschaftsvölkerstrafrecht)* (n 17).

72 Jonathan Clough, Punishing the Parent: Corporate Criminal Complicity in Human Rights Abuses (2008) 33 Brooklyn Journal of International Law 3.

73 *Prosecutor v Al Khayat* [2014] STL, Case No. STL-14-05/PT/AP/AR26.1, Decision on Interlocutory Appeal Concerning Personal Jurisdiction in Contempt Proceedings (discussing the decision of the Al-Jadeed case) (hereinafter *Al Khayat,* STL); Carsten Stahn, 'Liberals vs Romantics: Challenges of an Emerging Corporate International Criminal Law Corporations on Trial: International Criminal and Civil Liability for Corporations for Human Rights Violations' (2018) 50 Case Western Reserve Journal of International Law 91; Brent Fisse & John Braithwaite, The Allocation of Responsibility for Corporate Crime: Individualism, Collectivism and Accountability (1988) 11 Sydney Law Review 468, 483–88 (Their primary argument is functional autonomy of transnational corporations. These are organizations which have autonomy of action, capacity to change their policies, etc. They are not just the sum of individuals working for them.); Ratner, 'Corporations and HR' (n 2).

74 Antony Anghie and BS Chimni, 'Third World Approaches to International Law and Individual Responsibility in Internal Conflicts' (2003) Chinese Journal of International Law 77, 89.

75 Ibid.

relationships at play tend to imply that violence is endogenous to the Third World. Such implementation of international criminal law renders invisible the external actors and frameworks that contribute to local conditions of violence.[76] The choice of not including these structures within the ambit of international criminal legal institutions is a form of pre-selectivity that takes place even before the court comes into action. Such pre-selection reinforces bias into the structures of the law. This criticism not only speaks of an existing accountability gap but it also has implications for the legitimacy of international criminal justice as a system.[77]

Like Nuremberg, the option of corporate criminality was tabled in Rome as well. At the Rome Conference for establishment of the ICC in 1998, the French delegation proposed to include corporations in the jurisdiction of the ICC.[78] At the beginning of the Conference, the draft statute had a bracketed provision that granted ICC jurisdiction over both natural and legal persons.[79]

The French proposal was based on the recognition of legal personality for *personnes morales* and the declaration of organizations as criminal, following the precedent of the Nuremberg Trials, which would have resulted in corporations being outlawed, declared illegal, closed down, or even dissolved.[80] The proposal was essentially modelled after French domestic legal provisions where collective criminal responsibility does not displace individual responsibility, rather it is dependent on the individuals bearing criminal responsibility

76 See *Al Khayat*, STL (n 73) paras 82–83 (The prosecution of natural persons, rather than the legal persons that they serve, would fail to underline, and punish corporate cultures that condone and, in some cases, encourage illegal behaviour. Punishing only natural persons in such circumstances would be a poor response where the need for accountability lies beyond any one person.)

77 Joanna Kyriakakis, 'Corporations before International Criminal Courts: Implications for the International Criminal Justice Project' (2017) 30 Leiden Journal of International Law 221; Federic Mégret, 'What Sort of Global Justice is "International Criminal Justice"?' (2015) 13 Journal of International Criminal Justice 77.

78 Working Paper on Article 23 (3 July 1998) A/Conf.183/C.1/WGGP/L.5/Rev.2, paras 5 and 6. For an overview of the negotiations, see Clapham, 'Lessons from Rome' (n 23) 139–160.

79 Draft Article 23(5) and (6) which did not make the final cut read as '23 (5) The Court shall have jurisdiction over legal persons, with the exception of States, when the crimes committed were committed on behalf of such legal persons or by their agencies or representatives. (6) The criminal responsibility of legal persons shall not exclude the criminal responsibility of natural persons who are perpetrators or accomplices in the same crimes'. See UN Doc A/CONF.183/2/Add.1. The footnote following the text already indicated the controversy associated with the provisions: 'There is a deep divergence of views as to the advisability of including criminal responsibility of legal persons in the Statute. Many delegations are strongly opposed, whereas some strongly favour its inclusion. Others have an open mind. Some delegations hold the view that providing for only the civil or administrative responsibility/liability of legal persons could provide a middle ground. This avenue, however, has not been thoroughly discussed. Some delegations, who favour the inclusion of legal persons, hold the view that this expression should be extended to organizations lacking legal status'.

80 Clapham, 'Lessons from Rome' (n 23).

for the crimes in question.[81] Therefore, the primary jurisdiction of the Court, according to the proposal, would have concerned individuals and jurisdiction over the juridical persons in addition to the primary role of determining individual responsibility.[82]

The proposal came with complex questions of control, knowledge, and corporate guilt viewed divergently in national jurisdictions which made it difficult to figure out the complementarity implications of the provision.[83] In the absence of a unified standard for this liability, it was also feared that the principle of individual responsibility would be watered down. Furthermore, there were concerns that considerable problems gathering evidence when investigating corporations, which often operate internationally, would overtax the ICC's limited capacity.[84] In the end, the proposal was never even voted on but withdrawn for paucity of time in the negotiating process[85] and lack of consensus.[86] As Kai Ambos has argued, if there was genuine political will to include corporate responsibility within the ICC's ambit, the issue could have very well been passed on to a working group for future negotiations, like the crime of aggression.[87] Therefore, this absence may well be construed as a sign of political willingness rather than an outcome of legal complexity.

Even if the French proposal is not read as a sign of growing acceptance of the principle of corporate criminality as some of its advocates[88] would hope, there are some recent developments in the practice of international

81 This is based on the notion that corporations lack minds and thus a corporation can only be found guilty through its individual employees. See Anna Triponel, Comparative Corporate Responsibility in the United States and France for Human Rights Violations Abroad, in Andrew Morriss & Samuel Estreicher (eds), *Proceedings of the New York University 61st Conference on Labour* (2010) 80; Kaeb, 'Shifting Sands' (n 7); also see discussion in Section 6.III.

82 Clapham, 'Lessons from Rome' (n 23)152.

83 Kuntz, *Conceptualising Transnational Corporate Groups* (n 4) 25; William Schabas, *The International Criminal Court: A Commentary on the Rome Statute* (2nd edn, Oxford University Press 2016).

84 Kai Ambos, *Treatise on International Criminal Law* (Vol. I, Oxford University Press 2013) 83–84 (hereinafter Ambos, *Treatise on International Criminal Law*); Jendrik Adam, *Strafbarkeit juristischer Personen* (n 18) 80; Kaeb, 'Shifting Sands' (n 17) 353.

85 Summary Records of the Meetings of the Committee as a Whole, 26th Meeting, UN Doc.A/CONF.183/C.1/SR.26
(8 July 1998), at 10. Clapham, 'Lessons from Rome' (n 23)157.

86 The drafters of the ICC Statute noted that '[t]here is a deep divergence of views as to the advisability of including criminal responsibility of legal persons in the Statute'. See Official Records of the United Nations Diplomatic Conference of Plenipotentiaries on the Establishment of an International Criminal Court, Rome (15 June to 17 July 1998) Vol III, A/CONF.183/2, Article 23, para 6, note 71.

87 Ambos, 'IECL' (n 19) 519.

88 Clapham, 'Lessons from Rome' (n 23)140: (even though the negotiations in Rome failed to include legal persons within the jurisdiction of the Court, the debate highlighted the importance of considering ways to tackle corporate war crimes and the perceived difficulties of

criminal law, outside of the ICC,[89] indicating an understanding that corporations as legal persons can contribute to violations amounting to crimes under international law.

The Special Tribunal for Lebanon (STL) became the first international criminal judicial body to have decided in two cases that it had criminal jurisdiction over corporations in contempt of court cases.[90] In October 2014, the Appeals Panel examined a number of developments at the national level as well as treaties that refer to corporate criminal responsibility, and concluded that 'corporate criminal liability is on the verge of attaining, at the very least, the status of a general principle of law applicable under international law'.[91] Scholars have celebrated this finding for marking the broader trend towards holding corporations accountable and anticipate that there will be normative implications of this decision for domestic laws.[92]

In terms of an international statutory recognition of collective corporate accountability for crimes under international law,[93] Article 46 of the annex to the Malabo Protocol on Amendments to the Protocol on the Statute of the African Court of Justice and Human Rights explicitly distinguishes between individual criminal responsibility (Article 46B) and corporate criminal liability (Article 46C).[94] Therefore, the future African Court would have jurisdic-

devising rules of attribution.) Kuntz, *Conceptualizing Transnational Corporate Groups* (n 4) 27; ICJ, Corporate Complicity (n 17) 56.

89 In 2016, in its Policy Paper on Case Selection and Prioritisation, the OTP stated that it would prioritize the investigation and selection of cases whose manner of commission and impact may very likely include crimes where corporate actors participate by putting profit over vulnerable communities, grabbing their land and/or destroying the environment. The policy, however, does not expressly provide any indication that the OTP will focus on the accountability of corporate actors. See ICC OTP, Policy Paper on Case Selection and Prioritization, 2016, paras 40-1.

90 *Al Akbar Beirut SAL* (n 18) and *New TV SAL* (n 18). For a detailed discussion on both the cases, see Kaeb, 'Shifting Sands' (n 17); Bernaz (n 18).

91 Decision on Interlocutory Appeal Concerning Personal Jurisdiction in Contempt Proceedings, *New TV Karma Mohamed Tashin Al Khayat* [2014] ICC, Case No. STL-14-05/PT/AP/AR126.1, para 67. It should be noted that ruling was later rejected by the Contempt Judge in a related proceeding: STL-14-06/PT/CJ [2014].

92 Kaeb, 'Shifting Sands' (n 17) 353–54.

93 Seventeen other multilateral international instruments contain one or more provisions on corporate criminal liability. However, none of these instruments apply to crimes under customary international law over which international courts or tribunals have jurisdiction. See Bert Swart, 'International Trends Towards Establishing Some Form of Punishment for Corporations' (2008) 6 Journal of International Criminal Justice 947, 949.

94 Article 46C – Corporate Criminal Liability: '1. For the purposes of this Statute, the Court shall have jurisdiction over legal persons, with the exception of States. 2. Corporate intention to commit an offence may be established by proof that it was the policy of the corporation to do the act which constituted the offence. 3. A policy may be attributed to a corporation where it provides the most reasonable explanation of the conduct of that corporation. 4. Corporate knowledge of the commission of an offence may be establishes by proof that

tion over corporations as 'legal persons' for human rights violations. This Court would also have jurisdiction over a broader range of crimes, including money laundering, corruption, trafficking, and the illicit exploitation of natural resources. The scope of Court's jurisdiction is significantly broader as compared to other international/hybrid criminal tribunals and courts. Even if this development might remain a regional exception, this would have implications for corporations, regardless of their nationality, as long as they are operating in Africa and they will have to consider that they could be potentially prosecuted for crimes under international laws.

Finally, in 2017, as a part of International Law Commission's (ILC) Draft Articles on Crimes against Humanity, the following paragraph was adopted as draft Article 6(7):

> Subject to the provisions of its national law, each State shall take measures, where appropriate, to establish the liability of *legal persons* for the offences referred to in this draft article. Subject to the legal principles of the State, such liability of legal persons *may be criminal, civil or administrative*.[95]

Inclusion of liability for legal persons is a development in ILC's stance on the state of the norm as in its 1996 draft code of crimes, the Commission only addressed the criminal responsibility of 'an individual'.[96] By expanding the liability provision to include legal persons, the ILC issued a clarification that protected interests in the convention on crimes against humanity can be violated by a private corporation as well, in addition to an individual or a state.[97]

Scholars have written extensively on the added value of criminal liability of corporations where civil and administrative remedies are already available. Normative arguments justifying imposition of criminal accountability on corporations are also very well-rehearsed and do not warrant repetition here.[98]

---

the actual or constructive knowledge of the relevant information was possessed within the corporation. 5. Knowledge may be possessed within a corporation even though the relevant information is divided between corporate personnel. 6. The criminal responsibility of legal persons shall not exclude the criminal responsibility of natural persons who are perpetrators or accomplices in the same crime'. Available online at <https://au.int/en/treaties/protocol-amendments-protocol-statute-african-court-justice-and-human-rights> accessed 15 August 2021.

95 Article 6(7), Draft articles on Prevention and Punishment of Crimes against Humanity 2019 (emphasis added).

96 Article 2, Draft Code of Crimes against the Peace and Security of Mankind 1996.

97 See the commentary in the ILC's Annual Report 2016, UN Doc A/71/10, 262–265.

98 Mordechai Kremnitzer, 'A Possible Case for Imposing Criminal Liability on Corporations in International Criminal Law' (2010) 8 Journal of International Criminal Justice 909;

Therefore, on the basis of these recent developments in international law combined with the consensus emerging from the existing scholarship, it is fair to argue that corporate criminality has at least attained the status of a general principle under international law.[99] In other words, international criminal law has evolved since Nuremberg to recognize that even though corporations don't have a body to be kicked, a soul to be damned, still they cannot do as they like.[100]

III. Liability for Corporate Conduct

Given the nature of economic activity, there are two primary ways in which corporate conduct can be held liable: one, by way of holding the corporate culpable directly for its own conduct, and two, in the form of a derivative liability where the conduct of natural persons (managers/staff, etc.) is attributed to the corporation. The first model of liability would be organizational and the latter attribution model.[101]

Mordechai Kremnitzer and H. Genaim, 'The Criminal Liability of a Corporation', in A Barak (ed) *Shamgar Book* (Israel Bar Association, 2003) 33–113, 74; Larissa van den Herik, 'Subjecting corporations to the ICC regime: Analyzing the Legal Counterarguments' and Marc Engelhart, 'International Criminal Responsibility of Corporations', both in Christoph Burchard, Otto Triffterer, and Joachim Vogel (eds), *The Review Conference and the Future of the International Criminal Court* (Kluwer International 2010); Volker Nerlich, 'Core Crimes and Transnational Business Corporations' (2010) 8 Journal of International Criminal Justice 895; Harmen van der Wilt, 'Corporate Criminal Responsibility for International Crimes: Exploring the Possibilities' (2013) 12 Chinese Journal of International Law 43; Jendrik Adam, *Personen im Völkerstrafrecht* (n 18); Clapham, 'Lessons from Rome' (n 23) 147; Singelnstein, 'Grenzen eines internationalen Wirtschaftsstrafrechts zur Ahndung von Menschenrechtsverletzungen' and Zerbes, 'Globales Wirtschaftshandeln als Gegenstand des Straf- und Strafverfahrensrechts' both in Jeßberger, Kaleck, Singelstein (eds), *Wirtschaftsvölkerstrafrecht* (n 17) 145–6, 214, 230–231, 234; James G Stewart, 'Atrocity, Commerce and Accountability Antonio Cassese Prize for International Criminal Law Studies: A Book Proposal' (2010) 8 Journal of International Criminal Justice 314; Christina Chiomenti, 'Corporations and the International Criminal Court' in De Schutter (ed), *Transnational Corporations and Human Rights* (Hart Publishing 2006) 287; Joanna Kyriakakis. 'Corporations and the International Criminal Court: the Complementarity Objection Stripped Bare' (2008) 19 Criminal Law Forum 115–151 (hereinafter Kyriakakis, 'Corporations and ICC').

99 Some have gone even further to assert that the principle may have attained the status of customary international law; see Andrew Clapham, 'Extending International Criminal Law beyond the Individual to Corporations and Armed Opposition Groups' (2008) 6 Journal of International Criminal Justice 899 (hereinafter Clapham, 'Extending ICL to Corporations').

100 The following oft-repeated observation of British Chancellor Edward Thurlow '[c]orporations have neither bodies to be punished, nor souls to be condemned; they therefore do as they like' has been used to justify the absence of corporate criminality. See John Poynder, *Literary Extracts from English and Other Works; Collected During Half a Century: Together with Original Matter* (Vol. I, John Hatchard & Son 1844).

101 Ambos, 'IECL' (n 19) 531.

On the one hand, the organizational model assumes that corporations act as autonomous agents who carry out activities against the law while simultaneously having the option to act otherwise. This places the emphasis on 'capacity to act' and 'corporate responsibility', and does not depend on culpability (mental elements) derived from the individuals working within the organization.[102]

The attribution model, on the other hand, relies on the culpability of the staff and then creates a parallel liability for the corporation on the basis that such culpable conduct was carried out on behalf of or for the corporation itself. This model raises the question of conditions under which the conduct of an individual can be attributed to the company. Do they have to be decision-making managers of the parent company who exercise substantial control over the subsidiary or is the conduct of a staff member of a subsidiary sufficient to hold the (parent) corporation criminally liable?[103] In both of these cases, either the decision-making managers are acting as the corporation or the staff where the conduct was directed by/emanated from a failure of supervisory action was acting on behalf of the corporation. Building on the premise that essentially organizational actions are key in both the scenarios, Ambos argues that even the attribution model boils down to a 'hidden organizational model'.[104]

In that sense, the attribution model, where the organization's culpability is derived from the conduct of its individual members, is consistent with international criminal law's focus on individual criminal responsibility.[105] Attribution of individual conduct to the corporation and holding it accountable for the same takes into account the structure within which the responsible individual was acting.

Even if this broad normative understanding is adopted for attribution of conduct to the corporation, there are significant practical hurdles in prosecuting corporations, such as identification of most responsible individuals, corporate veil, aiding in the form of neutral multipurpose goods such as money, etc. The case studies in the following chapters deal with similar

102 Ibid 540.

103 See Kuntz, *Conceptualizing Transnational Corporate Groups* (n 4) 165; Stoichkova, *Towards Corporate Liability* (n 17).

104 Ambos, 'IECL' (n 19) 543.

105 In a case of individual criminal responsibility before the ICTR, *Musema*, the director of a tea factory, stood trial and was convicted on charges of genocide and extermination as a crime against humanity for ordering, aiding, and abetting or, as a superior having failed to prevent or repress such crimes committed by his subordinates against Tutsis. *Alfred Musema* [2000] ICTR-96-13-T, Judgment and Sentence; *Ruto & Sang* [2012] ICC – Decision on the Confirmation of Charges Pursuant to Article 61(7) (a) and (b) of the ICC Statute, paras 349, 367 (corporate executive of a media company subject to the prosecution of the ICC on charges of incitement to commit crimes against humanity). See Slye, 'Corporations, Veils' (n 17).

obstacles in one manner or the other, albeit in their respective domestic contexts. Therefore, before moving to the case studies, it would be worthwhile to have an overview of the forms of participation that can attract individual liability for conduct carried out through corporate structures under international criminal law.

1. Principal Liability

Broadly, there are two forms of individual criminal liability that can be attributed to corporate executives: either principal liability for *stricto sensu* 'commission' of a crime or accessory liability for contributing to crimes committed by others.[106] In case of corporate misconduct, it would inevitably be a situation where a number of individuals commit the crime 'jointly with another or through another' person as opposed to an individual committing the crime directly herself. The ICC Statute recognizes principal liability through co-perpetration under Article 25(3)(a) and it is distinguished from ordering a crime or contributing to a crime, both of which attract accessory liability.

Under Article 25(3)(a), in order to attract principal liability for co-perpetration, the perpetrator must knowingly and intentionally provide an 'essential contribution' to the joint criminal effort with the power 'to frustrate the commission of the crime by not performing their tasks'.[107] The quality of this contribution establishes joint control of the co-perpetrators over the crime.[108] ICC jurisprudence on this question relies heavily on German doctrine of functional control over the act (*Tatherrschaft*) to distinguish between principal and accessory liability.[109] The notion underpinning this approach is that principals to a crime are not limited to those who physically carry out the

106 *Lubanga* [2014] ICC, Appeals Chamber Judgment, para 469. The Appeals Chamber also opined that the principals to the crime, i.e. those who had actually committed the crime (whether by themselves, jointly with other, or 'through' another person), bore 'more blameworthiness' than the accessories to the crime, i.e. those who had *merely* contributed to the crime of someone else (Ibid, para 462) (emphasis added). Recently, the idea of degrees of blameworthiness was challenged in dissenting judgments by Judge Morrison and Judge Eboe-Osuji, who argued that the various provisions of Article 25(3) did not constitute a 'hierarchy of blameworthiness' but rather listed the many different forms of participation in an international crime, without attaching any normative significance to one form or another. *Bosco Ntaganda* [2021] ICC, Appeals Chamber (hereinafter *Ntaganda*, Appeals Chamber) Judge Morrison, paras 8–9; Judge Eboe-Osuji, paras 45–47.

107 *Lubanga* [2007] ICC, Trial Chamber, Confirmation of Charges Decision, paras 346–347 (hereinafter *Lubanga*, Confirmation of Charges).

108 Ibid para 341.

109 Claus Roxin, *Täterschaft Und Tatherrschaft* (Cram, De Gruyter & Co. 1963); See Thomas Weigend, 'Perpetration through an Organization, The Unexpected Career of a German Legal Concept' 9 Journal International Criminal Justice (2011) 91–111.

objective elements of the offence, but also include those who, in spite of being removed from the scene of the crime, control or mastermind its commission because they decide whether and how the offence will be committed.[110]

In case of committing a crime *through* another (indirect perpetration), the ICC has extended the scope of principal liability to include persons who commit a crime through an organization, in which they hold a superior position, and can accomplish the crime by ordering subordinates they control.[111] This would ideally be applicable on the structures of corporations, as well-provided structures included a sufficient number of subordinates in order to guarantee that the superiors' orders would be carried out, 'if not by one subordinate, then by another'[112] It should be noted, however, that the control theory has been subjected to strong criticism.[113] This discontent recently featured in two separate opinions to the Appeals Chamber judgment in the case of *Bosco Ntagnada* where the two dissenting judges favoured a plain reading of the word 'commission' in Article 25(3)(a) and adopted a narrow approach of 'sufficient nexus' between the crime and the accused.[114] Such an approach would essentially mean that only persons in some form of proximity to the commission of crime could be held liable as principals and cases of organizational criminality would eventually need to be dealt with under common purpose liability (see Section III.4).

The concept of co-perpetration was perceived as an improvement of ad hoc tribunal principle of joint criminal enterprise (JCE).[115] A number of material and mental elements distinguish the two concepts of imposing principal liability for co-perpetration.[116] To attract JCE liability, the contribution made by the accused 'need not be necessary or substantial, but it should at least

110 *Lubanga*, Confirmation of Charges (n 107) para 330, referring to the 'concept of control over the crime'.

111 *Germain Katanga* [2014] ICC, Trial Chamber Judgment.

112 *Germain Katanga and Mathieu Ngudjolo Chui* [2008] ICC, Pre-Trial Chamber, Decision of Confirmation of Charges, para 512.

113 See Leila Sadat and Jarrod Jolly, 'Seven Canons of ICC Treaty Interpretation: Making Sense of Article 25's Rorschach Blot' (2014) 27 Leiden Journal of International Law 755, 781–782; Jens Ohlin, Elies van Sliedregt and Thomas Weigend, 'Assessing the Control-Theory' (2013) 26 Leiden Journal of International Law 725, 731–732; Jens Ohlin, 'Co-Perpetration: German Dogmatik or German Invasion' in Carsten Stahn (ed.), The Law and Practice of the International Criminal Court (Oxford University Press 2015) 517, 527–531.

114 *Ntaganda*, Appeals Chamber (n 106) Judge Morrison, para 34, Judge Eboe-Osuji, para 24.

115 Ambos, *Treatise on International Criminal Law* (n 84) 152–153; Gerhard Werle and Boris Burghardt, 'Establishing Degrees of Responsibility: Modes of Participation in Article 25 of the ICC Statute' in Elies van Sliedregt and Sergey Vasiliev, Pluralism in International Criminal Law (Oxford University Press 2014) 316–317.

116 Elies Van Sliedregt and Lachezar Yanev, 'Co-perpetration Based on Joint Control over the Crime' in Jérôme de Hemptinne and others (eds), *Modes of Liability in International Criminal Law* (Cambridge University Press 2019) 85–120 (hereinafter Jérôme de Hemptinne and others (eds), *Modes of Liability*).

be a significant contribution to the crimes for which the accused is found responsible'.[117] The definitions of common plan are also different in the two forms of liability. Under co-perpetration theory, the said plan in itself does not need to be intrinsically a criminal plan.[118] Moreover, the 'extended' variant of JCE allows ascribing responsibility for 'incidental' crimes of the common plan on the basis of a *dolus eventualis* standard,[119] but this form of *mens rea* is excluded from the ICC legal framework of co-perpetration based on joint control.[120]

As the jurisprudence suggests, to hold corporate managers directly liable as principals committing a crime with another or through another, the element of control between the accused and the people who actually committed the crime will have to be established. To reproduce the degree of hierarchy and control as required to establish co-perpetration, which is usually exercised in military structures relationships, becomes very difficult in the case of corporate hierarchies,[121] as is exemplified in Chapter 4 when discussing the case of the military–corporate nexus during the military dictatorship in Argentina from 1976 to 1983.

2. *Accomplice Liability*

Corporations often do not act as principal perpetrators and the diffused structures may result in considerable physical distance between the place of decision-making and the place of commission of crimes. Attributing criminal conduct to a corporation and/or its individual officials requires some level of proximity to the 'zone of legal risk'.[122] Their status as accomplices or accessories to the crime requires a response to three fundamental questions: one, whether the company's conduct was sufficiently linked or to what extent did the company contribute, enable, or facilitate gross human rights abuses?; two, was there an element of knowledge or foreseeable knowledge present

117 *Krajišnik* [2009] ICTY, Appeals Chamber, IT-00-39-A, para 215.

118 Marco Milanović, 'An Odd Couple: Domestic Crimes and International Responsibility in the Special Tribunal for Lebanon' (2007) 5 Journal of International Criminal Justice 1139, 1146; Wayne Jordash and P. van Tuyl, 'Failure to Carry the Burden of Proof: How Joint Criminal Enterprise Lost Its Way at the Special Court for Sierra Leone' (2010) 8 Journal of International Criminal Justice 591, 600.

119 *Tadić* [1999] ICTY, Appeals Chamber, IT-94-1-A, paras 220, 228.

120 Ibid paras 36–37.

121 See Guénaël Mettraux, *The Law of Command Responsibility* (Oxford University Press 2009) 188 (hereinafter Mettraux, *The Law of Command Responsibility*); Hans Vest, 'Business Leaders and the Modes of Individual Criminal Responsibility under International Law' (2010) 8 Journal of International Criminal Justice 3, 870 (hereinafter Vest, 'Modes of Individual Criminal Responsibility').

122 ICJ, Corporate Complicity (n 17) 8.

in the decision-making that led to criminal conduct?; and three, how close was the company to the principal perpetrator of the crimes or the victims?[123]

Under the statutes of the ICC and the ad hoc tribunals for Yugoslavia and Rwanda,[124] a person can be responsible for committing,[125] planning,[126] ordering,[127] or instigating[128] a crime or for otherwise aiding and abetting a crime. Both international and national criminal laws commonly characterize a person who directly or physically commits a crime as a principal perpetrator. However, those who plan, order, or instigate might be described as either principal perpetrators or accomplices in various national laws.

According to the ILC's second version of the draft Code of Crimes against the Peace and Security of Mankind which was adopted in 1996 (ILC Code), any act other than the commission or the attempt to commit a crime fell within the general category of accomplice liability.[129] These forms of liability included ordering, failing to prevent or repress a crime as a superior, direct participation in planning or conspiring to commit a crime, or directly and publicly inciting a crime.[130] The ILC Code also provided that an individual will be held responsible if he 'knowingly aids, abets or otherwise assists, *directly and substantially*, in the commission of such a crime, including providing the means for its commission'.[131]

This interpretation is also consistent with the findings of the ad hoc tribunals.[132] Accordingly, under international criminal law the requisite *acts*

123 Ibid 9.

124 See Article 7(1) ICTY Statute; Article 6(1) ICTR Statute; Article 25 ICC Statute.

125 Committing refers to the physical participation of an accused in the actual acts, which constitute the material elements of a crime. *Rutaganda* [1999] ICTR, Trial Chamber, para 40 (hereinafter *Rutaganda*); *Galic* [2003] ICTY, Trial Chamber, para 168 (hereinafter *Galic*); see Article 25(3)(a) ICC Statute.

126 Planning occurs when one or several persons contemplate designing the commission of a crime at both the preparatory and execution phases. *Akayesu* [1998] ICTR, Trial Chamber, para 480 (hereinafter *Akayesu*); *Rutaganda* (n 125) para 37; *Galic* (n 125) para 168.

127 Ordering means a person in a position of authority using that authority to instruct another to commit an offence. *Akayesu* (n 126) para 483; *Rutaganda* (n 125) para 39; *Gacumbitsi* [2006] ICTR, Appeals Chamber paras 181–183 (hereinafter *Gacumbitsi*); see Article 25(3)(b) ICC Statute.

128 Instigating means prompting another to commit an offence which is actually committed, either through an act or omission. *Gacumbitsi* (n 127) para 129; see Article 25(3)(b) ICC Statute, which prohibits soliciting or inducing the commission of a crime.

129 ILC, Yearbook of the International Law Commission (Vol II, 1954) UN Doc. A/CN.4/SER.A/1954/Add.l, 18, 20.

130 Article 2(3)(b)–(f); see ILC Yearbook of the International Law Commission (Vol II, 1996) A/CN.4/SER.A/1996/Add.l, 18.

131 Ibid 21(emphasis added).

132 Article 7(1) ICTY Statute and Article 6(1) ICTR Statute on individual criminal responsibility include persons who have 'otherwise aided and abetted in the planning, preparation of execution of a crime'. 'The contribution of the aider and abettor may be provided at any stage – planning, preparation, or execution – of the criminal process' and 'may take the

reus is direct and substantial contribution and the *mens rea* of aiding and abetting is 'knowledge' that the acts performed assist the commission of the specific crime of the principal perpetrator. Article 25(3)(c) of the ICC Statute provides for criminal liability for assisting the direct perpetrator. The *actus reus* criterion of the provision has been interpreted by ICC that such assistance that has 'substantial effect' on the crime should suffice, it does not need to be a substantial contribution.[133] The *mens rea* standard is however different from that of ad hoc tribunals: 'for the purpose of facilitating the commission of such crime'.[134] The person assisting need not share the same intent with the primary perpetrators. Knowledge of the primary perpetrator's intent is sufficient.[135]

In national criminal laws, often these acts of aiding, abetting, instigating, and ordering are separate and distinct offences. They are consistent with international criminal law in the sense that such conduct is criminalized. Under national penal systems, mere knowledge may not be sufficient to prove the mental intent. Some national laws require a higher threshold of shared intent or at least a previous agreement between the principal perpetrator and the accomplice.[136]

Therefore, in a typical scenario where a company knowingly sells a product such as chemicals, weapons, computers, and technology, which are likely to be used for atrocity crimes and their contribution is unambiguous, would be held liable for aiding, facilitating, and assisting the direct perpetrator. However, cases of ambiguous support and complicity might not

form of a positive act or an omission, and it may occur before, during, or after the fact of the principal offender'. See *Blagojevic and Jokic* [2007] ICTY, Appeals Chamber, para 127; *Simic* [2006] ICTY, Appeals Chamber, para 86; *Blaskic* [2004] ICTY, Appeals Chamber paras 45–46; *Vasiljevic* [2004] ICTY, Appeals Chamber, para 102.

133 Marina Aksenova, *Complicity in International Criminal Law* (Hart Publishing 2016) 155 (hereinafter Aksenova, *Complicity in ICL*). Some would also argue that it is sufficient if an act facilitates or furthers a crime and it does not necessarily have to have a substantial effect on the commission of the crime. See Gerhard Werle and Florian Jeßberger, *Principles of International Criminal Law* (4th edn, Oxford University Press 2021) 260.

134 Kai Ambos, 'Article 25' in Otto Triffterer (ed), *Commentary on the Rome Statute of the International Criminal Court* (2nd edn, Beck-Hart-Nomos 2008) 760 marginal no. 23 (hereinafter Ambos, 'Art. 25'); Albin Eser, 'Individual Criminal Responsibility', in Antonio Cassese and others (eds), *The Rome Statute of the International Criminal Court: A Commentary* (Vol I, Oxford University Press 2002) 801; Chantal Meloni, *Individual Criminal Responsibility* (Oxford University Press 2020).

135 Werle and Jeßberger, *Principles* (n 133) 262; G. Mettraux, *International Crimes and the ad hoc Tribunals* (Oxford University Press 2005) 212; some scholars have also argued that the provision requires a higher mental threshold of shared intent; see Aksenova, *Complicity in ICL* (n 133) 155; Ambos, 'Art. 25' (n 134) 1009.

136 Anita Ramasastry and RC Thompson, *Commerce, Crime and Conflict: Legal Remedies for Private Sector Liability for Grave Breaches of International Law: A Survey of Sixteen Countries* (FAFO 2006) 18 (hereinafter FAFO Survey).

be criminalized until the higher threshold of mental element, stricter than knowledge, i.e. shared intent is met. Mere commercial engagements with the perpetrator would not be sufficient to incur liability.[137] Given the fact that different jurisdictions deal with the question of neutral assistance differently,[138] the situation of ambiguous support will be dealt with on a case-by-case basis. The manner in which the litigation around accomplice liability unfolds is exemplified by the *Lafarge* case discussed in Chapter 6.

3. *Common Purpose Liability*

Both national and international criminal laws include criminal liability for persons participating in a crime pursuant to a common purpose. In international criminal law, an individual can be held criminally liable if they are a part of a group of several people who share a common purpose and then embark on criminal activity in the execution of it. Whoever contributes to the commission of crimes by the group or some members of it, 'in any other way' according to Article 25(3)(d) ICC Statute, would incur liability.[139] With the 'lowest objective threshold for participation'[140] the required *mens rea* for Article 25(3)(d) is either (i) the 'the aim of furthering the criminal activity of criminal purpose of the group' or (ii) 'the knowledge of the intention of the group to commit a crime'.[141] Therefore, the complicit can either intend to further the crime or intentionally contribute with knowledge of the others' intention to commit the crime. Since the assistance is referring to a future conduct of a group of persons, the substantial likelihood that a certain crime will be committed may be enough.[142] The ICC Trial Chamber has distinguished this mode of liability from JCE, 'inasmuch as the accused will not be considered responsible for all of the crimes which form part of the common

137 ICJ, Corporate Complicity (n 17) 15 (company will not be held legally responsible merely for commercial engagement with the perpetrator).

138 For example, in Germany, the scholarly discussion on the 'neutral' assistance problem has produced a huge and complicated array of conflicting concepts. See Peter Rackow, *Neutrale Handlungen als Problem des Strafrechts* (Peter Lang 2007) 483; Vest, 'Modes of Individual Criminal Responsibility' (n 121).

139 In any other way than regulated in Article 25(3)(a)–(c) ICC Statute. Article 25(3)(d) constitutes an almost verbatim copy of a provision of a 1997 anti-terrorism convention and is part of customary international law. See Kai Ambos, 'The ICC and Common Purpose: What Contribution Is Required Under Article 25 (3)(d)?' in Carsten Stahn (ed), *The Law and Practice of the ICC: A Critical Account of Challenges and Achievements* (Oxford University Press 2015) 592 (hereinafter Ambos, 'The ICC and Common Purpose').

140 Ambos, 'Art. 25' (n 134) 761 marginal no. 25.

141 Ibid 761–762, marginal no. 26–28 .

142 See Christoph Burchard, 'Ancillary and Neutral Business Contributions to "Corporate – Political Core Crime": Initial Enquiries Concerning the Rome Statute' (2010) 8 Journal of International Criminal Justice 919.

purpose, but only for those to whose commission she or he contributed'.[143] Consequently, a person who stands charged pursuant to Article 25(3)(d) will not incur individual criminal responsibility for those crimes which form part of the common plan but they do not make a substantial contribution in commission of those crimes.[144] This person need not be a member of the group, nor does membership preclude criminal liability.

This form of accessory liability is different from aiding, abetting, etc. on the subjective level, because that demands the contribution to be made with the 'purpose of facilitating' the commission of a crime, i.e. more is required than general intent, as in Article 25(3)(d).[145]

National criminal jurisdictions punish common purpose criminality in the form of conspiracy underlining the requirement of an agreement.[146] Some countries consider acting in furtherance of common purpose warrants liability as co-perpetration and the others attribute it as accomplice liability. One representative example of how conduct of corporations acting with other actors with a common criminal purpose is highlighted in the *CACI case* discussed in Chapter 5.

4. Command Responsibility

Another mode of attributing responsibility to corporate leaders is through the principle of command or superior responsibility where superiors are inculpated for crimes committed by their subordinates on the basis of their failure to prevent or punish them.[147] The principle that military or civilian superiors may be held criminally responsible for the acts of their subordinates that they have effective control over is a well-established principle under international criminal law.[148] Applied by the Nuremberg and Tokyo tribunals,[149] included in the ILC Code and the ad hoc tribunals, it also found explicit mention in Article 28(b) of the ICC Statute.

143 *Germain Katanga* [2014] ICC, Trial Chamber Judgment, para 1619.

144 The question of what form of contribution has been answered varyingly. See Ambos, 'The ICC and Common Purpose' (n 139) 596–604.

145 Vest, 'Modes of Individual Criminal Responsibility' (n 121) 851, who refers to subparagraph (d) as a 'rescue clause' with respect to subparagraph (c).

146 The United States, Australia, France, the Netherlands, Belgium, Spain, Japan, and South Africa, see § 6 of the FAFO Survey Questions and Responses prepared for each of the aforementioned countries. FAFO Survey (n 136).

147 Roger O'Keefe, *International Criminal Law* (Oxford University Press 2015) 201.

148 Mettraux, *Law of Command Responsibility* (n 121) 5–11.

149 *United States of America v. Pohl et al.* [1947] Case No. 4, Military Tribunal II (Nuremberg) Vol V, 981–982; *United States of America et al. v. Araki et al.* [1948] Tokyo Tribunal in J. Pritchard and others (eds), *The Tokyo War Crimes Trial* (Garland 1981).

Essentially, the focus is on culpable omissions in the context of superior–subordinate relationships.[150] The superior becomes responsible when they have either *de jure* or *de facto* authority over their subordinate but failed to take all necessary and reasonable measures to prevent or punish the crimes committed by the subordinate.[151] In that sense, the relationship of hierarchy between the superior and subordinate involves exercise of 'effective power or control'.[152]

The element of effective control has been interpreted broadly when it comes to civilian superiors as opposed to military commanders. For instance, it suffices that civilian subordinate, through their position in the hierarchy, has the duty to report whenever crimes are committed and that in light of their position there is the likelihood that those reports will trigger an investigation or initiate disciplinary or criminal measures.[153] A noteworthy point in the context of complex corporate structures is that remote hierarchy, through intermediaries, can also incur liability on the basis of the principle of superior responsibility as long as the superior exercises effective control over the person committing the crimes.[154] The key issue is still the same: did the ultimate superior have the 'material ability' to prevent or punish the underlying crimes?[155]

The mental element for command responsibility requires that 'the superior knew or had reason to know that the criminal act was about to be or had been committed'.[156] It must be established that the superior had either active or constructive knowledge of the crimes being committed by the subordinate. Active knowledge can be established through direct or circumstantial evidence and constructive knowledge can be inferred from the fact that the superior 'had the reason to know' or had in their possession the information regarding a crime.[157] It is a higher threshold than mere negligence or 'should have known' standard.[158] Article 28 of the ICC Statute further distinguishes

150 See Miles Jackson, 'Command Responsibility' in Jérôme de Hemptinne and others (eds), *Modes of liability* (n 116).

151 See *Hadzihasanovic* [2006] ICTY, Trial Chamber, para 83; *Bagilishema* [2001] ICTR, Trial Chamber, paras 39, 44.

152 Boris Burghardt, *Die Vorgesetztenverantwortlichkeit im völkerrechtlichen Straftatsystem. Eine Untersuchung zur Rechtsprechung der internationalen Strafgerichtshöfe für das ehemalige Jugoslawien und Ruanda* (Berliner Wissenschafts-Verlag 2008) 114–115.

153 *Brdanin* [2004] ICTY, Trial Chamber, para 281.

154 *Oric* [2008] ICTY, Appeals Chamber, para 20.

155 Miles Jackson, 'Command Responsibility' in Jérôme de Hemptinne and others (eds), *Modes of Liability* (n 116) 415.

156 *Delalić et al.* [1998] ICTY, Trial Chamber Judgment, para 346.

157 *Akayesu* (n 126) paras 479, 489; ILC, Yearbook of the International Law Commission (1996) 26; ICJ, Corporate Complicity (n 17); *Ignace Bagilishema* [2002] ICTR, Appeal Judgement, para 42.

158 *Blaškić* [2014] ICTY, Appeals Chamber, para 62.

between military and non-military superiors, as the latter are liable if they 'either knew, or consciously disregarded information which clearly indicated, that the subordinates were committing or about to commit such crimes'.[159] This formulation is closer to the common law idea of wilful blindness.[160] Therefore, a situation of superior not preventing their subordinates from paying out money to rebel armed groups despite knowing or consciously disregarding the knowledge that they use these weapons to commit war crimes and the superior had the material ability to take necessary and reasonable measures to do so would be a typical case of command responsibility of civilian corporate leader under international criminal law.

IV. Conclusion

Against the backdrop of accountability of corporations and their persons in-charge for their involvement in crimes under international law, a general note on the idea of accountability as envisaged in this book is warranted at this stage. The book adopts an expansive notion of accountability to analyse the practice of strategic litigation seeking corporate accountability in different national jurisdictions. It includes domestic legal interventions against corporations *and* their persons in-charge carried out in domestic criminal law framework *as well as* civil and tort law framework. The book also takes into account practice where alternative civil or administrative liability is possible avenue to seek corporate accountability, as long as the litigation invokes norms derived from international criminal law. Such flexibility is intended to acknowledge and accommodate the diversity of approaches adopted within national legal systems. In that sense, this expansive notion of accountability in cases involving corporate accountability mirrors the current status of practice.

In conclusion, this chapter elaborates on the thematic focus of the thesis, accountability of corporations, and their persons in-charge responsible for their involvement in crimes under international law. The chapter highlights the decisions taken in the lead up to the Nuremberg trials that led to a missing international trial against corporate leaders and a prosecutorial strategy to prefer individual responsibility over collective corporate responsibility. The subsequent sections dealt with two key questions on corporate responsibility under international criminal law, respectively: one, the culpability of corporations as legal persons, and two, the question of attributing responsibility for corporate conduct under international criminal law.

159 Mettraux, *Law of Command Responsibility* (n 121) 195.
160 Miles Jackson, 'Command Responsibility' in Jérôme de Hemptinne and others (eds), *Modes of Liability* (n 116) 425.

References

Adam J, *Die Strafbarkeit juristischer Personen im Völkerstrafrecht* (Nomos Verlag 2015)

Ambos K, 'Art. 25' in Otto Triffterer (ed), *Commentary on the Rome Statute of the International Criminal Court* (2nd edn, Beck-Hart-Nomos 2008) 743–770

Ambos K, 'International Economic Criminal Law' (2018) 29 Criminal Law Forum 4, 500

Ambos K, 'The ICC and Common Purpose: What Contribution is Required Under Article 25 (3)(d)?' in Carsten Stahn (ed), *The Law and Practice of the ICC: A Critical Account of Challenges and Achievements* (Oxford University Press 2015) 592–607

Ambos K, *Treatise on International Criminal Law* (Vol. I, Oxford University Press 2013)

Ambos K, *Wirtschaftsvölkerstrafrecht: Grundlagen der völkerstrafrechtlichen Verantwortlichkeit von Unternehmen* (Dunker and Humblot 2018)

Baars G, 'Capitalism's Victor's Justice? The Hidden Stories Behind the Prosecution of Industrialists Post-WWII' in Kevin Heller and Gerry Simpson (eds), *The Hidden Histories of War Crimes Trials* (Oxford University Press 2013) 163–192

Batesmith A, 'Corporate Criminal Responsibility for War Crimes and Other Violations of International Humanitarian Law: The Impact of Business and Human Rights Movement' in Harvey, Summers and White (eds), *Contemporary Challenges to the Laws of War: Essays in Honour of Professor Peter Rowe* (Cambridge University Press 2014) 285–312

Beale SS, 'A Response to the Critics of Corporate Criminal Liability' (2009) 46 American Criminal Law Review 1481

Berghahn VR, 'Writing the History of Business in the Third Reich: Past Achievements and Future Directions' in Francis Nicosia and Jonathan Huener (eds), *Business and Industry in Nazi Germany* (Bergahn Books 2004) 129–148

Bernaz N, 'Corporate Criminal Liability Under International Law: The New TV SAL and Akhbar Beirut SAL Cases at the Special Tribunal for Lebanon' (2015) 13 Journal of International Criminal Justice 2, 313–330

Bloxham D, 'Defeat, Due Process, and Denial: War Crimes Trials and Nationalist Revisionism in Comparative Perspective' in J Macleod (ed), *Defeat and Memory: Cultural Histories of Military Defeat in the Modern Era* (Springer 2008) 117–136

Bloxham D, '"The Trial That Never Was": Why There Was No Second International Trial of Major War Criminals at Nuremberg' (2002) 87 History 285, 41

Bung J, 'Nauckes Narrative – politisches Wirtschaftstrafrecht statt Wirtschaftsvölkerstrafrecht?' in Jeßberger, Kaleck and Singelnstein (eds), *Wirtschaftsvölkerstrafrecht* (Nomos Verlag 2015) 129–144

Burchard C, 'Ancillary and Neutral Business Contributions to "Corporate–Political Core Crime": Initial Enquiries Concerning the Rome Statute' (2010) 8 Journal of International Criminal Justice 919

Burghardt B, *Die Vorgesetztenverantwortlichkeit im völkerrechtlichen Straftatsystem. Eine Untersuchung zur Rechtsprechung der internationalen Strafgerichtshöfe für das ehemalige Jugoslawien und Ruanda* (Berliner Wissenschafts-Verlag 2008)

Bush JA, 'The Prehistory of Corporations and Conspiracy in International Criminal Law: What Nuremberg Really Said Essay' (2009) 109 Columbia Law Review 1094

Chiomenti C, 'Corporations and the International Criminal Court' in De Schutter (ed), *Transnational Corporations and Human Rights* (Hart Publishing 2006) 287–312

Clapham A, 'The Question of Jurisdiction Under International Criminal Law Over Legal Persons: Lessons from the Rome Conference on an International Criminal Court' in MT Kamminga and S Zia-Zarifi (eds), *Liability of Multinational Corporations Under International Law* (Kluwer International 2000)

Clapham A, 'Extending International Criminal Law beyond the Individual to Corporations and Armed Opposition Groups' (2008) 6 Journal of International Criminal Justice 5, 899–926

Clough J, 'Punishing the Parent: Corporate Criminal Complicity in Human Rights Abuses' (2008) 33 Brooklyn Journal International Law 3

DuBois JE, *Generals in Grey Suits; The Directors of the 'I.G. Farben' Cartel, their Conspiracy and Trial at Nuremberg* (The Bodley Head 1953)

Engelhart M, 'International Criminal Responsibility of Corporations' in Christoph Burchard, Otto Triffterer and Joachim Vogel (eds), *The Review Conference and the Future of the International Criminal Court* (Kluwer International 2010) 175–190

Eser A, 'Individual Criminal Responsibility' in Antonio Cassese and others (eds), *The Rome Statute of the International Criminal Court: A Commentary* (Vol. I, Oxford University Press 2002)

Huisman W, Van Baar A and Gorsira M, 'Corporations and Transnational Crime' in Gerben Bruinsma (ed), *Histories of Transnational Crime* (Springer 2015) 147–170

ICC OTP, Policy Paper on Case Selection and Prioritization, 2016

International Commission of Jurists (ICJ), *Corporate Complicity & Legal Accountability* (Vol. II, Criminal Law and International Crimes 2008)

Jackson M, 'Command Responsibility' in Jérôme de Hemptinne and others (eds), *Modes of Liability in International Criminal Law* (Cambridge University Press 2019) 409–432

Jackson RH, *Report to the President of the United States* (State Bulletin, Vol. 12, 1945)

Jacobson KR, 'Doing Business with the Devil: The Challenges of Prosecuting Corporate Officials Whose Business Transactions Facilitate War Crimes and Crimes Against Humanity' (2005) Air Force Law Review 56

Jens O, 'Co-Perpetration: German Dogmatik or German Invasion' in Carsten Stahn (ed), *The Law and Practice of the International Criminal Court* (Oxford University Press 2015) 517–537

Jeßberger F, 'On the Origins of Individual Criminal Responsibility under International Law for Business Activity: IG Farben on Trial' (2010) 8 Journal of International Criminal Justice 3, 783–802

Jeßberger F and Geneuss J (eds), 'Transnational Business and International Criminal Law: Special Issue' (2010) 8 Journal of International Criminal Justice 2

Jeßberger F, Kaleck W and Singelnstein T (eds), *Wirtschaftsvölkerstrafrecht* (Nomos Verlag 2015)

Jiang Z, 'International Criminal Responsibility of the Corporate Entity for Complicity in International Crimes: A Policy and Legal Case' (2020) 5 Cambridge Law Review 1

Jordash W and Van Tuyl P, 'Failure to Carry the Burden of Proof: How Joint Criminal Enterprise Lost Its Way at the Special Court for Sierra Leone' (2010) 8 Journal of International Criminal Justice 591

Kaeb C, 'The Shifting Sands of Corporate Liability Under International Criminal Law' (2016) 49 George Washington International Law Review 351–403

Kaleck W and Saage-Maaß M, 'Corporate Accountability for Human Rights Violations Amounting to International CrimesThe Status Quo and Its Challenges' (2010) 8 Journal of International Criminal Justice 699

Kelly MJ, *Prosecuting Corporations for Genocide* (Oxford University Press 2016)

Kirsch S, *Völkerstrafrechtliche Risiken unternehmerischer Tätigkeit* (Neue Zeitschrift für Wirtschafts-, Steuer- und Unternehmensstrafrecht 2014)

Kolieb J, 'Through the Looking-Glass: Nuremberg's Confusing Legacy on Corporate Accountability under International Law Academy on Human Rights and Humanitarian Law: Articles and Essays on Transitional Justice, International Human Rights, and Humanitarian Law' (2016) 32 American University International Law Review [i]

Kremnitzer M, 'A Possible Case for Imposing Criminal Liability on Corporations in International Criminal Law' (2010) 8 Journal of International Criminal Justice 909

Kremnitzer M and Genaim H, 'The Criminal Liability of a Corporation' in A Barak (ed), *Shamgar Book* (Israel Bar Association 2003) 33–113

Kuntz M, *Conceptualizing Transnational Corporate Groups for International Criminal Law* (Nomos Verlag 2017)

Kyriakakis J, 'Corporations and the International Criminal Court: The Complementarity Objection Stripped Bare' (2008) 19 Criminal Law Forum 115–151

Kyriakakis J, 'Corporations before International Criminal Courts: Implications for the International Criminal Justice Project' (2017) 30 Leiden Journal of International Law 221

Kyriakakis J, 'Prosecuting Corporations for International Crimes: The Role for Domestic Criminal Law' in Larry May and Zachary Hoskins (eds), *International Criminal Law and Philosophy* (Cambridge University Press 2010) 108–137

Lauterpacht H (ed), *Annual Digest and Reports of Public International Law Cases - 1948* (Butterworth & Co., 1953)

Mégret F, 'What Sort of Global Justice is "International Criminal Justice"?' (2015) 13 Journal of International Criminal Justice 77

Meloni C, *Individual Criminal Responsibility* (Oxford University Press 2020)

Mettraux G, *The Law of Command Responsibility* (Oxford University Press 2009)

Milanović M, 'An Odd Couple: Domestic Crimes and International Responsibility in the Special Tribunal for Lebanon' (2007) 5 Journal of International Criminal Justice 1139

Naucke W, *Der Begriff der politischen Wirtschaftsstraftat – Eine Annäherung* (Vol. 33, LIT Verlag 2012)

Nerlich V, 'Core Crimes and Transnational Business Corporations' (2010) 8 Journal of International Criminal Justice 895

O'Keefe R, *International Criminal Law* (Oxford University Press 2015)

Oehm F, 'Grundlagen der strafrechtlichen Verantwortlichkeit von wirtschaftlichen Akteuren für Menschenrechtsverletzungen' in Markus Krajewski, Franziska Oehm and Miriam Saage-Maaß (eds), *Zivil-und strafrechtliche Unternehmensverantwortung für Menschenrechtsverletzungen* (Springer 2018) 177–194

Ohlin J, Van Sliedregt E and Weigend T, 'Assessing the Control-Theory' (2013) 26 Leiden Journal of International Law 725

Poynder J, *Literary Extracts from English and Other Works; Collected During Half a Century: Together with Original Matter* (Vol. I, John Hatchard & Son 1844)

Rackow P, *Neutrale Handlungen als Problem des Strafrechts* (Peter Lang 2007)

Ramasastry A and Thompson RC, *Commerce, Crime and Conflict: Legal Remedies for Private Sector Liability for Grave Breaches of International Law: A survey of Sixteen Countries* (FAFO 2006)

Ratner SR, 'Corporations and Human Rights: A Theory of Legal Responsibility' (2001) 111 The Yale Law Journal 443, 452–459

Robins N, 'Loot: In Search of the East India Company, the World's First Transnational Corporation' (2002) 14 Environment and Urbanization 79

Robins N, *The Corporation that Changed the World: How the East India Company shaped the Modern Multinational* (Pluto Press 2012)

Roxin C, *Täterschaft Und Tatherrschaft* (Cram, De Gruyter & Co. 1963)

Sadat L and Jolly J, 'Seven Canons of ICC Treaty Interpretation: Making Sense of Article 25's Rorschach Blot' (2014) 27 Leiden Journal of International Law 755

Schabas W, *The International Criminal Court: A Commentary on the Rome Statute* (2nd edn, Oxford University Press 2016)

Skinner G, 'Nuremberg's Legacy Continues: The Nuremberg Trials' Influence on Human Rights Litigation in US Courts under the Alien Tort Statute' (2008) 71 Albany Law Review 321

Slye R, 'Corporations, Veils, and International Criminal Liability' (2008) 33 Brook Journal of International Law 955

Soyer R, 'Unternehmensstrafrecht, Schutz von Menschenrechten und Strafzwecktheorien' in Kert and Lehner (eds), *Vielfalt des Strafrechts im Internationalen Kontext* (Festschrift für Frank Höpfel zum 65. Geburtstag 2018)

Stern P, 'The English East India Company and the Modern Corporation: Legacies, Lessons, and Limitations' (2015) 39 Seattle University Law Review 423

Stewart JG, 'Atrocity, Commerce and Accountability Antonio Cassese Prize for International Criminal Law Studies: A Book Proposal' (2010) 8 Journal of International Criminal Justice 314

Stewart JG, 'The Turn to Corporate Criminal Liability for International Crimes: Transcending the Alien Tort Statute' (2014) 47 New York University Journal of International Law and Politics 121–206

Stoichkova D, *Towards Corporate Liability in International Criminal Law* (Intersentia 2010)

Swart B, 'International Trends Towards Establishing Some Form of Punishment for Corporations' (2008) 6 Journal of International Criminal Justice 947

Taylor T, Final Report to the Secretary of the Army on the Nuremberg War Crimes Trials Under Control Council Law No. 10 (1949)

Taylor T, *The Anatomy of the Nuremberg Trials: A Personal Memoir* (Knopf 1992)

Triponel A, 'Comparative Corporate Responsibility in the United States and France for Human Rights Violations Abroad' in Andrew Morriss and Samuel Estreicher (eds), *Proceedings of the New York University 61st Conference on Labour* (2010) 59–158

Van Baar A, 'Corporate Involvement in the Holocaust and Other Nazi Crimes' in JG van Erp and others (eds), *The Routledge Handbook of White-Collar and Corporate Crime in Europe* (Routledge 2015) 133–150

Van den Herik L, 'Subjecting corporations to the ICC regime: Analyzing the legal counterarguments' in Christoph Burchard, Otto Triffterer and Joachim Vogel (eds), *The Review Conference and the Future of the International Criminal Court* (Kluwer International 2010) 155–174

Van der Wilt H, 'Corporate Criminal Responsibility for International Crimes: Exploring the Possibilities' (2013) 12 Chinese Journal of International Law 1, 43

Van Sliedregt E and Yanev L, 'Co-Perpetration Based on Joint Control Over the Crime' in Jérôme de Hemptinne and others (eds), *Modes of Liability in International Criminal Law* (Cambridge University Press 2019) 85–120

Vest H, 'Business Leaders and the Modes of Individual Criminal Responsibility under International Law' (2010) 8 Journal of International Criminal Justice 3, 870

Weigend T, 'Perpetration Through an Organization, the Unexpected Career of a German Legal Concept' 9 Journal International Criminal Justice (2011) 91–111

Werle G and Burghardt B, 'Establishing Degrees of Responsibility: Modes of Participation in Article 25 of the ICC Statute' in Elies van Sliedregt and Sergey Vasiliev (eds), *Pluralism in International Criminal Law* (Oxford University Press 2014) 31–319

Part II

Case Studies

Chapter 4

CELS and Transitional Justice in Argentina

The Ford Case

Argentina is often referred to as the world leader in transitional justice innovations.[1] In fact, the innovative components of Argentinian transitional justice process, referred to as '*memoria, verdad y justicia*' or 'memory, truth, and justice' (MTJ), have been a full-fledged subject of academic enquiry for decades.[2] The victims, survivors, and human rights groups have played a critical role in the implementation of these processes as well as in keeping the agenda of MTJ alive for over four decades.[3] Unlike most other transitional contexts, the systematic involvement of businesses and corporate actors in

1 Francesca Lessa, Leigh A Payne, and Gabriel Pereira, 'Overcoming Barriers to Justice in the Age of Human Rights Accountability' (2015) 37 Human Rights Quarterly 3, 728–754; see Leigh Payne and Gabriel Pereira, 'Accountability for Corporate Complicity in Human Rights Violations: Argentina's Transitional Justice Innovation?' in Horacio Verbitsky and Juan Bohoslavsky (eds), *The Economic Accomplices to the Argentine Dictatorship: Outstanding Debts* (Cambridge University Press 2016) 29–44 (hereinafter Verbitsky and Bohoslavsky (eds), *Outstanding Debts*).

2 Juan E Mendez, 'Accountability for Past Abuses' (1997) 19 Human Rights Quarterly 255; Victoria Basualdo, 'Business and the Military in the Argentine Dictatorship (1976–1983): Institutional, Economic, and Repressive Relations' in Victoria Basualdo, Hartmut Berghoff and Marcelo Bucheli (eds), *Big Business and Dictatorships in Latin America: A Transnational History of Profits and Repression* (Springer 2021) (hereinafter Basualdo and others, *Big Businesses and Dictatorships*); Willem de Haan, 'To Know or Not to Know: Silent Complicity in Crimes against Humanity in Argentina (1976–1983)' (2020) 62 Business History 1279 (hereinafter de Haan 'To Know or Not to Know'); Par Engstrom and Gabriel Pereira, 'From Amnesty to Accountability' in Francesca Lessa and Leigh A Payne (eds), *Amnesty in the Age of Human Rights Accountability* (Cambridge University Press 2012).

3 Valeria Vegh Weis, 'The Relevance of Victims' Organizations in the Transitional Justice Process: The Case of the Grandmothers of Plaza de Mayo in Argentina' (2017) 12 Intercultural Human Rights Law Review 1 (hereinafter Weis, 'Victims' Organizations'); Enrique Peruzzotti and Catalina Smulovitz (eds), *Enforcing The Rule Of Law: Social Accountability in the New Latin American Democracies* (University of Pittsburgh Publication 2006); Raluca Grosescu, 'Transnational Advocacy Networks and Corporate Accountability for Gross Human Rights Violations in Argentina and Colombia' (2019) 33 Global Society 400; David Crocker, 'Transitional Justice and International Civil Society: Toward a Normative Framework' (1998) 5 Constellations 492.

DOI: 10.4324/9781003405047-7

the egregious violations of human rights that took place during the last military dictatorship (1976–1983) has consistently been in the foreground in Argentina. Moreover, along with the truth commission, criminal accountability for historical wrongs has also been an integral part of the transitional justice processes. In that vein, it may not be surprising that Argentina has also gone the farthest in the world in holding domestic criminal trials for corporate complicity in crimes against humanity.[4]

The ongoing trials of corporate executives tell the story of a four-decade struggle that has rested on the shoulders of strategic legal interventions combined with the tenacity of the regime's victims and survivors. What makes Argentinian domestic trials particularly relevant for this study is the fact that lawyers and human rights defenders have consistently relied on international criminal law as an instrument in seeking justice for past violations. One of the protagonists of this political movement is an Argentinian organization called *Centro de Estudios Legales y Sociales* or Center for Legal and Social Studies (CELS). Their role in bringing international legal norms home and employing them strategically to seek accountability has been central to the MTJ movement. This chapter is an enquiry into their practice and legal innovations that resulted in domestic trials on corporate complicity in crimes against humanity.[5]

4 Juan Pablo Bohoslavsky and Veerle Opgenhaffen, 'The Past and Present of Corporate Complicity: Financing the Argentinean Dictatorship' (2010) 23 Harvard Human Rights Journal 157; See Horacio Verbitsky and Juan Pablo Bohoslavsky, *Cuentas Pendientes: Los Cómplices Económicos De La Dictadura* (Siglo XXI Editores, 2019).

5 Prohibition of 'crimes against humanity' is a peremptory norm of international law or *jus cogens*. See Questions relating to the Obligation to Prosecute or Extradite *Belgium v Senegal* [2012] ICJ 422, para 99; *Zoran Kupreškić et al.* [2000] ICTY, Trial Chamber, para 520; *William Samoei Ruto and Joshua Arap Sang* [2013] ICC, Trial Chamber, Decision on Mr. Ruto's Request for Excusal from Continuous Presence at Trial, para 90. Various definitions of 'crimes against humanity' have been used since 1945, both in international instruments and in national laws that have codified the crime, including the Nuremberg Charter (Article 6(c)), International Law Commission (ILC)1954 draft Code of Offences against the Peace and Security of Mankind (Article 2, para 11), ICTY Statute (Article 5), ICTR Statute (Article 3), and the ICC Statute (Article 7). The 2009 ILC Draft Convention on Prevention and Prosecution of Crimes Against Humanity kept the definition of the ICC statute (signed by 122 state parties) as reflective of current understanding of the crime under international law as the following: crimes as any of a series of acts 'when committed as part of a widespread or systematic attack directed against any civilian population, with knowledge of the attack'. An attack directed against any civilian population 'means a course of conduct involving the multiple commission of specific criminalized offences against any civilian population, pursuant to or in furtherance of a State or organizational policy to commit such attack'. See International Law Commission Draft articles on Prevention and Punishment of Crimes Against Humanity with commentaries (2019); Gerhard Werle & Florian Jeßberger, *Principles of International Criminal Law* (4th edn, Oxford University Press 2020).

For political context, the chapter discusses the nexus between private corporations and the military regime (Section I). Next, the overall state of transitional justice processes concerning the economic dimensions of large-scale violence will be discussed, relying on the Argentinian transitional justice journey as a case study (Section II). In the context of strategic litigation, the subject of this case study is CELS and their practice within the international criminal law framework (Section III). Finally, this chapter dives deeper into the case of the involvement of Ford Motors' managers in crimes against humanity to highlight the challenges faced in domestic trials against corporate actors in Argentina (Section IV). Essentially, the chapter analyses the attempts by CELS and other actors to instrumentalize the crimes against humanity framework in domestic law which resulted in corporate accountability.

I. Political Context

1. Violations under the Military Dictatorship (1976–1983)

In the late 1960s and early 1970s, Argentina had a powerful union movement constituted by a growing industrial working class.[6] Increased mobilization, as well as demands for greater political participation and better income distribution, culminated in the re-election of Juan Perón in September 1973.[7] Perón's term, which ended with his sudden death in July 1974, was taken over by his political successor and wife Isabel Perón. This period, however, was rife with guerrilla violence and severe economic crisis.[8] Argentina had seen a series of successful coups since 1930.[9] But in 1976, armed forces backed by the silent support of the US administration[10] led what the American rep-

6 Argentina had one of the most powerful union movements in Latin America, with the industrial working class, which had grown constantly since the 1930s, at its core. See Daniel James, *Resistance, and Integration: Peronism and the Argentine Working Class, 1946–1976* (Cambridge University Press 1988).

7 For more on Peronism and Juan Perón, see James Brennan (ed), *Peronism and Argentina* (Rowman & Littlefield 1998); Steven Levitsky, 'Institutionalization and Peronism: The Concept, the Case and the Case for Unpacking the Concept' (1998) 4 Party politics 1, 77–92.

8 The newspapers describe those years as 'just about every day a person whose name was widely known got gunned down in the street or was found, bullet-ridden, lying dead in a ditch' (Buenos Aires Herald, 27 March 2016) as quoted in de Haan 'To Know or Not to Know' (n 2) 1283.

9 The previous military coups lasted from 1930 to1932, 1943 to 1946, 1955 to 1958, 1962 to 1963, and 1966 to 1973. See Marcelo Larraquy, *Primavera Sangrienta: Argentina 1970–1973 un País a Punto de Explotar, Guerrilla, Presos Políticos y Represión ilegal* (Sudamericana 2017).

10 The insubordination of Argentina to the United States had changed because of American National Security Doctrine which was an integral part of the US strategy to consolidate global hegemony. This meant the creation of an institutionalized military participation in

resentatives at the time termed 'the best executed and most civilized coup in Argentine history'.[11] The military justified their intervention by citing lack of faith in the government that seemed unable to solve the political and economic crisis and the problems of escalating violence, rising inflation, and increasing unemployment.[12]

This coup was different from the ones before for multiple reasons. The Argentinian military regime from 1976 to 1983 was the most brutal one in terms of the severity of the repression and the number of civilians killed and/or disappeared.[13] The alliance between the army, the navy, and the air force, with the support of select civilian entities, developed a policy to counteract any political or economic opposition while funding a model of production based on the violent dispossession of workers.[14] Trade union activists and factory workers who required 'disciplining' became primary targets of repression aimed at implementing a neoliberal economic plan.[15] This violent campaign against political opponents has been referred to as a 'dirty war' by international observers,[16] but domestic advocates and activists prefer the description of 'state-terrorism' as it highlights the one-sidedness of repression carried out by the state against unarmed civilians.[17] To counteract all forms of political opposition, the state relied on despotic violence orchestrated

fighting international communism. The combination of ideological training and support for a stronger role of the armed forces paved the way for creation of dictatorial armed forces in the region. The army was prescribed with the function of not only fending off external threat but also their aim was to counteract – with force – any communist action in the societies. Patrice McSherry, 'Preserving Hegemony National Security Doctrine in the post-Cold War Era' (2000) 34 NACLA Report on the Americas 3, 26–34; Patrice McSherry, *Predatory States: Operation Condor and Covert War in Latin America* (Rowman & Littlefield Publishers 2012).

11 Department of State telegram, Buenos Aires, 2061, US Embassy (Hill) to secretary of state (Kissinger), March 29, 1976, quoted in William Schmidli, 'Institutionalizing Human Rights in US Foreign Policy: US-Argentine Relations, 1976–1980* (2011) Diplomatic History accessed through Wiley Online Library.

12 De Haan, 'To Know or Not to Know' (n 2) 1284.

13 Ibid.

14 Horacio Verbitsky and Juan Bohoslavsky, 'Introduction' in Verbitsky and Bohoslavsky (eds), *Outstanding Debts* (n 1) 1–16.

15 Laura García Martín, *Transitional Justice, Corporate Accountability and Socio-Economic Rights: Lessons from Argentina* (Routledge 2019) 125 (hereinafter Martín, *Lessons from Argentina*).

16 David Pion-Berlin, 'The National Security Doctrine, Military Threat Perception, and the "Dirty War" in Argentina' (1988) 21 Comparative Political Studies 3, 382–407.

17 Gabriel Pereira, 'Business Collaborators on Trial: Legal Obstacles to Corporate Accountability in Argentina' in Juan Espíndola Mata and Leigh A. Payne (eds), *Collaboration in Authoritarian and Armed Conflict Settings* (Oxford University Press 2022) (hereinafter Pereira, 'Business Collaborators on Trial').

by the armed forces.[18] The repression was carried out through a network of more than 600 detention and concentration camps across the country. Nearly 30,000 people were reported to be enforced disappeared, i.e. forcibly apprehended from their homes, workplaces, etc.[19] Victims were imprisoned, tortured, murdered, or exiled; their personal property seized; and, in hundreds of cases, the children of those who disappeared were kidnapped and given up for illegal adoption.[20] An estimated 250,000 people, in a population of 25 million, were forced into exile.[21] One-third of the victims were workers suspected of having been politically active as members of trade unions and/or workers' councils and these abductions and enforced disappearances were committed as part of a policy of 'annihilation of subversion in industrial centres'.[22]

2. *The Corporate–Military Nexus*

In Argentina, the complicity of economic actors in state repression was always in the foreground, to the extent that it became difficult to turn a blind eye to the economic structures that sustained the dictatorship and fuelled its repression. The 1976 military coup embraced economic liberalization and privatization in Argentina. The United States formally recognized the military government within two days, and the International Monetary Fund granted it a previously approved loan of US$127 million.[23] Terms and conditions for the US support to the military coup were implicit and understood: increased foreign capital in the country and participation in international commerce. As a result, in the following years, the junta invested a great amount in selling itself as investor-friendly to the US business community.[24] But this also

18 Guadalupe Basualdo, *Movilización legal internacional en dictadura: La visita de la CIDH y la creación del*, CELS (Teseopress 2019).

19 There is no official consensus on the exact number of victims. The human rights organizations insist the number is 30,000 because, though in their list they have gathered information of 10,000 disappeared and 2400 murdered people, they are just a fraction of the total number of disappeared. In many cases, the disappearance has not been denounced because of fear, disconnection with the family, lack of information on where to make the exposition, among other factors. See Weis, 'Victims' Organizations' (n 3) 10.

20 Emilio Crenzel, 'Introduction: Present Pasts: Memory(ies) of State Terrorism in the Southern Cone of Latin America' in Francesca Lessa and V. Druliolle (eds), *The Memory of State Terrorism in the Southern Cone* (Palgrave Macmillan 2011) 1–13.

21 Ibid.

22 Paul Cooney, 'The Dictatorship of the 70s, the IMF and the Shift to Neoliberalism' (2007) 11 Revista de Economia Contemporanea 1, 7, 11–14.

23 Jorge Taiana, 'Foreign Powers, Economic Support, and Geopolitics' in Verbitsky and Bohoslavsky (eds), *Outstanding Debts* (n 1) 70.

24 These public relations communications were carried out in coordination with the council for the Americas, an association founded by David Rockefeller, which still gathers the leading US companies with interests in Latin America. Ibid 69.

meant that potential obstacles to smooth foreign investment at home needed to be tackled.

José Alfredo Martínez de Hoz was appointed the Minister of Economy from 1976 to 1981. He was the CEO of Acindar, a steel company deeply implicated in labour repression from 1975 onwards. He, along with others, had also been advocating for liberalization and criticizing the previous policies of the 'interventionist' state and concentration of power at the hands of trade unions.[25] Since the trade unions still enjoyed considerable power, the sudden transition to the new economic model encountered resistance. In response, not only were labour rights violated,[26] but all forms of association and protests were brutally repressed.[27] Laws prohibiting all union activity such as workers' assemblies, reunions, congresses, and elections were put in place. These measures further enabled the military to intervene in business operations by appointing military personnel at the direction of companies to replace union representatives in the workers council.[28]

The crimes committed during the regime were motivated by the desire to preserve a given ideology, and to establish and defend an economic model with neoliberal values that would be free of threats from labour demands.[29] This resulted in an intricate relationship between corporate conduct, military regime's economic policy, and gross human rights violations against civilians that disproportionately targeted union and factory workers.

Workers targeted by the regime and their family members had been consistently insisting on the systematic joint perpetration of the crimes by the

25 According to them, the unions had too much power and the state taken on an overly active role in economic and social affairs. Victoria Basualdo, Hartmut Berghoff, Marcelo Bucheli, 'Crime and (No) Punishment: Business Corporations and Dictatorships' in Victoria Basualdo, Hartmut Berghoff, Marcelo Bucheli (eds), *Big Business and Dictatorships in Latin America: A Transnational History of Profit* (Springer 2020) 41 (hereinafter Basualdo and others, *Big Businesses and Dictatorships*).

26 The armed forces deployed military personnel to control the General Confederation of Labour (Confederación General del Trabajo) and many significant trade unions. Wage bargaining, the right to strike, and all other labour actions were suspended indefinitely; trade union privileges were eliminated; dismissal without cause was authorized for state employees; military supervisors were appointed to control the leading trade union organizations. See Héctor Recalde, 'Suppression of Workers Rights' in Verbitsky and Bohoslavsky, *Outstanding Debts* (n 1).

27 Victoria Basualdo, 'Business and the Military in the Argentine Dictatorship (1976–1983): Institutional, Economic, and Repressive Relations' in Basualdo and others, *Big Businesses and Dictatorships* (n 25) 39.

28 De Haan, 'To Know or Not to Know' (n 2) 1289; Juan Bohoslavsky and Veerle Opgenhaffen, 'The Past and Present of Corporate Complicity: Financing the Argentinean Dictatorship' (2010) 23 Harvard Human Rights Journal 157

29 Juzgado Federal de Jujuy No. 2, November 15, 2012, order initiating criminal proceedings in the case of sugar mill Ledesma; Ibid 92.

military and corporations.[30] The CONADEP truth commission report,[31] thousands of victim testimonies, court proceedings, and civil society research reports pointed out the systematic involvement of the private corporations in the crimes committed by the military state. However, the focus on unpacking the exact nature and extent of this relationship came much later around 2015.[32] Until then, most of the efforts by victims' groups and the state were largely directed against the military officials.

In 2014 and 2015, CELS, along with the Area of Economics and Technology of the Latin American Faculty of Social Sciences (FLACSO) and the Secretary of Human Rights from the Ministry of Justice and Human Rights of Argentina, conducted a far-reaching research analysing the involvement of businesses in state repression from 1976 to 1983.[33] The report raised a number of crucial questions in order to make the transition from documenting repressive business practices to examining the individual responsibility of corporate executives for crimes committed during the dictatorship. Their final report lists 25 companies from a wide range of sectors who allegedly made direct contributions to the criminal machinery set up by the military state.[34] One of the key factors that led to the inclusion of these companies in the report was that the army attributed significant importance to them, so they were either leaders in their respective branches of activity or they were providers of goods and services to the armed forces.[35]

The 2015 report contends that the businesses and military shared a common concern, i.e. conflict between capital and labour. To achieve their common objective, corporations contributed to the repression carried out by the dictatorship in varied forms, including logistical and material support, as well as the installation of clandestine detention centres on their factory

30 Interview with Gabriel Pereira, Law Professor at the National University of Tucuman (online, 28 June 2021).

31 Presidential Decree No. 187/83, 15 December 1983, reprinted in Anales de Legislacion Argentina (1984), Tomo XLIV-A, LA LEY, 137–138.

32 Truth Commission on Economic Complicity in Argentina was only established in 2015 to evaluate the role of economic actors who contributed to, benefited from, or directly participated in systematic international crimes. See statement in support of the Commission by five UN mandate holders and independent experts (10 November 2015). <https://www.ohchr.org/SP/NewsEvents/Pages/DisplayNews.aspx?NewsID=16733&LangID=S> accessed 09 February 2022.

33 CELS, FLASCO, and Ministry of Justice and Human Rights, 'Responsabilidad empresarial en delitos de lesa humanidad: represión a trabajadores durante el terrorismo de Estado' (Business responsibility in crimes against humanity: The repression of workers during state terrorism) (December, 2015) <https://www.cels.org.ar/web/2015/12/nuevo-informe-responsabilidad-empresarial-en-crimenes-de-lesa-humanidad-en-la-argentina/>accessed 09 February 2022 (hereinafter CELS Report on Business Responsibility).

34 There were many more which have either not been included in the study for they did not meet the selection criteria or they have been reserved for future research and action. Ibid.

35 See Introduction to CELS Business Responsibility Report (n 33) 1–25.

premises which were then used for torture and ill-treatment of union workers. An overall analysis of the nature of business involvement reflected a clear systematic pattern of corporate complicity in dictatorship crimes.[36] The following extract from the report underlines the extent of their complicity:

> In 88 percent of the cases, workers delegates were kidnapped from their workstations at the factories, while in 76 percent the companies provided private and sensitive information about the persecuted workers to the military. In 72 percent of the cases, the military had a presence within the private property of the firms, and military personnel exercised control and oversight over the workers, and in 68 percent, military officers participated in the board of directors or the managerial structure of the firms. Moreover, in 56 percent of the cases, there were major military operations carried out from within the factory premises. 52 percent of the cases found top officials present in the process of detention and kidnapping, and in some cases even torture. In nearly 50 percent of the cases, the companies temporarily granted space within their private property for the military to settle, while 48 percent of the firms made financial contributions to the armed forces, and in 40 percent they provided vehicles to the military to use in the repressive action. Finally, five of the 25 companies – Acindar, Astilleros Río Santiago, Ford, Ingenio La Fronterita, and the transportation company, La Veloz del Norte – had clandestine detention centres located on site. Workers were kept and tortured for different periods of time, ranging from hours to days, after which they usually disappeared or were imprisoned.[37]

Realizing the extent of corporate–military nexus and the systematic nature of the crimes committed during the regime led domestic observers and advocates to term the military rule as 'civilian–military' dictatorship instead.[38] The report establishes the role of corporations not merely as 'profiteers' of the dictatorship, but also as direct contributors to acts amounting to crimes under international law. The systematic nature of this corporate–military nexus underlined the reasoning that such large-scale crimes would not have taken place without the participation and complicity of the business actors.

36 Victoria Basualdo, 'Business and the Military in the Argentine Dictatorship (1976–1983): Institutional, Economic, and Repressive Relations' in Basualdo and others, *Big Businesses and Dictatorships* (n 25) 35–62.

37 Ibid 53–54.

38 Juan Pablo Bohoslavsky, Agustín Cavana, and Leonardo Filippini, 'Statute of Limitations in Actions for Complicity' in Verbitsky and Bohoslavsky (eds), *Outstanding Debts* (n 1).

II. The Economic Dimensions of Transitional Justice

1. *Transitional Justice Processes*

Despite the sometimes explicit nature of the business involvement in the large-scale violence, transitional justice processes find it difficult to attribute responsibility to the economic structures that caused and sustained large-scale violence. The potential of using law as a tool for political transformation takes a different meaning in a post-conflict/dictatorship context.

Transitional justice deals with the central question of how to respond to large-scale and systematic crimes committed in connection with dictatorship or armed conflict.[39] The responses to this question often mirror fundamental tensions and debates over how societies are going to deal with abuses carried out during the past conflicts.[40] The options include prosecutions for crimes as well as non-judicial responses such as granting amnesties, truth commissions, and reparation measures that envisage a broader conception of justice with an eye towards transition.[41] Truth commissions can acknowledge the atrocities while seeming less confrontational or burdensome than criminal prosecutions for large-scale violations.[42] Literature from the late 20th century has extensively dealt with questions on how the concept of transitional justice should be conceived in relation to the role of law during and after a conflict; the need to redress past violence without jeopardizing the newly acquired and fragile democratic structures;[43] when and how societies or negotiators choose particular mechanisms over others;[44] the corresponding benefits of 'top-down' and 'bottom-up' approaches to the design of transitional justice processes; and the merits of local versus national and international processes.[45]

39 Werle, Jeßberger, *Principles* (n 5) 108.

40 Neil Kritz, *Transitional Justice: How Emerging Democracies Reckon with Former Regimes* (United States Institute of Peace Press 1995); Diane F. Orenthlicher, "Settling Accounts' Revisited: Reconciling Global Norms with Local Agency' (2007) The International Journal of Transitional Justice 1, 12.

41 Mark Drumbl, *Atrocity, Punishment and International Law* (Cambridge University Press 2007) 187.

42 Naomi Roht-Arriaza, 'The New Landscape of Transitional Justice' in Naomi Roht-Arriaza and Javier Mariezcurrena (eds), *Transitional Justice in the Twenty-First Century: Beyond Truth versus Justice* (Cambridge University Press 2006) 3 (hereinafter Roht-Arriaza and Mariezcurrena, *Beyond Truth versus Justice*).

43 See Christine Bell, Colm Campbell and Fionnuala Ní Aoláin, 'Justice Discourses in Transition' (2004) 13 Social and Legal Studies 3, 305–328; Ruti Teitel, *Transitional Justice* (Oxford University Press 2000) 7 (hereinafter Tietel, *Transitional Justice*).

44 Jack Synder and Leslie Vinjamuri, 'Trials and Errors: Principles and Pragmatism in Strategies of International Justice' (2003) 28 International Security 3, 5–44.

45 Patricia Lundy and Mark McGovern, 'Whose Justice? Rethinking Transitional Justice from the Bottom Up' (2008) 35 Journal of Law and Society 2; Kieran McEvoy, and Kirsten McConnachie, 'Victims and Transitional Justice: Voice, Agency and Blame' (2013)

In one of the most significant works on transitional justice, Ruti Teitel discusses five legal responses implemented during transitions: criminal justice, historical justice, reparatory justice, administrative justice, and constitutional justice.[46] Weighing the pros and cons of both truth commissions and criminal prosecutions in achieving these goals, there has been an emerging consensus in viewing transitional justice processes as a 'package'.[47] A full package tends to include a combination of judicial and non-judicial mechanisms with different levels of international involvement and individual prosecutions, reparations, truth-seeking, institutional reform, vetting, and dismissals.[48]

In most situations, however, amidst the goals of reconciliation and reconstruction, an effective addressing of the economic dimension remains missing.[49] The continuation of economic and social marginalization in post-conflict countries risks making the goal of transition hollow. Naomi Roht-Arriaza succinctly lays down the potential economic dimensions to a conflict or large-scale violence which warrant addressing in a transitional justice

---

22 Social & Legal Studies 4, 489–513; Laura Arriaza and Naomi Roht-Arriaza, 'Social Reconstruction as a Local Process' (2008) 2 International Journal of Transitional Justice 2, 157–172; Paul Gready and Simon Robins, 'Transitional Justice and Theories of Change: Towards Evaluation as Understanding' (2020) 14 International Journal of Transitional Justice 2 (hereinafter Gready and Robins, 'TJ and Theories of Change').

46 Teitel, *Transitional Justice* (n 43) 6; Gerhard Werle and Moritz Vormbaum, *Transitional Justice* (Springer 2018).

47 Naomi Roht-Arriaza, 'The New Landscape of Transitional Justice' in Roht-Arriaza and Mariezcurrena, *Beyond Truth versus Justice* (n 42) 8; see Juan Méndez, 'Accountability for Past Abuses' (1997) Human Rights Quarterly 19, 255–282.

48 UN Secretary-General, *The Rule of Law and Transitional Justice in Conflict and Post-Conflict Societies* (2004) UNDocS/2004/616, para 8. For the United Nations, transitional justice refers to 'the full set of processes and mechanisms associated with a society's attempts to come to terms with a legacy of large-scale past abuse, in order to secure accountability, serve justice and achieve reconciliation.' Guidance Note of the Secretary-General: United Nations Approach to Transitional Justice (March 2010) <https://www.un.org/ruleoflaw/files/TJ_Guidance_Note_March_2010FINAL.pdf> accessed 09 February 2022.

49 Philipp Wesche, 'Business Actors, Paramilitaries and Transitional Criminal Justice in Colombia' (2019) 13 International Journal of Transitional Justice 3, 478–503; Leigh Payne and Gabriel Pereira, 'Accountability for Corporate Complicity in Human Rights Violations: Argentina's Transitional Justice Innovation?' in Verbitsky and Bohoslavsky (eds), *Outstanding Debts* (n 1) 11 (Despite the prevalence and significance of corporate complicity in human rights violations in armed conflicts and authoritarian regimes, transitional justice scholars and practitioners tend to ignore it, focusing instead on state actors. Such an approach fits the critique of the transitional justice field as liberal in orientation, rather than transformative.). On transformative justice, see Gready and Robins, 'TJ and Theories of Change' (n 45); Evelyne Schmid and Aoife Nolan, 'Do No Harm'? Exploring the Scope of Economic and Social Rights in Transitional Justice' (2014) 8 International Journal of Transitional Justice 3, 362–382; Anushka Sehmi, 'Judicializing Economic Violence as Means of Dismantling the Structural Causes of Atrocity in the Democratic Republic of Congo' (2020) 14 International Journal of Transitional Justice 3, 423–442.

context.[50] Patterns of economic inequality and exclusion, and lack of economic, social, and cultural rights, lie behind many conflicts. Authoritarian governments choose repression as a response to demands for greater social justice, or disaffected groups who have little left to lose take up arms against the regime.[51] Alternatively, once a de facto government/authority resorts to brutal repression, it is often armed, financed, informed, or otherwise supported by powerful economic actors.[52] Massive and systematic corruption can also play a role, as both a cause and a consequence of the conflict.[53]

Therefore, in order to address the varied economic dimensions of a conflict, a comprehensive transitional justice package would also ideally include the means to hold economic actors accountable for their role in the extraordinary violence carried out during the authoritarian rule or armed conflict.[54] However, it has not been the case in most situations, largely because of the practical and political obstacles in pursuing corporate accountability particular to a transitional justice context.

In order to establish the pattern and scale of violence, the judicial and non-judicial processes tend to focus on the more visible and responsible state agents or non-state armed actors. In these attempts, the background role and responsibilities of unarmed civilian third parties in carrying out the violations remain largely invisible. Unless the scale of documentation during the oppression is very comprehensive, as it was for instance in Germany during the 1930s and 1940s, it becomes a herculean task to trace the role of civilian entities and gather supporting evidence to seek effective accountability through transitional justice processes.[55]

Additionally, in situations where civil society organizations are driving the initiative to seek accountability of corporations, they are faced with the

50 Naomi Roht-Arriaza, 'Why Was the Economic Dimension Missing for So Long in Transitional Justice? An Exploratory Essay' in Verbitsky and Bohoslavsky (eds), *Outstanding Debts* (n 1) 19–28; Lisa Hecht and Sabine Michalowski, 'The Economic and Social Dimensions of Transitional Justice' (2012) 11.

51 See Jane Alexander, *A Scoping Study on Transitional Justice and Poverty Reduction* (The Department For International Development 2003) 64.

52 See Ingrid Samset, 'Conflict of interests or interests in conflict? Diamonds & War in the DRC' (2002) 29 Review of African Political Economy 93–94, 463–480.

53 See Ruben Carranza, 'Plunder and pain: Should transitional justice engage with corruption and economic crimes?' (2008) 2 The International Journal of Transitional Justice 3, 310–330.

54 Youseph Farah, 'Toward a Multi-directional Approach to Corporate Accountability' in Sabine Michalowski (ed), *Corporate Accountability in the Context of Transitional Justice* (Routledge 2013) 27–51.

55 Joris van de Sandt & Marianne Moor (eds), *Peace, Everyone's Business! Corporate Accountability in Transitional Justice: Lessons for Colombia* (PAX 2012) available online at <https://www.dejusticia.org/wp-content/uploads/2017/05/PAX_COL_PZ_BIZ_FINAL_WEB.pdf> accessed 9 February 2022.

challenge of power (or resource) imbalance. Challenging the economic elite often translates to economic and/or physical risk to those seeking to hold them accountable. Repercussions such as targeted physical violence, claims of libel/slander, and Strategic Litigation Against Public Participation (SLAPP) suits can be effective deterrents to such accountability initiatives.[56] While this challenge is not exclusively applicable to a transitional justice context, it is of particular interest here because unlike the political power exercised by former authoritarian regimes or armed groups, corporate capital travels well through the transition.

Naturally, an additional challenge stems from the fact that corporate accountability in most cases would not be in the economic interests of a country seeking to rebuild itself. The potential of alienating economic actors does not fare well with the economic reconstruction of a post-conflict country. As discussed in Chapter 3, this was one of the reasons behind the policy choices made concerning corporate accountability at the Nuremberg trials.[57] Impunity of corporate actors becomes a convenient choice in view of the overarching goals of peace-building and economic revival.

Nevertheless, there have been a few attempts to at least highlight the economic dimensions of a conflict through transitional justice mechanisms despite the aforementioned challenges. The Sierra Leone Truth Commission, for example, placed 'the central cause of the war' as 'endemic greed, corruption, and nepotism that deprived the nation of its dignity and that reduced most people to a state of poverty'.[58] The Liberian Truth Commission also highlighted the economic root causes, denouncing an 'entrenched political and social system founded on privilege, patronage ... and endemic corruption which created limited access to education, and justice, economic and social opportunities', as well as recognizing the centrality of 'historical disputes over land acquisition, distribution, and accessibility'.[59] It should be noted, however, that these were non-judicial mechanisms.

Against this background, it is said that 'no country has gone as far as Argentina'[60] in using domestic criminal law to hold corporate actors accountable for their complicity in crimes against humanity.

56 See Robert Abrams, 'Strategic lawsuits against public participation (SLAPP)' (1989) 7 Pace Environment Law Review 33.

57 See Section I of Chapter 3.

58 Report of the Sierra Leone Truth and Reconciliation Commission, 'Witness to Truth' (2004) Volume II, Chapter 2, Primary Finding 13.

59 Consolidated Final Report, Liberia Truth and Reconciliation Commission, Consolidated Final Report (2009) Volume II, 16–17.

60 Leigh Payne, Gabriel Pereira, and Laura Bernal-Bermúdez, 'Corporate Accountability from Below' in *Transitional Justice and Corporate Accountability from Below: Deploying Archimedes' Lever* (Cambridge University Press 2020) 36 (hereinafter Payne and others, *Deploying Archimedes' Lever*).

2. *Argentina's Quest for 'Memory, Truth, and Justice'*

Argentinian transitional justice process has garnered high praise with titles such as 'protagonist', 'world leader', and 'cascade instigators'[61] largely because of the ways in which Argentina activated new mechanisms to seek accountability for historical violations. These included, among others, the first ever published truth commission report; the creation of the first UN Working Group on Enforced Disappearances in 1980; the domestic trial of nine military leaders of the former authoritarian regime in 1985 (it was also the first of its kind in Latin America);[62] 'truth trials' and pioneering the so-called right to truth;[63] and holding domestic trials addressing corporate involvement in crimes under international law.

While the MTJ programme adopted by Argentina was a full package of judicial and non-judicial mechanisms, criminal accountability for violations committed during the last dictatorship has been a consistent demand by the victims, their families, and human rights activists and organizations who have played a key role in steering the MTJ process from the late 1970s till date.[64] With changing governments, the nature of the state response to these demands has also fluctuated drastically. Over the decades, MTJ has taken different forms and meanings in the domestic politics of Argentina. Gabriel Pereira, a law professor, describes it as follows:

> Initially, in 1980's MTJ was mainly, but not exclusively, a demand for retributive justice for the victims from the state in response to the violations committed against them. But in 1990's, that retributive demand became a democratic claim. The demands for memory, truth, and justice for historical wrongs became a pre-requisite for an effective democracy in Argentina. And in 2000's, the political precariousness of the country converted that democratic claim to a legitimacy resource for the elected governments.[65]

61 Kathryn Sikkink, 'From Pariah State to Global Protagonist: Argentina and the Struggle for International Human Rights' (2008) 50 Latin American Politics and Society 1 (hereinafter Sikkink, 'From Pariah State to Global Protagonist'); Kathryn Sikkink, 'Latin America's Protagonist Role in Human Rights' (2015) SUR International Journal on Human Rights 22, 207; Verónica Michel and Kathryn Sikkink, 'Human Rights Prosecutions and the Participation Rights of Victims in Latin America' (2013) 47 Law & Society Review 873.

62 Attempts that come close to such domestic trials of holding country's own former leaders accountable were follow-up trials in Germany after World War II and prosecution of the Greek colonels in Greece in 1974.

63 For more details, see Section III.1 of this chapter.

64 Weis, 'Victims' Organizations' (n 3).

65 Interview with Gabriel Pereira, Law Professor at the National University of Tucuman (online, 28 June 2021).

In 2003, the progressive president Néstor Kirchner was elected with a humble 22.25% of the vote-share. With much of the population questioning the legitimacy of Kirchner's presidency, he was forced to look for sources to gain political clout and build trust.[66] As we shall see in the following sections, this is where the importance of strategic litigation carried out by groups like CELS in keeping the MTJ agenda alive and pressing becomes apparent. The insistence on the importance of MTJ over the decades made it a source of legitimacy for a weak government. As a result, one witnesses a proactive involvement of the state in MTJ processes from 2003 onwards. This analysis becomes more clear in the following discussion on key milestones in the Argentinian transitional justice process.

Argentina's transition from dictatorship to democracy happened rather abruptly because of political mobilization. The military government collapsed because of the loss of the Falklands War in June 1982.[67] This is to say that there was no 'pact' before the shift in power took place which could have given a leeway to the former authoritarian regime. Such a transition laid down a more conducive atmosphere to seek accountability for human rights violations.[68] However, it also depended largely on the priorities of those in power in the subsequent years. Raúl Alfonsín of the Radical Party became the first democratic president after the military dictatorship and expressed strong commitment to the rule of law and accountability in contrast to his Peronist opponent who favoured respecting amnesty. For him, a mechanism to account for historical wrongs was non-negotiable as the 'foundation for an authentic democratic system'.[69]

66 During 2001–2002, Argentina was gripped by a severe economic crisis that threw the country into 'near anarchy'. There were frequent, widespread demonstrations in which the protestors chanted *'Que se vayan todos'* ('everybody goes') calling for the resignation of the political leadership and 'an end to impunity', meaning 'honesty, accountability and transparency in government and the liquidation of a system of privileges and corruption'. See Larry Rohter, 'Letter from South America: Now the Dirtiest of Wars Will Not Be Forgotten' (New York Times, 18 June 2003).

67 To read more about the Falklands War, see David Pion-Berlin, 'The Fall of Military Rule in Argentina: 1976–1983' (1985) 27 Journal of Interamerican Studies and World Affairs 55–76.

68 The army tried to issue a self-amnesty law in March 1983 covering the crimes committed between May 1973 and June 1982. Decree 2726/83 ordered the destruction of all documents relating to the State repression. However, human rights groups immediately reacted against those actions, and particularly against the self-amnesty. On 27 September 1983, the Buenos Aires Lawyers' Association filed a suit in a federal court, claiming that an unconstitutional government had no authority to declare an amnesty. The court declared that the self-amnesty was 'a flagrant violation of the law' and declared it 'null and void'. See Alejandro Garro and Enrique Dahl, 'Legal Accountability for Human Rights Violations in Argentina: One Step Forward and Two Steps Backward' (1987) 8 Human Rights Law Journal 283–344, 305.

69 Raúl Alfonsín, '"Never Again" in Argentina' (1993) 4 Journal of Democracy 15–19, 15 (hereinafter Alfonsin, 'Never Again').

The First Truth Commission Report

Alfonsín set up the Argentinian Truth Commission (*La Comisión Nacional Sobre la Desaparición de Personas* – National Commission on Disappeared Persons, CONADEP).[70] Within six months, the Commission released its final report titled *Nunca Más* (Never Again).[71] In 1983, before the establishment of ad hoc international criminal tribunals, the report stated that gross violations committed during the dictatorship, especially enforced disappearances, should be considered a crime against humanity. The report became popular and its findings continued to shape the narrative in Argentina on what happened during the dictatorship.[72] One of the recommendations of the report was to set up judicial processes to deal with the gravity of the allegations recorded by the Commission.

The First Domestic Junta Trials

Following up on the CONADEP report, a framework was devised to prosecute nine high-ranking military leaders considered most responsible for their planning, control, and organization of the state repression between 1976 and 1983.[73] The junta trials in 1985 were meant to distinguish between the armed forces as an institution that only needed reforms and the high-ranking military officers who were individually responsible for unleashing egregious violence.[74] These crimes were prosecuted under the provisions in domestic criminal code for unlawful deprivation of liberty, torture, theft, and murder committed against 711 victims (less than 8% of the CONADEP numbers).[75] Despite a few limitations, the fact that they were unprecedented and took place relatively quickly ensured a promising start.

The whole MTJ process, however, was brought to a sudden halt in 1986. Due to increased military pressure and the following unrest, the government

70 Presidential Decree No. 187/83, 15 December 1983, reprinted in Anales de Legislacion Argentina (1984), Tomo XLIV-A, LA LEY, 137–138.

71 Official translation to English, Alfonsin, 'Never Again' (n 69).

72 Beyond the systematic nature of the disappearance's violations, the narrative pushed forward by the report as the 'Theory of the Two Demons' and the absence of comprehensive addressing the machinery of state repression were criticized. It claimed that 'during the decade of the 1970s Argentina was torn by terror that was coming as much from the extreme right as from the extreme left', and adding that 'the armed forces responded to the terrorists' crimes with a terrorism far worse than the one they were combating, and after 24 March 1976 they could count on the power and impunity of an absolute State, which they misused to abduct, torture and kill thousands of human beings'. See Lucas Martin, 'On Innocent Victims and Demons in Argentina (1983–1985)' (2012) 3 African Yearbook of Rhetoric 2, 65–75.

73 *Juicio a las Juntas Militares,* Argentinean Military Junta Members Case [1985]. <http://www.internationalcrimesdatabase.org/Case/1118> accessed 18 February 2022.

74 Martín, *Lessons from Argentina* (n 15) 153.

75 Ibid.

passed two amnesty laws – 'Full Stop'[76] and 'Due Obedience'[77] – which effectively granted impunity to all the military officers of the former regime. It is questionable whether these developments can be attributed directly to the junta trials or to the large number of trials against mid-tier officers which began after the top nine leaders were convicted.[78] Regardless, the high costs and high risks suffered by the armed forces in the form of *junta* trials are proffered as central reasons for the military's continuous subordination to constitutional power since the 1980s.[79] In fact, this has been the longest time without a coup in over 200-year history of the Republic of Argentina.[80]

The First Truth Trials

Throughout the 1990s, the victims, their families, and human rights groups remained persistent in seeking alternative avenues. One advance was to request the courts to hold 'truth trials' where the civil rights groups argued that even though the amnesty laws blocked criminal proceedings, family members still had the right to know the truth about their loved ones. These right to truth actions, which have been credited to CELS (discussed in greater detail in the next section), paved the way for the democratic state to collect evidence which later fed into judicial processes.[81]

The First Domestic Trials Involving Crimes against Humanity

In May 2003, with the election of a Peronist President Néstor Kirchner, the political dimensions within the state finally lined up consistently in favour of the MTJ agenda. In his term, the state ratified the Convention on the

76 *Ley de Punto Final*, Law 23.492 of 23 December 1986 available at <http://www1.hcdn.gov.ar/dependencias/cdhygarantias/Leyes/ley23492.htm> accessed 18 February 2022. This provision barred criminal prosecution for those suspects or defendants who had not then been summoned to provide a statement in relation to the crimes described by Article 20, Law 23.049 of 13 February 1984 (basically, the dictatorship's crimes) within the compulsory 60-day period after the enactment of the law.

77 *Ley de obediencia debida*, Law 23.521 of 4 June 1987 <https://web.archive.org/web/20060515222256/http://www.nuncamas.org/document/nacional/ley23521.htm> accessed 18 February 2022. This law modified the interpretation of the due obedience clause, by changing a relative presumption into an absolute presumption (juris et de jure). The new presumption claimed that subordinated members of the armed forces and the police could not be considered guilty of the crimes because they had simply obeyed orders emanating from their superiors.

78 Compare Sikkink, 'From Pariah State to Global Protagonist' (n 61) with Martín, *Lessons from Argentina* (n 15).

79 See Sikkink, 'From Pariah State to Global Protagonist' (n 61).

80 Verbitsky and Bohoslavsky, 'Introduction' in Verbitsky and Bohoslavsky (eds), *Outstanding Debts* (n 1) 1–16.

81 *Carmen Aguiar de Lapacó v Argentina* [2000] IACHR, Report No. 21/00, Case 12.059.

Non-Applicability of Statutory Limitations to War Crimes and Crimes against Humanity, and appointed three new Supreme Court judges in the wake of broader vetting and institutional reforms.[82] Thus, when human rights groups (particularly CELS) reached the Supreme Court to challenge the constitutionality of the amnesty laws, the Supreme Court declared them null and void for being inconsistent with international law norms.[83] Consequently, the state was again mandated to investigate and sanction the dictatorship's crimes against humanity.[84]

The nullification of amnesty laws led to the reopening of judicial processes. It is in this context that multinational corporations have also been called before the court for their complicity in crimes against humanity committed by the military. By 2021, over 20 cases involving corporate complicity in crimes against humanity are pending before various courts in Argentina.[85]

However, despite clear signs of complicity, corporate accountability had been largely missing from the transitional justice package adopted by Argentina.[86] Until almost ten years after the amnesty laws were nullified, there were no serious attempts or even discussions on corporate involvement in state repression, either by the state or by human rights groups, including CELS.

The victims who were targeted because of their status as workers and their survivors had been persistently lobbying for corporate accountability since the very beginning. However, it was only when the trials of military officials had led to convictions and imprisonment that the unacknowledged hierarchy amongst the perpetrators became apparent to other stakeholders. As Gabriel Pereira notes,

82 See Francesca Lessa, 'Transitional Justice in Argentina (1983–2012)' in *Memory and Transitional Justice in Argentina and Uruguay* (Palgrave Macmillan 2013) 49–80. One of the reasons for such turn of political willingness, as Sikkink and Booth-Walling point out, Kirchner belonged to the generation of the Peronist party that had been severely repressed in the 1970s, see Kathryn Sikkink and Booth-Walling, 'Argentina's Contribution to Global Trends in Transitional Justice' in Roht-Arriaza and Javier Mariezcurrena (eds), *Beyond Truth versus Justice* (n 42) 301–324.

83 *Simón, Julio Héctor y otros s/privación ilegítima de la libertaz* [2005] Supreme Court of Argentina, S.1767. XXXVIII.

84 The case is known as Simón Case. Julio Simón was a police officer during the military regime and indicted for his involvement in the detention of Claudia Poblete's parents, as well as the appropriation of their child at a secret detention centre (the 'Olimpo') (discussed in the next section).

85 Pereira, 'Business Collaborators on Trial' (n 17); also see Ramiro Garcia Falconi, 'The Codification of Crimes against Humanity in the Domestic Legislation of Latin American States Latin American and International Criminal Law: The Codification of International Crimes in Latin America' (2010) 10 International Criminal Law Review 453.

86 See Juan Bohoslavsky, 'Tracking down the Missing Financial Link in Transitional Justice' (2012) 1 International Human Rights Law Review 54.

> we [the human rights groups, lawyers and legal scholars] were working with the realization that state-terrorism in the late 1970's was not just a criminal enterprise to eliminate political opponents by the military. It was a state-transformation plan where the economic actors played an equally important role.[87]

The period was being viewed as a 'military–civilian' dictatorship where the corporate elite and the military officers were collaborating to bring about a social, economic, and political transformation of the state through violent means. It later dawned upon them that by that logic the military and the economic actors were being treated differentially not just by the state but also by those non-state actors who were pushing the accountability agenda. The 'military–civilian dictatorship' framing highlighted the blind spot in their strategy, which resulted in a shift of focus from military officials to corporate managers as necessary accomplices to the violations amounting to crimes under international law.[88]

The domestic trials against corporations for crimes committed over 40 years ago is a milestone reached after many twists and turns in Argentina's quest for MTJ. Consistent actions by human rights groups and victims/survivors played a critical role in placing accountability for historical wrongs on the political agenda. Although various governments responded differently, even at the peak of state inaction in this regard, the human rights groups exhausted all possible international and national avenues to retain the importance of their demands for accountability. Within this process, self-criticism and reflection also resulted in the evolution of their strategy. The factor that remained constant, nevertheless, was their use of international legal norms and legal avenues in pursuit of the MTJ agenda. The next section takes a closer look at CELS who played an instrumental role in the internalization of 'crimes against humanity' framework into domestic law and state policy as a tool to seek accountability of political and economic actors.

III. Centro de Estudios Legales y Sociales

CELS is one of the oldest organizations pursuing strategic litigation, without officially labelling it as such.[89] The organization was founded in 1979 by a group of legal professionals whose children or relatives were direct victims of

87 Interview with Gabriel Pereira, Law Professor at the National University of Tucuman (online, 28 June 2021).

88 Ibid.

89 The organization officially does not claim the label of being a 'strategic litigation organization'. However, in addition to a couple of mentions on their website, they published a book, CELS, *La lucha por el derecho: Litigio Estratégico y Derechos Humanos* (*Strategic Litigation and Human Rights: The Struggle for Law*) (Siglo Editores 2008) discussing their

enforced disappearances by the military regime.[90] Unlike its North American and European counterparts, invoking international criminal law and seeking accountability for international crimes was not a matter of political choice for the founders of CELS. They engaged with the international criminal legal framework for pragmatic and circumstantial reasons. They were able to implement and initiate procedures which some of the most resourceful non-governmental organizations collectively would find difficult to execute, such as creation of the Working Group of Enforced Disappearances, conceiving and implementing the concept of truth trials and right to truth, and getting amnesty laws struck down – not once, but twice.[91] They were particularly adept in using the Inter-American system of human rights to challenge impunity in the periods when the political conditions were unfavourable within the country, particularly during the military regime (1976–1983) and then during the term of President Carlos Menem (1989–1999) when amnesty laws were enacted.[92] The Inter-American Commission made a two-week visit to Argentina in 1979 and released a country report on the human rights situation.[93] The report by the Commission strengthened the credibility of the Inter-American human rights system in the eyes of the civil society and later became a robust tool in the hands of CELS in legitimizing their accountability demands.[94]

strategies, lessons, and impact from the litigation in the past ten years (hereinafter CELS, *Strategic Litigation and Human Rights*).

90 See CELS official website <https://www.cels.org.ar/web/en/presentacion/fundadores-2/> accessed 18 February 2022.

91 The first one was in 1983. On September 26, 1983, CELS issued a statement to the relatives of the disappeared, offering to help them fight the constitutionality of the self-amnesty issued by the military before the elections. Moreover, on 27 September 1983, the Buenos Aires Lawyers' Association filed a suit in a federal court, claiming that an unconstitutional government had no authority to declare an amnesty. The court declared that the self-amnesty was 'a flagrant violation of the law' and declared it 'null and void'. The second one in 2003 during the term of President Kirchener. See text to the notes 70 and 71.

92 See Par Engstrom, 'A Special Relationship Gone Normal: Argentina and the Inter-American Human Rights System, 1979–2013' (2013) Pensamiento Propio 38 (hereinafter Engstorm 'A Special Relationship Gone Normal').

93 See Inter-American Commission on Human Rights Country Report: Argentina (1979) <http://www.cidh.org/countryrep/argentina80eng/introduction.htm> accessed 19 May 2021.

94 Compare Sikkink, 'From Pariah State to Global Protagonist' (n 61) with Engstrom 'A Special Relationship Gone Normal' (n 92); also see J Zalaquett, 'Victims Unsilenced: The Inter-American Human Rights System and Transitional Justice in Latin America' (2008) 2 International Journal of Transitional Justice 426. However, this strong relationship has not always been without problems, see Gerald Neumann, 'Import, Export and Regional Consent in the Inter-American Court of Human Rights' (2008) 19 European Journal of International Law 101.

Responding to violations by the military regime in the early 1980s as a first-aid measure, CELS' mandate was to establish truth and seek justice for the crimes committed during that time. During its early years, CELS mainly documented the violations while offering legal aid and assistance to the victims to whatever extent possible,[95] highlighting the systematic pattern in illegal behaviour of the state at the time. In hindsight, this documentation and building of a network with the victims and survivors proved to be essential legwork for prosecutions which are being held to this date. With the changing political realities of the country, however, the organization has also expanded its agenda to include human rights violations committed during democratic rule, their structural causes, and their relationship to social inequality.[96] Their mandate, strategies, and position on the political spectrum have evolved in over 40 years, but their use of legal tools to achieve social transformation has been consistent. Currently, their work also includes international interventions and they position themselves as a national organization with a global agenda.[97]

In 2009, the organization released a book titled 'Strategic Litigation and Human Rights: The Struggle for Law' (*La lucha por el derecho: litigio estratégico y derechos humanos)* to offer a detailed account of how they perceive their work as strategic litigation in various thematic fields, including international criminal law in general and crimes against humanity in particular. Generally, CELS views strategic litigation as bringing exemplary cases to the court along with the victims/survivors' groups for multiple objectives: one, to promote implementation of human rights; two, to question the substance or implementation of a given state policy; three, to make visible the rights that are absent from the agenda of political powers with a view to insert them into public discussions; and four, to question judicial power.[98]

An integral aspect of their strategy in initiating any litigation is case selection which primarily relies on involvement of those directly affected.[99] The selection of cases is informed by the belief that only those legal strategies obtain the best results which are accompanied by public activism and a process of mobilization.[100] As evidenced by their early documentation phase, CELS' work goes beyond the courtroom. Currently, CELS actively trains judges by conducting seminars and workshops on, for instance, inclusion of international law in case analysis. They have also been contributing to

95 CELS, *Strategic Litigation and Human Rights* (n 89) 13.
96 CELS official website <https://www.cels.org.ar/web/en/presentacion/> accessed 18 February 2022.
97 Ibid.
98 CELS, *Strategic Litigation and Human Rights* (n 89) 18.
99 Ibid.
100 Ibid 26.

judicial reforms.[101] At the same time, CELS regularly engages with the public discourse by means of literature as well as art with a view to modify perceptions on social problems and human rights violations.

Archetypical of Latin American human rights groups in general, CELS has been shuttling frequently to regional and international human rights mechanisms to seek support for their cause and to leverage an increased bargaining power against the state. They view the Inter-American system of human rights not only as the last recourse but also as a source of principles and minimum guarantees for human rights implementation which guide domestic institution-building processes.[102]

While the thematic areas they engage with are wide-ranging, the following section discusses their two key interventions engaging the framework of crimes against humanity (truth trials, nullification of amnesty laws)[103] to exemplify how they shaped the policy of the state on dealing with historical crimes. This discussion illustrates how CELS has always employed international criminal law in the context of their strategic litigation initiatives, before the final section of this chapter will show how they brought this approach to bear on economic accountability.

1. Truth Trials (juicios por la verdad)

When the amnesty laws were still in place, CELS challenged the courts' surrender to impunity. Even though criminal proceedings were paralysed, lawyers from CELS reached out to the courts invoking their right to truth and the right to the mourning of the families of the disappeared.[104] In order to convince the courts to admit these cases, they argued that the amnesty laws prevented indictment and punishment but not investigation. Therefore, it would be still lawful for the courts to use their powers to establish truth and thus allow victims to seek enforcement of their right to truth.[105]

The concept of invoking the right to truth before the courts came from the jurisprudence established by the Inter-American Commission on Human

101 Alba Ruibal, 'La Sociedad Civil en el Proceso de Reformas a la Corte Suprema Argentina' (2008) 70 Revista Mexicana de Sociología 725.

102 See Medellin-Urquiaga, 'The Normative Impact of the Inter-American Court of Human Rights on Latin-American National Prosecution of Mass Atrocities' (2013) 46 Israel Law Review 405; Raluca Grosescu, 'Transnational Advocacy Networks and Corporate Accountability for Gross Human Rights Violations in Argentina and Colombia' (2019) 33 Global Society 400.

103 Request for unconstitutionality of the Laws Final Point and Due Obedience (*Poblete* case), CELS, *Strategic Litigation and Human Rights* (n 89) 102, 223, 233.

104 Ibid 225.

105 Ibid.

Rights (IACHR).[106] The event that triggered these petitions was a public confession by a former naval officer, Captain Adolfo Scilingo, in March 1995, who confessed to being a part of the 'death flights' which were used to throw living prisoners into the river La Plata. This horrific confession led to the subsequent unravelling of the systematic nature of crimes committed by the military regime.

One of the founders of CELS explained the reason behind these legal interventions as follows:

> [T]he social impact caused by the declarations of the former naval officer (Scilingo) highlighted another crucial issue about state terrorism: the right of the relatives to know the final destiny of their loved ones and the right of society to know in detail the methodology used by the military dictatorship to exterminate tens of thousands of Argentines. It was this need to know (in both its aspects, the personal right of the relatives and the collective right of the whole community) that was presented to the courts, pleading the 'Right to the Truth'.[107]

To avoid preliminary legal objections, the first cases that were brought before the courts were chosen carefully. These were emblematic cases illustrating the systematic nature of the armed forces' criminal conduct. Moreover, these were cases of disappearances of the relatives of CELS founders so that the organization could claim legitimacy while initiating these proceedings. At the same time, they could also set precedents to be replicated in thousands of other similar cases.[108]

The two cases initially presented were those of Mónica Candelaria Mignone, the daughter of the late Emilio Mignone, founder of CELS, and of Alejandra Lapaco, whose mother, Carmen Aguiar de Lapaco, was a co-founder of the Grandmothers Association of Plaza de Mayo and a board member of CELS. Mónica Mignone was abducted in 1976 and taken to the detention site called 'School of Mecánica de la Armada' (ESMA). Alejandra Lapaco and her mother were abducted in 1977 and detained in the 'Athletic Club', an army detention centre in Buenos Aires. Her mother was released two days later but Alejandra was never seen again.[109]

In both cases, the first instance courts ordered the armed forces and ministry of defence to bring all existing evidence concerning the fate of these two

106 See James Sweeney, 'The elusive Right to Truth in Transitional Human Rights Jurisprudence' (2018) 67 International & Comparative Law Quarterly 2, 353–387; Klass Dykmann, 'Impunity and the Right to truth in the Inter-American System of Human Rights' (2007) 7 Iberoamericana 26, 45–66 (hereinafter Dykmann, 'Impunity and Right to Truth').

107 Martin Abregú, *CELS Annual Report* (1995) 88.

108 CELS, *Strategic Litigation and Human Rights* (n 89) 225.

109 Ibid.

victims on record. These orders, on their own account, meant a recognition of violations of the rights of the victims and their families.[110] The petitions were supported by *amicus curiae* submissions filed by international non-governmental organizations like Human Rights Watch, Amnesty International, and CEJIL based on international human rights law.[111] They argued that the state was under an obligation to investigate and inform the families of the fate of the disappeared.[112] The naval and armed forces, however, refused to cooperate. Later, the appellate courts, including the Supreme Court, also declared these petitions as inadmissible.[113]

In 1998, with the sponsorship of domestic human rights organizations, Lapaco's case was brought as a complaint before the IACHR alleging violation of their right to truth.[114] The complaint led to a settlement with the state. Argentina agreed to a series of commitments regarding the right to truth, inter alia, to exhaust all available means to achieve clarification about what happened to the missing people, to set up a special ad hoc prosecutorial body who would achieve specialization in this kind of investigation, and to ensure centralized circulation of information. In return, the complainants promised to halt their international action on this matter while the agreement was being implemented.[115] Thus, in 1999, the Inter-American Commission acted as a mediator between the Argentinian state and CELS to get the state to accept and guarantee the right to the truth which consists in the exhaustion of all means to obtain clarification of what happened to disappeared persons.[116] The agreement effectively meant that human rights investigations by courts could continue even in the wake of amnesty laws[117] – but they continue to this day even when the amnesty laws are no longer in place.

Holding truth trials was an innovative idea, later replicated in other Latin American states as well.[118] The courts now had the power to access confidential information which the civil society could have never managed to document with their limited resources. The courts could get the testimonies of those involved in these crimes as ordinary witnesses, for instance, doc-

110 Ibid 227.

111 See Human Rights Watch, *Argentina: Reluctant Partner* (2001) Vol 13.5, 26–30 <https://www.hrw.org/reports//pdfs/a/argentna/argen1201.pdf> accessed 18 February 2022 (hereinafter, HRW, *Argentina: Reluctant Partner*).

112 Ibid.

113 CELS, *Annual Report* (1999) 74–78.

114 The violation of the rights enshrined in Articles 1.1, 8 and 25 of the American Convention on Human Rights, and II and XVIII of the American Declaration of Rights and Duties of Man.

115 CELS, *Strategic Litigation and Human Rights* (n 89) 232.

116 See HRW, 'Argentina: Reluctant Partner' (n 111).

117 Dykmann, 'Impunity and Right to Truth' (n 106).

118 See Paula Sofia Cuellar, 'The Influence of Latin American Domestic Courts in the Development of the Right to Truth' (2014) Journal for the Study of Peace and Conflict 1.

tors who signed death certificates for unidentified victims and pilots who operated the 'death flights'.[119] Moreover, these trials went a step further from the truth commission reports as the victims were no longer reduced to mere numbers. Individual proceedings could ensure that details of fate for each complainant could be established to the maximum extent possible.

2. *Nullification of Amnesty Laws*

In 2003, the newly elected pro-accountability Peronist President Néstor Kirchner introduced a series of institutional and legal reforms that led to the national congress repealing the *punto final* (final point) and *obediencia debida* (due obedience) laws.[120] In 2005, the Supreme Court also endorsed the nullification and held that the two amnesty laws were unconstitutional.[121] These two key moments were a turning point in Argentinian transitional justice process and marked the incorporation of international legal norms into the domestic policy as well as the legal framework.

CELS played a key role in framing retributive claims of justice as enforceable international legal obligations before Argentinian courts. The annulment was based on the claims that amnesty laws violated binding international legal norms, particularly *aut dedere aut judicare*, the obligation of states to prosecute persons who committed crimes against humanity or to extradite them.

The *Julio Hector Simon case* is an exemplary illustration of strategic litigation on various counts. It arose from the fact that an 8-month-old Claudia

119 HRW, *Argentina: Reluctant Partner* (n 111) 5.

120 In the same session, the senate also voted unanimously to approve the ratification of the Convention on Non-Applicability of Statutes of Limitations to War Crimes and Crimes Against Humanity. These reforms helped the government gain approval from the resentful population which demanded an end to impunity and opposed his election earlier that year. See Sam Ferguson, 'The Unending War: Argentina's Quest for Justice' (Boston Review, 1 May 2008) <https://bostonreview.net/articles/ferguson-the-unending-war-argentina/> accessed 18 February 2022; Louise Mallinder 'The Ongoing Quest for Truth and Justice: Enacting and Annulling Argentina's Amnesty Laws', Working Paper No. 5 From Beyond Legalism: Amnesties, Transition and Conflict Transformation (Queen's University Belfast, May 2009). Earlier, in 2004, the Supreme Court had stated that the Convention on the Non-Applicability of Statutory Limitations to War Crimes and Crimes Against Humanity implied the recognition of the prohibition of crimes against humanity as a jus cogens norm.

121 *Simón, Julio Héctor y otros s/privación ilegítima de la Libertad* [2005] Supreme Court of Argentina S.1767. XXXVIII; see *Mazzeo, Julio Lilo y otros* [2007] Supreme Court of Argentina, Appeal Judgment, para 15 (recognizing the prohibition of crimes against humanity as jus cogens); *Priebke, Erich* [1995] Supreme Court of Argentina, paras 2–5 (recognizing the prohibition of crimes against humanity as *jus cogens*); see Alba Ruibal, 'Innovative Judicial Procedures and Redefinition of the Institutional Role of the Argentine Supreme Court' (2012) 47 Latin American Research Review 22.

Poblete was kidnapped by the military forces along with her parents José Poblete and Gertrudis Poblete on 28 November 1978. The three members of the same family were taken to a clandestine detention centre El Olimpo (Automotive Maintenance Division of the Police Federal Argentina) and according to testimonies, the couple was also tortured and ill-treated during their detention. [122]

Amnesty laws had a loophole, they allowed prosecutions for kidnapping of minors. As a result, Claudia's kidnapping was being investigated and tried at the initiation of the Grandmothers Association of Plaza de Mayo in 1998.[123] Judge Gabriel Cavallo, in charge of the Criminal Court and Federal Correctional Facility, had indicted two members of the security forces, Julio Héctor Simón and Juan Antonio Del Cerro, as perpetrators in the abduction of the girl.[124]

CELS' intervention in the case began in 2000 mainly because of the typical nature of the case. The facts highlighted the fundamental contradiction in the state of the law at the time: the judges could investigate and punish the perpetrator for a given conduct when Claudia (a minor) was the victim, but the courts could take no action against the same perpetrators when her parents were the victims of the same criminal act, as the latter was protected by amnesty laws. Arguing on the criminality of the conduct which could only be partly prosecuted under the existing laws at the time, CELS contended that the act of abduction and disappearance per se was criminalized not only under domestic law but also under international criminal law as abduction was a part of the systematic attack against civilian population qualifying it as a crime against humanity.[125]

A 1994 constitutional amendment allowed lawyers to challenge the constitutionality of amnesty laws based on international criminal law and international human rights law. Under the amended constitution, domestic courts not only had the power to prosecute crimes against humanity but also were obliged to investigate such allegations.[126] The Supreme Court declared the

122 This centre operated from August 1978 to February 1979, at the Headquarters of Area V, one of the seven areas into which it was divided the City of Buenos Aires for the purposes of the repression of terrorism of State.

123 In 1998, the Grandmothers Association of Plaza de Mayo had filed a criminal trial against the appropriators of Claudia Victoria Poblete, who raised her as a biological daughter and hid her true identity. In June 2001, a judgment was issued against Ceferino Landa, who was sentenced to serve nine years and half in prison, and his wife, sentenced to five and a half years. Case No. 17,889, 'Incident of appeal of Simón, Julio' – Judge – Federal Register No. 4, Secretariat No. 7, Buenos Aires, 9 November, 2001.

124 CELS, *Strategic Litigation and Human Rights* (n 89) 104.

125 Ibid.

126 The duty to try and punish those responsible for grave violations of human rights had its legal basis in international human rights law. In addition to international human rights treaties prescribing the duty to investigate and punish, the Inter-American court had been

amnesty laws unconstitutional in 2005[127] and held that it was possible to apply certain general principles of international law and international criminal law in its entirety by the federal courts of the country.[128]

In the meantime, the case had already influenced public discourse and reignited the demands of accountability for crimes during the military repression which had been relegated to the sidelines for a long time. The Supreme Court reaffirmed the decision, quoting IACtHR's *Barrios Altos* decision,[129] and concluded that 'in the current context of our domestic law, the validation and declaration of unconstitutionality the [amnesty laws] is not an alternative. It is an obligation'.[130]

In addition to the incorporation of international law within the constitutional framework and newly appointed progressive judges to the Supreme Court, there were several key tactics at play which, in combination, made this litigation strategic and resulted in the annulment of amnesty laws.

Firstly, case selection: it was a demonstrative case where the facts highlighted the inherent contradiction in law. Claudia's family was the 'ideal victim' who would enable the invocation of the crimes against humanity framework for the first time before the court of law.[131] Secondly, direct involvement of the victims and survivors: CELS did not initiate the proceedings on their own account but joined forces with the Grandmothers Association of the Plaza de Mayo as the group was directly engaging with the victims, and thus was involved in the case more effectively.[132] Thirdly, timing of this litigation: even though amnesty laws had been in place since 1986, the economic crisis had triggered public outrage which then further flared the demands to end impunity. Fourthly, capitalizing on international pressure: the pres-

---

emphasizing on this for over a decade then. For instance, *Velásquez Rodríguez* [1989], *Godínez Cruz* [1989], *El Amparo* [1996], *Castillo Páez* [1997], *Suárez Rosario* [1997], *Nicholas Blake* [1998]. Articles 75 and 118 of the Argentine Constitution (as amended in 1994), which refer, respectively, to the supremacy of human rights treaties over domestic law, and international law (Derecho de Gentes).

127 *Julio Simón et al. v. Public Prosecutor* [2005] Corte Suprema de Justicia de la Nación (Supreme Court), Argentina, No. 17.768, S. 1767. XXXVIII.

128 The Court in first instance considered the *Ley de Obediencia Debida* to have violated Articles 1, 2, 8, and 25 of the American Convention on Human Right, Articles 2 and 9 of the ICCPR, as well as the 1984 Convention Against Torture: Juzgado Criminal en lo Criminal Federal y Correccional N. 4, Judge Gabriel Cavallo, *Simón, Julio y Del Cerro, Juan s/sustracción de menores de 10 años* [2001] No. 8686/2000.

129 *Barrio Altos v Peru* [2001] IACtHR.

130 Ibid para 41; for an analysis of the Supreme Court decision, see Christine Bakker, 'A full stop to amnesty in Argentina: the Simon case' (2005) 3 Journal of International Criminal Justice 5, 1106–1120 (hereinafter, Bakker, 'the Simon case').

131 On the problems of creating the ideal victim, see Christine Schwöbel-Patel, *Marketing Global Justice: The Political Economy of International Criminal Law* (Cambridge University Press 2021).

132 For more on the group, see Weis 'Victims' organizations' (n 3).

sure from international arrest warrants was building at the time. Requests were being made by countries such as Spain to extradite those responsible for international crimes.[133] The Attorneys General were supportive of these claims and hence, did not put a strong contestation in the courts.[134] Finally, combining the law with the extra-legal lobbying: CELS supplemented the litigation by even lobbying at the IACHR to challenge the pressures by the government and armed forces on the judiciary.[135] As a result, the Supreme Court established the precedence of international customary and treaty law in Argentinian legal order and relied on this precedence to set up a domestic order that prosecutes crimes under international law.[136]

An international development that had a direct link to accountability initiatives within the country was issuance of arrest warrants as an exercise of universal jurisdiction against 50 officials (including some key leaders) by Spanish Judge Baltasar Garzón on charges of genocide and terrorism in 1999.[137] The warrants were a result of a 1996 complaint filed by the

133 One of the Supreme Court judges noted that the extradition requests presented by third states generate the legal option either to exercise the state's territorial jurisdiction or to admit its incapacity to do so, and thus to renounce an attribution of national sovereignty, ceding jurisdiction over facts committed on Argentine territory by Argentine citizens. See Bakker, 'The Simon case' (n 130) 1118.

134 CELS, *Strategic Litigation and Human Rights* (n 89) 109.

135 The organization requested reactivation of the case that was initiated before the IACHR when the amnesty laws were in place, which led to a pronouncement citation of the Commission (Report No. 28 of 1992) in which it resolved 'that the laws of full stop and due obedience and the decrees of pardon are incompatible with the Right to Justice enshrined in the American Declaration of the Rights and Duties of Man and in the American Convention on Human Rights'.

136 In *Simón,* one of the judges analysed the decisions of this regional judicial body concerning amnesty laws. He pointed to a jurisprudential evolution starting with the recognition that the duty of states to guarantee the rights protected by the Convention includes not only the duty to prevent, investigate, and punish violations of these rights, but also the obligation to organize all state organs involved in the exercise of public power in such a way that they are capable of ensuring human rights. See Justice Petracchi referring to the case *Velázquez Rodríguez* [1988] IACHR, para 18.

137 See Máximo Langer,'The diplomacy of universal jurisdiction: The political branches and the transnational prosecution of international crimes' (2011) 105 American Journal of International Law 1, 1–49 (The only universal jurisdiction case over international crimes to reach the trial phase in Spain was against retired Argentine captain Adolfo Scilingo, which evolved out of a broader investigation of mass atrocities in Argentina in the 1970s. Scilingo had gained notoriety in Argentina by telling a journalist that the navy had killed some 2000 people that it kidnapped and tortured by throwing them unconscious and naked from airplanes into the Rio de la Plata, which separates Argentina and Uruguay. On 6 October 1997, Scilingo travelled to Spain at the invitation of a Spanish television station that wished to interview him. Following Scilingo's arrival, investigating judge Baltasar Garzón interrogated him, then ordered his arrest. Garzón also issued incriminating decisions against about 120 people and arrest warrants against about 50 in the Argentine case, 1 of whom had been arrested in Mexico, and extradited first to Spain and then to Argentina.)

Progressive Association of Prosecutors (*Unión Progresista de Fiscales*) jointly with Argentine human rights groups in Spain and the political party Izquierda Unida (United Left).[138] The Argentine administration, unsurprisingly, refused to cooperate with the Spanish judiciary and argued this was a colonial interference at the expense of Argentina's sovereignty.[139] At the same time, while the investigation in Spain was pending from 1996 to 1999, the Argentinian courts placed the two most powerful leaders of the regime under preventive detention for crimes of kidnapping babies and falsifying public documents (the two crimes that were not covered in amnesty laws).[140] Arguably, these detentions of a few high-profile but at the time marginalized officers were intended to fend off political pressure to extradite them.[141] As a ripple effect, these international trials pushed the judges to keep the accountability processes going even when the government was actively against such efforts.

Another important dimension of the legal political environment of Argentina was domestication of international law. President Alfonsin had set up an Advisory Commission during his term. One of the mandated tasks of the Commission was to initiate constitutional reform. The Commission recommended that the President convened a Constitutional Assembly which would 'amplify and strengthen' individual rights and their status under the constitution.[142] In 1994, Argentina undertook a constitutional reform. Article 75(22) of the 1994 Constitution histrionically altered the status of international human rights law in Argentina as it included provisions such as its subclause (2) stating that 'all international treaties (currently ratified, as well as those that Argentina may ratify in the future) are superior to domestic laws' and subclause (3) providing that 'several human rights treaties enjoy constitutional status'.[143]

International law, regional institutions, and universal jurisdiction cases in third countries became potent tools used tactically by CELS, seizing on a favourable political opportunity structure.[144] Backed by mass mobiliza-

138 HRW, *Argentina: Reluctant Partner* (n 111).

139 In 1998, President Carlos Menem issued Decree 111/98, formally refusing to cooperate with Judge Garzón's investigation. Menem's successor, Fernando De la Rúa, reinforced this move in 2001 with Decree 1581/01, rejecting any extradition request for crimes committed on Argentine territory.

140 HRW, 'Argentina: Reluctant Partner' (n 111) 38.

141 Sikkink, 'From Pariah State to Global Protagonist' (n 61) 12.

142 See Laura Dickinson (ed), *International Law and Society: Empirical Approaches to Human Rights* (1st edn, Routledge 2017).

143 See Janet Koven Levit, 'The Constitutionalization of Human Rights in Argentina: Problem or Promise' (1998) Columbia Journal of Transnational Law 37, 281; Rogrigo Uprimny, 'The Recent Transformation of Constitutional Law in Latin America: Trends and Challenges' in *Law and Society in Latin America* (Routledge 2014) 105–123.

144 Katheryn Sikkink, 'From Pariah State to Global Protagonist' (n 61) 2–3; Martha Finnemore and Kathryn Sikkink, 'International Norm Dynamics and Political Change' (1998) 52

tion, their litigations opened the possibility to prosecute international crimes before domestic courts in Argentina. In the past two decades, the country has also witnessed the creation, involvement, and coordination of a series of state agencies that traditionally do not participate, at least not so actively, in cases involving crimes against humanity.[145] The favourable political opportunity structure leveraged by CELS, in addition to the other key interventions discussed above, laid the groundwork for corporate accountability cases.

IV. Prosecuting Historical Corporate Complicity: The Ford Case

Multiple enquiries examining the relationship between military and economic power reflect that the planned and systematic violations were aimed at not only silencing political dissent and militancy but also to discriminate against the working class mobilizing for imposition of limits on profits, authority, and the power enjoyed by the business elite.[146]

The CONADEP truth commission report pointed out the two aspects of the business–military relationship as early as 1983: one, the majority of the victims belonging to the working class; and two, abductions and arrests occurring within workplaces.[147] Many survivor testimonies indicated that companies had provided the repressive forces with personal data, photographs, and lists of union activists and delegates – who were later disappeared. However, this aspect of the dictatorship was only considered background information and contextual circumstance of the state repression in the report.[148] During the period when amnesty was in place in Argentina, Spanish judge Baltazar Garzon's investigation identified more than 10,000 workers who went missing.[149] Truth trials and large numbers of witness testimonies pointed towards the centrality of the repression of workers and trade unionists and to the different forms of participation of business sectors in pursuit.[150]

International Organization 887. The theory of political opportunity structure emerges from social movement studies. See Doug McAdam, John McCarthy, and Mayer Zald (eds), Comparative Perspectives on Social Movements: Political Opportunities, Mobilizing Structures, and Cultural Framings (Cambridge University Press 1996).

145 Leigh Payne and Gabriel Pereira, 'Accountability for Corporate Complicity in Human Rights Violations: Argentina's Transitional Justice Innovation?' in Verbitsky and Bohoslavsky (eds), *Outstanding Debts* (n 1) 44.

146 See Victoria Basualdo, 'Business and the Military in the Argentine Dictatorship (1976–1983): Institutional, Economic, and Repressive Relations' in Basualdo and others, *Big Businesses and Dictatorships* (n 25).

147 CONADEP Final Report, Part I, The Repression, 'The Profits of Repression' (n 69).

148 Martín, *Lessons from Argentina* (n 15) 163.

149 Ibid.

150 Ibid; see Verbitsky and Bohoslavsky (eds), *Outstanding Debts* (n 1).

As discussed above, the CELS research report in 2015 shifted the focus and brought corporate responsibility to the forefront.[151] It claimed that the corporate contributions to military conduct could be qualified as co-perpetration in violations amounting to crimes against humanity, both because of the characteristic form of the conduct but also because they contributed to the systematic nature of the attack by the state against workers.[152]

At the same time, when this comprehensive research was being released, there were other developments in the state machinery that facilitated domestic trials on corporate complicity. In 2007, the Office of the Public Prosecutor created the Prosecutorial Unity for Co-ordination and Monitoring of the cases of violation of human rights under state repression.[153] The Unity evolved in 2013 to the Attorney's Office for Crimes against Humanity. One of the new working targets of this new office was to precisely address the responsibility of civilians under the military regime, including government and judicial officials and business and economic groups.[154] The public discourse on accountability, at the time, had also been altered heavily towards corporate complicity.[155]

1. Legal Framework for Corporate Complicity in Crimes under International Law

The constitutional reforms of 1994 established the primacy of international human rights obligations over domestic law and gave them constitutional status. After the Argentinian Supreme Court nullified amnesty laws and declared them as unconstitutional, it became possible to initiate prosecutions before domestic courts. Therefore, because of the 1994 constitutional reforms, international crimes could be directly prosecuted before the domestic courts in Argentina even though Argentina only ratified the ICC Statute in 2007.[156]

Civil law claims against these violations were barred because of the limitation period.[157] But the prosecution for historical crimes was possible if it

151 Reasons for the delay and change in focus discussed in Section III.

152 See Introduction, CELS Business Responsibility Report (n 33).

153 Ministerio Público Fiscal, Procurador General de la Nación, Resolution PGN 1442/13 (2013).

154 Martín, *Lessons from Argentina* (n 15) 167.

155 Payne and Pereira recall posters and graffiti titled 'democracy or corporations' on the March 2014 commemoration of the 1976 coup. Leigh Payne and Gabriel Pereira, 'Accountability for Corporate Complicity in Human Rights Violations: Argentina's Transitional Justice Innovation?' in H. Verbitsky, and J. Bohoslavsky (eds), *Outstanding Debts* (n 1) 29.

156 Law 26.200 came into effect in January 2007 <http://servicios.infoleg.gob.ar/infolegInternet/anexos/120000-124999/123921/norma.htm> accessed 19 February 2022.

157 *Villamil, Amelia Ana vs. Estado Nacional sobre daños y perjuicios.* Villamil filed a claim against the Argentinian State for her son and her daughter-in-law's disappearances in 1977.

could be argued that these crimes were committed under the framework of crimes against humanity.[158] The existence of a larger criminal plan was judicially established in the 1985 juntas trial (Causa 13/84) by the Federal Court of the city of Buenos Aires.[159] Thus, these crimes could only be prosecuted under a crimes against humanity framework, as the domestic law bars any initiation of civil actions and criminal law proceedings from over decades ago.

The Argentine Criminal Code does not provide for the prosecutions of corporations as an entity.[160] Based on testimonies by victims collected during the CONADEP and truth trials processes, prosecutions are being held against those corporate managers who were identified to have directly contributed to the commission of crimes. Direct contribution, in these cases, included giving information to the military officers to abduct the workers, being present in the detention centres where workers were being tortured, providing material resources for instance, physical property, to install detention centres or cars to carry out the abduction.[161] The corporate managers are then prosecuted for 'complicity' in crimes of kidnapping, torture, murder, and enforced disappearance and the trials are regulated by domestic procedural law. Concerning the notion of complicity, the Argentinian Criminal Code punishes anyone who helps or cooperates with direct perpetrators, whether or not that collaboration was essential to the perpetration.[162]

On the question of standing, in 2009, Argentina's congress amended the law to allow non-governmental organizations to act as private prosecutors

A summary of the case and the sentence can be found at <www.cij.gov.ar/nota-25380-La-Corte-Suprema–por-mayor-a–ratific–su-precedente-sobre-la-prescripci-n-de-acciones-civiles-contra-el-Estadoen-juicios-de-lesa-humanidad.html> accessed 19 February 2022.

158 In 2005 the Supreme Court declared in the *Simón case* the non-applicability of statutory limitations to crimes committed under State repression and explicitly considered them as crimes against humanity, according to the ICC Statute. See *Arancibia Clavel, Enrique Lautaro* [2004] Appeal Judgment, Supreme Court of Argentina, para 28. Kirchner's government ratified the Convention on the Non-Applicability of Statutory Limitations to War Crimes and Crimes against Humanity. This ratification forced the State to punish such human rights violations and made extradition possible. See Kathryn Sikkink and Booth-Walling, 'Argentina's Contribution to Global Trends in Transitional Justice' in Roht-Arriaza and Mariezcurrena (eds), *Beyond Truth versus Justice* (n 42).

159 Victoria Basualdo, Quintana and Varsky, 'The Cases of Ford and Mercedes Benz' in Verbitsky and Bohoslavsky (eds), *Outstanding Debts* (n 1) 161.

160 Juan Bohoslavsky, 'Corporate Responsibility for Complicity: International and Local Perspectives' in Verbitsky and Bohoslavsky (eds), *Outstanding Debts* (n 1).

161 See CELS Report on Business Responsibility (n 33).

162 Sections 45–49, 210, 277ff. Laura García Martín, 'Overcoming Corporate-Related Human Rights Abuses in Transitional Justice: Lights and Shadows from the Case of Argentina' (2021) 20 Journal of Human Rights 547, 555 (hereinafter Martín, 'Lights and Shadows from the Case of Argentina').

in cases of crimes against humanity or grave human rights violations.[163] This possibility existed prior to the legislative change as well, but only on a case-by-case basis. State prosecutors continue to take the lead, but private prosecutors, or 'institutional plaintiffs', can also act independently, bringing their own evidence forward and making direct appeals to the judge. They often collaborate with the state prosecutors as well.[164]

Until 2023, the only case in Argentina where two managers of a corporation were convicted for their involvement in the crimes committed by the military are those who worked for Ford Motors. The following sections discuss the *Ford case*, its implications for the future cases, and obstacles in litigating these cases against corporations.

2. Ford Complicity in Crimes against Humanity

Clandestine Detention Centre at Ford Motors Co.

Ford Motors Co., a multinational corporation engaged in automotive manufacturing, had outsourced parts of its manufacturing process to Argentina as early as 1914. It was one of the first car manufacturers to have offices in Argentina.[165] By the time the 1976 military coup took place, Ford Motors Co. US (the parent company) was controlling an influential conglomerate in Argentina, including a full-fledged manufacturing plant in Buenos Aires called Ford Motor Argentina SA and a few other auto-parts firms.[166] Traditionally, the firm enjoyed a good reputation amongst workers for its relatively high wages.

The 1960s witnessed a period of growth in the country's automotive industry, but the 1970s brought a crisis in the sector. Ford Motors premises were also reflective of the political tensions ongoing in the country at large. Ford workers' dissatisfaction with long working hours and unhealthy work conditions resulted in increased mobilization and participation in national trade unions. In 1975, Argentina witnessed one of the largest workers' strikes where Ford workers were on the leading front.[167] The enhanced bargaining power in the hands of workers led them to avoid the imposition of austerity

163 Gastón Chillier, 'Prosecuting Corporate Complicity in Argentina's Dictatorship' (Open Democracy, 19 December 2014) <https://www.opendemocracy.net/en/openglobalrights-openpage-blog/prosecuting-corporate-complicity-in-argentinas-dictatorship/> accessed 19 February 2022

164 Ibid.

165 Eduardo Basualdo and Victoria Basualdo, 'Confronting Labor Power: Ford Motor Argentina and the Dictatorship (1976–1983)' in Basualdo and others, *Big Businesses and Dictatorships* (n 25) 216. Ford has been alleged to be involved in massive human rights violations in Brazil and South Africa as well.

166 Ibid; CELS Report on Business Responsibility, 'Ford' (n 33) 458.

167 Ibid 219.

measures, and enabled an agreement with Ford which was beneficial for the workers collectively.[168]

But the scales of power tilted drastically to the side of the management immediately after the military coup of 1976. The activists and union workers who were leading the protests in 1975 became primary targets. A victim testimony recounts a disturbing incident that took place a day after the coup: during the weekly meeting of the company's managers with the internal workers' commission, the managers announced that they were no longer going to recognize the commission as a workers' body. When one of the delegates asked the manager the reason for this interruption of the relationship with the union, the industrial relations manager, Guillermo Galarraga (who was put on trial later), replied that 'the Ford Motor Argentina company has become a military objective and priority'. He also later added, 'Amoroso, give my regards to Camps'.[169] The delegate did not know Camps – the newly appointed head of police by the regime – until he was later 'disappeared' by him.[170] As findings suggest, the management at Ford knew about the coup at the planning stages as well.[171] As soon as the coup took place, the company pulled itself back from any negotiations with the workers' union, dismissing their demands and undoing the bargains of the preceding year. At the same time, the company had plans to take violent retributive actions against the unionists with the help of the regime.[172]

Within two months of the military seizing power, 25 Ford workers were kidnapped.[173] Most of the members of the internal commission and active unionists remained 'disappeared' for 30–60 days.[174] Some of them were kidnapped from their homes, while the rest were arrested directly at the shopfloor or factory premise in Pacheco, near Buenos Aires where they were

168 Written statement by Pedro Troiani, a factory worker and delegate, given in the case *Rivero, Santiago Omar y otros s. privación ilegal de libertad, tormentos, etc.* [2004] Case file 142, Juzgado Federal en lo Criminal y Correccional no. 2, San Martín, Victoria Basualdo, Quintana and Varsky, 'The Cases of Ford and Mercedes Benz' in Verbitsky and Bohoslavsky (eds), *Outstanding Debts* (n 1) 168.

169 Ibid.

170 Ibid.

171 Eduardo Basualdo and Victoria Basualdo, 'Confronting Labor Power: Ford Motor Argentina and the Dictatorship (1976–1983)' in Basualdo and others, *Big Businesses and Dictatorships* (n 25) 228.

172 Victoria Basualdo, Quintana and Varsky, 'The Cases of Ford and Mercedes Benz' in Verbitsky and Bohoslavsky (eds), *Outstanding Debts* (n 1)160.

173 See Victoria Basualdo, Quintana and Varsky, 'The Cases of Ford and Mercedes Benz' in Verbitsky and Bohoslavsky (eds), *Outstanding Debts* (n 1); Eduardo Basualdo and Victoria Basualdo, 'Confronting Labor Power: Ford Motor Argentina and the Dictatorship (1976–1983)' in Basualdo and others, *Big Businesses and Dictatorships* (n 24); CELS Report on Business Responsibility, 'Ford' (n 33).

174 CELS Report on Business Responsibility (n 33) 469.

held and tortured for hours.[175] Later, they were taken to Tigre or Ingeniero Maschwitz police stations, where they were subjected to interrogations and unlawfully detained.[176] Through different presidential decrees, the workers were placed at the disposal of the National Executive Power and transferred to other prison units such as Devoto, La Plata, or Sierra Chica.[177] A few days after these trade unionists and activists were abducted, their families received telegrams from the management notifying them that these workers had been fired for walking out on the job without providing any reason.[178] The 2015 CELS report produced a verified account of 37 victims who were working for Ford Motors during this time, of which 24 cases presented evidence of direct involvement of company executives.[179]

Many testimonies suggested that the company executives gave the military a list of workers and trade union delegates asking them to be abducted. The lists were marked with IDs bearing photos to enable easy identification. As a family member of one of the victims recalls,

> the officer opened a drawer and pulled out a list typed on a sheet of paper with the Ford logo, which he told me had 'all the names that the company gave us of workers it wanted us to '*chupar*'.[180]

Chupar (literally, suck up) was a colloquial phrase being used for kidnapping and disappearing.[181] Ford workers and former conscript soldiers of the military offered similar details regarding the exchange of favours between Ford and the military. The testimonies corroborated each other's account that there was a detention camp operating at a recreational facility and that workers' locker rooms inside the plant were run by 50–80 soldiers who lived there.[182] The sections which were turned into military barracks were

175 Ibid.

176 Victoria Basualdo, Quintana and Varsky, 'The Cases of Ford and Mercedes Benz' in Verbitsky and Bohoslavsky (eds), *Outstanding Debts* (n 1) 162.

177 Argentina Ministry of Justice, *A dos años del veredicto en la Causa "Ford"*, 10 December 2020, <https://www.argentina.gob.ar/noticias/dos-anos-del-veredicto-en-la-causa-ford> accessed 6 March 2022.

178 CELS Report on Business Responsibility (n 33) 470.

179 Ibid.

180 In the case *Molinari, Antonio, personal Ford s. privación illegal de la Libertad*, statements requested by Pedro Troiani. Other statements also confirmed a list with approximately 20 or 30 typewritten names, Victoria Basualdo, Quintana and Varsky, 'The Cases of Ford and Mercedes Benz' in Verbitsky and Bohoslavsky (eds), *Outstanding Debts* (n 1) 160; CELS Report on Business Responsibility (n 33) 481.

181 Ibid.

182 'Denuncian a Ford por torturas y desaparición de obreros durante la dictadura Argentina' (El Mundo, 26 January 2004) <https://www.elmundo.es/elmundo/2004/01/24/economia/1074958411.html> accessed 19 February 2022.

cordoned off for workers,[183] and the soldiers present there were specifically tasked to combat subversion.[184]

In addition to giving the military shelter at the factory, Ford executives were alleged to have taken part in the interrogation of the kidnapped union delegates meant to extract information on trade union activities. One of the victims who was kidnapped and interrogated at the military installation at Ford factory premises, despite being hooded, could clearly identify the voice of the head of security chief, Héctor Francisco Sibilla, who was present in the same room.[185]

Several victims also testified that they were abducted in F100 pickup trucks provided by Ford to the military. These were custom-made anti-noise and untraceable cars manufactured by Ford for the military especially for the purposes of carrying out the abductions.[186] They were used so frequently by the military that these Ford Falcons became the symbol of the regime's operations to the extent that people came to fear them.[187]

Therefore, Ford and its executive staff participated in the crimes committed by the military in the following ways: one, by asking them to abduct its trade union representatives and workers; two, by hosting a clandestine detention centre; three, by taking part in torture of the workers to extract information from them; and four, by manufacturing customized cars to facilitate abductions for the military.

The Trial

After amnesty laws were struck down, a former trade union delegate, Pedro Troiani, sought to initiate proceedings as a private prosecutor (*querellante*) in a criminal case against Ford in November 2002. He was also accompanied by other trade union delegates in accusing the Ford executives as civilian accomplices of the crimes committed by the military. The case was taken up for prosecution in the Federal Court of Buenos Aires presided by Daniel Eduardo Rafecas, but the investigation had been delegated to the prosecutor's office headed by Federico Delgado.[188] In addition to the department of Federal Justice, the private prosecution (along with Ford workers) provided numerous pieces of evidence and testimonies, called on experts to add elements to

183 Victoria Basualdo, Quintana and Varsky, 'The Cases of Ford and Mercedes Benz' in Verbitsky and Bohoslavsky (eds), *Outstanding Debts* (n 1) 161.

184 Ibid.

185 Ibid 162.

186 Haley Anderson Nelson, *Selling Souls: The Economic Supporters of the 'Dirty War'* (Dissertation, University of North Carolina at Charlotte 2016) 35.

187 Ibid 34.

188 Victoria Basualdo, Quintana and Varsky, 'The Cases of Ford and Mercedes Benz' in Verbitsky and Bohoslavsky (eds), *Outstanding Debts* (n 1) 163.

analyse the company's records, and requested a search and on-site inspection of the plant.[189] The victims were represented by cooperating partners of CELS, Tomás Ojea Quintana[190] and Elizabeth Gómez Alcorta.[191] The National Human Rights Secretariat and the Buenos Aires Province Human Rights Secretariat were also named plaintiffs in the case. The documentation and investigations by CELS proved instrumental to complement direct testimonies given by the victims before the court.

In 2006, after gathering preliminary evidence, the private prosecutors summoned four people (one military officer and three Ford managers) who had been identified as co-participants in the crimes of kidnapping, torture, murder, and disappearance of persons, to give their statements in the preliminary investigation.[192] Two of them were managers of the company, Pedro Müller and Héctor Francisco Jesús Sibilla and former manager of labour relations, Guillermo Galarraga, who died before the trial began.[193] Santiago Riveros, the former head of the Military Institutes, was the only military official filed as direct perpetrator in the case.

Even though much of the investigations and evidence gathering was already done by the plaintiffs and private prosecution, it took 11 years for the trial to begin. In 2014, the case was assigned to Federal Oral Court No. 1 in San Martin, Province of Buenos Aires, and the trial finally began on 19 December 2017.[194] Some of the delays were caused by procedural obstacles such as jurisdictional disputes but there were certain challenges that are inherent to the trial of executive officers of a powerful corporation.

The case was stalled for almost a decade by the assigned judge Juan Maniel Yajl despite repeated petitions and complaints made by the plaintiffs.[195] In 2012, the San Martin Federal Court had a change in Bench, and the case was

189 Ibid.

190 An international human rights lawyer with vast experience litigating human rights cases, such as the abduction of children during the authoritarian regimes on behalf of the Grandmothers of the Plaza de Mayo.

191 An Argentine lawyer, professor, and politician. She was the first Minister of Women, Genders and Diversity from 2019 to 2022.

192 Victoria Basualdo, Quintana and Varsky, 'The Cases of Ford and Mercedes Benz' in Verbitsky and Bohoslavsky (eds), *Outstanding Debts* (n 1) 164.

193 The Ford case was the second case in the series of litigations against civilians for their complicity in crimes against humanity. The first case was against Carlos Pedro Blaquier, the 'sugar czar', one of the most powerful business tycoons of the country commonly known as the Ledesma case. See Alejandra Dandan and Hannah Franzki, 'Between Historical Analysis and Legal Responsibility: The Ledesma Case' in Verbitsky and Bohoslavsky (eds), *Outstanding Debts* (n 1); Hannah C Franzki, *Criminal Trials, Economic Dimensions of State Crime, and the Politics of Time in International Criminal Law* (Doctoral Dissertation 2018).

194 Martín, *Lessons from Argentina* (n 15) 185.

195 Victoria Basualdo, Quintana and Varsky, 'The Cases of Ford and Mercedes Benz' in Verbitsky and Bohoslavsky (eds), *Outstanding Debts* (n 1) 164.

assigned to new judge, Alicia Vence. Within a few months of taking charge, she admitted the private prosecutor's long-standing request and allowed on-site inspection of the Ford plant in Pacheco where the detentions and torture allegedly took place. Later in the same year, she ordered the four accused identified by the private prosecutors as co-perpetrators to appear for preliminary investigation.[196]

After preliminary investigations, in May 2013, Judge Venice initiated criminal proceedings against the three Ford executives for their criminal involvement in the illegal deprivation of liberty of the factory delegates and workers and torture inflicted on them. Despite and because of the procedural and practical hurdles, it was already a breakthrough development when a public and oral trial was scheduled to take place in 2014.

The Judgement

On 11 December 2018, in a courtroom packed with the victims, survivors, political leaders, and trade unionists, the three judges announced their judgment. They found the three accused (Galarraga having died during the process) guilty of having participated in crimes against humanity and sentenced them to 15 years (Santiago Omar Riveros), 12 years (Sibila), and 10 years (Müller) of effective imprisonment. While Santiago Riveros, the military officer, was found culpable for commission of the crimes, the judges found the two Ford managers Sibilla and Müller to be 'necessary participants' (*partícipes necesarios)* that their actions and contributions were necessary for the illegal detention and torture to take place. The court held that it was through the factory that business officials 'contributed to the repressive apparatus of the State, providing information, means and facilities to the execution of crimes against humanity'.[197]

The court made three far-reaching acknowledgements: one, reaffirming that the state is obligated to investigate and prosecute crimes against humanity based on customary international law; two, that corporations (Ford as well as others) effectively and systematically contributed to state repression; and three, that the military and the state worked with a common purpose to eliminate the trade unions.[198]

The judges also reaffirmed that the violations amounted to crimes against humanity under international law. The trial court judgment not only cited the Argentinian Supreme Court on this issue, but also relied on the ICC

196 Ibid.

197 Victoria Basualdo, 'The Ford Trial in Argentina: A Workers' Victory' (Justice Info, 1 April 2019) <https://www.justiceinfo.net/en/40813-the-ford-trial-in-argentina-a-workers-victory.html> accessed 19 February 2022.

198 Ibid.

Statute and jurisprudence of several international tribunals, to clearly affirm that civilians could indeed be perpetrators of such crimes.[199] The judges went to great lengths analysing the contributions made by Ford executives. These contributions were placed in the broader context of the strategic relationship between the military and the corporations. The court admitted the argument that the military and corporations worked with a common purpose to what they considered a 'normalization' of labour relations, and the profound transformation of the economic and social structure. Elimination of the internal commissions of the trade union at Ford and beyond was key for both the military and the corporations. Therefore, the judges held that the acts of abducting the workers, torturing, and murdering them were carried out in furtherance of this common purpose.[200]

It should be noted that in arriving at these findings, the court primarily relied on the testimonies given by workers and their relatives themselves. Inter alia, the court used the research report by CELS and others on corporate responsibility in crimes against humanity and expert witnesses (context witnesses) as 'clarifying and conclusive' evidence.[201] The Ford trial judgment, 40 years after the crimes were committed, builds on all the preceding processes in the Argentinian transitional justice framework: CONADEP, truth trials, nullification of amnesty laws, research reports, and intense public mobilization demanding accountability.

3. *Legal and Practical Obstacles*

The conviction in the *Ford case* does not mean smooth sailing for the other pending cases against corporate executives before the domestic courts. There are both legal and political obstacles which are particular to cases involving historical corporate complicity.

In the *Ford case*, attribution of responsibility for corporate conduct was a major challenge in these cases despite the availability of exceptionally strong evidence and testimonies. In many other cases, there is no comparable evidence testifying the presence of corporate executives at the location of crimes or any other form of direct contribution. Even if the argument is to be made that the accused corporate managers were acting through, for instance, the military personnel, a certain degree of control over those involved would be a necessary element to prove. Typically, de facto control by a civilian superior requires a degree of hierarchical integration and stability that is comparable to a military superior–subordinate relationship.[202] Given the special nature of

199 Ibid.
200 Ibid.
201 Ibid.
202 Werle and Jeßberger, *Principles* (n 5) 393 ff

the corporate–military nexus, the chain of control and hierarchy was not as clearly demarcated. In view of the time that has elapsed since the commission of crimes, it is unlikely that more strong evidence will surface in cases that are still pending against corporate executives to fulfil requirements of effective control. As a result, the judges are reluctant to find corporate executives liable under the crimes against humanity framework.[203]

In addition to these legal challenges, there are certain political and practical obstacles as well. Buying time is an effective strategy employed by multinational corporations. Similar to the trend highlighted in the case study on ATS in the United States (see Chapter 5),[204] Ford Motors also resorted to delaying and dilatory tactics.[205] These tactics turned out to be particularly effective when one defendant who was 93 years old died while the trial was still pending, and the others awaiting trial were 85, 90, and 94.[206] The death of the accused suspends the proceedings while saving significant reputational costs to the corporations. A combined study of all pending 20 cases before Argentinian courts notes that all of them were affected by severe delays at different stages of the litigation process.[207]

The implicated corporations continue to yield significant economic and political power in Argentina. A few months after the indictment was released and the trial was scheduled for a public hearing, it was reported that, in 2015, senior executives from Ford US, and Ford Argentina visited the President at the Government Palace and announced an investment of US$220 million in Argentina within the next two financial years.[208] The large sum was an unusual but timely investment for Ford.

Moreover, the lawyers defending corporate executives often add their weight to the political costs of these proceedings. The legal team defending the Ford management, for example, is regarded as a part of a select group of lawyers with a potential to influence judicial and political affairs in Argentina. Some of them have held influential government positions during authoritarian and democratic governments in Argentina. They have represented several

203 Interview with Gabriel Pereira, Law Professor at the National University of Tucuman (online, 28 June 2021).

204 See Chapter 5.

205 Quoting interview with Tomas Quintana, Martín, *Lessons from Argentina* (n 15) 196.

206 Public Prosecutor's Office, 'Causa Ford: suspendieron el juicio previsto para marzo y no fijaron una nueva fecha' (10 January 2017) https://www.fiscales.gob.ar/lesa-humanidad/causa-ford-suspendieron-el-juicio-previsto-para-marzo-y-no-fijaron-una-nueva-fecha/ accessed 19 February 2022.

207 Pereira, 'Business collaborators on Trial' (n 17).

208 'Cristina Kirchner recibió a los directivos de Ford' (El Tribuno, 29 May 2015). <https://www.eltribuno.com/jujuy/nota/2015-5-29-0-0-0-cristina-kirchner-recibio-a-los-directivos-de-ford-economia-cristina-kirchner-ford-ford-argentina-unidad-de-pronta-atencion≥ last accessed 19 February 2022.

other high-profile multinational companies operating in Argentina, high-profile politicians, and businessmen.[209]

A study based on Corporate Accountability and Transitional Justice (CATJ) database correlates how social, political, and economic power of the corporation charged with complicity in crimes against humanity has affected judicial processes in Argentina.[210] Gabriel Pereira notes this as the 'stop motion process' when a case presents controversial evidence that demands similarly controversial legal assessment and judicial practice, the judiciary is reluctant to move forward.[211] The case gets stuck, and sometimes shelved indefinitely to avoid pressure or criticism from both pro-accountability and pro-impunity camps.[212] This phenomenon has only been observed in cases against corporations and it could possibly explain why out of 20 cases, only one has reached its final stage.[213]

Against that backdrop, the existence of domestic trials for corporate complicity in crimes under international law may be only worthy of a partial celebration. Pending these legal and political obstacles, one successful conviction may not be considered as a wholesome moment of victory in the struggle for MTJ in Argentina.

V. Conclusion

Argentina is not the only country that has grappled with the economic fuelling of state repression but the way international criminal law has been strategically used to target the participation of the economic elite in atrocity crimes makes it a telling story for the purposes of this study. The enabling conditions and legal opportunities that became available to human rights groups like CELS in Argentina played a significant role in making space for non-state actors to participate in and contribute to domestic prosecutions. The legal framework, prosecutorial openness, and persistent pressure from the public are all factors that have contributed to Argentina's paving the path in the field of transitional justice and international criminal law. Against that backdrop, the following aspects stand out when strategic litigation carried out by the Argentinian organization, CELS, is seen through the TWAI(C)L framework:

209 Payne and others, *Deploying Archimedes' Lever* (n 60) 259.

210 Pereira, 'Business collaborators on Trial' (n 17).

211 Ibid.

212 Interview with Gabriel Pereira, Law Professor at the National University of Tucuman (online, 28 June 2021).

213 Ibid.

The Long Haul to Target Economic Structures

An exclusive focus on the most responsible political/military leadership often renders the economic structures that sustain and fuel large-scale violence as mere footnotes in the transitional justice process. TWAIL scholar Vasuki Nesiah terms the prioritization of prosecution of dictators such as Pinochet, Habre, etc. as the 'Despot Crusade', an effort to prosecute the radical evil and the monstrous.[214] Building on Hanna Arendt's argument on the banality of evil, Nesiah argues the dominant approach to criminal accountability, which emphasizes only on prosecuting high-ranking officials, does not allow the societies to confront the systematic nature of atrocities of their history. Mass atrocities require many actors: actors driven not by monstrous intent but by ambitions and ideologies which insidiously integrate governance and atrocity.[215] These individual prosecutions fail to channel the complex legacies of macroeconomic policy[216] (also see Section IV.4 of Chapter 1).

Arguably, there are some obstacles to challenging the macroeconomic policy through corporate accountability that are particular to a transitional justice framework, namely lack of comprehensive documentation, power imbalances, and the importance of big businesses in the rebuilding of a nation. The following is another conventional explanation for this perceived leniency towards the corporate elite over the political/military elite in a transitional justice context by drawing on the post–World War II German experience:

> As a rule, it is the political and occasionally also the military elites that are first 'overtaken'. By contrast, industry and business constitute a continuum in all societies, at least in such societies that accept the basic ideas of international criminal law today. This is an observation that can perhaps explain why there is often no energy for a determined legal 'settling up' in these [corporate complicity] cases.[217]

The changed regime often focuses on the 'fallen' political elite to seek political legitimacy and ends up relying on the support of the economic elite that continues to yield power in the fresh and fragile democratic setups.

214 Vasuki Nesiah, 'The Trials of History: Losing Justice in the Monstrous and the Banal' in Ruth Buchanan, Peer Zumbansen (eds), *Law in Transition: Human Rights, Development and Transitional Justice* (1st edn, Bloomsbury 2014) 298 (hereinafter Nesiah, 'The Trials of History').

215 See Hannah Arendt, *Eichmann in Jerusalem: A Report on the Banality of Evil* (Penguin Books 1994).

216 Nesiah, 'The Trials of History' (n 214) 297.

217 Florian Jeßberger, 'On the Origins of Individual Criminal Responsibility under International Law for Business Activity: IG Farben on Trial' (2010) 8 Journal of International Criminal Justice 3, 783–802, 800.

In that regard, the experience of Argentina illustrates the tensions highlighted by TWAI(C)L and the role of strategic litigation in countering those. On the one hand, the primary focus on the military leadership for the first two decades after the fall of the military regime confirms the TWAIL critique of shielding economic structures. On the other hand, because of the fact that the struggle for MTJ continued for four decades, it also shines a light on the long path of corporate accountability that unpacks and challenges the economic structures that contributed to historical atrocities.

Clearly, the corporate trials were an afterthought even in Argentina, where the transitional justice processes always foregrounded the systematic nature of the involvement of corporations in the crimes committed by the military. The truth commission report of 1983, the truth trials, and thousands of victim testimonies had been pointing out that the role played by corporations was more than that of an accessory to a repressive state. But it took almost three decades for corporate accountability to feature in the MTJ agenda.

In consideration of the political and legal challenges, the Argentine journey compels that accountability for mass atrocities must be viewed as a multi-step process where all stakeholders involved need to be in for the long haul. These trials against corporate executives in Argentina could be perceived to indicate that early prosecutions of the top military officers do not necessarily mean that all the other actors in the system are absolved of their contributions to the repressive machinery.

The time frame of 40 years spent in pursuit of accountability also underlines the temporal aspect of strategic litigation discussed in Section I of Chapter 2. Several legal interventions were carried out over the years that go beyond their immediate outcomes that contribute towards a long-term structural objective. The duration of the process allowed for these moments of reflection where litigators realized the blind spots in their strategy and evolved in the process. The shift in focus is also a reflection of their dynamic approach that draws heavily on the broader movements and changing political circumstances.

Reform-oriented Innovations

CELS is considered a protagonist of the MTJ movement primarily because of the many innovations in the process are to their credit. But these legal interventions in pursuit of MTJ were not only innovative but they also prioritized reform over repair (see Section III of Chapter 2) of the legal structure.

When the amnesty laws were in place, the organization conceived the idea of 'the right to truth' and went up to the Inter-American Commission to secure this right for the victims. In the process, these interventions critiqued the lack of accountability in the country at an international stage but also at the same time constructively engaged with the existing legal framework to secure evidence and documentation that would have been impossible for victims or their representatives to pursue on their own account. This is a good example to illustrate the TWAI(C)L stance of reform-oriented critique (see Section III.1 of Chapter 1)

Turning Accountability into a Legitimacy Resource for the State

The example of Argentina is reflective of the importance that state institutions hold in a sustained accountability process, be it against military/political leadership or corporations. Yet, at the same time, the role played by the victims and civil society organizations can be instrumental in essentially making it a non-negotiable demand from the state.

The 1983 transition to democracy in Argentina was abrupt and domestically induced. This meant that neither the outgoing repressive regime had the space to bargain amnesty agreements, nor there were any external actors facilitating the transition. On the one hand, the new government had the option to employ accountability measures to seek legitimacy. On the other hand, the absence of official commitments meant the victims, activists, and human rights groups had to consistently lobby to keep the political importance of historical accountability alive. In that process, it is noteworthy that CELS resorted to the vocabulary of international criminal law and 'crimes against humanity' framework to keep the importance of accountability processes alive and urgent in public consciousness. As had been argued in the chapter, this consistent emphasis placed the MTJ movement on high priority of national politics to the extent that it became a primary source of legitimacy for the Kirchner government in 2003. Those most directly affected by these violations contributed to the practice and implementation of international criminal law and the state responded to their notions of justice (see Section III.3 of Chapter 1).

Implementing the Universal through the Specific

Through these legal interventions in the last four decades, victims and strategic litigators have instrumentalized international law and international institutions against the injustices committed by their own state that finally resulted in trials against corporate executives for perpetrating crimes against humanity.

The *Ford Trial* discussed above presents a context-specific, locally informed implementation of the purportedly universal framework of crimes against 'humanity'. The legal system of Argentina is unique in that it incorporates international legal principles in the Constitution. But the unprecedented trials of corporate executives for historical crimes that took place in Argentina, with substantive international law and domestic procedural laws, contribute to the relative application of international criminal law, and challenges its hegemonic characterization (see Section III.2 of Chapter 1)

Even when pursued as an afterthought, it was a herculean task at the hands of victims and lawyers holding big corporations accountable. The trials are largely taking place in a void without set models of holding corporate executives accountable for a systematic attack against a civilian population. The nature of the evidence is diluting with time and judges are evidently reluctant to use creative models of attributing individual criminal responsibility in the 'dictator–civilian' hierarchical structure. The fact that the perpetrators continue to yield significant economic and social influence poses an additional challenge.

Regardless of whether the convictions in the *Ford case* will be replicated in the cases against other corporate managers or not, these attempts to prosecute corporations mark a leap in the way corporate accountability is addressed in post-conflict countries. The Argentinian case suggests that cases such as the *Ford trial* may even have an impact beyond the courtroom as there is more information in the public domain, the company is recognizable, and the violations are particularly abhorrent. Their visibility is likely to send a message not only to other subsidiaries of the transnational company or the industrial sector, but to all firms about the reputational, financial, and legal risks of becoming partners with authoritarian regimes and armed violent actors.

This practice demonstrates that economic collaborations with repressive regimes can be unpacked, foregrounded, and challenged legally. At the same time, this litigation also highlights that if owned and adapted to the context, international criminal law can also be a tool in the service of those directly affected by egregious state violence.

References

Abregú M, 'CELS Annual Report' (1995)

Alba R, 'La Sociedad Civil en el Proceso de Reformas a la Corte Suprema Argentina' (2008) 70 Revista Mexicana de Sociología 725

Alexander J, *A Scoping Study on Transitional Justice and Poverty Reduction* (The Department for International Development 2003)

Alfonsín R, '"Never Again" in Argentina' (1993) 4 Journal of Democracy 15–19

Arendt H, *Eichmann in Jerusalem: A Report on the Banality of Evil* (Penguin Books 1994)

Arriaza L and Roht-Arriaza N, 'Social Reconstruction as a Local Process' (2008) 2 International Journal of Transitional Justice 2, 157–172

Basualdo G, *Movilización legal internacional en dictadura: La visita de la CIDH y la creación del* (CELS, Teseopress 2019)

Basualdo V, Berghoff H and Bucheli M (eds), *Big Business and Dictatorships in Latin America: A Transnational History of Profits and Repression* (Springer 2021)

Basualdo V, 'The Ford Trial in Argentina: A Workers' Victory' (Justice Info, 1 April 2019) <https://www.justiceinfo.net/en/40813-the-ford-trial-in-argentina-a-workers-victory.html> accessed 19 February 2022

Basualdo V, Berghoff H and Bucheli M (eds), *Big Business and Dictatorships in Latin America: A Transnational History of Profits and Repression* (Springer 2021)

Basualdo V, Quintana TO and Varsky C, 'The Cases of Ford and Mercedes Benz' in H Verbitsky and J Bohoslavsky (eds), *The Economic Accomplices to the Argentine Dictatorship: Outstanding Debts* (Cambridge University Press 2016) 159–173

Bell C, Campbell C and Aoláin F, 'Justice Discourses in Transition' (2004) 13 Social and Legal Studies 3, 305

Bohoslavsky J, 'Corporate Responsibility for Complicity: International and Local Perspectives' in H Verbitsky and J Bohoslavsky (eds), *The Economic Accomplices to the Argentine Dictatorship: Outstanding Debts* (Cambridge University Press 2016) 130–142

Bohoslavsky J, 'Tracking Down the Missing Financial Link in Transitional Justice' (2012) 1 International Human Rights Law Review 54

Bohoslavsky J and Opgenhaffen V, 'The Past and Present of Corporate Complicity: Financing the Argentinean Dictatorship' (2010) 23 Harvard Human Rights Journal 157

Brennan J (ed), *Peronism and Argentina* (Rowman & Littlefield 1998)

Carranza R, 'Plunder and Pain: Should Transitional Justice Engage with Corruption and Economic Crimes?' (2008) 2 The International Journal of Transitional Justice 3, 310–330

CELS, FLASCO, and Ministry of Justice and Human Rights, 'Responsabilidad empresarial en delitos de lesa humanidad: Represión a trabajadores durante el terrorismo de Estado' (Business responsibility in crimes against humanity: The repression of workers during state terrorism) (December 2015) <https://www.cels.org.ar/web/2015/12/nuevo-informe-responsabilidad-empresarial-en-crimenes-de-lesa-humanidad-en-la-argentina/> accessed 5 March 2022

CELS, *La lucha por el derecho: Litigio estratégico y derechos humanos (Strategic Litigation and Human Rights: The Struggle for Law)* (Siglo Editores 2008)

Chillier G, 'Prosecuting Corporate Complicity in Argentina's Dictatorship' (Open Democracy, 19 December 2014) <https://www.opendemocracy.net/en/openglobalrights-openpage-blog/prosecuting-corporate-complicity-in-argentinas-dictatorship/> accessed 19 February 2022

Consolidated Final Report, Liberia Truth and Reconciliation Commission (2009)

Cooney P, 'The Dictatorship of the 70s, the IMF and the Shift to Neoliberalism' (2007) 11 Revista de Economia Contemporanea 1, 7

Crenzel E, 'Introduction: Present Pasts: Memory(ies) of State Terrorism in the Southern Cone of Latin America' in F Lessa and V Druliolle (eds), *The Memory of State Terrorism in the Southern Cone* (Palgrave Macmillan 2011) 1–13

Crocker D, 'Transitional Justice and International Civil Society: Toward a Normative Framework' (1998) 5 Constellations 492

De Haan W, 'To Know or Not to Know: Silent Complicity in Crimes against Humanity in Argentina (1976–1983)' (2020) 62 Business History 1279

Dickinson L (ed), *International Law and Society: Empirical Approaches to Human Rights* (1st edn, Routledge 2017)

Dykmann K, 'Impunity and the Right to Truth in the Inter-American System of Human Rights' (2007) 7 Iberoamericana 26, 45–66

Engstrom P and Pereira P, 'From Amnesty to Accountability' in F Lessa and LA Payne (eds), *Amnesty in the Age of Human Rights Accountability* (Cambridge University Press 2012) 97–122

Engstrom P, 'A Special Relationship Gone Normal: Argentina and the Inter-American Human Rights System, 1979–2013' (2013) Pensamiento Propio 38, 28

Falconi RG, 'The Codification of Crimes against Humanity in the Domestic Legislation of Latin American States Latin American and International Criminal Law: The Codification of International Crimes in Latin America' (2010) 10 International Criminal Law Review 453

Farah Y, 'Toward a Multi-directional Approach to Corporate Accountability' in S Michalowski (ed), *Corporate Accountability in the Context of Transitional Justice* (Routledge 2013) 27–51

Ferguson S, 'The Unending War: Argentina's Quest for Justice' (Boston Review, 1 May 2008) <https://bostonreview.net/articles/ferguson-the-unending-war-argentina/> accessed 18 February 2022

Finnemore M and Sikkink K, 'International Norm Dynamics and Political Change' (1998) 52 International Organization 887

Final Report of the Truth, Justice and Reconciliation Commission of Kenya (2013)

Garrison C and Misculin N, 'Ex-Ford Argentina Executives Convicted in Torture Case; Victims May Sue in U.S.' (Reuters, 11 December 2018) <www.reuters.com/article/us-argentina-rights-ford-motor/ex-ford-argentina-executivesconvicted-in-torture-case-victims-may-sue-in-u-s-idUSKBN1OA25H> accessed 19 February 2022

Grosescu R, 'Transnational Advocacy Networks and Corporate Accountability for Gross Human Rights Violations in Argentina and Colombia' (2019) 33 Global Society 400

Franzki H, *Criminal Trials, Economic Dimensions of State Crime, and the Politics of Time in International Criminal Law* (PhD Thesis 2018)

Human Rights Watch, *Argentina: Reluctant Partner* (Vol 13.5, 2001) <https://www.hrw.org/reports//pdfs/a/argentna/argen1201.pdf> accessed 18 February 2022

Inter-American Commission on Human Rights Country Report – Argentina (1979) <http://www.cidh.org/countryrep/argentina80eng/introduction.htm> accessed 19 May 2021

James D, *Resistance, and Integration: Peronism and the Argentine Working Class, 1946–1976* (Cambridge University Press 1988)

Jeßberger F, 'On the Origins of Individual Criminal Responsibility Under International Law for Business Activity: IG Farben on Trial' (2010) 8 Journal of International Criminal Justice 3, 783–802

Kritz N, *Transitional Justice: How Emerging Democracies Reckon with Former Regimes* (United States Institute of Peace Press 1995)

Langer M, 'The Diplomacy of Universal Jurisdiction: The Political Branches and the Transnational Prosecution of International Crimes' (2011) 105 American Journal of International Law 1, 1–49

Larraquy M, *Primavera Sangrienta: Argentina 1970-1973 un País a Punto de Explotar, Guerrilla, Presos Políticos y Represión illegal* (Sudamericana 2017)

Lessa F, *Memory and Transitional Justice in Argentina and Uruguay* (Palgrave Macmillan 2013)

Lessa F, Payne L and Pereira G, 'Overcoming Barriers to Justice in the Age of Human Rights Accountability' (2015) 37 Human Rights Quarterly 728

Levit JK, 'The Constitutionalization of Human Rights in Argentina: Problem or Promise' (1998) 37 Columbia Journal of Transnational Law 281

Levitsky S, 'Institutionalization and Peronism: The Concept, the Case and the Case for Unpacking the Concept' (1998) 4 Party Politics 1, 77–92

Lutz E and Sikkink K, 'The Justice Cascade: The Evolution and Impact of Foreign Human Rights Trials in Latin America International Human Rights Law in Practice' (2001) 2 Chicago Journal of International Law 1

Mallinder L, 'The Ongoing Quest for Truth and Justice: Enacting and Annulling Argentina's Amnesty Laws', Working Paper No. 5 From Beyond Legalism: Amnesties, Transition and Conflict Transformation (Queen's University Belfast 2009)

Martin L, 'On Innocent Victims and Demons in Argentina (1983–1985)' (2012) 3 African Yearbook of Rhetoric 2, 65–75

Martín LG, *Transitional Justice, Corporate Accountability and Socio-Economic Rights: Lessons from Argentina* (Routledge 2019)

McSherry P, 'Preserving Hegemony: National Security Doctrine in the Post-Cold War Era' (2000) 34 NACLA Report on the Americas 3, 26–34

Medellin-Urquiaga X, 'The Normative Impact of the Inter-American Court of Human Rights on Latin-American National Prosecution of Mass Atrocities' (2013) 46 Israel Law Review 405

Mendez JE, 'Accountability for Past Abuses' (1997) 19 Human Rights Quarterly 255

Michel V and Sikkink K, 'Human Rights Prosecutions and the Participation Rights of Victims in Latin America' (2013) 47 Law & Society Review 873

Nelson CM, 'An Opportunity for Constitutional Reform in Argentina: Re-Election 1995' (1993) The University of Miami Inter-American Law Review 283–317

Nelson HA, *Selling Souls: The Economic Supporters of the "Dirty War"* (Dissertation, University of North Carolina at Charlotte 2016)

Nesiah V, 'The Trials of History: Losing Justice in the Monstrous and the Banal' in R Buchanan and P Zumbansen (eds), *Law in Transition: Human Rights, Development and Transitional Justice* (1st edn, Bloomsbury 2014) 289–308

Neumann G, 'Import, Export and Regional Consent in the Inter-American Court of Human Rights' (2008) 19 European Journal of International Law 101

Orenthlicher DF, '"Settling Accounts" Revisited: Reconciling Global Norms with Local Agency' (2007) 1 The International Journal of Transitional Justice 1, 10–22

Payne L and Pereira G, 'Accountability for Corporate Complicity in Human Rights Violations: Argentina's Transitional Justice Innovation?' in H Verbitsky and J Bohoslavsky (eds), *The Economic Accomplices to the Argentine Dictatorship: Outstanding Debts* (Cambridge University Press 2016) 29–46

Payne L, Pereira G and Bernal-Bermúdez L, *Transitional Justice and Corporate Accountability from Below: Deploying Archimedes' Lever* (Cambridge University Press 2020)

Pereira G, 'Business collaborators on Trial: Legal Obstacles to Corporate Accountability in Argentina' in JE Mata and LA Payne (eds), *Collaboration in Authoritarian and Armed Conflict Settings* (Oxford University Press 2022) 222–243

Peruzzotti E and Smulovitz C (eds), *Enforcing the Rule of Law: Social Accountability in the New Latin American Democracies* (University of Pittsburgh Press 2006)

Pion-Berlin D, 'The Fall of Military Rule in Argentina: 1976–1983' (1985) 27 Journal of Interamerican Studies and World Affairs 55–76
Pion-Berlin D, 'The National Security Doctrine, Military Threat Perception, and the "Dirty War" in Argentina' (1988) 21 Comparative Political Studies 3, 382–407
Report of the Sierra Leone Truth and Reconciliation Commission, 'Witness to Truth' (2004) <https://www.sierraleonetrc.org/index.php/view-the-final-report/table-of-contents> accessed 2 July 2023.
Recalde H, 'Suppression of Workers Rights' in Verbitsky H and Bohoslavsky J (eds), *The Economic Accomplices to the Argentine Dictatorship: Outstanding Debts* (Cambridge University Press 2016) 217–234
Roht-Arriaza N, 'Why Was the Economic Dimension Missing for So Long in Transitional Justice? An Exploratory Essay' in H Verbitsky and J Bohoslavsky (eds), *The Economic Accomplices to the Argentine Dictatorship: Outstanding Debts* (Cambridge University Press 2016) 19–28
Roht-Arriaza N and Mariezcurrena J (eds), *Transitional Justice in the Twenty-first Century: Beyond Truth versus Justice* (Cambridge University Press 2006)
Rohter L, 'Letter from South America: Now the Dirtiest of Wars Will Not Be Forgotten' (New York Times, 18 June 2003) <https://www.nytimes.com/2003/06/18/world/letter-from-south-america-now-the-dirtiest-of-wars-won-t-be-forgotten.html> accessed 31 March 2023
Ruibal A, 'Innovative Judicial Procedures and Redefinition of the Institutional Role of the Argentine Supreme Court' (2012) 47 Latin American Research Review 22
Samset I, 'Conflict of Interests or Interests in Conflict? Diamonds & War in the DRC' (2002) 29 Review of African Political Economy 93–94, 463–480
Schmidli W, 'Institutionalizing Human Rights in U.S. Foreign Policy: U.S.-Argentine Relations, 1976–1980' (2011) 35 Diplomatic History 2, 351–377
Schwöbel-Patel C, *Marketing Global Justice: The Political Economy of International Criminal Law* (Cambridge University Press 2021)
Sikkink K and Booth-Walling C, 'Argentina's Contribution to Global Trends in Transitional Justice' in N Roht-Arriaza and J Mariezcurrena (eds), *Transitional Justice in the Twenty-first Century: Beyond Truth versus Justice* (Cambridge University Press 2006) 301–324
Sikkink K, 'From Pariah State to Global Protagonist: Argentina and the Struggle for International Human Rights' (2008) 50 Latin American Politics and Society 1
Sikkink K, 'Latin America's Protagonist Role in Human Rights' (2015) 22 SUR International Journal on Human Rights 207
Sweeney J, 'The Elusive Right to Truth in Transitional Human Rights Jurisprudence' (2018) 67 International & Comparative Law Quarterly 2, 353–387
Synder J and Vinjamuri L, 'Trials and Errors: Principles and Pragmatism in Strategies of International Justice' (2003) 28 International Security 3, 5–44
Statistics from the Office of the Prosecutor for Crimes against Humanity, as published 16 December 2021, <https://www.fiscales.gob.ar/lesa-humanidad/a-45-anos-del-golpe-de-estado-suman-1025-las-personas-condenadas-por-crimenes-de-lesa-humanidad-en-254-sentencias/> accessed 31 March 2023
Teitel R, *Transitional Justice* (Oxford University Press 2000)
Taiana J, 'Foreign Powers, Economic Support, and Geopolitics' in H Verbitsky and J Bohoslavsky (eds), *The Economic Accomplices to the Argentine Dictatorship: Outstanding Debts* (Cambridge University Press 2016) 61–74

UN International Law Commission Draft Articles on Prevention and Punishment of Crimes Against Humanity (2019) <https://legal.un.org/ilc/texts/instruments/english/draft_articles/7_7_2019.pdf> accessed 2 July 2023

UN Secretary-General, The Rule of Law and Transitional Justice in Conflict and Post-Conflict Societies (UNDoc S/2004/616, 23 August 2004)

Van de Sandt J and Moor M (eds), Peace, Everyone's Business! Corporate Accountability in Transitional Justice: Lessons for Colombia (PAX 2012) available online at <https://www.dejusticia.org/wp-content/uploads/2017/05/PAX_COL_PZ_BIZ_FINAL_WEB.pdf> accessed 9 February 2022

Verbitsky H and Bohoslavsky J (eds), *The Economic Accomplices to the ArgentineDictatorship: Outstanding Debts* (Cambridge University Press 2016)

Werle G and Jeßberger F, *Principles of International Criminal Law* (4th edn, Oxford University Press 2020)

Zalaquett J, 'Victims Unsilenced: The Inter-American Human Rights System and Transitional Justice in Latin America' (2008) 2 International Journal of Transitional Justice 426, 28

Chapter 5

CCR and Alien Tort Statute

The CACI Case

Using courts as 'forums for protest'[1] is a rather established tradition for social and political movements in the United States. In the 19th century, movement leaders frequently resorted to courtrooms and litigations in order to challenge unjust policies and structural injustices.[2] Often unsuccessful in the courtroom, these litigations were used to highlight legal blind spots while creating space for rights-based discourse. This tradition of tying law with political movements was carried forward into the 20th century by political movements and lawyers alike. The lines between law and politics blurred further when resistance lawyering attained a somewhat institutional form with organizations such as the American Civil Liberties Union, Centre for Constitutional Rights, and National Lawyers Guild. These organizations held official mandates to use law and courts to build political resistance to oppressive government policies. Unsurprisingly, their ventures also meant an unending streak of courtroom losses over the years.[3]

In the last several decades, this practice of using courts as forums for protest has also been extended to matters affecting citizens of third countries. Since the conduct of the US government and non-state actors increasingly bears consequences on people beyond its borders, US courts and legal frameworks have become an avenue for international and transnational matters. As a result, this long-standing tradition of strategic political engagement with the law now frequently interacts with international human rights law and occasionally, international criminal law as well.

1 See Jules Lobel, 'Courts as Forums for Protest' (2004) UCLA Law Review 52, 477.

2 The practice of slavery was brought up to challenge before the US courts consistently through 1840s and 1850s and such actions grew in number post–civil war, leading up to *Plessy v. Ferguson* [1896] 163 US 537. See Melissa Milewski, 'From Slave to Litigant: African Americans in Court in the Postwar South, 1865–1920' (2012) 30 Law and History Review 3, 723; D. S. Farbman, 'Resistance Lawyering' (2019) California Law Review 107, 1877.

3 See Jules Lobel, *Success Without Victory: Lost legal Battles and the Long Road to Justice in America* (Vol 70, NYU Press 2006) (hereinafter Lobel, *Success Without Victory)*.

DOI: 10.4324/9781003405047-8

Concerning multinational corporations' involvement in crimes under international law, corporate executives could be potentially prosecuted in the United States under the provisions of the War Crimes Act of 1996, the Genocide Convention Implementation Act of 1987, etc. However, these provisions remain underused. Notably, the tort law framework provides an alternative remedy for violations of international law through the Alien Tort Statute (ATS),[4] which has become a potent tool to bring claims against corporations based in the United States for their misconduct in other countries.

The invocation of international criminal law within the domestic tort law framework to hold US corporations accountable for their misconduct abroad is the subject of this case study. The focus is on strategic litigation practice of the Center for Constitutional Rights based in New York (hereinafter, the Center or CCR) mainly because of their involvement with the ATS framework in general and the ongoing cases involving corporate accountability for crimes under international law.

Three distinguishing features of CCR's strategic litigation practice that make it relevant for this study are as follows: one, the synergy between their litigation and the social and the political actors outside of the courtrooms; two, their transnational practice involving not only collaborations with partners abroad but also the cases involving violations and crimes committed in other parts of the world; and three, their active reliance on international criminal law before the domestic courts. Each of the three elements will be discussed in the following sections.

Given CCR's role in reviving ATS as a remedy for human rights violations, the structure of this chapter is slightly different from the other two case studies. The chapter begins with a discussion on how CCR has been strategically using international law to achieve broader political goals and then explores CCR's role in the revival of ATS. The second section traces the trajectory of ATS through the years as relevant context to highlight the stakes involved in the case against the private military security company CACI. Finally, the third section dives deeper into the *CACI case* involving torture and mistreatment of detainees by its employees during the Iraq war. What makes the case strategic and important for this book is that while it emanated from the broader opposition to the Iraq war, it also highlights the implications of privatization of war and how private corporations are used to outsource violence and avoid accountability in an armed conflict. The case's journey over the last decade is indicative of the obstacles in using a civil law framework

4 Used to be interchangeably referred as Alien Tort Claims Act (ATCA), Alien Tort Act (ATA), or Alien Tort Statute (ATS) until the US Supreme Court in the case of *Sosa v. Alvaraiz-Machain* [2004] referred to the statute as the Alien Tort Statute (ATS) and it has held that name since then.

against mega corporations for violations amounting to crimes under international law.

I. Center for Constitutional Rights

The Center was founded in 1966 as Law Center for Constitutional Rights by lawyers Morton Stavis, Arthur Kinoy, Ben Smith, and William Kunstler to provide legal support to the ongoing civil rights movement.[5] Today, the organization classifies their work as 'social justice work' and identifies its mission as 'the creative use of law as a positive force for social change'.[6] The organization is guided by a responsibility to bring legal interventions, despite the low odds of winning, with the underlying aim of continuing to create legal precedents that contribute to progressive social and political change.[7]

The organization has evolved significantly and gone through several leadership transfers with each successive generation of lawyers becoming prominent faces of human rights litigation in the country of their time. Michael Ratner, one of the former presidents of CCR, describes the Center in the 1970s as 'a small, low-budget, ambitiously radical organization'.[8] Five decades later, only the last bit remains true. The innovative nature of their work that remains constant includes relying on underutilized rules and rulings, giving space to stories of individuals and communities impacted by injustice, and understanding the interplay between law, politics, and social change.[9] Their cases are placed in a larger movement, for instance, the anti-war movement, anti-militarism, or anti-torture.

In its early years, the identity of the founders and their associates as 'civil rights radical lawyers' informed most of the organization's work.[10] Their engagement with international law may be credited to Peter Weiss. In his autobiography, while recounting how international law arguments were

5 CCR, 'Envision the World You Want to See' <https://ccrjustice.org/home/blog/2021/03/09/envision-world-you-want-see-center-constitutional-rights-celebrates-55-years> accessed 20 March 2022.

6 Mission Statement, Center for Constitutional Rights <https://ccrjustice.org/home/how-we-work/creative-legal-strategies> accessed 14 March 2022.

7 Just after filing a suit in Washington District Court challenging George Bush's declaration of war on Iraq in 2003, a reporter asked the team 'What makes you think you have a snowball's chance in hell [of winning the lawsuit]?' to which Dellums' response was: 'Cynics don't change the world. Those of us standing here are idealistic enough and optimistic enough to believe that we have a responsibility to try to act. If we simply said we don't have any chance, then we would not act'. See Lobel, *Success Without Victory* (n 1) 30.

8 Michael Ratner, *Moving the Bar: My Life as a Radical Lawyer* (OR Books 2021) 131 (hereinafter Ratner, *Moving the Bar*).

9 Ibid.

10 Ibid 139.

added to Ratner's legal briefs as an afterthought on the insistence of Peter Weiss, Ratner says:

> Long before it was fashionable, Peter's insistence on including human rights claims in almost every case we litigated was prescient and provided the basis for many of our big cases in the decades ahead.[11]

Although CCR has a strong legacy of representing civil rights activists, anti-war demonstrators, offshore prisoners, etc., in recent years, the organization also seems to have adopted an expansionist approach in incorporating international legal norms into domestic jurisprudence.[12] CCR brought at least a dozen lawsuits seeking to expose and end rendition, illegal drone strikes, the wars in Afghanistan and Iraq, and the torture at Guantánamo and other US secret prisons. These lawsuits, relying extensively on international law claims, turned out to be impactful legal interventions. These interventions are also emblematic of their use of law as the tool to challenge unchecked political power. Therefore, before discussing their encounters with ATS and the incorporation of international criminal law, the next section discusses their choice to defend Guantánamo detainees as an illustration of their strategic engagement with law.

1. Habeas Corpus on Behalf of Guantánamo Detainees

In the wake of the 'war on terror', several consecutive executive orders were issued by the US government to bring a radical overhaul in the way international law was being practiced and respected. One such controversial order issued by President Bush stated that the president could direct the US Secretary of Defense to detain any non-citizen from anywhere in the world.[13] Once the president designated the person, on a mere suspicion that they were a terrorist, the United States could arrest, capture, or kidnap the person without complying with extradition laws or worrying about their country's borders.[14] All fair trial and due process guarantees were waived, and the detainees could be held in prison indefinitely and secret military commissions

11 Ibid 140.

12 See Beth Stephens and others (eds), *International Human Rights Litigation in US courts* (Martinus Nijhoff Publishers 2008); Lobel, *Success Without Victory* (n 1), Wolfgang Kaleck and others (eds), *International Prosecution of Human Rights Crimes* (Springer 2006) (hereinafter Kaleck and others, *International Prosecutions*).

13 Military Order of 13 November 2001, Detention, Treatment, and Trial of Certain Non-Citizens in the War Against Terrorism <https://fas.org/irp/offdocs/eo/mo-111301.htm> accessed 7 April 2021; see also Authorization for Use of Military Force Joint Resolution (Public Law 107–40, 115 Stat. 224).

14 See US Military Order of 13 November 2001.

could try detainees on charges that carried the death penalty.[15] These military orders were intended to remain in force until every effective terrorist network in the world was dismantled.[16] The rights at stake with such blanket power-ordaining executive orders were obvious and the extent of their misuse imaginable.

CCR, who had already been representing vulnerable Muslim immigrants in the United States, decided to challenge the detentions carried out under these executive orders. It was not a litigation that arose from someone reaching out for help and support, it was a political decision of the organization to challenge the misuse of executive powers that violated basic due process rights of people within and outside the nation.

Ratner recalls the team's thought process behind their decision:

> We met at CCR and made the decision that we would represent the first person detained and/or tried under this Military Order. … CCR, in more normal times, was more used to defending the rights of those we generally agreed with, those involved in making progressive social change such as civil rights workers in the South or opponents of the US-Contra war in Nicaragua in the 1980s. This was something new. We might well be involved in the representation of those involved in the planning of the 9/11 attacks. … While we understood that every defendant deserves and is entitled to vigorous defense, some of us were not sure those legal defenders should be us. … We would be setting ourselves up as targets.[17]

In addition to the personal risks, there were also practical challenges facing CCR lawyers, such as not being able to find allies, unfavourable legal precedents, and most importantly, not knowing or having access to their clients.

Two CCR lawyers, Michael Ratner and Bill Goodman, started the legal fight with a public declaration through the *New York Times*. On 30 November 2001, the paper published an article headlined 'Center Girds for Long Legal Fight on New Bush Anti-Terror Policies' with the picture of two lawyers

15 Ibid; see ME O'Connell, 'The Legal Case Against the Global War on Terror' (2004) 36 Case Western Reserve Journal of International Law 349; Rebecca Sanders, 'Human Rights Abuses at the Limits of the Law: Legal Instabilities and Vulnerabilities in the 'Global War on Terror'' (2018) 44 Review of International Studies 2.

16 See Silvia Borelli, 'Casting Light on the Legal Black Hole: International Law and Detentions Abroad in the "War on Terror"' (2005) 87 International Review of the Red Cross 857, 39–68; Daniel Moeckli, 'The Selective War on Terror: Executive Detention of Foreign Nationals and the Principle of Non-Discrimination' (2005) Brooklyn Journal of International Law 31, 495.

17 Michael Ratner, 'Litigating Guantánamo' in Kaleck and others (eds), *International Prosecutions* (n 12) 202.

declaring war against the White House to protect the Constitution.[18] As anticipated, their mailboxes were filled with hate mail soon thereafter.[19]

This was six weeks after 9/11, recalls Ratner, and the voices within the organization and the well-wishers outside unanimously wondered: 'are we going to be defending terrorists?'[20] Years later, at a Panel Discussion at Columbia Law School when an Arab woman thanked the Center for not worrying about hate, hostility, and bad precedent, Ratner explained, 'we see the law as a malleable instrument that has some flexibility. We believe it can effect social change, even with losses'.[21]

CCR found their first client in January 2002, David Hicks, an Australian detainee held incommunicado in Guantánamo, through a newspaper clipping.[22] Hicks had converted to Islam and travelled to Afghanistan. He had been captured unarmed in the back of a truck by a Northern Alliance warlord and was sold to the US Special Forces for 5,000 USD.[23] However, Hicks could not become the face of this fight, as his pictures with a gun over his shoulders from the Kosovo war had made enough rounds in the media. Instead, CCR chose to file the case on behalf of a 24-year-old British citizen Shafiq Rasul who had travelled to Pakistan to visit his relatives and was rounded up by warlords to be sold to the US forces. Hence, the name of the landmark case came to be *Rasul v. Bush*.[24]

Guantánamo Bay being a 'foreign' territory,[25] the question of jurisdiction was a complicated matter for the US courts. However, Guantánamo was a familiar terrain for CCR lawyers as the organization had already represented Haitian and Cuban refugees, and HIV positive refugees who were detained at Guantánamo in the 20th century.[26]

In this case, however, the Center ended up filing petitions seeking *habeas corpus* rights, including access to counsel, freedom from interrogations, and

18 Ratner, *Moving the Bar* (n 8) 253.
19 Ibid.
20 Ibid 254.
21 Ibid 258.
22 Michael Ratner, 'Litigating Guantánamo' in Kaleck and others (eds), *International Prosecutions* (n 12) 202.
23 Ibid.
24 Ratner, *Moving the Bar* (n 8) 264.
25 The United States occupies the naval base in Cuba called Guantanamo Bay, which comprises 45 square miles of land and water along the southeast coast of Cuba, pursuant to a 1903 Lease Agreement executed with the newly independent Republic of Cuba in the aftermath of the Spanish-American War. Lease of Lands for Coaling and Naval Stations, 23 February, 1903, U.S.-Cuba, Article III, TS No. 418; Treaty Defining Relations with Cuba, 29 May 1934, US-Cuba, Article III, 48 Stat. 1683, TS No. 866.
26 Michael Ratner, 'How We Closed the Guantánamo HIV Camp: The Intersection of Politics and Litigation Practitioners' (1998) 11 Harvard Human Rights Journal 187.

access to a court of tribunal.[27] The petitions on behalf of Hicks, Rasul, and 13 others reached the Supreme Court in 2004 after the lower courts dismissed the case for lack of jurisdiction. The argument on behalf of the petitioners was that they were not nationals of countries at war with the United States, and they were denying that they engaged in or plotted acts of aggression against the United States; they had never been afforded access to any tribunal, much less charged with and convicted of wrongdoing; and for more than two years they had been imprisoned in territory over which the United States exercises exclusive jurisdiction and control.[28]

In June 2004, the Supreme Court found that the US courts had jurisdiction over Guantánamo Bay detainees. The Supreme Court primarily relied on an expanded notion of territorial jurisdiction for the common law writ of *habeas corpus* to include the offshore prison over which the United States had exclusive jurisdiction.[29] Therefore, the courts in the United States could now entertain matters on legality of the detention of non-citizen detainees.

In addition to the *habeas corpus* petitions, the Center had put in a sustained advocacy effort over months to bring crucial publicity to the conditions of Guantánamo prison.[30] The court victory, along with the increasing public pressure over the years brought Guantánamo and its illegality to light. These proceedings fuelled further actions challenging the misuse of executive power by the US administration and brought law to a law-free zone. This led to further mobilization within the legal community, which meant that each of the Guantánamo detainees got competent representations by US lawyers before the Courts.[31] The case was reported as the most important civil rights case in 50 years.[32]

Legal interventions such as these are driven with the purpose to engage with the democratic potential of law where judicial relief is not an all-encompassing goal in itself, and neither is any particular piece of litigation brought

27 The claim was initially prepared under ATS as well but later removed on the suggestion of Prof. Harold Koh in the fear of jeopardizing future human rights claims under it. Ratner, *Moving the Bar* (n 8) 268. However, the Supreme Court while upholding the jurisdiction of US courts over Guantanamo detainees also relied on ATS in addition to common law history and scope of habeas corpus petitions. *Rasul v. Bush* [2004]. Also see, Juliet Stumpf, 'Citizens of an Enemy Land: Enemy Combatants, Aliens, and the Constitutional Rights of the Pseudo-Citizen' (2004) 38 UC Davis Law Review 79.

28 *Rasul v. Bush* [2004] 542 USC 466, 476.

29 Ibid 482.

30 Michael Ratner, Ellen Ray, and Anthony Lewis, *Guantanamo: What the World Should Know* (Chelsea Green Publishing 2004); Gillian Slovo's documentary, 'Guantanamo: Honor Bound to Defend Freedom'.

31 See David Cole, 'Michael Ratner's Army' *NY Books* (New York, 15 May 2016). <https://www.nybooks.com/daily/2016/05/15/michael-ratner-army-fight-against-Guantánamo/> accessed 7 April 2021.

32 Ratner, Moving the Bar (n 8).

with the intention of a clear and conclusive political outcome. It is the synergy of the legal and political in the interventions which makes this litigation strategic in the longer run.

Another strategic legal intervention that can be credited to CCR is the revival of ATS as a remedy for human rights violations. The possibility to use domestic tort framework to claim relief for violations of international law comes from the Judiciary Act of 1789. The civil remedy witnessed a revival in 1980 after having been ignored for almost 200 years with the *Filártiga* case.[33] The following section discusses how the case was developed by CCR and the political context which led to the revival of ATS.

2. *Filártiga and Revival of ATS*

In 1979, Dr. Joel Filártiga and Dolly Filártiga were put in touch with CCR by their immigration lawyer to help them catch hold of the Paraguayan police officer who had tortured Dolly's brother Joelito Filártiga and then fled to the United States, pending criminal proceedings in his home country. CCR, who had already discovered ATS during the Vietnam War,[34] thought the civil remedy was 'tailor-made' for *Filártiga*. They filed a case in the Eastern District of New York, two days before the accused police officer Pena Duarte was about to be deported back to Paraguay.[35]

Three years before, Joelito had been abducted, tortured, and killed in Asuncion as a reprisal for his father Joel's outspoken criticism and opposition to the then president, General Alfredo Stroessner.[36] In the criminal proceedings in Paraguay, Pena Duarte argued the defence of 'crime of passion' and hoped to avoid jail. However, soon after he fled to the United States with his accomplice.[37] He ended up overstaying the visa and was later picked up by the immigration officers to be deported – creating conditions that gave rise to a very long and explicit engagement of US courts with international law.

33 See Kenneth C. Randall, 'Federal Jurisdiction over International Law Claims: Inquiries into the Alien Tort Statute' (1986) 18 NYU Journal of International Law and Politics15–16 (noting that the ATS was cited only 21 times from its inception to when *Filártiga* was decided).

34 During the Vietnam War, attorneys at CCR had researched the possibility of using the ATS to sue US officials on behalf of a young victim of a massacre in Vietnam, a case that never materialized. CCR also cited, but did not pursue, the statute as a basis for jurisdiction in a case challenging the 'baby lift' that evacuated thousands of Vietnamese children to the United States for adoption in the last days of that war in *Nguyen Da Yen v. Kissinger*, [2975] 9th Cir., 528 F.2d 1194, 1201–02. See Beth Stephens and others (eds), *International Human Rights Litigation* (n 12) 8.

35 Peter Weiss, 'ATS Lives: Al Shimari Survives Kiobel' (2015) 19 UCLA Journal of International Law and Foreign Affairs 19, 20.

36 *Dolly and Joel Filártiga v. Americo Norberto Pena-Irala* [1980] 630 F.2d 876 (2nd Circuit) (hereinafter *Filártiga*).

37 Ibid.

The Second Circuit Court of Appeals, surprisingly, held that an alien temporarily residing in the United States could be sued for an act of torture resulting in death, committed in a foreign country against another foreigner (an alien).[38] The Court held that the ATS reference to 'law of nations' implied evolving rules of international law and not just the rules at the time the statute was drafted.[39] As for the nature of the prohibition on torture, both the scholars' and the US government's *amicus curiae* briefs agreed on the binding nature of the norm on the prohibition of torture.[40] The Carter administration strongly supported the view that governments can be held liable under international law for their mistreatment of their own citizens and that accountability for such abuses in US courts is desirable.[41]

Litigation seeking accountability of a foreign officer for the crime of torture led to a 10 million USD award in damages and, most importantly, triggered a new movement of transnational justice and accountability in the United States. The core holding of *Filártiga* has been followed by courts around the country: an alien may sue for violations of 'universal, definable and obligatory' international law norms.[42]

To put things in context, the timing and the facts of *Filártiga* made it a strategic legal intervention. It was filed in the time of an expanding human rights movement driven by networks of non-governmental organizations.[43] The US government had been insistent on its human rights project with the Congress linking foreign aid to the human rights records of would-be recipients. In the early years of his term, President Carter was making human rights issues frontpage news with his protests against the treatment of Soviet dissidents.[44]

38 Ibid.

39 Ibid; WJ Aceves, 'Filártiga v. Pena-Irala: The Birth of Transnational Litigation' in *The Anatomy of Torture: A Documentary History of Filartiga v. Pena-Irala*' (Brill Nijhoff 2007) 17–76; Karen McFarlane, 'Torture as a Violation of the Law of Nations: Interpreting the Alien Tort Statute: Filartiga v. Pena-Irala' (1981) Brooklyn Journal of International Law 7, 413.

40 'Memorandum of the United States Submitted to the Court of Appeals for the Second Circuit, *Filartiga*', reprinted in (1988) 12 Hastings International & Comparative Law Review 34, 35 (hereinafter US Filartiga Brief).

41 Ibid 36.

42 The standard was first elaborated in *Forti v. Suarez-Mason* [1987] 672 E Supp. 1531, 1540 (N.D. Cal.); For cases following *Filartiga* approach, see *Wiwa v. Royal Dutch Petroleum Co.* [2000] 226 F.3d 88 (2nd Circuit); *Beanal v. Freeport-McMoran Inc.* [1999] 197 F.3d 161 (5th Circuit); *Martinez v. City of Los Angeles* [1998] 141 F.3d 1373, 1383–84 (9th Circuit).

43 Kenneth Cmiel, 'The Emergence of Human Rights Politics in the United States' (1999) 86 The Journal of American History 1231 (noting that by the end of the 1970s, there were over 200 human rights organizations in the United States).

44 Irving Kaufman, 'A Legal Remedy for International Torture' (NYT Magazine, 9 November 1980).

Internationally, during the eight months when the *Filártiga* appeal was pending, the Shah of Iran was ousted and found refuge in the United States. This led to an outcry over United States becoming a safe haven for perpetrators of human rights abuses, arguably, influencing the court's deliberations over the matter.[45]

Contrary to the clarity reflected in the *amicus* brief supporting Filártigas' view on the matter, there were substantial debates on concerns such as the US courts and government becoming 'self-appointed policemen for the world' and potentially creating 'tensions in foreign relations'.[46] (The latter concerns overpower judicial discretion and the stance of the administration in 2013, leading to an increasingly narrow scope of the remedy.) In the end, however, the government brief made critical arguments: one, that the ATS incorporates an evolving body of international law;[47] two, that there is a consensus in the international community that the right of judicial redressal is protected and there is little danger that judicial enforcement will impair the government's foreign policy efforts. Furthermore, it was contended that a refusal to recognize a private cause of action in these circumstances might seriously damage the credibility of the nation's commitment to the protection of human rights.[48] Three, the brief affirmed that international law afforded individual rights that can be directly enforced in domestic courts.[49] Plaintiffs continue to make the same arguments to date, albeit in different political circumstances.

When viewed against the backdrop of a favourable political atmosphere, extensive media coverage, and supporting executive briefs, CCR's *Filártiga* petition seemed set up for success. However, one of the law clerks who drafted the opinion for Judge Kaufman later confessed that the judge was 'bending over backwards not to open any floodgates', and 'rhetoric notwithstanding,

45 Harold Hongju Koh, 'Filartiga v. Pena-Irala: Judicial Internalization into Domestic Law of the Customary International Law Norm Against Torture' (2007) International Law Stories 45, 50–51 (quoting a memorandum written by former clerk to Judge Irving R. Kaufman: 'The Iran hostage crisis began in the middle of all this, and the nation felt itself under siege more than it would again for another 22 years. Everyone knew that if the panel didn't take the easy way out ... we'd be sailing into uncharted waters ... No one seemed to doubt that a finding of jurisdiction comported with our national ideals; the honest question we all had was whether it comported with our national interests as well'.)

46 Roberts B. Owen (Legal Adviser, US Department of State), 'Address at the Annual Dinner of the American Branch of the International Law Association' (1980) as quoted in William J. Aceves, *The Anatomy of Torture: A Documentary History of Filartiga v. Pena Irala* (Brill 2007) 481–82.

47 US Filartiga Brief (n 40) 4–5.

48 Ibid 22–23.

49 Ibid 20–21.

to decide as little as possible'.[50] Ultimately, the Court decided as little as possible, but still ended up opening the floodgates for human rights litigation.

At the time, the case was hailed as an 'enormous victory'.[51] In hindsight, several factors highlight the strategic nature of the *Filártiga* case: the innovative nature of invoking a forgotten underused provision; the choice of perpetrator who, although a foreign state actor, had fled their home country, thereby minimizing foreign policy concerns; the case being built on a transnational collaboration which involved directly affected victims; and the invoking the provision at a favourable political timing.

Decades later, ATS not only continues to be frequently used to litigate human rights violations taking place in other countries, but it is also proffered as an alternative to criminal prosecutions for crimes under international law.[52] Its language of 'law of nations' accommodates a range of international human rights law violations, including those amounting to crimes under international law.[53]

However, in the last decade, the scope of this remedy has been tapered by judicial interpretation. The following section of the chapter discusses the origin and the increasingly narrowing scope of ATS as a remedy, particularly with regard to corporate conduct, as necessary context to the importance of the ongoing cases against private military contractors such as CACI, the main case discussed in greater detail in subsequent sections.

II. ATS and Corporate Accountability: A Tale of Narrowing Landscape

ATS is a jurisdictional provision that emanates from a single sentence in the US Judiciary Act of 1789:

50 Beth Stephens, 'Curious History of the Alien Tort Statute' (2014) 89 Notre Dame Law Review 1467, 1470 (hereinafter, Stephens, 'Curious History').

51 See Dolly Filartiga, 'Foreword' to Stephens and others (eds), *International Human Rights Litigation*, (n 12) (describing her family's lawsuit against the man who tortured her brother to death as 'an enormous victory' for human rights and the pursuit of justice).

52 Katherine Gallagher, 'Alternatives to Prosecutions: Accountability through Civil Litigation for Human Rights Violations by Private Military Contractors' in N. Jørgensen (ed), *The International Criminal Responsibility of War's Funders and Profiteers* (Cambridge University Press 2020) 396–422 (hereinafter Gallagher, 'Alternatives to Prosecution'); Ernest A Young, 'Universal Jurisdiction, the Alien Tort Statute, and Transnational Public-Law Litigation after Kiobel' (2014) 64 Duke Law Journal 1023.

53 Most international human rights cases in US courts rely upon one of four federal statutes: the Alien Tort Statute, 28 USC Section 1350; the Torture Victim Protection Act, 28 USC Section 1350; the 'state sponsors of terrorism' exception to the Foreign Sovereign Immunities Act, 28 USC Section 1605(a)(7); or the Anti-Terrorism Act, 18 USC Sections 2333–2338.

> The district courts shall have original jurisdiction of any civil action by an alien for a tort only, committed in violation of the law of nations or a treaty of the United States.[54]

The clause lacks a definitive legislative history[55] which could also explain the rather haphazard application of the remedy by the US courts over the past decades. But there are various historical accounts speculating on the intent and purpose of the remedy.[56] Nearly every scholarly work on ATS devotes a section to its origins and development through the decades, seemingly in search of guidance for its scope, applicability, and consequent repercussions which are still ambiguous.

The remedy was possibly conceived to grant the newly created federal government power over foreign affairs,[57] or as a national security measure to appease European nations,[58] or to encourage foreign merchants to conduct business in the new nation by offering them a form of relief in the event of injury or other tortious conduct.[59] Some accounts take a moralistic stance stressing that perhaps the drafters were motivated by the conviction that upholding the law of nations was an obligation of nationhood.[60]

54 28 USC Section 1350.

55 William S Dodge, 'Corporate Liability Under the US Alien Tort Statute: A Comment on Jesner v. Arab Bank' (2019) 4 Business and Human Rights Journal 131; See *Sosa v. Alvarez-Machain* [2004] 542 US 692, 718–19 ([D]espite considerable scholarly attention, it is fair to say that a consensus understanding of what Congress intended [in passing the ATS] has proven elusive.) (hereinafter *Sosa*)

56 One plausible version of the original intent and purpose of the remedy goes like this: Oliver Ellsworth drafted much of the Judiciary Act and the ATS clause based on an earlier law enacted by the Connecticut Congress, providing criminal sanctions for violation of the law of nations. Ellsworth, who had been a member of the Connecticut Congress when the law was being drafted, intended ATS to be a work of political compromise. To prevent British creditors to enforce the 1783 Treaty of Paris in Federal Courts under which Americans owed them money, the Act allowed district courts' original jurisdiction over claims of violation of the law of nations. The state courts had already turned hostile to British claims and denied them a remedy. So that they could not claim breach of contracts in federal courts, which were more likely to be sympathetic to British claims, Ellsworth limited the jurisdiction of ATS to torts only. William Casto, 'SOSA *v.* Alvarez-Machain and the End of History Remarks' (2011) 43 Georgetown Journal of International Law 1001, 1002

57 William S. Dodge, 'The Historical Origins of the Alien Tort Statute: A Response to the "Originalists"' (1996) 19 Hastings International & Comparative Law Review 221, 222; Stephens, 'Curious History' (n 50).

58 Thomas H Lee, 'The Three Lives of the Alien Tort Statute: The Evolving Role of the Judiciary in US Foreign Relations' (2013) 89 Notre Dame Law Review 1645, 1650.

59 Ibid; See Dina H Arouri, 'Will Capitalism Kill Compassion - An Analysis of the Future of Corporate Liability under the Alien Tort Statute Note' (2019) 71 Florida Law Review Forum 1.

60 Anne-Marie Burley, 'The Alien Tort Statute and the Judiciary Act of 1789: A Badge of Honor' (1989) 83 American Journal of International Law 461, 487 (hereinafter Burley,

Regardless, it is hard to argue that the drafters would have even dreamt of the form it ended up taking at the dawn of this century. In allowing US federal courts jurisdiction over any civil action by and against an 'alien' for violation of customary international law,[61] ATS made it possible to litigate human rights violations without a clear link or involvement of the state. Subject to personal jurisdiction over the defendant, ATS allowed a remedy for violation of specific, universal, and obligatory norms of international law.[62]

The attention that ATS has received within the courts, by lawyers, human rights organizations, and the scholarship is discernible in many ways. The birth – or resurgence – of ATS was an outcome of the search by civil society for a forum to enforce human rights standards.[63] Immediately thereafter, scholars hailed ATS decisions as illustrious as another '*Brown v. Board of Education*' that 'inaugurated the era of transnational public law litigation in which we now live'.[64] Ernest Young called it a form of 'civil-side universal jurisdiction'.[65] The human rights community started wearing it as a badge of honour.[66] It has been a subject of intense discussion in academia ever since the first decision and each of the four Supreme Court decisions on this provision has been dissected and analysed in comprehensive detail.[67]

At its core, in Beth Stephens' apt description, the discussions on ATS in fact reflect its role in a long-standing struggle for control over the interpretation and enforcement of international law.[68] It is precisely for this reason that the role of the CCR in the enforcement of international criminal law through ATS is being discussed in this book.

'ATS: A Badge of Honor').

61 See Katherine Gallagher, 'Civil Litigation and Transnational Business: An Alien Tort Statute Primer' (2010) 8 Journal of International Criminal Justice 745.

62 See *Sosa* (n 55) 732.

63 See Sarah H Cleveland, 'The Alien Tort Statute, Civil Society, and Corporate Responsibility Symposium 2004: Citizen Participation in the Global Trading System: Panel II: The Alien Tort Claims Act' (2003) 56 Rutgers Law Review 971.

64 Harold Hongju Koh, 'Transnational Public Law Litigation' (1991) 100 Yale Law Journal 2347, 2366.

65 Ernest A Young, 'Universal Jurisdiction, the Alien Tort Statute, and Transnational Public-Law Litigation after Kiobel' (2014) 64 Duke Law Journal 1023.

66 Burley, 'ATS: A Badge of Honor' (n 60) (As controversy builds over the correct interpretation of the ATCA, the modest impact of the statute is often lost in the hyperbole. Over the life of the statute, approximately 120 cases have raised ATCA claims: of 20 of those, all but 2 were unsuccessful predated *Filartiga*. Most of the *post-Filartiga* cases have been dismissed, most often for failure to allege a violation of international recognized human rights, for *forum non conveniens*, or because of the immunity of the defendant. Despite this modest success, controversy over this line of litigation has exploded in the past few years.)

67 *Sosa* (n 55); *Kiobel v. Royal Dutch Petroleum Co.* [2013] 569 US 108 (hereinafter *Kiobel*); *Jesner v. Arab Bank, PLC* [2018] 138 S. Ct. 1386 (hereinafter *Jesner*); Nestlé & Cargill *v.* Doe [2021] 141 S. Ct. 1931 (hereinafter *Nestlé*)

68 Stephens, 'Curious History' (n 50) 1467.

1. Doe v. Unocal

Until the mid-1990s, the US courts continued to apply the *Filártiga* doctrine, with little dissent, and the executive kept a hands-off position throughout these years. The expansionist rhetoric of ATS facilitated the civil society to make bold choices in terms of the actors they were suing. Lawsuits began to be filed against politically and economically powerful defendants: multinational corporations, foreign government officials, and the US government itself. Unsurprisingly, these choices came at the price of backlash.

After over two decades of the resurgence of ATS, the first case was brought against a corporate defendant – *Doe v. Unocal.* The remarkable coincidence which conceived this consequential litigation is also an illustration of how transnational mobilization can influence the implementation of international human rights law. *Doe v. Unocal* was initiated as a result of conversations between a US law student and the general secretary of the Federation of Trade Unions of Burma. [69]

The case involved the construction of a natural gas pipeline in Burma by California-based energy giant Unocal. It was charged for its alleged complicity in abuses committed by the Burmese military.[70] The plaintiffs, villagers from the Tenasserim region of Burma (now Tanintharyi region of Myanmar), claimed that Unocal was complicit in the intimidation and relocation of villages, enslavement, forced labour, rape, torture, and murder of the villagers. In 1996, a claim under ATS was brought before the US District Court of California against Unocal. The District Court dismissed the claim and found there was no evidence to suggest that Unocal could be held accountable for the actions of the Burmese military. However, in appeal, the Ninth Circuit Court disagreed with the District Court and held that certain crimes such as rape, torture, and summary execution, while ordinarily requiring state action under ATS, do not need to be committed under 'colour of law' if done so in furtherance of other more heinous crimes, such as slave trading, genocide, or war crimes.[71] *Jus cogens* crimes, the Court held, do not require state action and are so egregious that they violate the law of nations regardless of whether they are committed under 'colour of law'.[72] The Court found the 'aiding and abetting' test set by the ICTY and ICTR instructive to determine whether a private actor could be held responsible for their complicity in these crimes. Reliance was placed on ICTY's *Furundzija* decision to apply the test of 'reasonable knowledge' on the part of the defendant that their actions will

69 See Cheryl Holzmeyer, 'Human Rights in an Era of Neoliberal Globalization: The Alien Tort Claims Act and Grassroots Mobilization in Doe *v.* Unocal' (2009) 43 Law & Society Review 271.

70 *Unocal I* [1997] 963 F. Supp. 884–85.

71 *Unocal III* [2002] 395 F.3d 932 (9th Circuit), para 945–47.

72 Ibid 949.

assist the perpetrator in the commission of the crime.[73] Finally, the Court held that the plaintiffs had furnished sufficient evidence to prove that Unocal aided and abetted the forced labour practices of the Burmese military.[74]

This judgment would have set a clear precedent that even if the actors who actually perpetrated the crime were outside of the United States, US-based corporations complicit in serious violations of international law could be held accountable for their conduct.[75] Although later an *en banc* order of the Ninth Circuit Court vacated the previous ruling in favour of the plaintiffs and held that the decision could not be cited as a precedent in future cases.[76] It was only days before the case could go on trial in December 2004 when Unocal and the plaintiffs, represented by Earth Rights International, agreed on an out-of-court confidential settlement which would drop all proceedings against Unocal on the matter.[77]

Even though the case could not hold precedential value, the victims got compensation, and the knowledge that an expansive interpretation of ATS could potentially allow these claims served as a guidepost for those seeking corporate accountability for violation of international norms. In response, a 2002 column in *The Nation* noted that Wall Street was 'paying attention', 'watching and waiting to see if Third World locals screwed by transnationals can obtain justice in [US] courts far from their villages'.[78]

2. Sosa v. Alvarez-Machain

The Supreme Court decision in *Sosa*[79] is a definitive illustration of the absurdities of judicial law-making. Academic titles following the judgment predicted either an extreme sense of doom or hope, with references to ajar doors, wide floodgates, and the end of history. Rife with uncertainties, one sentence in the judgment made the corporations and human rights lawyers both believe they had won.[80]

73 Ibid 951.

74 Ibid 953.

75 See Armin Rosencranz & David Louk, 'Doe v. Unocal: Holding Corporations Liable for Human Rights Abuses on Their Watch' (2005) 8 Chap. Law Review 135.

76 Ibid 978–79.

77 Duncan Campbell, 'Energy Giant Agrees Settlement with Burmese Villagers' (The Guardian, 15 December 2004) <https://www.theguardian.com/world/2004/dec/15/burma.duncan-campbell≥ accessed 10 November 2020.

78 David Corn, 'Corporate Human Rights' (The Nation, July 15 2002) http://www.thenation.com/article/corporate-human-rights accessed 20 November 2020.

79 *Sosa* (n 55) 697.

80 Outside Counsel for Unocal said that the decision represented a 'sound rejection' of the way that human rights groups were using the ATS. On the other hand, a representative of the Center for Constitutional Rights in New York remarked 'that businesses and government's effort to eliminate the statute as a basis for relief was defeated'. Robert S. Greenberger

In *Sosa*, a Mexican doctor, Alvarez, sued a group of Mexican nationals (Sosa and others) who were hired by the US Drug Enforcement Agency (DEA) for abducting and detaining Alvarez to be extradited to the United States as he had been indicted in the United States for torture and murder of a DEA agent. In a DEA-approved action, Sosa and others 'abducted Alvarez from his house, held him overnight in a motel, and brought him by private plane to El Paso, Texas, where he was arrested by US federal officers'.[81] After Alvarez was acquitted by a US District Court in 1992, he filed a civil suit for damages against Sosa and others for arbitrary arrest and detention.

Factors such as the involvement of the US government, a split decision of the Ninth Circuit Court on whether ATS was applicable in this matter, and the generally increasing controversy over correct interpretation of ATS made it fitting for the Supreme Court to take up an ATS matter for review, for the first time.

The Supreme Court held that the remedy was originally 'available to enforce a small number of international norms that a federal court could properly recognize as within the common law enforceable without further statutory authority'.[82] This meant that claims under ATS could be brought only for violation of customary international law. The Court was quick to issue the qualifier that ATS does not confer jurisdiction on federal courts for claimed 'violations of any international norm with less definite content and acceptance among 'civilized' nations than the historical paradigms familiar when [the ATS] was enacted'.[83] Thus, ATS could only be applicable for violations of 'specific, universal, and obligatory' norms under international law.[84] The onus of the determination of norms which meet the standard of universal specificity and resemblance to 1789 version of 'law of nations' was left to the restrained 'residual common law discretion' of lower federal courts – leading scholars to comment that the door was left ajar, subject to vigilant door keeping.[85] In making this determination, the courts were supposed to give 'serious weight to the Executive Branch's view of the case's impact on foreign policy'.[86]

& Pui-Wing Tam, 'Supreme Court Limits Foreigners' Ability to Act' (Wall Street Journal, 30 June 2004); Tim Kline, 'A Door Ajar or a Floodgate: Corporate Liability after *Sosa v. Alvarez-Machain*' (2005) 94 Kentucky Law Journal 691 (hereinafter Kline, 'Door Ajar or Floodgate').

81 *Sosa* (n 55) 698.

82 Ibid 729.

83 Ibid 732.

84 Ibid 733.

85 Kline, 'Door Ajar or Floodgate' (n 80); Beth Stephens, 'Sosa v. Alvarez-Machain - The Door Is Still Ajar for Human Rights Litigation in US Courts Comment' (2004) 70 Brooklyn Law Review 533.

86 *Sosa* (n 55) 733.

Notably, the circumstances setting the stage for this decision in 2004 were drastically different from those in 1979. The 'war on terror' of the Bush administration was at its peak and the US government was no longer desperate to become the poster child for upholding human rights standards. Moreover, multinational corporations were lobbying heavily, alarmed by the increasing number of claims against them.[87]

This standard was to serve as the framework for the US courts to incorporate international legal norms into domestic law in a restrained cautious manner. The ambiguity in the decision led to contradictory judgments from different circuit courts,[88] yet signalled hope for human rights advocates.[89] The subject matter jurisdiction of ATS was rather clear on situations of egregious violations of international law, including, torture, genocide, and war crimes, while 'modern claims' such as those based on environmental harm could also be potentially brought in ATS ambit if sufficient international consensus emerged to back them.

While there was some clarity about the subject matter of claims, the question of whether they could be brought against corporations was addressed merely in a footnote.[90]

Footnote 20 of the decision stated:

> A related consideration is whether international law extends the scope of liability for a violation of a given norm to the perpetrator being sued if the defendant is a private actor such as a corporation or individual. Compare, Tel-Oren v. Libyan Arab Republic, 726 F.2d 774, 791-795 (D.C. Cir. 1984) (Edwards, J., concurring) (insufficient consensus in 1984 that torture by private actors violates international law), with Kadic v Karadzic, 70 F.3d 232, 239-241 (2d Cir. 1995) (sufficient consensus in 1995 that genocide by private actors violates international law).[91]

87 See Carolyn A. D'Amore, 'Sosa *v.* Alvarez-Machain and the Alien Tort Statute: How Wide Has the Door to Human Rights Litigation been Left Open' (2006) 39 Akron Law Review 593.

88 Compare *Enahoro v. Abubakar* [2005] 408 F.3d 877, 883–86 (7th Circuit) (holding that torture and extrajudicial killings are not actionable under the ATS) with *Aldana v. Del Monte Fresh Produce, Inc.* [2005] 416 F.3d 1242, 1250–53 (11th Circuit) (holding that torture is actionable under the ATS).

89 See Donald J. Kochan, 'The Political Economy of the Production of Customary International Law: The Role of Non-Governmental Organizations in U.S. Courts' (2004) 22 Berkeley Journal International Law 240, 250; Elizabeth F. Defeis, 'Litigating Human Rights Abuses in United States Courts: Recent Developments' (2004) 10 ILSA Journal of International & Comparative Law 319.

90 As it was not a question pertinent to the case, the US Supreme Court did not intend to lay down any rules on private actors' liability.

91 *Sosa* (n 55).

Not only the question whether corporate liability falls within the scope of ATS goes unanswered, the footnote – by making these two references – opened another relevant question, i.e. source of law: in these cases, procedural rules will be governed by domestic or international law.

Plaintiffs argue that international law comes into play only to determine the 'nature of the violation' but is not (or not exclusively) to be used as the source of law on questions concerning the secondary rules on who will be liable and under which model of liability, i.e. aiding or abetting. On the contrary, corporate defendants argue that there are no universally accepted international norms implying corporate liability by way of aiding and abetting.[92]

International law's lack of specificity in this case gives way to the risk of not having the substantial norms enforced at all. Therefore, human rights practitioners insist on a dual framework which rests substantively on international law but proceeds within the remits of US procedural law.

Nevertheless, the footnote left the question confusingly open with that passing reference. The confusion is apparent from the subsequent litigation at the Circuit Courts.[93] Soon after, in *Re South African Apartheid Litigation*, the Second Circuit Court asked 'whether customary international law recognizes corporate criminal liability'.[94]

Therefore, by 2004, the US Courts had come to the decision that violations of customary international law can be brought under ATS. Whether the scope of liability extends to private actors and which law would be the determinant source to decide this question remained up for debate.

3. Kiobel v. Royal Dutch Petroleum Co.

In an already full bag of questions puzzling ATS on subject matter, cause of action, choice of law, and scope of liability, with *Kiobel*,[95] in 2013, the presumption against extraterritoriality came as a surprising new stumbling block.[96] The presumption against extraterritoriality implies that any 'legislation of Congress, unless a contrary intent appears, is meant to apply only within the territorial jurisdiction of the United States'.[97]

92 Katherine Gallagher, 'Civil Litigation and Transnational Business: An Alien Tort Statute Primer' (2010) 8 Journal of International Criminal Justice 745.

93 For a comparative analysis of Circuit Courts and their ATS analysis post-SOSA, see Kline 'Door Ajar or Floodgate) (n 80).

94 *In re South African Apartheid Litigation* [2015] (2nd Circuit).

95 *Kiobel* (n 67).

96 Eugene Kontorovich, 'Kiobel Surprise: Unexpected by scholars but consistent with international trends' (2013) Notre Dame Law Review 89, 1671 (hereinafter Kontrovich, 'Kiobel Surprise').

97 *Morrison v. Nationall Austl. Bank Ltd.* [2010] 561 US 247, 255.

Kiobel used the presumption against extraterritoriality as an attempt to end the cosmopolitan life of ATS.[98] After considering the text of the law, the Court held in *Kiobel* that nothing in the statutory language provided a clear indication that the statute was intended to have an extraterritorial reach.[99] The Supreme Court held that the presumption of extraterritoriality also applies to claims brought for violations of customary international law that occurred abroad. However, plaintiffs could potentially overcome the presumption by showing that a claim '*touches and concerns*' the territory of the United States with sufficient force; although a mere business presence in the United States would not be sufficient to overcome the presumption.[100]

A group of Nigerian nationals residing in the United States had brought a suit against Nigerian, British, and Dutch oil companies. They alleged that the named corporations had abetted and aided the Nigerian military and police in committing widespread, violent atrocities against the people of the Niger Delta. The Second Circuit dismissed the suit on the ground of absence of any international norm supporting corporate liability. The Court found that executives, individual managers, and individuals within the corporation might be sued, but not the corporation itself.[101]

Although the matter had reached the US Supreme Court on the question of corporates as a class of defendants, the SC ordered the restoring of the case for a second round of arguments on a different question, i.e. extraterritoriality and ended-up ruling only on this question. This was not the first time when the Supreme Court passed up the opportunity to decide on corporate liability under ATS.[102]

98 See Thomas H. Lee, The Three Lives of the Alien Tort Statute: The Evolving Role of the Judiciary in U.S. Foreign Relations (2013) 89 Notre Dame Law Review 1645.

99 Ibid 1669.

100 *Kiobel* (n 67) 114.

101 *Kiobel* [2010] 621 F.3d 111 (2d Circuit) 149. The holding was exceptional and 'odd' given the Court had already allowed an ATS claim against Pharma-giant Pfizer for killing 11 Nigerian children in an illegal human trial without informed consent. (*Rabi Abdullahi v. Pfizer Inc.* [2003] 77 Fed.Appx. 48, 53 (2nd Circuit)) Since *Unocal* until 2012, approximately 60 cases had been filed claiming ATS jurisdiction involving corporations. Before the Supreme Court granted a petition for certiorari in *Kiobel*, the Seventh, Ninth, Eleventh, and D.C. Circuits had rejected this reasoning holding that ATS does permit suits against corporate defendants. Nevertheless, it was the split amongst the Circuits that led the Supreme Court to review Kiobel. Ralph Steinhardt, 'Kiobel and the Multiple Futures of Corporate Liability for Human Rights Violations Keynote Address: Symposium: Extraterritorial Post-Kiobel: International and Comparative Legal Perspectives', (2013) 28 Maryland Journal of International Law 1, 6 (hereinafter Steinhardt, 'Kiobel and Multiple Futures').

102 After the court in *Talisman* dismissed the case against a Canadian oil company alleged to have aided and abetted war crimes in Sudan, the plaintiffs filed a petition for certiorari. See Petition for Writ of Certiorari at 10, *Presbyterian Church of Sudan v. Talisman Energy Inc.* [2010] WL 1602093 (No. 09-1262). Defendant Talisman filed a cross-petition in which it presented the Court with the question of whether corporations can be held liable under the

In *Kiobel*, the Supreme Court affirmed the Second Circuit Court's dismissal, however, on the ground that the matter did not 'touch and concern' the United States with sufficient force to displace the presumption against extraterritorial application[103] and that ATS did not rebut the presumption against extraterritoriality.[104]

Although the judgment did not offer much guidance on the contours of this 'touch and concern' test, it explained that a mere corporate presence was not enough.[105] The Court stated that 'corporations are often present in many countries, and it could reach too far to say that mere corporate presence suffices'.[106] The policy reasons offered behind the decision to uphold the extraterritoriality presumption were two-fold: one, to protect against unintended clashes between (domestic) laws and those of other nations, which could result in international discord; and two, to avoid unwarranted judicial interference in the conduct of foreign policy.[107]

Therefore, the so-called foreign-cubed cases, where claims are brought by non-citizens against non-citizens based solely on extraterritorial conduct, were rendered outside the purview of ATS. Even though, *Kiobel* did not overrule *Filártiga* or the subsequent developments, it would be incorrect to say that ATS, in this form, could function as the civil side of universal jurisdiction – or if it functioned as such for natural persons (given the previous line of cases had not been overruled), it would at least not do so for corporate conduct.[108]

Arguably, the growing trend of hostility towards universal jurisdiction could have been relevant to the presumption against extraterritoriality in

ATS. See Cross-Petition of Defendant at 14, *Talisman*, 2010 U.S. S. Ct Briefs LEXIS 1830 (No. 091418). The Court denied certiorari in both cases. See *Saleh v. Titan* [2010] No. 09-1313, 131 S. Ct. 379 (addressing whether non-state actors can be held liable for war crimes under the ATS).

103 *Kiobel* (n 67).

104 Ibid 1669. Chief Justice Roberts noted that the presumption usually applies to statutes that regulate conduct as opposed to those that set norms. See Issac Ramsey, 'Hidden Renvoi: The Search for Corporate Liability in Alien Tort Statute Litigation Notes' (2019) 107 California Law Review 2071 on whether corporate liability rules are conduct regulating or norm setting and the consequences of this on policy considerations implications.

105 See Justice Kennedy's one-paragraph concurring opinion 'the presumption against extraterritorial application may require some further elaboration and explanation' *Kiobel* (n 67) 1669.

106 Ibid 1908; See A. Don, 'Clarifying Kiobel's 'Touch and Concern' Test (2017) 130 Harvard Law Review 1902, 1904 (hereinafter Don, 'Clarifying Kiobel').

107 *Kiobel* (n 67) 1664–1665. (In principle, extraterritoriality is a device to escape conflict of choice-of -law. The ATS, however, is only a jurisdictional statute. But because ATS suits can have harmful foreign policy consequences, the Court held that the presumption against extraterritoriality should similarly apply to ATS causes of action.)

108 The concurring opinions seemed to assume that corporations can be defendants in ATS lawsuits; however, the lack of mention ensured that the question remained unanswered.

Kiobel. Kontrovich argues that this presumption was more against universality than extraterritoriality. He placed *Kiobel* as a part of a global trend against universal jurisdiction by nations that had enthusiastically embraced it in the 1990s.[109] In that sense, parallels could be drawn with the cautious approach adopted by Western European states in pursuing politically inexpensive cases only against those who were present on their territory and not adopting 'pure universal jurisdiction' models.[110] Beyond the extraterritorial aspects of the remedy, its narrowing scope should also be seen in the context of 'hostility against tort law at large in the US for the last 40 years'.[111]

Since *Kiobel*, the US Supreme Court had the chance to address the specific question of corporate liability under ATS in *Jesner v. Arab Bank* (2018)[112] and in *Nestlé USA, Inc. v. Doe* (2021).[113] On both occasions, however, the Court passed the opportunity to resolve the question of whether and under what conditions corporates can be held liable under ATS. The *Jesner* case was against the Arab Bank, an entirely 'foreign' corporation in the US context, for allegedly financing terrorist organizations. The Supreme Court, in a 5:4 split ruling, held that 'foreign' corporations cannot be held liable under ATS.[114] The judgment limits the scope of the remedy by explicitly stating the boundary; however, the reasoning was not much of a departure from *Kiobel.*[115] In the *Nestlé* case, US corporations were being alleged to have aided and abetted child slavery and forced labour at cocoa farms in Ivory Coast. Although the judges recognized that corporations were not exempt from liability under ATS,[116] the Supreme Court dismissed the case, inter alia, on the grounds of presumption of extraterritoriality. The Court upheld the presumption as laid down in *Kiobel.* However, it did not rely on the 'touch and concern' test, instead it adopted a stricter requirement to rebut the presumption of extraterritoriality that the plaintiffs must allege more domestic conduct than general corporate activity.[117] The Court found that in this

109 Kontrovich, 'Kiobel Surprise' (n 67) 1671.

110 See discussion in Section I of Chapter 6.; also see Kalika Mehta, 'Other Examples of Domestic Implementation of the ICC Statute' in Chantal Meloni, Florian Jeßberger and Maria Crippa (eds.) *Domesticating International Criminal Law* (Routledge 2023).

111 Interview with Katherine Gallagher, Senior Staff Attorney, CCR (online, 18 March 2021).

112 *Jesner* (n 67).

113 *Nestlé* (n 67).

114 *Jesner* (n 67).

115 The Court found that litigation involving 'foreign corporate defendants create unique problems. And courts are not well suited to make the required policy judgments that are implicated by corporate liability in cases like this one'. Opinion of J. Kennedy, *Jesner* (n 67) 25–26.

116 See concurring judgment of Justice Gorsuch, J. and Justice Sotomayor, joined by Justice Breyer and Justice Kagan, states that she and 'four other Justices' would reject corporate immunity. *Nestlé* (n 67)148.

117 *Nestlé* (n 67) 1936.

case the conduct relevant to the allegations of slavery was not sufficiently connected to the US corporate defendants.[118]

From being a beacon of modern human rights litigation to being subjected to an increasing number of limitations, the ATS has been a story of legal possibility that mirrors the politics of its time. Metaphorically, it has been a loyal weapon in CCR's arsenal through the decades. While tracing the journey of CCR's long-standing case of corporate liability, *Al-Shimari v. CACI*, a case that precedes *Sosa* and is pending after *Nestlé,* it might be worthwhile to reflect on the relationship between law as it is and the political considerations that determine the conditions in which it is applied.

III. Challenging Privatization of War: The CACI Case

In May 2004, a classified internal investigation report written by US Army Major General Antonio Taguba landed in the hands of the media. The report listed institutional failures of the US army prison system in Iraq, including numerous instances of 'sadistic, blatant, and wanton criminal abuses' at the Abu Ghraib detention camp outside Baghdad.[119] It was filled with stunning testimonial and photographic evidence supporting the allegations of torture in US-managed detention facilities in Iraq. More importantly, it explicitly named US soldiers, military-intelligence teams, including Central Intelligence Agency (CIA), officers, linguists, and interrogation specialists from private security contractors who were involved in these violations between 2003 and 2004.[120]

News outlet CBS broke the story on their show '60 Minutes II', broadcasting disturbing pictures of US soldiers torturing and sexually humiliating Iraqi prisoners, including a picture of naked Iraqi prisoners at Abu Ghraib piled up to form a human pyramid as the US soldiers watched; and another picture

118 According to William S. Dodge, this has serious implications for cases involving extraterritorial violations and might end the *Filartiga* kind of cases. See William S. Dodge, 'The Surprisingly Broad Implications of Nestlé USA., Inc. *v.* Doe for Human Rights Litigation and Extraterritoriality' (Just Security, 18 June 2021). Concerning claims against US corporations, Desirée LeClercq argues, 'it would simply mean that plaintiffs must more specifically allege that the corporate conduct in the United States specifically aided and abetted the human rights violations abroad'. Desirée LeClercq, 'Nestlé United States, Inc. *v.* Doe. 141 S. Ct. 1931' (2021) 115 American Journal of International Law 115, 694–700.

119 Rebeca Leung, 'Abuse at Abu Ghraib' (CBS News, 5 May 2004) < https://www.cbsnews.com/news/abuse-at-abu-ghraib/> accessed 13 March 2021; Seymour M. Hersh, 'Torture at Abu Ghraib' (The New Yorker, 30 April 2004) <https://www.newyorker.com/magazine/2004/05/10/torture-at-abu-ghraib> accessed 13 March 2021.

120 Ibid.

of a hooded detainee with his outstretched hands attached to electric wires to gather intelligence information from the detainees.[121]

The Abu Ghraib detention facility was administered by the US Army in the wake of the Iraq invasion by a UNSC mandated coalition force led and composed almost entirely of troops from the United States and Great Britain in March 2003. The invasion was initially premised on the threat of and in search of weapons of mass destruction in Iraq, and the promise of liberation of the Iraqi people from Saddam Hussein's oppressive regime. The attack on Iraq led to the defeat of the Iraqi military regime and the capture and execution of Saddam Hussein setting up a provisional establishment, namely the Coalition Provisional Authority.[122]

The detention facility was previously and notoriously under the control of Saddam Hussein but was taken under control by the US Army in 2003. Upon assuming control of the facility, the US military used the prison to detain (1) common criminals, (2) security detainees accused or suspected of committing offenses against the Coalition Provisional Authority, and (3) 'high-value' detainees who might possess useful intelligence (insurgency leaders, for example), including women and juveniles.[123] The Taguba report cited gross differences between the actual number of prisoners and the number officially recorded.[124] Even of those recorded, the majority were civilians unjustifiably detained at Abu Ghraib.

The exposé posed many inescapable questions on the Iraq invasion, on the legality of the US invasion and the Coalition Provisional Authority, and on the extent of its compliance with the international norms. Notwithstanding, one significant part of the spotlight also fell on the substantial contribution made by private military contractors (PMCs) to the US war effort.

The concept of mercenaries – paid soldiers – was neither new nor exclusive to the United States.[125] The outsourcing of war to transnational corporations primarily gained prominence after the Cold War ended, when millions of former military personnel found themselves free from duty because of

121 Abu Ghraib Abuse Photos (CBS, 21 May 2004) <https://www.cbsnews.com/pictures/abuse-photos-ii/5/> accessed 13 March 2021.

122 United Nations Security Council Resolution 1483, S/RES/1483, 22 May 2003. See James Dobbins and others, *Occupying Iraq: A History of the Coalition Provisional Authority* (RAND Corporation 2009); Mark Phythian, 'The Perfect Intelligence Failure? US Pre-War Intelligence on Iraqi Weapons of Mass Destruction' (2006) 34 Politics & Policy 2, 400–424.

123 Atif Rehman, 'The Court of Last Resort: Seeking Redress for Victims of Abu-Ghraib Torture Through the Alien Tort Claims Act' (2005) 16 Ind. International l & Comparative Law Review 493.

124 Seymour M. Hersh, 'Torture at Abu Ghraib' (The New Yorker, 30 April 2004) <https://www.newyorker.com/magazine/2004/05/10/torture-at-abu-ghraib> accessed 13 March 2021.

125 See Antonio Cassese, 'Mercenaries: Lawful Combatants or War Criminals' (1980) 40 Zeitschrift für Ausländisches Öffentliches Recht und Völkerrecht 1.

downsizing of the military. Many found their place in private sector companies.[126] This was a corporate form of the age-old practice of specialized mercenaries providing services intricately linked to warfare.[127] Because of the scale and scandal, however, the Iraq war became one of the first conflicts where the role of PMCs came to the forefront.

While the US military had roughly 150,000 troops stationed in Iraq, the number of contractors ranged from 100,000 to 180,000 (possibly, more than the military personnel).[128] Indisputably, the private military industry contributed more forces to Iraq than any other member state of the US-led coalition which led scholars to rename President Bush's 'Coalition of the Willing' to the 'Coalition of the Billing'.[129]

But the critical role that PMCs were playing in Iraq cannot be foregrounded by numbers alone. The wide-ranging nature of their work included handling of logistics, guarding military camps, training local forces, secret intelligence gathering, and operational support.[130] Their role was not merely restricted to filling the gaps with ancillary functions in places where the state armed forces were absent. They had been working alongside the state boots on the ground, providing tactical military services such as interrogation and intelligence. They also provided on-the-ground security for senior government officials or at military bases, identified targets for drone attacks, developed interrogation techniques, and served as interrogators in detention facilities.[131]

The scale of their involvement posed huge questions on the traditional distinction between combatants and civilians and made determinations of legality of their conduct in conflict zones increasingly difficult.[132]

126 David Isenberg, 'Shadow Force: Private Security Contractors in Iraq' (Praeger Security International 2009) 2.

127 Peter Warren Singer, *The Private Military Industry and Iraq: What have we learned and where to next?* (Geneva Centre for the Democratic Control of Armed Forces 2004) 1–2, <https://www.dcaf.ch/private-military-industry-and-iraq> accessed 3 July 2023 (hereinafter Singer, 'Private Military and Iraq'); Peter Warren Singer, 'Outsourcing War' (2005) 84 Foreign Affairs 119.

128 The US government officially claimed the number of contractors employed in war effort tallied up to 25,000. See Jeremy Cloward 'An Examination of the Top Private Military Firms in the United States War with Iraq (2003–2008) and Their Impact on Democratic Government' (PhD Thesis, The Claremont Graduate University 2009) <https://search.proquest.com/docview/304863851/abstract/F1F67AF9AF624F33PQ/1> accessed 15 March 2021.

129 Singer, 'Private Military and Iraq' (n 127) 4.

130 See Filiz Zabci, 'Private Military Companies: 'Shadow soldiers' of Neo-Colonialism' (2007) 31 Capital & Class 2, 1–10.

131 Gallagher, 'Alternatives to Prosecutions' (n 52).

132 See Jennifer K. Elsea, Moshe Schwartz, and Kennon H. Nakamura, *Private security contractors in Iraq: Background, Legal Status, and Other Issues* (Library of Congress Washington DC 2008).

Against that background, employees of CACI International and Titan corporations who were contracted to work as military interrogators and translators in the prison camps administered by the United States in Iraq were also part of abuses that took place in Abu Ghraib.

Employees from CACI International Inc. made up more than half of all the analysts and interrogators at Abu Ghraib, while all the translators who made it possible for the interrogators and guards to communicate with the prisoners were employees of the Titan Corp.[133]

Almost two decades after the war, if there are any clear winners emerging from the war, it is corporations such as CACI International and Titan Corporation living up to the label of 'war profiteers'.[134] Despite being explicitly identified by government reports for having participated in criminal abuses, neither the companies nor any of their employees have been ever prosecuted or sanctioned by the state. Meanwhile, CACI crossed the 1 billion USD mark in revenue generation for the first time in 2004. If not monetarily, the Company did not seem to have lost much in reputation and standing either. Since the scandal and drastic drop in share value in 2004, CACI managed to recover its reputation. With words such as 'ethics', 'integrity', and 'character' sprinkled for emphasis all over its official communication, it takes pride in being listed as the 'Fortune Most Admired Company' ten times in a row by 2021.[135] Although CACI has been out of the interrogation business (only one per cent of the company's revenue source)[136] since 2005, the following year a strong lobby in Washington[137] secured them a place as one of seven contractors chosen by the US Army to provide technology and engineering services worth as much as 19 billion USD over a ten-year period.[138] By 2021, it was a 5.7 billion USD company[139] which continues to 'play a vital

133 Peter Singer, 'The Contract That Military Needs to Break' (Brookings, 12 September 2004) <https://www.brookings.edu/opinions/the-contract-the-military-needs-to-break/> accessed 15 March 2021.

134 PC Light, 'The True Size of Government: Tracking Washington's Blended Workforce - 1984–2015' (Volcker Alliance Inc, October 2017) 3.

135 CACI International Official Website <https://investor.caci.com/news/news-details/2021/CACI-Named-a-Fortune-Worlds-Most-Admired-Company/default.aspx> accessed 15 March 2021.

136 Charlie Cray, 'Meet the War Profiteers' (2006) Multinational Monitor, 27–33. <https://search.proquest.com/magazines/meet-war-profiteers/docview/208869443/se-2?accountid=11262≥ accessed 15 March 2021.

137 In 2020, a Former White House Chief of Operations was appointed as the Strategic Corporate Advisor of CACI International (Bloomberg, 5 February 2021) <https://www.bloomberg.com/press-releases/2020-02-05/caci-appoints-former-white-house-chief-of-operations-daniel-walsh-as-corporate-strategic-advisor≥ accessed 15 March 2021.

138 War Resisters' International (April 2010) <https://wri-irg.org/en/story/2010/war-profiteer-month-caci> accessed on 15 March 2021.

139 As of 15 March 2021, retrieved from CACI's official website <https://www.caci.com/about-caci> accessed 27 February 2022.

role in US national security, safeguarding troops, and enabling government to deliver cost-effective and high-quality support for people in the US'.[140]

This scale of privatization and the enormous profits made by the contractors like CACI and Titan were not accidental. Organizations like CCR had already been highlighting the fact that 'this was a war of choice, that this war was not about weapons of mass destruction but this was a war for profit'.[141] When the Taguba report revealed that these contractors were holding leadership positions in the detention centres, the facts reaffirmed CCR's anti-war and anti-privatization stance. Hence, these cases were initiated 'not because they were convenient or trendy' but rather because they highlighted the consequences of the privatization of war and war becoming a profit-making business.[142]

The case is about their conduct and the treatment of detainees in Abu Ghraib which constituted a violation of universally applicable prohibition of torture. As private military contractors who engage in wide-ranging tasks of a traditional military in a war for profit-making, they enjoy substantive impunity despite being associated with serious violations of international law. ATS being a tool that makes it possible to not depend on prosecutors to initiate action for crimes, multiple civil action suits were brought around these violations by corporations.

These lawsuits were a continuation of the movement after *Dellums v. Bush* litigation as well as the anti-war advocacy CCR, along with others, had been undertaking outside the courts.[143] They wanted to bring a challenge against the PMCs on the ground who were not only taking orders but were also enjoying leadership positions and performing essential military functions. One of these cases that is still ongoing, *Al-Shimari et al. v. CACI Premier Technology*, is discussed in greater detail here.

1. Building a Transnational Litigation

The leak of the Taguba report to the media essentially confirmed what Haidar Muhsin Saleh, an Iraqi civilian, was trying to convince his family in the United States and other local lawyers: that he had been arbitrarily detained and tortured at Abu Ghraib at the hands of US citizens.[144] Before leaving the

140 Ibid.

141 Interview with Katherine Gallagher, Senior Staff Attorney, CCR (online, 18 March 2021).

142 Ibid.

143 See Michael Ratner, Jennie Green, and Barbara Olshansky, *Against War with Iraq: An Anti-War Primer* (Seven Stories Press 2011); Michael Ratner, 'The United Nations Charter and the Use of Force Against Iraq' (2002) <http://www.lawyersagainstthewar.org/legalarticles/ratner. html> accessed 27 February 2022.

144 Saleh opposed Saddam Hussein, who had him imprisoned and tortured in the Abu Ghraib prison in Iraq. After being released from prison, Plaintiff Saleh fled from Iraq to Sweden.

prison, a US military officer had let him keep his identity badge confirming his detention at Abu Ghraib so that he could go to the United States and seek justice for the mistreatment he had endured.[145] When the Taguba report was released, Saleh and his local Michigan civil rights lawyer Shereef Akeel, along with CCR, were looking to gather facts and wondering how they could bring an action challenging what was happening in the detention facilities in Iraq.

Although it was not the first time CCR would be approaching the courts for the rights of foreigners detained by the United States, what was new this time was that these detainees were being tortured in the context of an active armed conflict on another continent. The Taguba report, written by a state official, identifying the names of US corporations engaged in mistreatment of detainees proved to be the missing puzzle piece.

Saleh had been insisting that he was not the only one who had endured mistreatment in detention centres in Iraq, indicating a systematic nature of torture and mistreatment ongoing at the time. Upon further confirmation by the Senate Report, Shreef Akeel travelled with Saleh to meet other detainees in Iraq. One of his Iraqi-American friends, who happened to be the grandson of a former Iraqi Prime Minister, helped him undertake this near impossible feat of convincing Iraqis to trust someone from the United States and his promise to fight for their rights on their behalf in the United States.[146] Over 300 Iraqis from all walks of life met a disguised Akeel in discrete locations to diligently answer his questions on whether Geneva Conventions were violated during their detention at Abu Ghraib.[147]

The following excerpt from an interview with Shereef Akeel hints at the tensions caused by nationalities while forging a transnational relationship such as this one:

> The thing that helped was that they realized that we were risking our lives and we were in a lot of danger. So, they opened up. Iraqis knew the risk. At that time, the Egyptians and Americans were being kidnapped and here I was, being both. So, they realized the danger. Iraqi victims

After the fall of the Hussein regime, Plaintiff Saleh responded to United States' plea for expatriates to return and help rebuild Iraq. Plaintiff Saleh returned to Iraq with funds to invest and rebuild the country. Upon his arrival on or about 25 September 2003, he was detained, sent to the same Abu Ghraib prison where he had been tortured by Saddam Hussein, and was tortured, abused, and otherwise mistreated. Retrieved from official complaint filed before the court a <https://ccrjustice.org/sites/default/files/assets/Second-Amended-Complaint-With-Exhibits.pdf> accessed 10 March 2021.

145 Interview with Shereef Akeel, Civil Rights Lawyer (online, 2 April 2021).

146 Ibid.

147 Ibid.

– women, men, teenagers – they saw the sincerity in our efforts, and this is where their guards went down.[148]

Since then, a total of over 300 Iraqi civilians who were detained and tortured at the hands of US actors in detention facilities and then released without ever being charged have reached the US courts seeking compensation against PMCs under ATS through American lawyers.

In challenging the US government policies, these US nationals end up representing those who have been oppressed by their own state. Be it Australian or British Guantánamo detainees, Haitian or Cuban refugees, political activists from Paraguay, or those illegally detained in Iraq – in choosing to turn to the US legal system for justice – they also choose their allies in the country. Be it a collaboration out of desperation or an escape to the last resort, overcoming inherent struggles in building and sustaining these relationships, to an extent, also indicates an active choice on the part of the affected communities. Although the exact nature of their collaboration is hard to determine, arguably, a somewhat basic alignment on the intended outcome of the litigation becomes a pre-condition for such litigations. After all that the victims have been subjected to at the hands of the United States, it is indeed 'miraculous' that 'they still believe in the US justice system and still want to tell their story to a US jury'.[149]

An engagement between the directly affected communities in countries which are the sites of violence and legal practitioners who have access to these avenues exemplifies the possibility of a plural practice of international law through transnational litigations.

2. *Procedural Timeline*

The first federal class action suit against CACI International, Titan Corporation, and three of their employees for their role in torture and other illegal acts committed at Abu Ghraib was filed on behalf of 252 Iraqis in June 2004 before the District Court for the Southern District of California. The claim was based on ATS claims as well as state law claims. The district court dismissed the petitioners' claims based on ATS, citing the lack of consensus on whether private acts of torture violate the law of nations but allowed the claims based on state law.[150]

148 Ibid.

149 Baher Azmy, Legal Director of the CCR quoted in Elise Swain, 'Iraqis Tortured by the U.S. in Abu Ghraib Never Got Justice' (The Intercept, 17 March 2023) https://theintercept.com/2023/03/17/iraq-war-torture-abu-ghraib/

150 *Haidar Muhsin Saleh, et al. v. Titan Corporation* [2009] 580 F.3d 1.

Because of the difference in their chain of command hierarchies, the District Court ordered in favour of Titan but against CACI International on state law claims. Both these orders were challenged in appeal. In 2009, the Appeals Court, in a 2:1 decision, dismissed the claims against CACI as well.[151] The decision was appealed before the Supreme Court, which asked the US government to submit a brief expressing their views on the case. The brief filed by the Obama administration argued against consideration of these claims under both ATS and state law. Consequently, the Supreme Court declined review.[152]

The loss of this class action suit, however, was not a total loss for all the victims.[153] The dismissal released future plaintiffs from this suit which made filling of the two subsequent suits possible.[154] The case on behalf of 71 former detainees against Titan resulted in a settlement for an undisclosed amount, the only pay out so far for crimes committed by US military contractors in Iraq.[155]

On 30 June 2008, CCR, along with Shereef Akeel and a private law firm, filed a civil complaint before the US District Court of Ohio against CACI International, Inc. and CACI Premier Technology, Inc. (a wholly owned subsidiary of CACI International) on behalf of Al-Shimari and three others based on ATS, federal and state law claims for acts amounting to torture, war crimes, and cruel and inhuman degrading treatment.[156] The case is yet to go on trial.

Suhail Najim Al-Shimari, an innocent Iraqi civilian, was arrested, placed in a cage, and threatened with death on 7 November 2003. He was moved to the 'hard site' at Abu Ghraib prison where he was detained for approximately two months before being transferred to another local prison (Camp Bucca) in Iraq. Imprisoned for more than four years in total before being finally released on 27 March 2008, he was never charged with any crime.[157]

The stories of other plaintiffs – Taha Yaseen Arraq Rashid, Sa'ad Hamza Hantoosh Al-zuba'E, and Salah Hasan Nusaif Jasmim Al-Ejaili – also follow a similar pattern. Rashid, detained for almost two years (from September

151 Ibid.

152 Brief for the United States as Amicus Curiae in *Haidar Muhsin Saleh et al. v. Titan Corporation* on petition for a writ of certiorari to the United States Court of Appeals for the District of Columbia Circuit in May 2011.

153 Interview with Katherine Gallagher, Senior Staff Attorney, CCR (online, 18 March 2021).

154 Ibid.

155 *Al-Quraishi v. Nakhla and L-3 Services, Inc.* [2012] 679 F.3d 205 (4th Circuit).

156 Ibid. The first complaint also explicitly named Timothy Dugan and other CACI employees as defendants who were later dropped from the proceedings for the suit finally against the parent company – CACI International.

157 *Al-Shimari v. CACI,* third amended complaint filed on 4 April 2013. <https://ccrjustice.org/sites/default/files/assets/Al%20Shimari%20TAC%20redacted.pdf> accessed 27 February 2022.

2003 to May 2005), was forcibly subjected to sexual acts by a female officer as he was cuffed and shackled to cell bars, hung from the ceiling by a rope tied around his chest, and forced to watch as the conspirators raped a female prisoner. Hamza, who was held from November 2003 to October 2004, was imprisoned in a solitary cell in conditions of sensory deprivation for almost a full year. Salah Al-Ejaili, an Al-Jazeera reporter and later producer, was held in detention from November 2003 to February 2004. All the plaintiffs were civilians who were arrested, detained, and tortured at Abu Ghraib during interrogation, and then eventually released without having been charged of any crime.[158]

The complaint alleged that CACI and its employees conspired with the military personnel to torture the prisoners detained at the 'hard site' of Abu Ghraib prison.[159] The employees not only tortured the detainees themselves but also enjoyed leadership positions at the detention centres where they ordered other military personnel to 'soften up' the detainees before they were brought in for questioning.[160] The plaintiffs contended that CACI employees, jointly acting with other actors, instigated, ordered, participated in, and aided and abetted conduct towards prisoners that violated the Geneva Conventions, US Army Field Manuals, and the laws of the United States.[161] According to the complaint, the acts of CACI employees could be attributed to the parent company in the United States, CACI International.[162]

The complaint relied on the decision-making hierarchy of the corporation to attribute the conduct of its employees to US-based CACI International. The employees who were deployed at the detention centres worked for CACI Premier Technology, a wholly owned subsidiary of CACI International Inc. Both registered in Virginia, the former controlled by the latter as one of its corporate divisions. CACI International had the ability to control, direct, and influence the actions of the employees in question and could have prevented them from torturing Al-Shimari and others, thus making it responsible for the acts of CACI Premier Technology and its employees.[163] Moreover, CACI employees held leadership positions at Abu Ghraib, where they gave specific directions to the military personnel on how the detainees were to be confined.[164]

The case is based on the argument that employees as well as the corporation in question knew that the use of torture and other cruel, inhuman, degrading treatment was absolutely prohibited and that their acts were in

158 Ibid 68–77.
159 Ibid 78–81.
160 Ibid 120.
161 Ibid 22.
162 Ibid 33.
163 Ibid.
164 Ibid 96.

violation of international law. Therefore, the corporation acted negligently and wrongfully by failing to prevent its employees from engaging in foreseeable and predictable wrongful acts. Based on this conduct, the plaintiffs brought not only ATS, but also federal and state law claims against CACI International for acts amounting to war crimes, torture, and cruel and inhuman degrading treatment.[165]

Since 2008, the case has done several rounds to appellate courts leading to a very complicated and winding procedural history. Related litigation with the same plaintiffs started before the *Sosa* decision (see above Section II.2) and this particular case (*Al-Shimari v. CACI Premier Tech. Inc.*) started before *Kiobel* and *Jesner* decisions (see above section II. 3). In the meantime, the scope of the remedy has been altered substantially. Each of these decisions also became an additional setback (temporally if not substantively) for this litigation.

Upon closer examination of the proceedings, two factors stand out as detrimental in shaping the course of this litigation from 2008 to 2021: one, the attitude and posturing of the district court judges towards this litigation; and two, the defences and tactics used by CACI and their implications for the litigation. The following two sections discuss each of these critical factors in detail with the aim to highlight the nature of challenges pertinent to a transnational litigation against a resourceful corporate defendant alleging violations of international law.

3. *The Judges and Corporations*

US Supreme Court has passed up the opportunity three times to settle the question of corporate liability under ATS.[166] Even when the Supreme Court did lay down the framework of the scope of applicability of ATS, it has come down to the discretionary powers of the lower courts to apply imprecise tests on a case-by-case basis. The uncertainty at the top court has resulted in lower court judges enjoying a decisive position in shaping the practice of this remedy.

The long duration of *Al-Shimari* litigation provides an opportunity to make comparative reflections and determine the effect of the attitude of a domestic court judge on the implementation of international law. Two district court judges have dealt with the case in the last 14 years – Judge Lee and Judge Brinkema – and the contrast with which both of them managed the case is inescapable and consequential.

165 For a detailed account of the factual allegations and the harms suffered by the plaintiffs, see *Al Shimari v. CACI Premier Tech., Inc.* [2018] 324 F. Supp. 2d 668, 673–82.

166 See discussion in section II of this Chapter.

Judge Lee's Discomfort with ATS and International Law

In his first preliminary decision in March 2009, Judge Gerald Bruce Lee, District Court Virginia, Alexandra Division, upheld all claims of the plaintiffs except the claim based on ATS jurisdiction. His reason for dismissal was that tort claims against government contractor interrogators were too recent and too novel to satisfy the *Sosa* requirements for ATS jurisdiction – that of 'universal, specific, and obligatory' norms of international law.[167]

His order begins with justifications for the invasion of Iraq, which offers a partial reflection of his stance on the narrative at the time.[168] His reasoning for dismissal of ATS claim based on the *Sosa* test indicated confusion regarding the scope of ATS as well as of the workings of international law. The *Sosa* test only applied to the nature of violation for which the tort claim is brought and not to the subsidiary questions such as rules of evidence, nature of defendants, etc. Judge Lee's order transposed the requirement of specificity and universality applicable to the norm and the nature of violation to the scope of liability for these claims. The search for universality in these questions would be inconsistent with the international legal framework where the enforcement is directly left to the domestic courts. Perhaps, a better ground for Judge Lee would have been to examine whether ATS allowed claims against corporate defendants or not, and the answer to this question in 2009 (before *Kiobel* and *Jesner*) would have been affirmative.

The confusion about the *Sosa* test and the scope of ATS may have been combined with an unwillingness to sail into new waters. The court in its own words was 'particularly wary of exercising too much discretion in recognizing new torts'.[169] In one of the transcripts of a subsequent court hearing where Baher Azmy, CCR's legal director, was arguing for the reinstatement of ATS charges before Judge Lee, the judge expresses his reservations on how he did not want to be the second judge (after *Kadic*) in the whole country to send a private actor on trial for an ATS claim.[170]

In 2012, Judge Lee was confronted with the same matter again when CCR filed for reinstatement of ATS claims after a favourable order from the Fourth Circuit Court of Appeals. This time he reinstalled all the ATS claims of war crimes, torture, and cruel and inhuman degrading treatment against CACI by observing, as somewhat of a departure from his earlier stance, that 'a growing body of law ... suggests that plaintiffs' claims ... are within the purview

167 *Sosa* (n 55) 733.

168 See Court Order (18 March 2009) <https://ccrjustice.org/sites/default/files/assets/3.18.09%20Al%20Shimari%20decision.pdf> accessed 27 February 2022.

169 Transcript for Motion Hearing on 1 November 2012 available at <https://ccrjustice.org/sites/default/files/assets/Al%20Shimari%20v.%20CACI%20%2011-1-12.PDF> accessed 7 March 2021.

170 Ibid.

of international law'.[171] By 2012, the stakes of this decision did not seem that high as the US Supreme Court was soon going to decide on the question in *Kiobel* and therefore his decision either way would not have stood on its own.

The Kiobel Intervention

After *Kiobel*, the question was not whether private contractors' liability falls under ATS jurisdiction or not but whether the facts in this case were sufficient to satisfy the 'touch and concern' test and rebut the presumption against extraterritoriality.[172] Given that the Supreme Court specifically mentioned that 'mere corporate presence in the country'[173] was not sufficient without providing any further guidance, this made Judge Lee one of the first judges interpreting the 'touch and concern' test in a case against a US corporation involved in misconduct outside the country against nationals of a third country.

It was the plaintiffs' duty to displace the presumption and prove that this case was not as 'foreign-cubed' as the defendants would claim. CCR argued that there were three critical facts that distinguished *Al-Shimari* from *Kiobel* on this account: one, the provisional control of the United States over the Iraqi territory during the time the alleged crimes took place; two, CACI's base and headquarters in the United States meant more than a mere presence as opposed to the corporation in *Kiobel*, which was essentially a foreign entity with an investor relations office in the United States; and three, a lot of the executive decisions, contractual activity between the government and CACI, did in fact take place on the US territory.[174]

In addition to the factual distinctions, a case like *Al-shimari* also differs on the policy consideration elements of the judicial decision-making. The primary policy considerations behind the *Kiobel* decision were to avoid interference with international comity and foreign government's interests – none of which posed a serious risk, in this case alleging torture by US actors.

Disregarding these distinctions, Judge Lee interpreted the *Kiobel* test very narrowly by holding that the presumption against extraterritoriality can only be rebutted by a legislative act and not judicial decision.[175] Although he admitted that it would be a fair reading for these facts to be considered under

171 Ibid.

172 *Kiobel* (n 67).

173 Ibid.

174 See Plaintiff's Opposition to CACI's Appeal to Dismiss on the basis of *Kiobel* (3 May 2013) <https://ccrjustice.org/sites/default/files/assets/399_2013-05.03%20Opposition%20ATS%20re%20Kiobel.pdf> accessed 27 February 2022.

175 Judge Lee's Order (25 June 2013) 16 <https://ccrjustice.org/files/Shimari_Opinion%20Dismissing%20ATS%20Claims%206.26.13.pdf> accessed 7 March 2021.

the 'touch and concern' test, he retained ground in holding that it was not a judicial role to make that determination.[176] It appears counter-intuitive for a judge to send a Supreme Court order of a fact-based case analysis back to the legislature or executive. As a result, once again, Judge Lee dismissed the case altogether.

On appeal, a three-judge bench at the Fourth Circuit Court[177] overturned the opinion of Judge Lee and concluded that the *Kiobel* ruling does not foreclose claims under ATS such as the one brought forth in this case.[178] The Court held that not only the 'touch and concern' test was a matter of judicial determination (as opposed to what Judge Lee had concluded) but also that claims of torture and other war crimes in Iraq against a US corporation fulfil the 'touch and concern' test as laid down by the Supreme Court in *Sosa*.[179]

The Fourth Circuit relied on distinction of facts in *Al-Shimari* and concluded that language in *Kiobel* provides guidance to the federal courts when ATS claims *involve substantial ties* to the US territory.[180] CACI's status as a US corporation, the US citizenship of CACI employees, upon whose conduct the ATS claims were based, the interrogation services contract between CACI and the US Department of the Interior being issued in the United States, and tacit complicity in or covering up or encouragement of said conduct by CACI managers also taking place in the United States, were all sufficient factors for the court to hold that the case held substantial ties to US territory.[181]

Consequently, in 2014, after having returned from the Circuit Court, the same case was put before Judge Lee for the third time. This time CACI filed a motion to dismiss on the ground of 'political questions doctrine', discussed in further detail in Section IV. Judge Lee dismissed the plaintiff's claims again. And for the third time, the Circuit Court overturned his judgment and remanded the matter back to the District Court. Almost six years into the litigation, the case had not even reached the stage of depositions primarily because the district court judge was arguably hesitant.

Judge Brinkema – The Change of Course

As far as dramatic turns in courtrooms are concerned, the significance of Judge Lee's recusal from this case cannot be overstated. After Judge Lee

176 Ibid 18.

177 *Al-Shimari v. CACI International Inc.* [2014] 758 F.3d 516 (4th Circuit) 6-7 (The order, while noting the facts, lists down all occasions where the high offices of the United States condemned these abuses and underlying the abhorrent nature of the conduct in question).

178 Ibid.

179 Ibid.

180 Ibid 27.

181 Ibid.

recused himself,[182] Judge Leonie Brinkema entered the case nine years after the litigation began, in January 2017. The hearing transcripts indicate that she was upfront with her intention to seek finality in this long-standing case. Her approach reflected a sense of urgency with which she addressed the matter. As it was a tort claim against a major corporation with claimants abroad,[183] she swiftly suggested CACI to settle and to read on the signal that Fourth Circuit might be giving by sending the case back on three different occasions.[184]

Within six months, Judge Brinkema resolved the question of applicable law and held that claims for torture, cruel, inhuman, and degrading treatment, and war crimes can be brought under ATS against private actors. This preliminary judgment based on the video depositions made by the victims helped a great deal in finally offering an acknowledgement and recognition to the injustice they had been subjected to in 2003.[185]

However, shortly before the case was set to go on trial, CACI challenged it on the grounds of 'derivative immunity' (details in Section IV). Judge Brinkema issued a comprehensive judgment displaying a sound understanding of the questions involving international law. She held that even the United States is not entitled to immunity for *jus cogens* violations, therefore, leaving no immunity for CACI to 'derive' as a governmental contractor.[186] The CCR lawyer working on this case called it a 'small victory' for this case.[187]

The Fourth Circuit Court, albeit in a split majority, dismissed CACI's appeal for lack of jurisdiction and for being improper to the effect that it did not raise any 'abstract' issue of law justifying an intermediary appeal.[188] As an anticlimax, it is an intermediary appeal concerning derivative sovereign immunity that reached the Supreme Court in 2019 instead of the questions on CACI liability for violation of international law. The Court denied CACI's

182 Recusal Order (21 October 2016) available at <https://ccrjustice.org/sites/default/files/attach/2016/10/562_10-21-16_Order%20recusing%20Judge%20Lee%20and%20requesting%20reassignment.pdf> accessed 27 February 2022.

183 Transcript of status conference before Judge Brinkema on 16 December 2016 <https://ccrjustice.org/sites/default/files/attach/2017/01/Al%20Shimari%20v.%20CACI%2012-16-16.pdf> accessed 27 February 2022.

184 Ibid (Plaintiffs have maintained for several years that they would be willing to settle if CACI offered).

185 See District Court Order (21 February 2018) <https://ccrjustice.org/sites/default/files/attach/2018/07/678_2-21-18_Opinion%20on%20MTD_Unsealed%203-1-18_web.pdf> accessed 27 February 2022.

186 See District Court Order (22 March 2019) <https://ccrjustice.org/sites/default/files/attach/2019/03/1183_3-22-19_Memorandum_Opinion_web.pdf> accessed 27 February 2022.

187 Interview with Katherine Gallagher, Senior Staff Attorney, CCR (online, 18 March 2021).

188 Unpublished Opinion of the 4th Circuit Court (23 August 2019) <https://ccrjustice.org/sites/default/files/attach/2019/08/8.23.19%20DIsmissal%20of%20Appeal.pdf> accessed 27 February 2022.

petition to issue a certiorari pending the decision in the *Nestlé* case and the case is finally back to Judge Brinkema. As of March 2023, two decades after the violations took place, the case is yet to go on trial.

As a final note, the following section discusses some key defences used by CACI, or in other words, legal doctrines which may serve as shields to create an accountability gap for corporations acting on behalf of a state party.

IV. CACI's Defences

During the long course of this litigation, CACI has been consistently using delaying tactics. Beginning from summary dismissal on grounds of statute of limitations,[189] CACI has appealed every possible interlocutory order to the extent that the case has been sent back to the district courts from the appeals court four times. In 2013, CACI moved to seek a dismissal as a sanction for the inability to appear in the United States for depositions as the state department prevented them to fly to the United States.[190] Such delay has directly benefitted CACI with an increasingly narrowing landscape of the ATS (as more conservative Justices are appointed to the Supreme Court) and fading of war's memory from the public conscience in clear contrast to the situation at the time of filling of these complaints back in 2004.[191]

CACI has invoked several doctrines to shield itself from liability: government contractor's defence; political question doctrine; combatant activities exception; and finally, derivative sovereign immunity (the one reviewed by the Supreme Court in 2021). These doctrines are applicable in situations where a corporation is playing a delegated essential sovereign function. They are briefly discussed here in so far as their definitions form the basis of CACI's defences and how the circuit court has responded to each of them.

Government's Contractor Defence

Because of the federal structure of US legal system, points of conflict often arise between state and federal laws. In cases of conflict of laws, the federal law stands, and state law is pre-empted owing to the 'supremacy clause' of the US Constitution. A federal statute, the Federal Tort Claims Act (FTCA) allows for the defence of 'combatant activities' exception where civilian

189 On 10 October 2008, CACI filed a motion for a partial summary dismissal on the grounds of Statutes of Limitation arguing that the claims of the latter plaintiffs were time-barred. The court held that filing of class action *Saleh v. Titan* filed in 2004 which essentially made the same material claims extended the time period under Statutes of Limitations based on the principle of equitable tolling under the US law.

190 Copy of the Motion (5 April 2013) available at <https://ccrjustice.org/sites/default/files/assets/258_2013-04-05(Public)DefsMotionforSanctions.pdf> accessed 27 February 2022.

191 Interview with Katherine Gallagher, Senior Staff Attorney, CCR (online, 18 March 2021).

contractors supporting the bona fide military personnel in wartime combatant conduct will be immune from liability. Additionally, the Act does not apply to either contractors or 'employees of the government'. Given the fact that CACI engaged in combatant activities on the directions and instructions of the federal government, it would therefore not be liable under the federal law claims.[192] Essentially, according to CACI, this exception pre-empted the applicability of state laws as well.

Given that the Titan Co. had successfully defended their way out of the litigation arising from the same facts in *Saleh v. Titan*, CACI resorted to this doctrine as their primary defence. Judge Lee at the District Court allowed the defence, as did the Fourth Circuit Court.[193] However, on the basis of a strong dissenting judgment at the Circuit Court, plaintiffs filed for an *en banc* hearing.[194] In the *en banc* decision, the Circuit Court upheld the claims of the plaintiffs as well as the opinion of the Obama administration at the time, who filed an *amicus* brief on the question.[195] The plaintiffs and the supporting *amicus* brief from the Justice Department argued that such immunity was not available in acts of torture.[196] The Circuit Court, *en banc* in an 11:3 split, accepted this reasoning and concluded that, in any event, allegations of torture do not implicate uniquely federal interests or present an irreconcilable conflict with state law.[197] Therefore, they rendered the defence unavailable in cases involving torture and other serious violations of international law.

Political Question Doctrine

The 'political question doctrine' derives from the principle of separation of powers and deprives courts of jurisdiction over 'controversies which revolve around policy choices and value determinations constitutionally committed' to Congress or, as alleged in this case, to the executive branch.[198] CACI argued on 'political questions doctrine' before the District Court as well as the Circuit Court of Appeals. CACI contended, inter alia, that reference to 'ghost detainees' practices necessarily implicated the official programme of the CIA, high-level determinations made as part of the United States' war

192 See *Saleh v. Titan Corp.* [2009] 580 F.3d 1 (DC Circuit) and *Koohi v. U.S.* [1992] 976 F.2d 1328 (9th Circuit).
193 Ibid.
194 It is an exceptional procedure invoked only in matters of exceptional public importance, but the plea was accepted, and a full bench of the Fourth Circuit Court of Appeals heard the matter again. Petition for Rehearing En Banc filed on 5 October 2011, available at <https://ccrjustice.org/sites/default/files/assets/Al%20Shimari%20en%20banc%20filed.pdf> accessed 27 February 2022.
195 *Al Shimari v. CACI* [2012] F.3d 205 (4th Circuit).
196 Ibid.
197 Ibid.
198 *Japan Whaling Association v. Am. Cetacean Soc'y* [1986] 478 US 221, 230.

effort. This determination is 'traditionally reserved to the political branches and removed from judicial review'.[199]

The political question challenge required the Court to answer two inherent questions[200]: (1) whether CACI was under the 'plenary' and 'direct' control of the military, and (2) whether national defence interests were so 'inextricably intertwined' with the military decisions governing CACI's conduct, such that a decision on the merits 'would require the judiciary to question actual, sensitive judgments made by the military'.[201] To both these questions, Judge Lee answered in the affirmative. He robustly argued that the court lacked judicially manageable standards in adjudicating the merits of this case.[202]

In appeal, the Fourth Circuit Court did not agree with the determination made by Judge Lee and held that the 'political question doctrine' does not shield from judicial review intentional acts by a government contractor that were unlawful at the time they were committed.[203]

The Circuit Court evaluated the test of 'direct' and 'plenary control' of the military in a broader meaning of actual control without restraining itself to formalistic contractual conditions of control. From the evidence produced, the Court found that it was apparent that although contractually the CACI interrogators were under direct command and control of the military officers running the camp, the actual practice was that there were no senior military officers to supervise, which allowed CACI interrogators to order low-level officers to torture the detainees. Therefore, in effect, the military did not have 'actual control' over the actions of CACI employees in the detention facility and the conduct in question was unlawful.[204]

On the second question, whether the conduct was so closely intertwined with the interest of defence that the courts would end up making a judicial determination of the conduct of the military, the court held that any acts of the CACI employees that were unlawful when committed, irrespective whether they occurred under actual control of the military, are subject to judicial review.[205] The Circuit Court ruled that these claims were justiciable

199 See *Smith v. Reagan* [1988] 844 F.2d 195, 198 (4th Circuit).

200 Concerning characteristics of political questions cases, see *Baker v. Carr*, 369 U.S. 186, 217 (1962). Also see, *Taylor v. Kellogg Brown & Root Services, Inc* [2011] 658 F.3d at 411 which distilled the test further to these two questions.

201 Ibid.

202 District Court Order (18 June 2015) available at <https://ccrjustice.org/sites/default/files/attach/2015/06/20150618%20PDQ%20decision.pdf> accessed 18 March 2022.

203 *Al Shimari v. CACI., Inc.* [2016] 840 F.3d 147 (4th Circuit).

204 Ibid.

205 The Court relied on *Zivotofsky* [2012] 132 S. Ct. at 1427, 1430; see also *El-Shifa* [2010] 607 F.3d at 836 (DC Circuit). (Justice Kavanaugh, concurring in the judgment 'the Supreme Court has never applied the political question doctrine in a case involving alleged statutory violations'.) The adjudication of such a claim requires a court only to engage in the traditional judicial function of 'say[ing] what the law is', and of determining how that law

to the extent that the challenged conduct violated settled international law or criminal law citing *Hamdi v. Rumsfeld*, explaining that 'a state of war is not a blank check for the President' with respect to individual rights.[206]

Battlefield Pre-emption

The Fourth Circuit Court, at the first instance, accepted CACI's defence of the 'Battlefield Pre-emption' on the ground that the case would have an adverse impact on the uniquely federal interests of interrogating detainees in foreign battlefield. The majority opinion notes:

> The potential liability under state law of military contractors for actions taken in connection with US military operations overseas would similarly affect the availability and costs of using contract workers in conjunction with military operations. In this case, that uniquely federal interest was especially important in view of the recognized shortage of military personnel and the need for assistance in interrogating detainees at Abu Ghraib prison .... Moreover, such interference with uniquely federal interests would be aggravated by the prison's location in the war zone. Finally, potential liability under state tort law would undermine the flexibility that military necessity requires in determining the methods for gathering intelligence.[207]

The judges relied on the recent dismissal of similar claims by the Supreme Court in *Saleh v. Titan*[208] where the court coined the term 'battlefield pre-emption' referring that the federal government occupies the field when it comes to warfare, and its interest in combat is always 'precisely contrary' to the imposition of a non-federal tort duty.[209] However, the Circuit Court opinion was not unanimous on this novel and far-reaching defence. Judge Robert King wrote a lengthy and forceful dissent, strongly arguing that discovery of this new form of pre-emption in the matter was unjustified by the

applies to the facts of a particular case, rather than passing judgment on a discretionary policy choice. *Burn Pit,* 744 F.3d at 334.

206 542 U.S. 507, 536 (2004) (opinion of Justice O'Connor)

207 *Al Shimari v. CACI Inc.* [2011] 658 F.3d 413 (4th Circuit) 8.

208 27 June 2011, the Supreme Court declined without comment to take up the case after a federal appeals court in Washington dismissed the case. The Court in Saleh adopted the following rule: 'During wartime, where a private service contractor is integrated into combatant activities over which the military retains command authority, a tort claim arising out of the contractor's engagement in such activities shall be pre-empted'. 580 F. 3d at 9.

209 *Al Shimari v. CACI, Inc.* [2011] 658 F.3d 413 (4th Circuit) 11.

Supreme Court precedent which prescribed to apply a 'limiting principle' to ensure that pre-emption in contractor cases was narrowly applied.[210]

The 11:3 judgments by the *en banc* panel primarily offered the same reasoning as Judge King's dissenting order and held that there was no conflict between tort law claims against the contractors and the federal duties to prisoners. The court held that 'battlefield pre-emption' was inapplicable in the case as the federal policy is clear on torture and the government could not make the contractor engage in torture, which was the basis of the claims under tort law.[211] As Gallagher notes, this sweeping defence to liability effectively serves as a block to the enforcement of international law through civil actions which can be particularly dangerous when corporate actors are so deeply intertwined with the business of war.[212]

Derivative Sovereign Immunity

CACI also claimed that the corporation is immune from liability for it derives its immunity from 'the government's unquestioned need to delegate governmental functions', and is a recognition that '[i]mposing liability on private agents of the government would directly impede the significant governmental interest in the completion of its work'.[213] CACI argued that in this case the government *did* 'stand in the contractor's shoes', or in other words, the government interrogators and CACI employees wore the same shoes.[214] Therefore, CACI derives sovereign immunity from being a government contractor.

Derivative sovereign immunity protects a government contractor from suit when (1) the United States would be immune from suit if the claims had been brought against it, (2) the contractor performed services for the sovereign under a validly awarded contract, and (3) the contractor adhered to the terms of its contract.[215]

As mentioned above, Judge Brinkema at District Court dismissed the argument holding that even the government is not immune from suits alleging violations of *jus cogens* norms, thus leaving no immunity for its contractors.[216]

210 Ibid 37.

211 *Al Shimari v. CACI Int'l, Inc.* [2012] 679 F.3d 205 (4th Circuit) 69–70.

212 Gallagher, 'Alternatives to Prosecutions' (n 52) 418.

213 *Butters v. Vance Int'l, Inc.* [2000] 225 F.3d 462, 466 (4th Circuit); *Mangold v. Analytic Servs., Inc.* [1996] 77 F.3d 1447–48 (4th Circuit).

214 Memorandum Filed by CACI (28 February 2019) 10, available at <https://ccrjustice.org/sites/default/files/attach/2019/03/1150_2-28-19_CACI%20memo%20MTD%20derivative%20immunit> accessed 27 February 2022

215 See *Cunningham v. Gen. Dynamics Info. Tech., Inc.* [2018] 888 F.3d 640, 649 (4th Circuit).

216 *Al Shimari v. CACI Premier Tech. Inc.* [2019] 368 F. Supp. 3d 935, 970. After concluding that CACI cannot avail itself of a sovereign immunity that the United States does not possess, the district court further observed that, alternatively, it is not clear that CACI would

Nevertheless, CACI approached the Supreme Court for review, arguing that the contractors were performing a government function as an extended arm of the state and are therefore entitled to the benefit of the immunity for discretionary acts for which the US military would have been immune.[217]

CACI argued that if the Circuit Court ruling was allowed to stand, it would have a chilling effect on federal contractor's willingness to provide vital services to the US military, and permit district courts and juries to second-guess the judgments of the US military and executive as well as legislative branches about the most sensitive aspects of military operations and intelligence. They asked for the ruling to be overturned in order to avoid 'hampering the war effort and undermining the private public cooperation and discipline necessary for the execution of military operations'.[218] The Supreme Court, however, denied CACI's petition claiming immunity from the torture allegations in the Iraq war, sending the matter back to District Court.[219]

These defences reflect the grey zone in which private military security corporations function, thereby allowing potential impunity resulting from the privatization of war. The government delegates its sovereign functions to private contractors and evades responsibility and when held accountable for violations the contractors ironically argue immunity because they were performing governmental functions. It remains to be seen if, through this case, this accountability gap can be filled. In any case, regardless of their outcome, each of these defences has managed to successfully delay the trial for the benefit of CACI.

V. Conclusion

In some ways, the tort cases brought against corporations in the United States for their misconduct abroad also paved the way for European lawyers and human rights organizations to pursue corporate accountability in their respective jurisdictions.[220] The role played by CCR in reviving ATS, which allowed federal courts in the United States to entertain civil law suits by

be granted derivative immunity under *Campbell-Ewald*, because of the factual allegations that the contractor violated federal law and international regulations in conspiring with military personnel in committing acts of torture.

217 *CACI Premier Tech. Inc. v. Al-Shimari and Ors*, Petition for a Writ of Certiorari filed before the US Supreme Court (15 November 2019) available at https://ccrjustice.org/sites/default/files/attach/2019/11/11-15-19_CACI-Cert-Petition_w.pdf accessed 27 February 2022.

218 Ibid 12.

219 As of March 2022, for latest updates on the case, see <https://ccrjustice.org/home/what-we-do/our-cases/al-shimari-v-caci-et-al> accessed March 2022.

220 Wolfgang Kaleck and Miriam Saage-Maaß, 'Corporate Accountability for Human Rights Violations Amounting to International Crimes' (2010) 6 Journal of International Criminal Justice 699, 703.

non-US nationals for violations of international law, has been instrumental. The Center's reliance on international criminal law in a tort framework provides a fascinating example for analysis of strategic litigation and various ways of international norm-internalization. Although this illustration may be unique to the United States, the ATS jurisprudence highlights the possibility of an expansive notion of accountability in the international criminal justice system as well. Against that backdrop, the following are some of the key takeaways from CCR's strategic legal practice and proceedings against the so-called war profiteers in the context of TWAI(C)L.

Law as a Means to Critique

Conceived as a legal ally to social and political movements, the long history of CCR exhibits the workings of organizational strategic litigation. The Center has consistently used existing legal avenues creatively to critique unjust policies of the state and the misuse of executive power. Each of their litigations reflects a combination of the legal and extra-legal in a way that their success is best measured outside the courtrooms (see Section II of Chapter 2).

Although the Guantánamo Bay detention camp is still open, CCR's early legal intervention was critical in bringing the offshore prison within judicial oversight in the first place. This intervention was path-breaking, as the Centre became the first actor to resist the misuse of executive power by the United States on the pretext of the war on terror when no one in the legal community was ready/willing to speak up. Moreover, the use of ATS to make claims based on international human rights law was innovative as well as far-sighted.

Each of these interventions has created new avenues to seek justice for the unheard and unaddressed – 'the aliens', the outsiders – who are affected by the conduct of the United States but not recognized as legitimate rights holders before its courts. At the same time, these litigations are also about achieving progressive political aims which are bigger than the litigation itself. For instance, the *CACI case* as much as it is about the civilians who were arbitrarily detained and tortured by the US actors, the case also strengthens the critique of the Iraq war being a war for profit, and CCR's anti-privatization stance (see Section I of Chapter 2).

This practice also speaks to the dilemma of engaging with the law while acknowledging its inherent flaws. These legal interventions are a good illustration of what the reform-oriented practice informed by TWAI(C)L (see Section III.1 of Chapter 1) could look like, in so far as it challenges and critiques the (mis-)use of legal framework by the executive while at the same time does not dismiss the emancipatory potential of the international legal order. It uses international criminal law innovatively to pose a challenge on behalf of those most directly affected by such violations.

Civil Remedy and Relative Application of International Criminal Law

Internationalist scholars have argued that transnational networks like the CCR serve as legal norm-entrepreneurs in bringing international law home by provoking interaction, provoking interpretation, and consequently provoking norm-internalizations through a judicial process.[221] In this process of norm-internalization, these legal interventions present a set of concrete practices of how the universal is relativized to accommodate plural ideas of justice and accountability (see Section III.2 of Chapter 1).

Admittedly, ATS' explicit mention of the 'law of nations' makes it conducive to incorporate international human rights and criminal law to support tort claims. The vocabulary of international legal norms not only helps underline the gravity of the violations in question but also brings in other practical advantages. Allegations of violations of international law subject the reputation of transnational companies to a greater risk, potentially leading to a higher monetary settlement. In some ways, the use of international laws makes the legal process for victims abroad more meaningful as it relies on a unified (universal) framework.

Existing scholarship has debated over the efficacy of ATS as a remedy in a cost–benefit analysis for the plaintiffs and survivors.[222] A tort claim offers certain clear advantages such as liberal pre-trial discoveries, lesser evidentiary thresholds, jury trials in civil litigation, higher compensation, including punitive damages, and most of all, the possibility of an out-of-court settlement.[223] However, a civil framework is not free of challenges either. Beyond the intimidating might of the adversary, transnational non-state driven

221 See Harold Koh, 'Transnational Legal Process The 1994 Roscoe Pound Lecture' (1996) Nebraska Law Review 181; Harold Koh, 'How Is International Human Rights Law Enforced?' (1999) 74 Indiana Law Journal 23; Harold Koh, 'The 1998 Frankel Lecture: Bringing International Law Home Address' (1998) Houston Law Review 623.

222 See Beth Stephens, 'Translating Filartiga: A Comparative and International Law Analysis of Domestic Remedies for International Human Rights Violations' (2002) 27 Yale Journal of International Law 1; Anna Grear and Burns Weston, 'The Betrayal of Human Rights and the Urgency of Universal Corporate Accountability: Reflections on a Post-Kiobel Lawscape' (2015) 15 Human Rights Law Review 21; Roger Alford, 'The Future of Human Rights Litigation after Kiobel' (2013) 89 Notre Dame Law Review 1749; Issac Ramsey, 'Hidden Renvoi: The Search for Corporate Liability in Alien Tort Statute Litigation Notes' (2019) 107 California Law Review 2071; Gwynne Skinner, 'Beyond Kiobel: Providing Access to Judicial Remedies for Violations of International Human Rights Norms by Transnational Business in a New (Post-Kiobel) World' (2014) 46 Columbia Human Rights Law Review 158; Christopher Whytock, Donald Childress, and Michael Ramsey, 'After Kiobel - International Human Rights Litigation in State Courts and under State Law Human Rights Litigation in State Courts and Under State Laws: Foreword' (2013) 3 UC Irvine Law Review 1.

223 See Roger Alford, 'Apportioning Responsibility Among Joint Tortfeasors for International Law Violations'(2011) 38 Pepp. Law Review 233 (discussing public, private, and hybrid approaches to apportioning liability).

litigations may be subject to peculiar practical, political, and legal setbacks. Unaccounted barriers such as limited access to resources, and as we saw in the *CACI* case, the survivors not being present in the country of litigation can become potentially huge limitations. Most importantly, even if this case resulted in a favourable outcome, those high-ranking US government officials 'most responsible' for these violations will continue to enjoy impunity.

While acknowledging that each legal framework comes with its own limitations, the use of tort law to incorporate international criminal law exemplifies a dual interplay between domestic and international law. While domestic law benefits from the weight that international norms lend to these processes, international criminal law also stands to gain from its expanded implementation and augmented credibility through judicial processes such as these.

The 14-year delay in these proceedings has also foregrounded one specific form of provocation in the process of norm-internalization. The way the networks engage with the judges and how the judges' posturing changes over the years is reflective of the increased comfort with international law as the governing framework. The impact is so critical that the whole litigation against CACI can be categorized in two phases: the phases of Judge Lee and Judge Brinkema. The two judges are representatives of two very different approaches to judicial discretion, which are perhaps not exclusive to the United States.

Certainly, neither of these approaches guarantees a favourable outcome for the victims and with the trial pending, commentary on that account must be withheld. However, what needs to be highlighted is the role a judge of a district court can play in the implementation of international criminal law. The extent of apprehension with which the domestic judges (even those in the lower courts) approach the litigation can potentially impact the essence, efficiency, and purpose of these legal interventions. An exhibit of this drastic difference is that the CACI case could have been before the Supreme Court for review before *Kiobel*, and could have potentially set a different precedent for future litigations.

Therefore, the outcome of provocation of interaction and interpretation depends as much on the judicial approach to international law as it does on networks such as CCR serving as norm-entrepreneurs. Litigations such as these only offer a different (more local) site of negotiation, while the structural terms and conditions largely remain the same.

Addressing Economic Structures Fuelling an Active Armed Conflict

In the United States, most ATS cases until the last decade filed against corporations did not implicate corporations as direct perpetrators.[224] Instead,

224 Donald Earl Childress, 'The Alien Tort Statute, Federalism, and the Next Wave of Transnational Litigation' (2011) Georgetown Law Journal 709.

they alleged complicity using aiding and abetting as the modes of secondary liability for corporate actions taken in conjunction with government officials.[225] This approach works with the conventional understanding of the extent and nature of corporate complicity – that corporations are never the ones actually 'pulling the trigger' and their responsibility can be accounted sufficiently within accomplice liability – for aiding and abetting the crimes but not committing them.[226]

Private military security companies, such as CACI, serve as good exhibits to challenge this conventional understanding and therefore push for direct liability as well as continued ATS jurisdiction over corporations when their conduct violates the 'laws of nations'. In this case, CACI is alleged to be co-perpetrators in acts amounting to torture and inhuman or degrading treatment of Iraqi detainees at the Abu Ghraib prison. The plaintiffs' lawyer remarks that the conspiracy argument in this case was intended to highlight that CACI was not only complicit in torturing the plaintiffs, but its employees were also effectively holding leadership positions, ordering other personnel on the ground to commit violations. [227]

While the lawsuit and settlement efforts are still ongoing, the case has already had some positive impact in addressing the macroeconomic realities of armed conflicts. The case strengthened the anti-war and anti-privatization-of-war movement not only in the United States but also internationally.[228] At the same time, the victims got a platform to share their truth and found consequent acknowledgement in the findings of the district judge.

Moreover, legal interventions such as these may be construed as attempts to challenge the distinction between law, economics, and politics (see Section III.4 of Chapter 1). They go a step beyond challenging the legality of the war on the face of it but unpack the economic structures that sustain (if not create) the conditions of violence in the 'Third World'. It makes abundantly clear that transnational business actors headquartered in the West play a significant role in fuelling armed conflicts.

225 Ibid 724; C. Keitner, 'Conceptualizing Complicity in Alien Tort Cases' (2008) 60 Hastings Law Journal 61, 61–63.

226 Tarek F Maassarani, 'Four Counts of Corporate Complicity: Alternative Forms of Accomplice Liability under the Alien Tort Claims Act' (2005) NYUJ International Law & Politics 38, 47.

227 Interview with Katherine Gallagher, Senior Staff Attorney, CCR (online, 18 March 2021).

228 The allegations against CACI International and others prompted states to adopt a more robust regulation of private military security companies at the national and international levels, in particular the 2008 Montreux Document on Pertinent International Legal Obligations and Good Practices for States Related to Operations of Private Military and Security Companies during Armed Conflict and the 2010 International Code of Conduct for Private Security Service Providers. See Annyssa Bellal, 'New Grammars of War: Article 3 – The Privatisation of War' (2019) 5 Global Challenges <https://globalchallenges.ch/issue/5/the-privatisation-of-war/> accessed 18 March 2022.

References

Aceves W, *The Anatomy of Torture: A Documentary History of Filartiga v Pena Irala* (Brill 2007)

Alford R, 'Apportioning Responsibility Among Joint Tortfeasors for International Law Violations' (2011) 38 Pepperdine Law Review 233

Alford R, 'The Future of Human Rights Litigation after Kiobel' (2013) 89 Notre Dame Law Review 1749

Arouri DH, 'Will Capitalism Kill Compassion - An Analysis of the Future of Corporate Liability Under the Alien Tort Statute Note' (2019) 71 Florida Law Review Forum 1

Avant D, *The Market for Force: The Consequences of Privatizing Security* (Cambridge University Press 2005)

Burley AM, 'The Alien Tort Statute and the Judiciary Act of 1789: A Badge of Honor' (1989) 83 American Journal of International Law 461

Campbell D, 'Energy Giant Agrees Settlement with Burmese Villagers' (The Guardian, 15 December 2004) <https://www.theguardian.com/world/2004/dec/15/burma.duncancampbell> accessed 10 November 2020

Cassese A, 'Mercenaries: Lawful Combatants or War Criminals' (1980) 40 Zeitschrift für Ausländisches Öffentliches Recht und Völkerrecht 1

Casto W, 'SOSA v Alvarez-Machain and the End of History Remarks' (2011) 43 Georgetown Journal of International Law 1001

Childress DE, 'The Alien Tort Statute, Federalism, and the Next Wave of Transnational Litigation' (2011) 100 Georgetown Law Journal 709

Cleveland SH, 'The Alien Tort Statute, Civil Society, and Corporate Responsibility Symposium 2004: Citizen Participation in the Global Trading System: Panel II: The Alien Tort Claims Act' (2003) 56 Rutgers Law Review 971

Cloward J, 'An Examination of the Top Private Military Firms in the United States War with Iraq (2003–2008) and Their Impact on Democratic Government' (PhD Thesis, The Claremont Graduate University 2009) <https://search.proquest.com/docview/304863851/abstract/F1F67AF9AF624F33PQ/1> accessed 15 March 2021

Cmiel K, 'The Emergence of Human Rights Politics in the United States' (1999) 86 The Journal of American History 1231

Cole D, 'Michael Ratner's Army' NY Books (New York, 15 May 2016) <https://www.nybooks.com/daily/2016/05/15/michael-ratner-army-fight-against-Guantánamo/> accessed 7 April 2021

Corn D, 'Corporate Human Rights' (The Nation, July 15 2002) http://www.thenation.com/article/corporate-human-rights accessed 20 November 2020

Cray C, 'Meet the War Profiteers' (2006) 6 Multinational Monitor 27–33

D'Amore CA, 'Sosa v Alvarez-Machain and the Alien Tort Statute: How Wide Has the Door to Human Rights Litigation Been Left Open' (2006) 39 Akron Law Review 593

Defeis EF, 'Litigating Human Rights Abuses in United States Courts: Recent Developments' (2004) 10 ILSA Journal of International & Comparative Law 319

Dickinson L, 'Public Law Values in a Privatized World' (2006) 31 Yale Journal of International Law 384

Dobbins J and others, *Occupying Iraq: A History of the Coalition Provisional Authority* (RAND Corporation 2009)
Dodge W, 'Corporate Liability Under the US Alien Tort Statute: A Comment on Jesner v Arab Bank' (2019) 4 Business and Human Rights Journal 131
Dodge W, 'The Historical Origins of the Alien Tort Statute: A Response to the "Originalists"' (1996) 19 Hastings International & Comparative Law Review 221
Dodge W, 'The Surprisingly Broad Implications of Nestlé USA., Inc. v Doe for Human Rights Litigation and Extraterritoriality' (Just Security, 18 June 2021)
Don A, 'Clarifying Kiobel's 'Touch and Concern' Test' (2017) 130 Harvard Law Review 1902
Elsea JK, Schwartz M and Nakamura KH, *Private Security Contractors in Iraq: Background, Legal Status, and Other Issues* (Library of Congress 2008)
Farbman DS, 'Resistance Lawyering' (2019) 107 California Law Review 1877, 1
Gallagher K, 'Alternatives to Prosecutions: Accountability through Civil Litigation for Human Rights Violations by Private Military Contractors' in N Jørgensen (ed), *The International Criminal Responsibility of War's Funders and Profiteers* (Cambridge University Press 2020) 396–422
Gallagher K, 'Civil Litigation and Transnational Business: An Alien Tort Statute Primer' (2010) 8 Journal of International Criminal Justice 745
Grear A and Weston B, 'The Betrayal of Human Rights and the Urgency of Universal Corporate Accountability: Reflections on a Post-Kiobel Lawscape' (2015) 15 Human Rights Law Review 21
Hersh SM, 'Torture at Abu Ghraib' (The New Yorker, 30 April 2004) <https://www.newyorker.com/magazine/2004/05/10/torture-at-abu-ghraib> accessed 13 March 2021
Holzmeyer C, 'Human Rights in an Era of Neoliberal Globalization: The Alien Tort Claims Act and Grassroots Mobilization in Doe v Unocal' (2009) 43 Law & Society Review 271
Isenberg D, *Shadow Force: Private Security Contractors in Iraq* (Praeger Security International 2009)
Kaleck W and Saage-Maaß M, 'Corporate Accountability for Human Rights Violations Amounting to International Crimes' (2010) 6 Journal of International Criminal Justice 699, 703
Kaleck W and others (eds), *International Prosecution of Human Rights Crimes* (Springer 2006)
Kaufman I, 'A Legal Remedy for International Torture' (NYT Magazine, 9 November 1980)
Keitner C, 'Conceptualizing Complicity in Alien Tort Cases' (2008) 60 Hastings Law Journal 61
Kochan DJ, 'The Political Economy of the Production of Customary International Law: The Role of Non-Governmental Organizations in U.S. Courts' (2004) 22 Berkeley Journal International Law 240
Koh HH, 'Filartiga v. Pena-Irala: Judicial Internalization into Domestic Law of the Customary International Law Norm Against Torture' (2007) International Law Stories 45
Koh HH, 'How Is International Human Rights Law Enforced?' (1999) 74 Indiana Law Journal 23

Koh HH, 'The 1998 Frankel Lecture: Bringing International Law Home Address' (1998) 35 Houston Law Review 623

Koh HH, 'Transnational Legal Process the 1994 Roscoe Pound Lecture' (1996) 75 *Nebraska Law Review* 1, 181

Koh HH, 'Transnational Public Law Litigation' (1991) 100 Yale Law Journal 2347

Kontorovich E, 'Kiobel Surprise: Unexpected by Scholars but Consistent with International Trends' (2013) 89 Notre Dame Law Review 1671

LeClercq D, 'Nestlé United States, Inc. v Doe. 141 S. Ct. 1931' (2021) 115 American Journal of International Law 694–700

Lee TH, 'The Three Lives of the Alien Tort Statute: The Evolving Role of the Judiciary in US Foreign Relations' (2013) 89 Notre Dame Law Review 1645

Leung R, 'Abuse at Abu Gharaib' (CBS News, 5 May 2004) <https://www.cbsnews.com/news/abuse-at-abu-ghraib/> accessed 13 March 2021

Light PC, 'The True Size of Government: Tracking Washington's Blended Workforce - 1984–2015' (Volcker Alliance Inc, October 2017)

Lobel J, 'Courts as Forums for Protest' (2004) 52 UCLA Law Review 47

Lobel J, *Success Without Victory: Lost legal Battles and the Long Road to Justice in America* (Vol. 70, NYU Press 2006)

Maassarani TM, 'Four Counts of Corporate Complicity: Alternative Forms of Accomplice Liability Under the Alien Tort Claims Act' (2005) 38 NYUJ International Law & Politics 39

Markusen A, 'The Case Against Privatizing National Security, Governance' (2003) 14 International Journal of Policy, Administration, and Institutions 471–501

Milewski M, 'From Slave to Litigant: African Americans in Court in the Postwar South, 1865–1920' (2012) 30 Law and History Review 3, 723

O'Connell ME, 'The Legal Case Against the Global War on Terror' (2004) 36 Case Western Reserve Journal of International Law 349

Owen R, 'Address at the Annual Dinner of the American Branch of the International Law Association' (14 November, 1980)

Politi, 'Winning Contractors - An Update: As the Number of Contracts Rises, Problems Continue to Plague the Contracting Process' (The Center for Public Integrity, 7 July 2004)

Ramsey I, 'Hidden Renvoi: The Search for Corporate Liability in Alien Tort Statute Litigation Notes' (2019) 107 California Law Review 2071

Randall KC, 'Federal Jurisdiction over International Law Claims: Inquiries into the Alien Tort Statute' (1986) 18 NYU Journal of International Law and Politics 1

Ratner M, 'How We Closed the Guantánamo HIV Camp: The Intersection of Politics and Litigation Practitioners' (1998) 11 Harvard Human Rights Journal 187

Ratner M, 'Litigating Guantánamo' in Kaleck W and others (eds), *International Prosecution of Human Rights Crimes* (Springer 2006) 201–212

Ratner M, *Moving the Bar: My Life as a Radical Lawyer* (OR Books 2021)

Ratner M, 'The United Nations Charter and the Use of Force Against Iraq' (2002) <http://www.lawyersagainstthewar.org/legalarticles/ratner.html> accessed 27 February 2022

Ratner M, Green J and Olshansky B, *Against War with Iraq: An Anti-War Primer* (Seven Stories Press 2011)

Rehman A, 'The Court of Last Resort: Seeking Redress for Victims of Abu-Ghraib Torture Through the Alien Tort Claims Act' (2005) 16 Indiana International & Comparative Law Review 493

Rosencranz A and Louk D, 'Doe v. Unocal: Holding Corporations Liable for Human Rights Abuses on Their Watch' (2005) 8 Chapman Law Review 135

Sanders R, 'Human Rights Abuses at the Limits of the Law: Legal Instabilities and Vulnerabilities in the "Global War on Terror"' (2018) 44 Review of International Studies 2

Silverstein K, *Private Warriors* (Verso 2000)

Singer P, 'Outsourcing War' (2005) 84 Foreign Affairs 119

Singer P, 'The Contract That Military Needs to Break' (Brookings, 12 September 2004) <https://www.brookings.edu/opinions/the-contract-the-military-needs-to-break/> accessed 15 March 2021

Singer P, The Private Military Industry and Iraq: What Have We Learned and Where to Next? *Geneva Centre for the Democratic Control of Armed Forces* (2004) <https://www.dcaf.ch/private-military-industry-and-iraq> accessed 3 July 2023

Skinner G, 'Beyond Kiobel: Providing Access to Judicial Remedies for Violations of International Human Rights Norms by Transnational Business in a New (Post-Kiobel) World' (2014) 46 Columbia Human Rights Law Review 158

Steinhardt R, 'Kiobel and the Multiple Futures of Corporate Liability for Human Rights Violations Keynote Address: Symposium: Extraterritorial Post-Kiobel: International and Comparative Legal Perspectives' (2013) 28 Maryland Journal of International Law 1

Stephens B and others (eds), *International Human Rights Litigation in US Courts* (Martinus Nijhoff Publishers 2008)

Stephens B, 'Curious History of the Alien Tort Statute' (2014) 89 Notre Dame Law Review 1467, 1483

Stephens B, 'Sosa v. Alvarez-Machain - The Door Is Still Ajar for Human Rights Litigation in U.S. Courts Comment' (2004) 70 Brooklyn Law Review 533

Stephens B, 'Translating Filartiga: A Comparative and International Law Analysis of Domestic Remedies for International Human Rights Violations' (2002) 27 Yale Journal of International Law 1

Stumpf J, 'Citizens of an Enemy Land: Enemy Combatants, Aliens, and the Constitutional Rights of the Pseudo-Citizen' (2004) 38 UC Davis Law Review 79

Swain Elise, 'Iraqis Tortured by the U.S. in Abu Ghraib Never Got Justice' (The Intercept, 17 March 2023) <https://theintercept.com/2023/03/17/iraq-war-torture-abu-ghraib/> accessed 30 march 2023

The Center for Public Integrity, *Making a Killing: The Business of War* (Public Integrity Books 2003)

United Nations Security Council Resolution 1483, S/RES/1483 (22 May 2003)

Weiss P, 'ATS Lives: Al Shimari Survives Kiobel' (2015) 19 UCLA Journal of International Law and Foreign Affairs 19

Whytock C, Childress D and Ramsey M, 'After Kiobel - International Human Rights Litigation in State Courts and under State Law Human Rights Litigation in State Courts and Under State Laws: Foreword' (2013) 3 UC Irvine Law Review 1

Young EA, 'Universal Jurisdiction, the Alien Tort Statute, and Transnational Public-Law Litigation after Kiobel' (2014) 64 Duke Law Journal 1023

Zabci F, 'Private Military Companies: 'Shadow soldiers' of Neo-Colonialism' (2007) 31 Capital & Class 2

Chapter 6

ECCHR and Extraterritorial Prosecutions in Europe

The Lafarge Case

Historically, European corporations have served as the flag-bearers of the colonizing mission, often preceding the colonial state in the territory to be colonized. In our current understanding, many abuses carried out by colonial corporations while serving that role would qualify as crimes under international law.[1] Such involvement of European corporations in crimes that are taking place in the formerly colonized world continues to this day (see Annexure for details of many of these cases).

In response, there has been a progressively consistent reliance on criminal law, inter alia, in France (in *Lafarge* and *Amesys* cases among others),[2] Italy (*RWM Italia SpA* case),[3] Switzerland (*Argor-Heraeus* case),[4] and Sweden (*Lundin Oil* case)[5] to hold European corporations and their executives accountable for their complicity in gross violations taking place in third countries. Thus far, only two cases of corporate complicity in crimes under international law have resulted in convictions. Both took place in the Netherlands and were held on the basis of the active-nationality principle. In 2009, Frans van Anraat, a Dutch businessman, was convicted and sentenced to 17 years of imprisonment for complicity in genocide and war crimes, for supplying the chemical gas thiodiglycol (TDG) to the regime of Saddam Hussein.[6] Guus

1 For instance, in 1621, the Dutch East Indies Trading Company annihilated the total population of the Banda Islands in modern-day Indonesia, because they were unwilling to work on the company's nutmeg plantations; see Wim Huisman, Annika van Baar, and Madelijne Gorsira, 'Corporations and Transnational Crime' in *Histories of Transnational Crime* (Springer 2015) 147–170. The West Indies Trading Company (WIC) was responsible for the shipment of over half a million slaves from Africa to the Americas; see Kerry Ward, *Networks of Empire: Forced Migration in the Dutch East India Company* (Cambridge University Press 2009).
2 See Annexure case nos. 2 and 22.
3 See Annexure case no. 31.
4 See Annexure case no. 4.
5 See Annexure case no. 23.
6 TDG was used by Saddam Hussein for the production of chemical weapons that were later deployed during the war between Iraq and Iran in 1988, most notably in the city of Halabja. The Dutch trial court convicted Van Anraat as an accessory to war crimes committed through

DOI: 10.4324/9781003405047-9

Kouwenhoven, another Dutch businessman, controlled several companies in Liberia, including the Royal Timber Company (RTC) and the Oriental Timber Company (OTC). In 2003, the NGO Global Witness reported that Kouwenhoven was an important business partner of Charles Taylor, the former president of Liberia, and had financed the civil war in Liberia and Sierra Leone between 1999 and 2003. In 2017, Kouwenhoven was convicted for aiding and abetting war crimes committed by Taylor's troops.[7]

Arguably, the ICC's lack of jurisdiction over corporations for their involvement in crimes under international law has not directly translated into impunity in the domestic legal frameworks as well. In Europe, the use of domestic criminal law to challenge corporate activity facilitating crimes under international law may be attributed to the recently enacted 'international crimes' laws.[8]

These newly enacted provisions flowing from the ICC Statute, when combined with the existing national legal frameworks, allow for a varied degree of corporate responsibility for crimes under international law across jurisdictions. The combination of substantive international criminal law and domestic procedural framework offers strategic litigation organizations renewed avenues to seek accountability in different forms. In that vein, the use of

the use of chemical weapons, since it was evident that the quantity of TDG was not used for agricultural purposes, but relevant to military activity on the basis of Article 8 War Crimes Act (Wet Oorlogsstrafrecht). The Court of Appeal used a stricter *mens rea* standard of 'positive knowledge' finding that 'the defendant was very aware of the fact that – "in the ordinary [course] of events" – the gas was going to be used'. In 2009, the Supreme Court upheld the ruling by the Court of Appeal. See S. Onate and others, 'Lessons Learned: Chemicals Trader Convicted of War Crimes' (2007) 2 Hague Justice Journal 1.

7 It was reported that Kouwenhoven's security personnel, many of whom were also former militia members, had committed violence against the civilian population and that Kouwenhoven had smuggled weapons for Taylor's army. In addition, Kouwenhoven was accused of violating the Dutch Sanctions Act (Sanctiewet), which implemented the UN and EU regulations that prohibited the supply of weapons to Liberia. The Court held that Mr Kouwenhoven 'must have been aware' that 'in the ordinary course of events' the weapons and ammunition he supplied and helped import would be used. See Dieneke de Vos, 'Corporate Accountability: Dutch court convicts former "Timber baron" of war crimes in Liberia' (14 April 2017) <https://me.eui.eu/dieneke-de-vos/blog/corporate-accountability-dutch-courtconvicts-former-timber-baron-of-war-crimes-in-liberia/> accessed 21 February 2022; *Prosecutor v. Kouwenhoven*, Court of Appeal, Judgment, 21 April 2017 <https://uitspraken.rechtspraak.nl/inziendocument?id=ECLI:NL:GHSHE:2017:1760> accessed 21 February 2022.

8 See Joanna Kyriakakis, 'Developments in International Criminal Law and the Case of Business Involvement in International Crimes' (2012) 94 International Review of the Red Cross 887, 981–1005; Joanna Kyriakakis, 'Corporations before International Criminal Courts: Implications for the International Criminal Justice Project' (2017) 30 Leiden Journal of International Law 221; Wolfgang Kaleck and Miriam Saage-Maaß, 'Corporate Accountability for Human Rights Violations Amounting to International Crimes' (2010) 6 Journal of International Criminal Justice 699, 703 (hereinafter, Kaleck and Saage-Maaß, 'Corporate Accountability').

extraterritorial criminal trials against corporations for their involvement in crimes under international law forms the subject matter of this case study.

Distinct domestic legal orders and their somewhat complementary approach towards the implementation of international criminal law have led to strategic litigation taking a different shape in Europe as compared to the two cases discussed earlier.

The impunity of transnational corporations headquartered in Europe for outsourcing violence is being challenged creatively by transnational collaborations of strategic litigation organizations under the framework of extraterritorial prosecutions. One such case in which, for the first time, a corporate entity is being charged with complicity in crimes against humanity for the conduct of its subsidiary outside of Europe is ongoing in France against cement giant Lafarge. Criminal proceedings against the global cement leader were initiated on the basis of complaints filed by two non-governmental organizations: Berlin-based European Center for Constitutional and Human Rights (ECCHR) and Paris-based Sherpa. This case is discussed in greater detail to enunciate the workings of strategic litigation in Europe while seeking corporate accountability.

The first section of this chapter lays down the legal basis for extraterritorial prosecutions as conceived under international criminal law, followed by a discussion of the politics and practice of universal jurisdiction in the second section. The third section paints a broad stroke picture of the practice of strategic litigation in Europe before zooming in on ECCHR and their practice within the framework of international criminal law. Finally, the last section of the chapter discusses the Lafarge case, and the legal and practical challenges inherent in extraterritorial prosecutions of corporations.

I. Universal Jurisdiction and Extraterritorial Prosecutions

Extraterritorial criminal jurisdiction of a state refers to 'jurisdiction over the activities of legal persons in situations where such activities have taken place, in totality or in part, outside the national territory'.[9] The fact that it is explicitly termed 'extraterritorial' highlights the primacy of a 'territorial' notion of exercising sovereignty in the form of criminal jurisdiction.[10] Although all bases for jurisdiction are theoretically equal in criminal law,[11] clearly,

9 James R Fox, *Dictionary of International and Comparative Law* (3rd edn, Oceana Publications 2003) 114.

10 Jurisdiction refers to the 'power of a sovereign to affect the rights of persons, whether by legislation, by executive decree, or by judgment of a court'. See Ian Brownlie, *Principles of Public International Law* (5th edn, Oxford University Press 1998) 313 (hereinafter Brownlie, *Principles PIL)*.

11 *S.S. 'Lotus'* [1927] Permanent Court of International Justice, Series A, No. 10, 18–20.

territorial jurisdiction has a certain place of pride.[12] With respect to crimes under international law, when the territorial state is unwilling or unable to prosecute,[13] domestic courts of other states can resort to extraterritorial jurisdiction to prevent impunity.[14] An exercise of extraterritorial jurisdiction is justified on the basis of several recognized principles: the active personality principle, the passive personality principle, the protective principle, or the universality principle.[15]

Given the multiplicity of the principles on the basis of which extraterritorial prosecutions can be conducted, the jurisdiction to prosecute genocide, crimes against humanity, and war crimes may overlap between two or more national courts. In that context, international law envisions a model of concurring jurisdictions. There is no established hierarchy among these types of jurisdiction that would determine the venue for prosecution.[16] Thus, practical factors such as the whereabouts of the suspect and the availability of evidence end up deciding where a crime is finally prosecuted.[17] Against this backdrop, the broad term of 'extraterritorial prosecutions' is used to discuss the developing practice of enforcement of international criminal law in domestic courts.

Under this broad umbrella, however, the principle of 'universality' warrants further discussion. Universal jurisdiction is understood as a derivative jurisdiction. It is defined as the assertion by a state (the so-called 'third state') of criminal jurisdiction over crimes allegedly committed by non-nationals against non-nationals on the territory of another state with the crime posing

12 Frédéric Mégret, '"Do Not Do Abroad What You Would Not Do at Home?": An Exploration of the Rationales for Extraterritorial Criminal Jurisdiction over a State's Nationals' (2020) 57 Canadian Yearbook of International Law/Annuaire canadien de droit international 1, 8 (hereinafter Mégret, 'Do Not Do Abroad What You Would Not Do at Home?').

13 Dubbed as conditional subsidiarity of the exercise of extraterritorial jurisdiction by Florian Jeßberger, Wolfgang Kaleck and Andreas Schüller, 'Concurring Criminal Jurisdictions under International Law' in Morten Bersmo (ed), *Complimentarity and the Exercise of Universal Jurisdiction for Core International Crimes* (FICHL Publication Series No. 7, TOAEP 2010) 239 (hereinafter, Jeßberger and others, 'Concurring Criminal Jurisdictions').

14 Brownlie points out that the customary law and general principles of law relating to jurisdiction, such as territoriality, active and passive personality, and protection, 'are emanations of the concept of domestic jurisdiction and its concomitant, the principle of non-intervention in the internal affairs of states. These basic principles do not apply to or do not apply very helpfully to . . . crimes under international law. In these areas, special rules have evolved'. Brownlie, *Principles PIL* (n 10) 314.

15 For an overview, see Cedric Ryngaert, *Jurisdiction in International Law* (Oxford University Press 2015), 85–133.

16 Jeßberger and others, 'Concurring Criminal Jurisdictions' (n 13) 237.

17 Florian Jeßberger, 'International v. National Prosecution of International Crimes' in Antonio Cassese and others (eds), *Oxford Companion to International Criminal Law* (Oxford University Press 2009) 211 (hereinafter, Jeßberger, 'International v. National Prosecution').

no direct threat to the vital interests of the state asserting jurisdiction.[18] When exercising universal jurisdiction, the third state is acting as an agent of the 'international community',[19] an express manifestation of universalist claims made by international criminal law while seeking 'global justice'.

However, as has been argued, what is labelled as the universal is essentially European or Western.[20] It should be noted that even in the current practice of international criminal law, European jurisdictions and European actors continue to occupy a central place in the implementation of international criminal law.[21] In other words, the future terms and conditions of the nascent practice of universal jurisdiction and domestication of international criminal law are also largely being determined in Europe today.

While it is important to critique the fact that the substantive origins lie in, and the practice is being determined by, a 'few Western states', a critique that stops there would be perfunctory. In view of the multi-faceted understanding of the global 'North' and 'South' or 'the First' and 'Third World', a nuanced analysis of the application of the 'principle of universality' will locate both its hegemonic tendencies and counter-hegemonic practices.[22] Its practice is marked by dichotomies and contrasting positions.[23] It has gone through various phases in the European context itself. For instance, in the late 1990s and early 2000s, the practice of exercising universal jurisdiction in European

18 Council of the European Union, AU-EU Technical Ad Hoc Expert Report on the Principle of Universal Jurisdiction, 8672/1/19, Brussels, 16 April 2009, 42. On the principle of universality, see Gerhard Werle and Florian Jeßberger, *Principles of International Criminal Law* (4th end, Oxford University Press 2020) (hereinafter Werle and Jeßberger, *Principles*) 95–103; Julia Geneuss, 'Fostering a Better Understanding of Universal Jurisdiction: A Comment on the AU–EU Expert Report on the Principle of Universal Jurisdiction' (2009) 7 Journal of International Criminal Justice 5, 945–962.

19 This justification rests on the conviction that the international community has a collective interest in deterring crime. Consequently, the international community has an interest in ensuring that serious offenders do not escape prosecution when the host state wishes to prosecute but cannot do so. See Dapo Akande, 'The Jurisdiction of the International Criminal Court over Nationals of Non-Parties: Legal Basis and Limits' (2003) Journal of International Criminal Justice 1, 618, 626.

20 See discussion in Chapter 1.

21 See Anne-Marie Slaughter and William Burke-White, 'The Future of International Law Is Domestic (or, the European Way of Law)' (2006) 47 Harvard International Law Journal 327 (It is important to note here that the authors move from prediction to prescription, suggesting ways that the European way of law should become the future of international law writ large).

22 Martti Koskenniemi, *From Apology to Utopia: The Structure of the International Legal Argument* (Cambridge University Press 2005) 241.

23 Debates include issues such as the presence of the offender as a prerequisite to exercising jurisdiction, immunity of state officials before foreign courts, the substantive crimes over which universal jurisdiction can be asserted by states, justification and content of the principle. See Aisling O'Sullivan, *Universal Jurisdiction in International Criminal Law: The Debate and The Battle for Hegemony* (Routledge 2017) (hereinafter O'Sullivan, *The Debate and The Battle for Hegemony*).

courts suddenly rose to prominence, displacing the well-established international legal principles of non-interference and sovereignty. A series of investigations and trials were initiated concerning international crimes committed, inter alia, in Argentina, Chile, Guatemala, and Haiti, followed by Rwanda, Congo, Algeria, and Afghanistan.

This post-2002 era of initiating universal jurisdiction trials, again primarily in Europe, can be attributed to the complementarity regime set-up by the ICC Statute and implementing legislations which incorporated international crimes in domestic legal frameworks.[24] These enabling legislations fell in the hands of enthusiastic international lawyers, some of whom along with NGOs had been passionately lobbying for an international criminal court in the years before.[25] Pinochet was arrested rather sensationally around the same time.[26] These events motivated and empowered human rights organizations, lawyers, prosecutors, and judges in Europe to prosecute egregious human rights violations in domestic and international fora and further their 'anti-impunity' positions.[27] As a result of this initial enthusiasm, the early years witnessed geopolitically expensive investigations against the United States or China initiated domestically in third states.[28]

Unsurprisingly, these events attracted political backlash and were dismissively labelled as politically motivated.[29] Responding to the backlash, along

24 Joanna Kyriakakis, 'Australian Prosecution of Corporations for International Crimes: The Potential of the Commonwealth Criminal Code' (2007) 5 Journal of International Criminal Justice 4; 809–826; also see the results of a study covering 16 countries coordinated for the Fafo by Anita Ramasastry and RC Thomas, *Commerce, Crime and Conflict. Legal Remedies for Private Sector Liability for Grave Breaches of International Law. A Survey of Sixteen Countries* (FAFO 2006).

25 See Harmen van der Wilt, '"Sadder but Wiser"?: NGOs and Universal Jurisdiction for International Crimes' (2015) 13 Journal of International Criminal Justice 237 (hereinafter van der Wilt, 'Sadder but Wiser'); Zoe Pearson, 'Non-Governmental Organizations and the International Criminal Court: Changing Landscapes of International Law' (2006) 39 Cornell International Law Journal 243; Máximo Langer, 'The Archipelago and the Wheel — The Universal Jurisdiction and the International Criminal Court Regimes' in Minow, True-Frost and Whiting (eds), *The First Global Prosecutor: Promise and Constraints* (University of Michigan Press 2015) 204–250, 221.

26 See Ariel Dorfman, *Exorcising terror: The Incredible Unending Trial of General Augusto Pinochet* (Seven Stories Press 2011); Naomi Roht-Arriaza, 'The Pinochet Precedent and Universal Jurisdiction' (2000) 35 New England Law Review 311.

27 Wolfgang Kaleck, 'From Pinochet to Rumsfeld: Universal Jurisdiction in Europe 1998–2008' (2008) 30 Michigan Journal of International Law 927, 929.

28 Christine Bakker, 'Universal Jurisdiction of Spanish Courts over Genocide in Tibet: Can it Work?' (2006) 4 Journal of International Criminal Justice 3, 595–601; Katherine Gallagher, 'Universal Jurisdiction in Practice: Efforts to hold Donald Rumsfeld and other high-level United States officials accountable for torture' (2009) 7 Journal of International Criminal Justice 5, 1087–1116 (hereinafter Gallagher, 'Universal Jurisdiction in Practice').

29 See O'Sullivan, *The Debate and The Battle for Hegemony* (n 23).

with the ICJ's *Arrest Warrant* judgment,[30] the states rapidly retreated and started downsizing the expansive scope of universal jurisdiction. This led many scholars to jump to the conclusion that universal jurisdiction had lost its ground and the 'bell was tolling' for the principle of universality.[31]

Nevertheless, the subsequent decades have proved those observations wrong. In scholarship, the 'rise and fall' narrative of universal jurisdiction has been adequately challenged.[32] In practice, genuine legal problems have been clearly demarcated from the *realpolitik* of international criminal law.

Contemporary practice of universal jurisdiction has gained solid ground in some respects, yet it remains marked with certain inconsistencies. The following sections identify broad trends in current practice of universal jurisdiction in Europe.

1. Increasing Democratization of Universal Jurisdiction

As opposed to the initial years when only a few select lawyers and professors were familiar with international criminal law and its intricacies, the tool of universal jurisdiction has been 'quietly expanding'[33] and has become increasingly accessible. In quantitative terms, there has been a sharp increase in the number of petitions filed on the basis of universal jurisdiction,[34] organizations which claim to be using universal jurisdiction as a tool to fulfil their mandates on international accountability and justice,[35] and scholarly attention to the

30 Arrest Warrant of 11 April 2000, *Democratic Republic of the Congo v. Belgium* [2002] ICJ.

31 See Antonio Cassese, 'Is the Bell Tolling for Universality? A Plea for a Sensible Notion of Universal Jurisdiction' (2003) 1 Journal of International Criminal Justice 589; Luc Reydams, 'The Rise and Fall of Universal Jurisdiction' in *Routledge Handbook of International Criminal Law* (Routledge 2012); Ben-Ari, 'Universal Jurisdiction: Chronicle of a Death Foretold?' (2014–2015) 43 Denver Journal of International Law and Policy 165; Moral de la Rasilla, 'The Swan Song of Universal Jurisdiction in Spain' (2009) 9 International Criminal Law Review 777.

32 Máximo Langer, 'Universal Jurisdiction is Not Disappearing: The Shift from "Global Enforcer" to "No Safe Haven" Universal Jurisdiction' (2015) 13 Journal of International Criminal Justice 2, 245; Florian Jeßberger, 'Towards a "Complementary Preparedness" Approach to Universal Jurisdiction – Recent Trends and Best Practices in the European Union' in European Parliament, *Universal jurisdiction and international crimes: Constraints and best practices* (2018) 46 <http://www.legal-tools.org/doc/fb2d88/> accessed 22 February 2022 (hereinafter Jeßberger, 'Towards a Complementary Preparedness Approach')

33 Máximo Langer and Mackenzie Eason, 'The Quiet Expansion of Universal Jurisdiction' (2019) 30 European Journal of International Law 3, 779–817.

34 Ibid. The paper is based on findings from Langer's database on universal jurisdiction cases originally compiled by Máximo Langer.

35 Florian Jeßberger and Leonie Steinl, 'Strategic Litigation in International Criminal Justice: Facilitating a View from Within' (2022) Journal of International Criminal Justice (hereinafter Jeßberger and Steinl, 'Strategic Litigation: A View from Within').

subject.[36] These factors speak volumes on the expanding interest, knowledge, and practice of international criminal law in general and universal jurisdiction in particular. This enhanced accessibility suggests a trend towards increasing democratization of universal jurisdiction as a tool. A 2022 review of universal jurisdiction found that extraterritorial prosecutions (universal as well as active-nationality jurisdiction) are taking place in 16 jurisdictions for crimes under international law committed in 22 different countries against over 100 suspects.[37] But an overwhelming amount of these proceedings have only taken place in Western Europe (with the few exceptions of Argentina,[38] Senegal,[39] etc.). In that sense, accessibility is still bound within the geographical limitations of affluent European countries.

Beyond numerical expansion, the democratization of universal jurisdiction as a tool also implies that the initiation of criminal proceedings is not exclusively dependent on a handful of prominent individual figures. A substantial amount of work in the formative years of international criminal law rested on the shoulders of individual personalities such as the Spanish Judge Baltazar Garzón.[40] It is laudable how his work helped the Spanish judiciary become accustomed to the idea that they could prosecute the crimes of the Argentine military dictatorship in the 1970s or the massacre at Srebrenica.[41] But at the same time, excessive reliance on individuals meant that universal jurisdiction prosecutions were essentially dependent on the docket of one proactive judge or one enthusiastic prosecutor, which did not bode well for the ideal of 'global justice'. Similarly, the number of domestic prosecutors competent

36 See Google Books Ngram < https://books.google.com/ngrams/graph?content=universal+jurisdiction&year_start=1990&year_end=2019&corpus=26&smoothing=3> accessed 22 February 2022 (not conclusive, albeit one indicator of consistently increasing scholarly attention since 2002).

37 TRIAL International and others, Universal Jurisdiction Annual Review (UJAR) 2022 < https://trialinternational.org/wp-content/uploads/2022/03/TRIAL_International_UJAR-2022.pdf > accessed 30 March 2023.

38 See Promueven Querella Criminal por la Comisión de los Delitos de Genocidio y/o de Lesa Humanidad que Tuvieron Lugar en España en el Período Comprendido entre el 17 de Julio de 1936 y el 15 de Junio de 1977, [2010]; Juzgado Nacional Criminal y Correccional Federal 1 [2013] CFP 4591/2010 'N.N. s/ genocidio'

39 Reed Brody, *Victims Bring a Dictator to Justice: The Case of Hissène Habré* (2017) 9 (updated edition after the final April 2017 verdict).

40 Daniel Rothenberg and Baltasar Garzón, 'Let Justice Judge: An Interview with Judge Baltasar Garzón and Analysis of His Ideas' (2002) 24 Human Rights Quarterly 4, 924–973; Peter Burbidge, 'Waking the dead of the Spanish Civil War: Judge Baltasar Garzon and the Spanish Law of Historical Memory' (2011) 9 Journal of International Criminal Justice 3, 753–781; John Carlin, 'Spain's Man of Law With Cojones of Steel' (2002) 131 New Statesman 4611, 20–21; regarding allegations of judicial misconduct, see <https://www.ecchr.eu/en/case/trial-of-spanish-judge-garzon/> accessed 22 February 2022.

41 Wolfgang Kaleck, *Double Standards: International Criminal Law and the West* (TOAEP 2015) 64, 65, 73 (hereinafter Kaleck, *Double Standards*).

in the framework of international criminal law to go after international perpetrators was very low. To some extent, this reliance on a few individuals to enforce the law, particularly on prosecutors familiar with this framework, might still be present. Nevertheless, this slow yet steady proliferation has led to an increased competency of the domestic courts to deal with situations involving international crimes in third countries.

2. *Politically Inexpensive Cases*

In recent years, international lawyers who would use universal jurisdiction have shifted to a more cautious and realistic gear. The early years of using universal jurisdiction were marked by the high-profile arrests of Pinochet and Videla, and criminal complaints against Rumsfeld and Bush.[42] Two decades later, the youthful naivety appears to have come of age. The wisdom gathered over the years is reflected in the fact that most of the perpetrators charged in universal jurisdiction cases range from low- to mid-level in the hierarchy.[43] This focus on low-cost defendants and defendants who are already present or residing in the prosecuting state, arguably, prevents universal jurisdiction from becoming a tool of global vigilante justice. Also, going after the 'small fish' makes the avenue of universal jurisdiction more sustainable.

In that sense, the idea of attributing individual criminal responsibility to the 'most responsible' or persons in 'leadership positions' does not hold a strong ground in the present-day practice of universal jurisdiction. Scholarship has dubbed this inconsistency as the big fish versus small fish dilemma.[44] It must be noted that universal jurisdiction practice is not unique to have rested on the horns of this dilemma. The ad hoc tribunals and the ICC have also been asked the question if they have the teeth to go after the most responsible perpetrators.[45] The ICC, in the past, has also recognized the need for 'a strategy of gradually building (cases) upwards'.[46] Therefore, this

42 Ibid 61–76; see Michael Ratner, *The Trial of Donald Rumsfeld: A Prosecution by Book* (The New Press 2008).

43 See TRIAL International Annual Universal Jurisdiction Reports 2014, 2015, 2016.

44 See Melanie O'Brien, 'Prosecutorial Discretion as an Obstacle to Prosecution of United Nations Peacekeepers by the International Criminal Court: The Big Fish/Small Fish Debate and the Gravity Threshold' (2012) 10 Journal of International Criminal Justice 3, 525–545 (hereinafter O'Brien, 'The Big Fish/Small Fish Debate').

45 Carsten Stahn, 'Daedalus or Icarus? Footprints of International Criminal Justice Over a Quarter of a Century' (2017) ZaöRV 77, 371–408.

46 OTP, Strategic Plan 2012–2015, para 22 (The Office would therefore first investigate and prosecute a limited number of mid- and high-level perpetrators in order to ultimately have a reasonable chance to convict the most responsible. Such a strategy will in the end be more cost-effective than having unsuccessful or no prosecutions against the highest placed perpetrators.)

disconnect between the principle of prosecuting the 'most responsible' for the 'most serious crimes', and the actual practice of prosecuting low-to-mid ranking perpetrators could be an ubiquitous feature of international criminal justice at large.

However, scholars such as Melanie O'Brien have questioned the fixation on senior leaders and what it means for the purposes set out for international criminal justice.[47] She argues that the victims' perspective must be taken into account in this debate and the most important perpetrators for the victims are those who committed the crime, not those who ordered its commission.[48]

On a more practical note, the basic justification is that the prosecutions of small fish in third states are inexpensive. It is important to consider the factor of limited resources of any given country to seek enforcement of these proceedings against high-level perpetrators as opposed to international tribunals. This results in states prosecuting only those perpetrators who are either their nationals or are on their territory for some reason. Most importantly, the foreign policy of the state conducting investigations and trials carries substantial weight given that the criminal law set-up is exclusively dependent on prosecutorial discretion and thus, the state.

However, this practice disregards the normative justification that international prosecutions should have a qualitatively precedential and quantitatively subsidiary function. International prosecutions are supposed to be qualitatively precedential in the sense that they should deal with those persons who bear the main responsibilities for international crimes.[49] Prosecuting low-ranking officers when they were directly involved in the commission of crimes does not often create qualitative precedents capable of being replicated.

Therefore, the current trend indicates that, despite the increased democratization outlined in sub-section 1, the principle of universality is still mostly being enforced by select Western states prosecuting mid- to low-level perpetrators from countries of conflict and consequently, it is also subject to the political interests of enforcing states.

3. *Coordinated Efforts to Overcome Practical Challenges*

Victims and perpetrators from conflict-torn countries taking refuge in Europe have been a major factor in facilitating extraterritorial prosecutions. Relatively easier access to evidence, little to no accountability in the countries where crimes are committed, and territorial control over the defendants give a rather direct link for the so-called third states to act as agents of the international community.

47 O'Brien, 'The Big Fish/Small Fish Debate' (n 44).
48 Ibid 531.
49 Jeßberger, 'International v. National Prosecution' (n 17) 214.

Institutional changes have also been initiated across jurisdictions to overcome practical barriers in gathering evidence and carrying out complex prosecutions. For instance, the creation of special international crimes divisions in the police and/or in the office of the prosecutor or among investigating judges.[50] Moreover, there is an increasingly transnational division of labour to conduct these prosecutions.[51] The European Union (EU) member states have strengthened their coordination and cooperation among themselves.[52] The formation of multinational 'joint investigative teams' focused on the prosecution of transnational crimes,[53] training programs dedicated to investigating international crimes,[54] and Europe-wide institutions such as EUROPOL and the European Arrest Warrant (EAW)[55] are a few examples of this new collaborative outlook.

The coordinated networks establish an institutional nexus within which officials involved in law enforcement, immigration, intelligence, or other relevant fields can share information. As a result, highly specialized expertise and resources are pooled together, resulting in more focused investigations and expedited proceedings.

50 For instance, Central Unit for the Fight against War Crimes and Further Offenses pursuant to the German Code against Crimes under International Law - *Zentralstelle zur Bekämpfung von Kriegsverbrechen und weiteren Straftaten nach dem Völkerstrafgesetzbuch* (Germany); War Crimes Prosecution Unit within Office of Federal Prosecutor (Germany); Police War Crimes Unit (Sweden); Specialized War Crimes Unit within Prosecution Authority (Sweden); L'Office central de lutte contre les crimes contre l'humanité, les génocides et lsses crimes de guerre (OCLCH) (France).

51 Jeßberger, 'Towards a Complementary Preparedness Approach' (n 32) 4.

52 See for instance, EU Genocide Network <https://www.eurojust.europa.eu/judicial-cooperation/practitioner-networks/genocide-network> accessed 22 February 2022. This initiative brings together representatives from the EU member states and representatives from Norway, Switzerland, Canada, and the United States to discuss legal and practical issues related to their work and to share information on specific cases. The network's success has inspired the African Union to begin efforts to establish a similar network of prosecutors from African countries. See Human Rights Watch, 'Long Arm of Justice: Lessons from Specialized War Crimes Units in France, Germany, and the Netherlands' <https://www.hrw.org/report/2014/09/16/long-arm-justice/lessons-specialized-war-crimes-units-france-germany-and#_ftnref1> accessed 22 February 2022 (hereinafter, HRW, 'Long Arm of Justice').

53 Council Framework Decision on Joint Investigation Teams (13 June 2002) 2002/465/JHA.

54 The Institute for International Criminal Justice regularly hosts such trainings for domestic investigators and other legal professionals. See <https://iici.global/> accessed 22 February 2022. INTERPOL has offered such trainings to war crimes investigators as well. See Interpol, 'War crimes investigators join INTERPOL simulation exercise' (29 November 2019).

55 Council Framework Decision on the European Arrest Warrant (EAW) and the Surrender Procedures Between Member States [2002] 2002/584/JHA. The EAW replaces the process of extradition between EU member states and abolishes dual criminality for many categories of crimes. For more details, see <https://ec.europa.eu/info/law/cross-border-cases/judicial-cooperation/types-judicial-cooperation/european-arrest-warrant_en> accessed 22 February 2022.

A Human Rights Watch report, based on interviews with practitioners, prosecutors, and judges on this issue, recalls the French experience in this context. It notes that without specialized war crimes units, authorities often find these challenges daunting and consequently choose not to prioritize universal jurisdiction cases.[56] For example, investigations into Rwandan genocide suspects living in France sat idle for years, in large part due to prosecutors' and investigative judges' lack of experience, resources, and time, resulting in criticism from the ECtHR in 2004. It was not until the establishment of a specialized unit of prosecutors and investigative judges in Paris in 2012 that these cases could be meaningfully pursued.[57]

This coordination is not only taking place on account of the states. NGOs and practitioners who bring these complaints, or contribute to the proceedings,[58] also work in a coordinated collaborative manner to bring these highly complex cases.

To summarize, the three trends that mark the ongoing practice of the principle of universality are increasing democratization of universal jurisdiction as a tool, preference for low-ranking politically inexpensive defendants, and transnational coordination and collaboration between states and other actors within Europe. The understanding and application of universal jurisdiction has shifted from the patronizing 'global-enforcer approach', wherein the states viewed universal jurisdiction as a tool to prevent and punish international crimes committed anywhere in the world. These developments indicate that the gears have now been moved to a narrower, more cautious, and realistic 'complementary preparedness' approach where various actors work together to prevent their territory from becoming a refuge for suspects involved in the commission of international crimes. As Jeßberger notes, the idea of international solidarity in the enforcement of international criminal law through the different stakeholders has become an integral part of the current understanding of universal jurisdiction.[59] However, the international solidarity – at least for now – is largely limited to European institutions and states, and is subject to their policy considerations.

Therefore, despite some positive developments, the practice of universal jurisdiction has largely failed to shed its hegemonic tendencies, thus allowing for competing claims concerning its impact and potential. Even in its most decentralized form, it continues to be a state-driven practice. Moreover,

56 See HRW, 'Long Arm of Justice' (n 52).

57 Ibid.

58 See Jeßberger and Steinl, 'Strategic Litigation: A View from Within' (n 35).

59 Jeßberger, 'Towards a complementary preparedness approach' (n 32) 3; see Wolfgang Kaleck and Patrick Kroker, 'Syrian Torture Investigations in Germany and Beyond: Breathing New Life into Universal Jurisdiction in Europe?' (2018) 16 Journal of International Criminal Justice 1, 165–191 (hereinafter Kaleck and Kroker, 'Syrian Torture Investigations in Germany and Beyond').

Europe being its almost exclusive place of practice calls for valid criticism on grounds of its Eurocentricity. The question then comes down to whether domestic implementation of international criminal law, in its current form, leaves any space for the critical legal practitioners to write resistance into the legal order.

II. ECCHR and Transnational Strategic Litigation

1. *The Many Faces of Strategic Litigation in Europe*

The scope of bringing legal claims against corporations for their misconduct abroad is very narrow. In this context, the innovative use of existing legal frameworks against corporate complicity has taken the shape of extraterritorial prosecutions, as discussed above. The litigations tend to be highly complex and technical, thus often dependent on transnational collaborations. As shown in the case-mapping table (see Annexure), even if most of the complaints are initiated in states such as France or Germany, these cases are primarily built on shared labour of transnational collaborations of non-state organizations. The transnational element of strategic litigation, in this context, does not merely suggest connections between the actors in the country of commission and the country of prosecution. It also implies partnerships between actors with similar mandates across European jurisdictions built on specialized legal and technical expertise.

Having acknowledged that collaborations are an integral part of this practice, it becomes not only difficult but also unfair to narrow down to one primary face of strategic litigation to represent the broader practice. Ascribing the acclaim of being a pioneer or a protagonist to one organization employing international criminal law to achieve political strategic objectives in this context would be misleading, for the following two reasons: one, the absence of a pan-European entity with a broad expertise and presence in jurisdictions where such cases can be brought. Diversity of jurisdictions requires a broad range of expertise and a much larger playfield in terms of engaging with judicial and non-judicial institutions. Different legal frameworks have resulted in a plurality of actors with their exclusive expertise that responds to the needs of their base jurisdiction. Some organizations might have offices and competence in multiple countries, such as Redress (with offices in London and The Hague),[60] but there is no one major actor in this context. Two, institutionalizing the use of law as a means to stage political protest is a rather new phenomenon in this context. Historically, lawyers, legal organizations, and political activists have been using criminal law and trials to achieve strategic

60 See their official website <https://redress.org/> accessed 22 February 2022.

political objectives.[61] However, the form this institutionalization has taken today is novel: the non-governmental organizations established by lawyers pursuing progressive sociopolitical objectives through persistent use of available legal means.

Therefore, most of the strategic litigation organizations in Europe are relatively young to have established such a long-standing reputation as compared to the ones in the United States or Argentina discussed in other case studies. Some of the organizations that claim to be strategically litigating international criminal cases in European jurisdictions are ECCHR, Berlin; TRIAL International, Switzerland; Civitas Maxima, Switzerland; Sherpa, Paris; *Fédération Internationale Pour Les Droits Humains* (FIDH), France; Redress (UK/Netherlands); and Global Legal Action Network (UK/Ireland).[62] The list is not exhaustive; however, it does highlight the fact that most of these organizations are based in Western Europe.

Despite the competition within the non-profit sector that heavily depends on donor-funding, strategic litigation organizations in Europe have managed to build project-based partnerships and pool their respective expertise to initiate complicated litigations. The collaborations range from producing research reports, field updates, such as Universal Jurisdiction Annual Review (TRIAL International co-produces it, inter alia, with FIDH, ECCHR, and Redress),[63] to filing criminal complaints, submitting *amicus* briefs, etc.

It should also be noted that not all of the aforementioned organizations fit neatly within the conceptualization of strategic litigation as laid down in Chapter 2, mainly because not all of them explicitly engage in the political examination of their work and its contribution to the inegalitarian nature of legal structures. Nevertheless, their practice does reflect a de-centring of focus from states in the realm of international criminal law.[64] The golden thread that binds them is their forward-looking approach to bring cases that have a broader political impact and their focus on states/corporations enjoying impunity for their involvement in egregious violations of human rights. For the purposes of this book, an extensive discussion on all of their cases is neither feasible nor warranted. In keeping with the representative nature

61 There are numerous examples of individual lawyers and legal organizations using trials and criminal legal proceedings to highlight the structural injustices of the system. For instance, see the work of Communist Party Legal Organization and others during the Weimar Republic in Henning Grunwald, *Courtroom to Revolutionary Stage: Performance and Ideology in Weimar Political Trials* (Oxford University Press 2012); Douglas Morris, *Legal Sabotage: Ernst Fraenkel in Hitler's Germany* (Cambridge University Press 2020).

62 See Jeßberger and Steinl, 'Strategic Litigation: A View from Within' (n 35).

63 See TRIAL International Annual Universal Jurisdiction Reports <https://trialinternational.org/latest/reports-and-publications/> accessed 22 February 2022.

64 Jeßberger and Steinl, 'Strategic Litigation: A View from Within' (n 35).

of the case study, this section only deals with the explicitly political strategic litigation practice of the Berlin-based ECCHR.

2. *ECCHR's Use of the Symbolism of International Criminal Law*

'Using the law. For a world free from torture, exploitation, and fortressed borders'.[65]

ECCHR's website flashes open with this motto outlining their mandate. In 2007, Wolfgang Kaleck, a German human rights lawyer, set up this organization in Berlin. The small team of ambitious lawyers, backed by renowned lawyers and professionals from Germany and across the globe, aimed to challenge the impunity enjoyed by powerful states and multinational corporations for violation of human rights. Even before setting up this entity, the legal interventions against high-ranking US officers in the preceding years had set the stage for ECCHR's mission to challenge political and economic hegemony in the global order.

In 2004 and 2006, along with lawyers Michael Ratner and Peter Weiss from CCR-New York, Kaleck filed two complaints before the Federal Prosecutor in Germany, on behalf of Iraqi survivors, alleging that, inter alia, former US Secretary of Defense Donald Rumsfeld held direct and command responsibility for the torture and mistreatment of detainees in US-run prisons in Guantanamo Bay, Cuba, and Abu Ghraib, Iraq.[66] The complaint was based on universal jurisdiction as prescribed under the newly enacted German Code of Crimes Against International Law (CCAIL).[67] It enabled the German Federal Prosecutor to investigate and prosecute international crimes, irrespective of the location of the defendant or plaintiff, the place where the crime was carried out, or the nationality of the persons involved.[68]

65 See ECCHR's official website < https://www.ecchr.eu/en/> accessed 22 February 2022.

66 Wolfgang Kaleck, *Law versus Power* (OR Books 2019) 150 (hereinafter Kaleck, *Law versus Power*); For a comprehensive description of US torture policy and the contents of the complaints, see Gallagher, 'Universal Jurisdiction in Practice' (n 28).

67 The English translation of CCAIL <http://www.iuscomp.org/gla/statutes/VoeStGB.pdf> accessed 22 February 2022.

68 Section 1 of the CCAIL reads: 'This Act shall apply to all criminal offenses against international law designated under this Act, to serious criminal offences designated therein even when the offence was committed abroad and bears no relation to Germany'. The Explanatory Memorandum to the CCAIL states that 'the primary objective' of the CCAIL is to fight impunity for international crimes 'by solidarity in prosecution. ... [t]he investigation and prosecution duty is not limited to crimes which have a German connection: even if there is no connection, the results of investigations initiated in Germany could be valuable for proceedings before a foreign or international criminal court'. Government Explanatory Memorandum as quoted in Salvatore Zappalà, 'The German Federal Prosecutor's Decision

It was unsurprising, that the German Prosecutor refused to initiate an investigation on both occasions.[69] For the lawyers, the actual initiation of investigation and issuance of arrest warrants was an aspirational goal with an eye on other intermediate achievable milestones. These criminal complaints against Rumsfeld and others were as much about politics as much as they were about the law. Kaleck and CCR lawyers had already capitalized on the publicity garnered by the criminal complaints even before they were filed.[70] In alleging that Donald Rumsfeld was directly responsible for abuse of detainees, the broader objective behind the case was to contextualize the unlawful torture policy of the United States.[71] In a tactical move, just after Rumsfeld's resignation, at the peak of a public discussion about his career, they leaked the information about their criminal complaints a week before they were going to be filed.[72] Widely reported by international outlets, they had successfully created a discourse around his impunity even before actually

not to Prosecute a Former Uzbek Minister: Missed Opportunity or Prosecutorial Wisdom?' (2006) 4 Journal of International Criminal Justice 602, 608–609.

69 The reason given for the 2004 decision was that investigations in Germany are only permitted if the competent state, either the state where the criminal acts took place, the home state of the victim, or of the perpetrator's home state, is unwilling or unable to itself carry out an investigation. Kaleck lodged an appeal against the decision, which was rejected by the Appeal Court in Stuttgart on 13 September 2005. The 2006 complaint was rejected once again. This time, the prosecution justified its decision by arguing that the suspects did not reside, or expect to do so, on German soil, thus adding an additional barrier to the initiation of legal proceedings against the United States. For more details, see case report. <https://www.ecchr.eu/fileadmin/Fallbeschreibungen/Case_Report_Rumsfeld.pdf> accessed 22 February 2022; A Fischer-Lescano, 'Decision of the General Federal Prosecutor at the Federal Court of Justice: *Center for Constitutional Rights et al. v. Donald Rumsfeld et al.*' (2006) 45 International Legal Materials 119–121.

70 See, for example, Mark Landler, '12 Detainees Sue Rumsfeld in Germany, Citing Abuse' (NY Times, 15 November 2006) <https://www.nytimes.com/2006/11/15/world/europe/15german.html> accessed 22 February 2022; 'War Crimes Lawsuit Filed Against Rumsfeld in Germany' (Deutsche Welle, 14 November 2006) <https://www.dw.com/en/war-crimes-lawsuit-filed-against-rumsfeld-in-germany/a-2237323>; 'Human Rights groups seek criminal investigation in Germany of Rumsfeld and other high-ranking US officials for authorizing torture in the 'war on terror' (FIDH, 13 November 2006) <https://www.fidh.org/en/region/americas/usa/USA-Guantanamo-Abu-Ghraib/Human-Rights-groups-seek-criminal> accessed 22 February 2022.

71 Gallagher, 'Universal Jurisdiction in Practice' (n 28) 1090–99; A. Fischer-Lescano, 'Torture in Abu Ghraib: The Complaint against Donald Rumsfeld under the German Code of Crimes against International Law' (2005) 6 German Law Journal 689–724, 689.

72 Kaleck, *Law versus Power* (n 66) 155.

going to court.[73] Rumsfeld was reported to have cancelled his trip to Munich for fear of arrest in Germany.[74]

In a memoir, Kaleck recalls the day they filed the second complaint:

> We give interview after interview, explaining the background of our legal action ... By submitting complaints against individuals, we are making use of the drama of the criminal law ... we try to draw attention to the broader system of torture that still needs to be fought through legal and political battles.[75]

Since 2007, ECCHR has been consistently building on this reputation of employing the symbolism of law to fight political battles. With respect to international criminal law, they have been tinkering with universal jurisdiction domestically and have submitted several communications to the Officer of the Prosecutor (OTP)-ICC challenging selectivity and double standards in the practice of international criminal justice.[76] The organization views highlighting and challenging double standards as a source of legitimacy for a European organization in the business of international justice.[77] The cases discussed in the following section serve to illustrate their approach of strategic litigation as relevant context to the case against Lafarge.

3. *Strategic Litigation and Challenging Political–Economic Power*

The approach of challenging political–economic power may have found a home in the form of an organization with an official mandate and a devoted team of lawyers, but their practice has significantly evolved and perhaps become 'cautiously innovative' over the years.

73 Jana Simon, 'Einer gegen Rumsfeld' (Die Zeit, 9 November 2006) <https://www.zeit.de/2006/46/Einer_gegen_Rumsfeld> accessed 22 February 2022; 'The Insider's Guide to Putting World Leaders on Trial' (CNN, 14 November 2006). <http://edition.cnn.com/2006/WORLD/europe/11/14/insider.trials/index.html> accessed 22 February 2022

74 'Arrest Threat to Rumsfeld' (BBC, 4 February 2005) <http://news.bbc.co.uk/2/hi/americas/4236489.stm>

75 Kaleck, *Law versus Power* (n 66) 160.

76 Excerpts from ECCHR's website: 'No politician or military officer from a Western state has ever sat on the defendants' bench at the ICC or gone on trial in a third state for international crimes. Despite many steps forwards, we still seem to be quite far from a truly international system of criminal justice for crimes against international law. With its legal interventions ..., ECCHR sends a clear message against double standards: even powerful perpetrators can face prosecution'. <https://www.ecchr.eu/en/cluster/double-standards-democracies/> accessed 19 July 2021.

77 Interview with Claire Tixeire, Senior Legal Advisor, ECCHR (online, 31 August 2021).

An illustrative example is the filing of criminal complaints that led to trials and convictions of Syrian officials for war crimes and crimes against humanity before domestic courts in Germany. ECCHR supported 17 torture survivors from Syria in the so-called Al-Khatib proceedings, 7 of whom were admitted as joint plaintiffs, in the world's first trial of state torture committed by the Syrian regime. The trial involved violations including torture, killings, and sexual violence carried out at the infamous Al-Khatib prison in Damascus run by Branch 251 of the Syrian General Intelligence Service between April 2011 and September 2012.[78]

In February 2021 and January 2022, the Koblenz Higher Regional Court convicted Anwar R.[79] and Eyad A.[80] for their involvement in crimes against humanity under CCAIL. Anwar was chief of the investigative unit at Al-Khatib prison and Eyad worked as one of his subordinates who would arrest people from anti-government protests and bring them to Al-Khatib. Both of them had defected from the Syrian regime and sought asylum in Germany several years before the trial began.[81]

78 See ECCHR, 'Dossier on Human Rights Violations in Syria: Torture under Assad' (March 2021) < https://www.ecchr.eu/fileadmin/Sondernewsletter_Dossiers/Dossier_Syria_2021March.pdf> accessed 22 February 2022.

79 Anwar R. was sentenced to life imprisonment for killing, torture, serious deprivation of liberty, rape, and sexual assault as crimes against humanity under section 7 para 1, no. 1, 5, 6, 9 of the CCAIL, and section 211 paras 1, 2 (murder); section 177 paras 1, 2, and 3 (sexual assault); and section 25 para 2 (joint perpetration) of the German Criminal Code. Oberlandesgericht Koblenz, Life imprisonment due to crimes committed against humanity and murder – sentencing of a suspected member of the Syrian secret service (17 January 2022) <https://olgko.justiz.rlp.de/de/startseite/detail/news/News/detail/life-imprisonment-due-to-crimes-committed-against-humanity-and-murder-sentencing-of-a-suspected-me/> 22 January 2022.

80 The judges found him guilty of aiding and abetting torture and severe deprivation of liberty as crimes against humanity. They found that he was involved in the arrest of 30 people and their transfer to Branch 251 in September or October 2011. According to the judges, he could have escaped the situation and a defence of duress was therefore not applicable. After weighing the aggravating and mitigating factors based on the totality of evidence (namely his self-incriminating interview with the German asylum authority), Eyad Al-Gharib was sentenced to 4.5 years imprisonment. See SAJC Trial Monitoring Report <https://syriaaccountability.org/library/inside-the-raslan-trial-the-al-gharib-verdict-in-detail/> accessed 6 March 2022; see official press release by Higher Regional Court Koblenz < https://olgko.justiz.rlp.de/de/startseite/detail/news/News/detail/urteil-gegen-einen-mutmasslichen-mitarbeiter-des-syrischen-geheimdienstes-wegen-beihilfe-zu-einem-ver/> accessed 21 March 2022.

81 Anwar Raslan, who sought asylum in Germany in 2014, himself walked into a Berlin police station in February 2015 to demand protection. He claimed that he was feeling threatened, since he had led interrogations, 'including by force', during his time as a senior Syrian intelligence officer. See 'Erster Zeuge im Prozess um Mutmaßliche Syrische Staatsfolter' (Die Welt, 23 April 2020) <https://www.welt.de/regionales/rheinland-pfalz-saarland/article207447011/Erster-Zeuge-im-Prozess-um-mutmassliche-syrische-Staatsfolter.html> accessed 22 February 2022; Caroline Fehl, 'The Partial Return of Universal Jurisdiction: Syrian Torturers on Trial in Germany' (Global Policy Journal, 12 May 2020) <https://www.globalpolicyjournal

These proceedings were largely possible because the violations in Syria have been comprehensively documented by international bodies,[82] and Syrian organizations such as the Syrian Network for Human Rights,[83] the Syrian Observatory for Human Rights,[84] and the Violations Documentation Centre.[85] Their testimonies have proven critical in these trials and investigations.[86] Notably, the Syrian civil society has been the driving force and strongly advocated for these trials.[87] After unsuccessfully waiting on the international avenues,[88] the politicized exiled community took to organizations such as ECCHR and mobilized resources towards these investigations. Syrian lawyers and experts have been intimately involved in conceptualizing, encouraging, and proving these cases.[89] These critical collaborations between

.com/blog/12/05/2020/partial-return-universal-jurisdiction-syrian-torturers-trial-germany> accessed 22 February 2022.

82 For instance, Independent International Commission of Inquiry on the Syrian Arab Republic; International, Impartial and Independent Mechanism to assist in the investigation and prosecution of persons responsible for the most serious crimes under International Law committed in the Syrian Arab Republic since March 2011.

83 A non-profit organization that documents and monitors human rights violations in Syria. For more, see their official website <https://sn4hr.org/> accessed 23 February 2022.

84 Official website <https://www.syriahr.com/en/> accessed 23 February 2022.

85 The Center documents all kinds of human rights violations in Syria to provide a reference not only for the media, but also for all future accountability and justice-related procedures for Syria. See official website <https://www.vdc-sy.info/index.php/en/about> accessed 23 February 2022.

86 'Refugees in Germany Reporting Dozens of War Crimes' (Deutsche Welle, 11 April 2016) <https://www.dw.com/en/refugees-in-germany-reporting-dozens-of-war-crimes/a-19179291> (noting that German police are receiving dozens of reports per day about war crimes from arriving refugees and asylum seekers); Stine Jacobsen, 'Norway Police Search for Syrian War Criminals Among Asylum Seekers' (Reuters, 15 January 2016) <https://www.reuters.com/article/uk-europe-migrants-warcrimes-norway-idUKKCN0UT1FG> accessed 23 February 2022.

87 See Kaleck and Kroker, 'Syrian Torture Investigations in Germany and Beyond' (n 59); Alexandra L. Kather, "Water Finds Its Way"? Universal Jurisdiction as an Avenue for Justice in Syria' (Lieber Institute, 28 July 2021) <https://lieber.westpoint.edu/water-finds-way-universal-jurisdiction-justice-syria/> accessed 23 February 2022.

88 A referral by the UN Security Council, the other avenue for the ICC to be granted jurisdiction, was vetoed by the permanent UN Security Council Members Russia and China in May 2014 (UN Doc. S/2014/348). In addition to this, Russia has so far almost systematically vetoed all resolutions containing condemnation of human rights violations or calls for accountability for crimes committed by Syrian government forces or their allies (On a draft resolution for accountability for chemical attacks in Syria: S/2017/712, S/PV.7893; 5 December 2016: UN Doc. S/2016/1026, S/PV.7825; 8 October 2016: UN Doc. S/2016/846, S/PV.7785; 22 May 2014: UN Doc. S/2014/348, S/PV.7481; 19 July 2012: UN Doc. S/2012/538, S/PV.6810; 4 February 2012: UN Doc. S/2012/77, S/PV.6711; 4 October 2011: UN Doc. S/2011/612, S/PV.6627).

89 Beth Van Schaak, 'National Courts Step Up: Syrian Cases Proceeding in Domestic Courts' in Imagining Justice for Syria, Lieber Studies Series (Online edn, Oxford Academic 2020).

the Syrian community and actors such as ECCHR put the wheels of universal jurisdiction cases in motion, paving the way for a new model of hybridity and complementarity.[90]

The standard critique of these cases often includes the narrative of a 'Global North' state prosecuting individuals for crimes that took place in the 'Global South'.[91] However, this critique, inter alia, disregards the efforts and concerns of the exiled communities or the diaspora at the margins awaiting justice in one form or the other.[92]

However, beyond the 'western saviour going after the savages' critique, the current universal jurisdiction practice in states like Germany can be criticized on several grounds. As discussed above, these trials depend on the so-called third states and their policies. The 'safe haven' approach adopted by the Federal Prosecutor of Germany,[93] that is the choice to only initiate prosecutions against defendants who are on German territory, contributes to shaping a selective and narrow narrative of a very complex conflict. Moreover, concerns have been raised about the lack of transparency,[94] absence of competent witness protection mechanisms, or psycho-social support necessary for victims testifying in cases of such gravity.[95] Mohammed Al-Abdallah, the Director of Syrian Justice and Accountability Center, has poignantly pointed out how these cases might be reproducing the existing structures of domination within these organizations.[96]

90 See Espen Stokke & Eric Wiebelhaus-Brahm, 'Syrian diaspora mobilization for prospective transitional justice in the absence of transition' (2022) Journal of Human Rights 1–17.

91 Thamil Ananthavinayagan, 'A Tale of German Global Criminal Justice: A TWAIL Perspective on the Syrian Torture Trial' (Just Security, 30 June 2020) <https://www.justsecurity.org/70986/a-tale-of-german-global-criminal-justice-a-twail-perspective-on-the-syrian-torture-trial/> accessed 23 February 2022.

92 Mohammed Al-Abdallah, 'Syrian civil society: Strategic Litigation With No Strategy' (5 November 2020) <https://www.aljumhuriya.net/en/content/syrian-civil-society-%E2%80%9Cstrategic-litigation%E2%80%9D-no-strategy> accessed 23 February 2022 (hereinafter Al-Abdallah, 'Strategic Litigation with No Strategy').

93 There are some exceptions to this policy as well, for instance, Argentinian perpetrators living in Berlin. See Bojan Pancevski and Ryan Dube, 'Luis Esteban Kyburg, Ex-Commander in Argentina's 'Dirty War', Is Living Quietly in Berlin, Prosecutors Say' (Wall Street Journal, 22 July 2021) <https://www.wsj.com/articles/luis-esteban-kyburg-ex-commander-in-argentinas-dirty-war-is-living-quietly-in-berlin-prosecutors-say-11595339405> accessed 23 February 2022.

94 Alexander Dünkelsbühler, Alexander Suttor, Lea Borger, 'Universal Jurisdiction Without Universal Outreach?: The Al-Khatib trial in Koblenz and the Limits of Domestic Criminal Procedure in the Adjudication of International Crimes' (Völkerrechtsblog, 13 January 2021) <10.17176/20210113-181614-0> accessed 23 February 2022.

95 Susann Aboueldahab, Fin-Jasper Langmack, 'The End of the Al-Khatib Trial: A Historic Verdict and a Trial of Missed Opportunities' (Völkerrechtsblog, 07 February, 2022) <10.17176/20220207-120946-0> accessed 23 February 2022.

96 Al-Abdallah, 'Strategic Litigation with No Strategy' (n 92).

Despite the limitations, such trials may be viewed as an illustration of non-state actors forging collaborations to leverage all possible avenues to seek accountability.

Beyond universal jurisdiction, ECCHR also resorts to regional or international courts to call out the double standards of the European states and their selective implementation of international criminal law. They went up to the European Court of Human Rights to challenge the absence of a criminal trial against a German Commander for carrying out an unlawful aerial strike killing civilians in Kunduz, Afghanistan.[97] They were also responsible for ICC's first preliminary examination against a European state.[98]

The organization considers itself a part of the broader network of social movements and lawyers combining the legal and the extra-legal by researching, investigating, and coordinating communication strategies to help raise awareness and lobby for the social, political, or economic objectives of the litigation.[99] Writings by those involved with the organization also indicate an outspoken political self-examination of their role and the dangers of their work.[100] A continuous reflection on whether these proceedings serve their long-term strategies and objectives often appears as a central concern. As Kaleck notes, the litigations are conducted in a politically aware manner, with an eye to utopian potential. Using to legal proceedings in order to pursue some further-reaching aims in the interest of the marginalized who are most frequently located in the Global South.[101] Selectivity is key when choosing situations, defendants, partners, and legal arguments.[102] This self-reflection strengthens the long-term strategic objective of reforming the system through legal means while addressing the structural inequalities and relations of subordination.

In line with such political self-reflection, they have also brought cases against multinational corporations to highlight the violence caused by the

97 *Hanan v. Germany* [2021] ECtHR; see Kalika Mehta, 'Hanan v. Germany (Eur. Ct. HR)' (2022) 61 International Legal Materials 1, 61–123.

98 In 2014, the ICC OTP re-opened a preliminary examination into British war crimes in Iraq for widespread and systematic abuse of hundreds of detainees by UK armed forces in Iraq between 2003 and 2008. In 2017, the OTP confirmed that there was a reasonable basis to believe that members of UK forces committed war crimes in Iraq. In December 2020, the ICC's OTP decided to close the preliminary examination. For more details, see <https://www.ecchr.eu/en/case/war-crimes-by-uk-forces-in-iraq/> accessed 23 February 2022.

99 See their official website <https://www.ecchr.eu/en/ecchr/enforcing-human-rights-through-legal-means/> accessed 23 February 2022.

100 Kaleck, 'From Pinochet to Rumsfeld' (n 27); Kaleck and Saage-Maaß, 'Corporate Accountability: Status Quo and Challenges' (n 8); Kaleck, *Double Standards* (n 41); Karina Theurer and Wolfgang Kaleck (eds), *Dekoloniale Rechtskritik und Rechtspraxis* (Nomos Verlag 2020).

101 Wolfgang Kaleck, *Double Standards* (n 41)118.

102 Interview with Claire Tixeire, Senior Legal Advisor, ECCHR (online, 31 August 2021).

European economic actors outside of Europe.[103] Particularly in the context of Syria, ECCHR worked with Syrian individuals to submit a criminal complaint to the German Federal Public Prosecutor against high-ranking employees of the Syrian military intelligence service, Syrian telecom, and a German software company Utimaco for contributing to state surveillance mechanisms.[104] The 2018 complaint alleged that Utimaco by selling its software to the Syrian intelligence service aided and abetted crimes against humanity and war crimes.[105]

Another way in which multinational corporations headquartered in Europe contribute to the violence in the Third World is by actively facilitating the parties to the conflict through money or weapons. One paradigm-shifting Article 15 communication was submitted to the ICC by ECCHR and partners requesting the OTP to initiate an investigation that would determine the legal responsibility of corporate and political actors from Germany, France, Italy, Spain, and the United Kingdom for aiding and abetting war crimes in Yemen through the supply of weapons.[106]

But the case that forms the subject matter of this chapter is the one involving the responsibility of a European parent company for the crimes committed through its subsidiary in Syria. The *Lafarge case* is a rare example of domestic enforcement of international criminal law through extraterritorial prosecution involving corporate complicity – a case of parent corporation being charged for complicity in crimes against humanity for the conduct of its subsidiary over which it exercises substantial financial and operational control.

103 One of their major cases is the KiK case, see Miriam Saage-Maaß, Peer Zumbansen, Michael Bader, and Palvasha Shahab (eds.), *Transnational Legal Activism in Global Value Chains: The Ali Enterprises Factory Fire and the Struggle for Justice* (Springer 2021).

104 See Fatima Hansia, 'French Tribunal Investigates Qosmos Over Surveillance Software Use In Syria' (Corpwatch, 21 July 2015) < https://www.corpwatch.org/article/french-tribunal-investigates-qosmos-over-surveillance-software-use-syria> accessed 21 February 2022. Also, see case no. 36 in the Annexure.

105 It is worth noting here the work of FIDH before French Courts on the roles and responsibilities of European information and communication technologies (ICT) companies, who provide products and services to oppressive and authoritarian regimes, thereby enabling the monitoring and surveillance of communications. See 'Surveillance Technologies 'Made in Europe': Regulation Needed to Prevent Human Rights Abuses' (FIDH, 2014).

106 For more details see 'Made in Europe, Bombed in Yemen: How the ICC Could Tackle the Responsibility of Arms Exporters and Government Officials' (February 2020) < https://www.ecchr.eu/fileadmin/Fallbeschreibungen/CaseReport_ECCHR_Mwatana_Amnesty_CAAT_Delas_Rete.pdf> accessed 23 February 2022.

III. Prosecuting a Parent Corporation: The Lafarge Case

On 21 June 2016, the French newspaper *Le Monde* published the investigative work of a Syrian news outlet *Zaman Al-Wasl* and French journalist Dorothée Myriam Kellou exposing evidence that the French company Lafarge SA, in order to continue the corporations' operations in Syria, had paid out millions of euros to armed groups, including the Islamic State (IS).[107] The allegations against the French company and its officials were connected to a massive plant in Jalabiya in Northeast Syria operated through its subsidiary Lafarge Cement Syria. They included financing of terrorism by paying out to groups such as the IS, violating the EU trade embargo, and subjecting its Syrian staff members to inhuman working conditions and endangering their lives.

The timing of the crucial exposé made the investigation politically urgent. Less than a year before the details of transactions between Lafarge and the IS were revealed, Paris had witnessed one of the deadliest terrorist attacks since World War II carried out by the IS.[108] The revelation that a French company had contributed substantially to the group's operations in preceding years was met with huge public outcry, newspaper coverage, and a quick response by the French authorities.

Although a Parliamentary report concluded that no connection, direct or indirect, could be established between Lafarge and the financing of Daesh,[109] in October 2016, the French Ministry of Finance filed a complaint against Lafarge, claiming that it had breached the sanctions imposed by the EU against the Syrian regime and the ban on trading with terrorist organizations in Syria.[110] The Swiss giant Holcim (Lafarge merged with Holcim in

107 Dorothée Myriam Kellou and others, 'Syrie : Les Troubles Arrangements de Lafarge avec l'Etat islamique' (Le Monde, 9 June 2016) <https://www.lemonde.fr/syrie/article/2016/06/21/syrie-les-troubles-arrangements-de-lafarge-avec-l-etat-islamique_4955023_1618247.html> accessed 23 February 2022 (hereinafter, Dorothée Myriam Kellou (Le Monde, 9 June 2016)) ; 'French cement maker Lafarge 'made deals with IS group in Syria' (France 24, 21 June 2016) <https://www.france24.com/en/20160621-france-lafarge-islamic-state-group-jalabiya-syria> accessed 23 February 2022.

108 Nicholas Rushworth, 'November 2015 attacks: A timeline of the night that shook the French capital' (France 24, 8 September 2021) <https://www.france24.com/en/france/20210908-paris-november-2015-attacks-a-timeline-of-the-night-that-shook-the-city> accessed 23 February 2022.

109 Rapport d'information (13 July 2016) <https://www2.assemblee-nationale.fr/static/14/daech/rapport-daech-tome1.pdf> accessed 23 February 2022; 'Lafarge n'aurait pas participé au financement de Daesh (rapport parlementaire)' (Batiactu, 21 July 2016) <https://www.batiactu.com/edito/lafarge-n-aurait-pas-participe-au-financement-daesh-45737.php> accessed 23 February 2022.

110 Mathilde Golla, 'Financement du Terrorisme en Syrie: La Chronologie de L'affaire Lafarge' (Le Figaro, 9 December 2017) <https://www.lefigaro.fr/societes/2017/12/09/20005-20171209ARTFIG00115-financement-du-terrorisme-en-syrie-la-chronologie-de-l-affaire-lafarge.php> accessed 23 February 2022.

2014) also admitted later that Lafarge had financed armed groups in Syria by recognizing that 'unacceptable practices had been employed to maintain the activity and security of its plant'.[111] Former executive Director-General of Operations, Christian Herrault, declared that the company had bowed to racketeering and 'provided funds to third parties to work out arrangements with a number ofarmed groups'.[112] The judicial inquiry has since identified that these 'arrangements' amounted to at least 13 million euros in payments.[113]

However, the discourse and legal actions against Lafarge's misconduct operated primarily in a counterterrorism paradigm until November 2016. That is when the Paris-based organization Sherpa, along with ECCHR and 11 Syrian former employees of Lafarge all acting as civil parties (*partie civile)*, filed a criminal complaint before the specialized War Crimes and Crimes Against Humanity Unit of the Paris *Tribunal de Grande Instance* (Office of the Public Prosecutor), alleging that the economic payout to armed groups in Syria and endangering the safety of its workers imply complicity in crimes under international law as well.[114]

Syrian former employees of Lafarge are plaintiffs to the criminal complaint. Based on evidence from plaintiffs, the two organizations alleged that the French company Lafarge was complicit in crimes against humanity through the operations of its Syrian subsidiary between 2012 and 2014.[115] The complaint argued that Lafarge and its former directors not only financed listed terrorist groups but also failed to take the necessary steps to either evacuate or appropriately protect its employees and pressured them to come to work, thereby possibly exposing them to kidnappings, disappearances, and attempted murder – elements that may establish complicity in crimes

111 Alexandru Tofan, 'The Lafarge Affair: A First Step Towards Corporate Criminal Liability for Complicity in Crimes against Humanity' (Doing Business Right, 2 October 2018) <https://www.asser.nl/DoingBusinessRight/Blog/post/the-lafarge-affair-a-first-step-towards-corporate-criminal-liability-for-complicity-in-crimes-against-humanity-by-alexandru-tofan> accessed 23 February 2022.

112 Lafargeholcim Responds to Syria Review (2 March 2017) <https://www.holcim.com/LafargeHolcim-responds-syria-review> accessed 24 February 2022.

113 Claire Tixeire, Cannelle Lavite, Marie Laura Guislain, 'Holding Transnational Corporations Accountable for International Crimes in Syria: Update on the Developments in the Lafarge Case (Part I)' (Opinio Juris, 27 February 2020) <https://opiniojuris.org/2020/07/27/holding-transnational-corporations-accountable-for-international-crimes-in-syria-update-on-the-developments-in-the-lafarge-case-part-i/> accessed 24 February 2022 (hereinafter Tixeire and others, 'Updates in the Lafarge Case (Part I)').

114 See ECCHR case report on Lafarge case <https://www.ecchr.eu/fileadmin/Fallbeschreibungen/Case_Report_Lafarge_Syria_ECCHR.pdf> accessed 24 February 2022.

115 Submission from SHERPA and ECCHR on an indictment of Lafarge for complicity in crimes against humanity (Sherpa, 15 May 2018) <https://www.asso-sherpa.org/submission-from-sherpa-and-ecchr-on-an-indictment-of-lafarge-for-complicity-in-crimes-against-humanity> accessed 24 February 2022.

against humanity.[116] This marked the beginning of the first of its kind criminal prosecution of a parent company as an entity for the conduct of its subsidiary involving crimes under international law.

The case has witnessed several twists and turns since the official opening of the investigation in June 2017. The prosecutors accepted the charges of financing of terrorism, endangering the lives of employees, as well as complicity in crimes against humanity. However, the Paris Court of Appeal in 2019 dismissed the crimes against humanity charge and ECCHR/Sherpa's status as civil parties. Both these rulings were appealed before the French Supreme Court, which reinstated the charge of crimes against humanity in September 2021.[117] After this decision, it is only ECCHR which can act as a civil party (and not Sherpa) and only on charges associated with crimes against humanity (and not on other charges in the case).[118] As of March 2023, the case is pending before the Supreme Court again on a related question.

The following section briefly discusses the collaboration between Sherpa and ECCHR and their connection to the plaintiffs which led to the initiation of the proceedings. This is followed by a discussion on the business activity and corporate structure of Lafarge that elicited criminal charges. The legal basis and the framework that allows for corporate criminality is discussed in further detail. The final sections are devoted to two pressing legal challenges in attributing criminal responsibility to a corporate entity: piercing the corporate veil, and relevant *mens rea* threshold.

1. *Sherpa Putting the Wheels in Motion*

Sherpa, a small Paris-based organization, founded in 2001, defends victims of economic crimes as their mission to build a world where law works in service

116 Tixeire and others, 'Updates in the Lafarge Case (Part I)' (n 113); Claire Tixeire, 'Can the Lafarge case be a Game Changer? French Multinational Company Indicted for International Crimes in Syria' (31 August 2018, BHRRC) <https://www.business-humanrights.org/en/blog/can-the-lafarge-case-be-a-game-changer-french-multinational-company-indicted-for-international-crimes-in-syria/> accessed 24 February 2022 (hereinafter, Tixeire, 'Can Lafarge Case be a Gamechanger?).

117 'Historic victory before French Supreme Court on the indictment of multinational Lafarge for complicity in crimes against humanity' (Sherpa, ECCHR, 7 September 2021) <https://www.asso-sherpa.org/historic-victory-before-french-supreme-court-on-the-indictment-of-multinational-lafarge-for-complicity-in-crimes-against-humanity> accessed 24 February 2022.

118 Article 2-4 of the French Criminal Code allows an association fighting against crimes against humanity and genocide to apply for civil party status. The court did not recognize Sherpa's status as civil party because the organizational mandate of Sherpa did not specifically include crimes under international law, even though most of their work includes corporate accountability also in context of atrocity crimes.

of a more mindful globalization.[119] Their work revolves around tackling new forms of impunity linked with globalization in two primary forms: the human rights costs of globalization and related accountability, and addressing illicit transnational financial flows. In addition to advocacy, developing new tools, education, and capacity-building, they claim that they engage in strategic litigation. Their view of strategic litigation mainly involves using a variety of legal tools to demonstrate the existence of violations and their dramatic consequences on populations, and expose limitations in the legal framework.[120]

The organization works to address a lack of recognition/legal framework of responsibility of corporations and their managers for their involvement in crimes. Sherpa also regularly collaborates with other, bigger organizations in bringing these complaints.[121] For instance, along with the *Collectif des Parties Civiles pour le Rwanda* (CPCR) and Ibuka France, they filed a complaint against BNP Paribas (a French international banking conglomerate), alleging complicity in genocide, crime against humanity, and war crimes.[122] They argued that the officers of the bank necessarily knew the destination of the funds and that these funds would contribute to the Rwandan genocide;[123] this was also the first time a complaint targeting a bank involved in a conflict setting was filed in France.

Regarding Lafarge, when investigations revealed the evidence supporting the financial relationship between Lafarge SA and armed groups in Syria, the former employees of Lafarge started reaching out individually to Sherpa seeking potential avenues for justice against the parent corporation in France.[124] The plaintiffs did not come as an already mobilized united group, rather Sherpa engaged with them individually to collect evidence and gather testimonies that formed the basis of the initial complaint.[125]

In 2016, Sherpa reached out to ECCHR with a well laid-out case.[126] Sherpa and ECCHR had been long-standing partners but their collaboration on this case was driven by the need to combine their respective expertise.

119 See Sherpa's website <https://www.asso-sherpa.org/mandate> accessed 24 February 2022.

120 Ibid.

121 They are a member of international coalition groups such as the OECD Watch, European Coalition for Corporate Justice etc.

122 Involvement of the BNP Paribas in the Tutsi Genocide in Rwanda: Opening of the Legal Inquiry and Nomination of an Investigation Judge' (Sherpa, 26 September 2017) <https://www.asso-sherpa.org/involvement-of-the-bnp-paribas-in-the-tutsi-genocide-in-rwanda-opening-of-the-legal-inquiry-and-nomination-of-an-investigation-judge>accessed 24 February 2022.

123 Ibid.

124 Interview with Cannelle Lavite, Co-Director Business and Human Rights, ECCHR (online, 6 August 2021).

125 Ibid; Interview with Claire Tixeire, Senior Legal Advisor, ECCHR (online, 31 August 2021).

126 Ibid.

When Sherpa had done most of the preliminary work on the case, ECCHR contributed with their experience and specialization in international criminal law and extraterritorial prosecutions.[127] As soon as the complaints were filed, more former employees reached out to the two organizations wanting to enlist themselves as plaintiffs on the case. In 2023, over 50 former employees are being represented by Sherpa and ECCHR and many more are listed as plaintiffs represented by other local lawyers.[128]

2. *Lafarge and Its Syrian Business: 'An ATM for ISIS'*

Lafarge, a French company incorporated in 1833, is a global leader in construction material and cement/concrete production. Following its merger with Swiss company Holcim, the company has a presence of 2,500 factories in 61 countries.[129] The Middle East has been an important market for the company, with almost 5,500 employees in the region. In 2007, Lafarge bought Syrian Cement Company – later renamed Lafarge Cement Syria – as part of its acquisition of the Egyptian cement conglomerate ORASCOM, the cement leader in the Middle East and the Mediterranean Basin.[130] As a result, Lafarge Cement Syria is a subsidiary 98.7% owned by the French group Lafarge with the remaining 1% owned by Mr. Firas Tlass (a friend of the Assad regime who continued to oversee its operations and work for Lafarge after the merger).[131]

The Jalabiya plant was officially inaugurated in 2010 after a huge investment of some 680 million euros.[132] Although under dictatorial rule at the time, the political situation in Syria was relatively stable when the investment was made. A few months later, the civil war began and by September 2011, the EU had placed an embargo against some of the Syrian goods.[133]

127 Ibid.

128 Ibid.

129 'A New Leader for a New World: Lafargeholcim Officially Launched Around the Globe' (Lafarge, 15 July 2015) <https://www.holcim.com/a-new-leader-a-new-world-lafargeholcim-officially-launched-around-globe> accessed 24 February 2022.

130 'Lafarge Acquires Orascom Cement, The Leading Cement Group in The Middle East and The Mediterranean Basin' (Lafarge, 10 December 2007) <https://www.holcim.com/lafarge-acquires-orascom-cement-leading-cement-group-middle-east-and-mediterranean-basin> accessed 24 February 2022.

131 Case Dossier (Sherpa, Nov 2018) <https://www.asso-sherpa.org/french-company-lafarge-sued-forfinancing-isis-and-complicity-in-war-crimes-and-crimes-against-humanity-in-syria> accessed 24 February 2022.

132 See Nathalie Belhoste and Bastien Nivet, 'The Organization of Short-sightedness: The Implications of Remaining in Conflict Zones. The Case of Lafarge During Syria's Civil War' (2021) 60 Business & Society 7, 1573–1605 (hereinafter Belhoste and Nivet, 'The Organization of Short-sightedness').

133 The embargo list was expanded to include cement by January 2012, see Council Regulation (EU) No. 36/2012 of 18 January 2012 concerning restrictive measures in view of the

From 2012, where other foreign companies, such as Shell and Suncor, were abandoning their local plants, Lafarge's business was peaking, which led the observers to label the company as 'the big cash cow'.[134] With the escalating conflict in Syria, Lafarge capitalized on the opportunity to make exponential profits because of the rise in cement prices and absence of competitors in the market.[135]

Between 2012 and 2014, to keep the business going, the company kept paying 20,000 euros per month to various armed groups, including the IS, to maintain the plant's production.[136] There are also allegations that Lafarge purchased large amounts of oil and pozzolan from the IS to continue its massive production. The sale of natural resources accounted for 80% of the IS's financing.[137] As a group, it was the IS's economic policy to exploit economic assets domestically to ensure financial self-sufficiency, rather than being financed from abroad as is the case with groups such as al-Qaeda.[138]

These transactions enabled Lafarge to access raw materials, and to secure the passage of its trucks and employees. The factory continued to operate in a violent, explosive context, even as the local staff suffered repeated kidnappings for which the company kept paying hefty ransom amounts.[139]

After repatriating its non-Syrian staff in 2012, the company allegedly exerted undue pressure on its local employees to come to work under inhuman conditions. The former employees describe it 'as extremely authoritarian and noncompliant with basic health, safety, environment, and quality policies'.[140] When the IS violently overtook the factory in September 2014,

situation in Syria and repealing Regulation (EU) No 442/2011.

134 'LafargeHolcim's Reputation at Risk over Alleged Links with ISIS' (Financial Times, 19 March 2017) <https://www.ft.com/content/406b06fe-05b6-11e7-aa5b-6bb07f5c8e12> accessed 24 February 2022.

135 On the competitive advantage of investing in conflict areas, see generally, C.H. Oh and Jennifer Oetzel, 'Once Bitten Twice Shy? Experience Managing Violent Conflict Risk and MNC Subsidiary-Level Investment and Expansion' (2017) Strategic Management Journal 38, 714–731.

136 In September 2017, French businessman Bruno Pescheux, the then director of Lafarge Cement Syria, in the context of the judicial inquiry admitted to the French police that IS received money from his company between 2013 and 2014.

137 Tixeire, 'Can Lafarge Case be a Gamechanger? (n 116).

138 In 2013, the Islamic State took gradual control of the cities and roads surrounding the factory. The city where most of the factory's employees were housed also fell to ISIL in March 2014. For more details, see Imogen Richards, 'Islamc State's Financial Practices' in *Neoliberalism and Neo-Jihadism* (Manchester University Press 2020).

139 The Jalabiya Plant Security Manager recalled events from mid-2012 onwards: 'at first, we had just over one incident per month. Then it was once or twice a week. Sometimes they stole the cement, sometimes they made the customer pay so that the driver would be released and could get the goods and the truck back'. Kellou (*Le Monde*, 9 June 2016) (n 107).

140 Belhoste and Nivet, 'The Organization of Short-sightedness' (n 132) 1590.

employees realized that there was no evacuation plan in place for them and that they were left to fend for themselves.[141] As the evidence of financial transactions amounting to over 13 million euros was circulating in 2016, the French public were reportedly calling Lafarge the ATM for IS.[142] Because of the 2015 terrorist attack in Paris, the public discourse in France was exclusively around their contribution to an armed group that attacked French soil, instead of their abuse of workers or complicity in violations committed by the group in Syria.

3. *The Legal Basis and Case Strategy*

Against that backdrop, the complaint filed by ECCHR and Sherpa along with 11 former employees alleged the crime of financing terrorism and complicity in crimes against humanity.[143] The complaint identified actors in France most responsible for crimes committed on the Syrian territory: the French entity Lafarge SA,[144] its CEO at the time of conduct (between 2012 and 2014), Bruno Lafont, the Syrian subsidiary Lafarge Cement Syria, along with its CEO until June 2014 Bruno Pescheux, and its CEO since June 2014 Frédéric Jolibois.

It finds its legal basis primarily on two grounds: one, the international legal consensus that IS (and other armed groups in Syria) had perpetrated war crimes and crimes against humanity in north-eastern Syria between 2012 and 2014; two, the fact that the domestic criminal law framework in France recognizes criminal liability of corporations in addition to the incorporation of the international crimes flowing from the ICC Statue in its criminal code, since 2005. Consequently, the complainants alleged the aforementioned actors to be liable for financing of a terrorist enterprise;[145] complicity in crimes against

141 Case Dossier (Sherpa, Nov 2018) <https://www.asso-sherpa.org/french-company-lafarge-sued-forfinancing-isis-and-complicity-in-war-crimes-and-crimes-against-humanity-in-syria> accessed 24 February 2022.

142 LafargeHolcim's Reputation at Risk over Alleged Links with ISIS' (Financial Times, 19 March 2017) <https://www.ft.com/content/406b06fe-05b6-11e7-aa5b-6bb07f5c8e12> accessed 24 February 2022.

143 Case Dossier (Sherpa, Nov 2018) <https://www.asso-sherpa.org/french-company-lafarge-sued-forfinancing-isis-and-complicity-in-war-crimes-and-crimes-against-humanity-in-syria> accessed 24 February 2022; Lafarge Case Report (ECCHR, November 2018) <https://www.ecchr.eu/fileadmin/Fallbeschreibungen/Case_Report_Lafarge_Syria_ECCHR.pdf> accessed 24 February 2022.

144 According to Article 121-2 of the French Criminal Code, legal persons may be held liable for criminal offences committed on their behalf by any of their representatives or bodies.

145 Article 421-2-2 of the French Criminal Code.

humanity;[146] deliberate endangerment of people;[147] exploitative labour work, undignified working conditions, and forced labour.[148]

The two organizations, along with the former employees, sought to take part in the proceedings on the basis of their status as *partie civile* (civil party).[149] In France, the Office of Judicial Police can open criminal investigations on receiving a complaint by victims or third parties.[150] The concept of *partie civile* is essentially a feature of civil law incorporated in all its essence into the French criminal law. A *partie civile* is a part of the criminal proceedings as if in a civil case. The provision simply allows for the possibility to bring evidence and legal arguments, and to get damages for the person who suffered prejudice as the result of an act which it defines as criminal.[151]

The two organizations had access to strong evidence, including reports by the media, the testimonies of factory workers and Lafarge employees, passes issued by IS (handwritten as well as officially stamped) to allow passage of raw materials to the factory in return of remuneration, and transcripts of communication between French Lafarge directors and their subsidiary's staff indicating that the company had hired intermediaries to negotiate with and finance local armed groups.[152] The strength of the evidence helped in linking the criminal conduct to individual officers of the company. The email chains and other internal documents of the corporation helped trace the decision-making within the corporate structure.

Based on the legal framework, the criminal complaint pursued a compounded case strategy. In addition to charging the corporation of financing terrorism, for which there is direct evidence and confessions from the company officials placed on record, the two organizations pursued the charges of complicity in war crimes and crimes against humanity as well. According to one of the lawyers working on the case, pursuing the charges of financing of terrorism was a risk they had to take to get their foot in the door.[153] The exceptional nature of available evidence combined with public pressure around financing terrorism made this a strong case which would not be easily dismissed. Once that charge was accepted, it offered them the opportunity

146 Article 212-1 of the French Criminal Code.

147 Article 223-1 of the French Criminal Code.

148 Article 225-13, 225-14-1 and 225-14-2 of the French Criminal Code.

149 Article 2-4 French Criminal Code allows an association fighting against crimes against humanity and genocide to apply for civil party status.

150 O.P. Lapie, 'The Partie Civile in the Criminal Law of France' (1928) Journal of Comparative Legislation and International Law 33–45; Jacqueline Hogson, 'Suspects, Defendants and Victims in the French Criminal Process: The Context of Recent Reform' (2002) 51 International and Comparative Law Quarterly 4 781, 792–93.

151 Ibid.

152 Tixeire, 'Can Lafarge Case be a Gamechanger? (n 116).

153 Interview with Claire Tixeire, Senior Legal Advisor, ECCHR (online, 31 August 2021)

to bring human rights to the heart of the case by arguing for complicity in crimes against humanity.[154]

This compounding strategy is not a case of pressing cumulative charges to enhance the prospects of a court victory but a strategic political move. Under the French Criminal Code, financing of terrorism is a relatively easier charge to prove. The criminalization of the financing of terrorism is particularly extensive and allows for the prosecution of all persons (natural and legal) who in some way participate in the financing of terrorism, as long as they are aware of the intended use of the funds for that purpose.[155] To constitute this offence of terrorist financing, it is not necessary that the funds raised were in fact used; it is sufficient that they were raised for the purpose of committing a terrorist act, which also allows prosecution of attempt as an offence. In contrast, to constitute a crime against humanity, the funds provided – to different groups in Syria in this specific case – needed to be attached to a specific underlying crime in the general category of crimes against humanity.

Discounting the charges of complicity in war crimes and crimes against humanity, the case – although easier to prove – would only comprise of charges of financing of terrorism, thus reducing it to the counterterrorism paradigm centred around the questions of national security. In that case, even if the corporation could have been held liable for their misconduct in Syria on terror-related charges, it would set a limiting precedent enhancing the political agendas of the state without even an acknowledgement of the Syrian victims of these violations.[156]

On the contrary, the charges on crimes against humanity bring to the fore the large-scale and systematic nature of violations against the Syrian population carried out by the armed groups partly sponsored by the French company. The victims of the crimes against humanity charge are Syrians, not only workers whose lives were directly endangered at Lafarge Cement Syria factory but also the civilians who were subjected to murders, rape, torture, and mistreatment at the hands of the armed groups that were economically supported by Lafarge in France.

Thus, the decision to combine the charges, one may argue, is another attempt at using the law to highlight (and counter) the structural biases of the legal system. ECCHR lawyers who worked on this case explain:

> The financing of terrorism became the focus of the scandal, if not to say its driving force. Yet, it would be a setback for the legal case to stay

154 Tixeire, 'Can Lafarge Case be a Gamechanger? (n 116).

155 Article 421-2-2 of the French Criminal Code.

156 Jelena Aparac, 'Business and Armed Non-State Groups: Challenging the Landscape of Corporate (Un) accountability in Armed Conflicts' (2020) 5 Business and Human Rights Journal 2, 270–275.

> locked within the counter-terrorism paradigm. Counter-terrorism legislation usually prioritizes national security over human rights and civil liberties – at times even putting them wholly aside.
>
> Combating terrorism is indeed primarily a matter of state security based on a government's political agenda – which can fluctuate with time. Human rights, however, have been built to protect the inalienable rights to which a person is entitled by virtue of being human, regardless of any political agenda. Reaffirming the fundamental superiority of human rights norms over fluctuating counter-terrorism regimes has been at the heart of ECCHR's and partners' work.[157]

In that sense, the legally risky choice was made to capitalize on the opportunity provided by public attention which could potentially create a judicial precedent, not only in France but also internationally. At the same time, this highlights that a strategic legal objective goes beyond a conviction or a court victory (that might have been more probable with the lower threshold of terrorism charges) to highlight the systematic complex nature of atrocity crimes, and contributions made by economic actors based in Europe for crimes committed elsewhere.

A few years since the beginning of these proceedings, there is an emerging practice of cumulative charging of terror-related charges along with core international crimes from European states prosecuting foreign terrorist fighters.[158] The following section discusses how the judges responded to this strategy and two of the most challenging aspects of this prosecution: piercing of the corporate veil and the mental element.

IV. Legal and Practical Challenges

1. *Timeline*

In June 2017, a judicial investigation[159] was launched following the criminal complaint filed by Sherpa and ECCHR. In December 2017, six high-level

157 Tixeire, 'Can Lafarge Case be a Gamechanger? (n 116).

158 Genocide Network, 'Cumulative Prosecution of Foreign Terrorist Fighters For Core International Crimes and Terrorism-Related Offences' (May 2020) <https://www.eurojust.europa.eu/sites/default/files/Partners/Genocide/2020-05_Report-on-cumulative-prosecution-of-FTFs_EN.PDF> accessed 24 February 2022.

159 The French *magistrature* (judiciary) has two branches: one is the standing judiciary and the other is the sitting judiciary. The standing judiciary represents prosecutorial functions and consists of a public prosecutor (*ministère public or procureur de la République*). Public prosecutors are hierarchically subordinate to the minister of justice and the executive. The other branch of the judiciary is the sitting judiciary, which is composed of the investigating magistrate (*juge d'instruction*) and the trial judge (*magistrat*), who represent the investigative and adjudicative functions, respectively. In the preliminary stage, the Office of the Judicial Police supervised by the Prosecutor gathers preliminary evidence.

executives of Lafarge were indicted on two separate charges of financing terrorism and endangering other people's lives.[160] In an ordinance dated 18 April 2018, the three judges in charge of the investigation considered the accusations against Lafarge as a legal person. The investigating judges, in a historic move, concluded that the allegations against Lafarge, as an entity, for financing terrorism and complicity in crimes against humanity warranted further investigation.[161] On 28 June 2018, nearly two years after *Le Monde*'s revelations, they indicted Lafarge for crimes against humanity under Articles 212-1 and 461-2, the financing of a terrorist enterprise under Article 421-2-2, endangerment of other people's lives under Article 223-1of the French Criminal Code, and the breach of an embargo (the latter stemming from the original investigation of the Ministry of Finance). As a result, the company was placed under judicial supervision and was asked to submit a bond of 30 million euros as the trial continues.[162]

The indictment was challenged by Lafarge before the Paris Court of Appeals. In October 2019, the Investigation Chamber of the Paris Court of Appeals rejected the admissibility of Sherpa and ECCHR as civil parties which rendered it impossible for them to continue to file submissions in the case.[163] Arguably, this move could be attributed to a noticeable

The Prosecutor then decides, on the basis of the evidence collected, weather to pursue the charges or not. Once the decision is made, further investigation is carried out by the investigation magistrates. See Jacqueline Hodgson, 'The Police, the Prosecutor and the *juge d'instruction*: Judicial Supervision in France, Theory and Practice' (2001) 41 British Journal of Criminology 2, 342–361.

160 Frédéric Jolibois (the Director of the plant since the summer of 2014), Bruno Pescheux (his predecessor) and Jean-Claude Veillard (the Director of Security), Bruno Lafont (the former CEO of Lafarge between 2007 and 2015), Christian Herrault (the former Director-General of Operations), and Éric Olsen (the Director of Human Resources at the time of the allegations. Two more executives were later indicted in April and May 2018: Sonia Artinian, who was Lafarge's Director of Human Resources between September 2013 and July 2018 and former Safety Director at Lafarge Cement Syria, Jacob Waerness.

161 Case Dossier (Sherpa, Nov 2018) <https://www.asso-sherpa.org/french-company-lafarge-sued-forfinancing-isis-and-complicity-in-war-crimes-and-crimes-against-humanity-in-syria> accessed 24 February 2022; Lafarge Case Report (ECCHR, November 2018) <https://www.ecchr.eu/fileadmin/Fallbeschreibungen/Case_Report_Lafarge_Syria_ECCHR.pdf> accessed 24 February 2022.

162 Case Dossier (Sherpa, Nov 2018) <https://www.asso-sherpa.org/french-company-lafarge-sued-forfinancing-isis-and-complicity-in-war-crimes-and-crimes-against-humanity-in-syria> accessed 24 February 2022; Lafarge Case Report (ECCHR, November 2018) <https://www.ecchr.eu/fileadmin/Fallbeschreibungen/Case_Report_Lafarge_Syria_ECCHR.pdf> accessed 24 February 2022.

163 The two organizations challenged this decision before Supreme Court and ECCHR was reinstated as *partie civile* by the French highest court. ECCHR, Press Release (7 September 2021) <https://www.ecchr.eu/en/press-release/historic-victory-before-french-supreme-court-on-the-indictment-of-multinational-lafarge-for-complicity-in-crimes-against-humanity-in-syria/> accessed 24 February 2022.

shift in jurisprudence, restraining the involvement of non-governmental organizations as *partie civile* in criminal proceedings in France.[164]

On 7 November 2019, the Paris Court of Appeals upheld all the other charges except for the most serious charge of complicity in crimes against humanity committed in Syria.[165] The only ground cited for dismissal of this charge was Lafarge's lack of shared intent to contribute to the crimes committed by the armed groups in Syria. Two years later, on 7 September 2021, the French Supreme Court held that the *mens rea* requirement for complicity was lower, i.e. mere knowledge of the crimes was sufficient, and reinstated the charge of complicity in crimes against humanity.[166] The two contrasting decisions reflect two of the most difficult aspects of prosecuting a multinational corporation as an autonomous agent for its complicity in crimes under international law: attribution of responsibility and *mens rea* standard each discussed in greater detail in the following sections. In May 2022, the French Court of Appeals enforced the order by the Supreme Court and charged the corporation with complicity in crimes against humanity and financing of terrorism.[167]

2. *Piercing the Corporate Veil*

One of the biggest obstacles in attributing responsibility to the parent corporation for the conduct of its subsidiary is the principle of a separate legal entity, the corporate veil.[168] The concept of corporate veil comes from tradi-

164 Interview with Cannelle Lavite, Co-Director Business and Human Rights, ECCHR (online, 6 August 2021); also see Sherpa, Press Release (24 October 2019) <https://www.asso-sherpa.org/10533-2> accessed 24 February 2022.

165 'Sherpa and ECCHR to Appeal Decision in Lafarge/Syria Case at French Supreme Court' (ECCHR, Sherpa, 7 November 2019) <https://www.ecchr.eu/en/press-release/sherpa-and-ecchr-to-appeal-decision-in-lafargesyriacase-at-french-supreme-court/> accessed 24 February 2022.

166 ECCHR, Press Release (7 September 2021) <https://www.ecchr.eu/en/press-release/historic-victory-before-french-supreme-court-on-the-indictment-of-multinational-lafarge-for-complicity-in-crimes-against-humanity-in-syria/> accessed 24 February 2022.

167 Sandra Cossart and others, 'Multinational Lafarge Facing Unprecedented Charges for International Crimes: Insights Into the French Court Decisions' (Opinio Juris,15 November 2022) <http://opiniojuris.org/2022/11/15/multinational-lafarge-facing-unprecedented-charges-for-international-crimes-insights-into-the-french-court-decisions/#:~:text=In%20a%20groundbreaking%20decision%2C%20French,the%20Supreme%20Court%20is%20awaited> accessed 16 March 2023 (hereinafter Cossart, 'Insights into the French Court Decisions').

168 Anil Yilmaz Vastardis and Rachel Chambers, 'Overcoming the Corporate Veil Challenge: Could Investment Law Inspire the Proposed Business and Human Rights Treaty?' (2017) 67 International and Comparative Law Quarterly, 389–423 (hereinafter Vastardis and Chambers, 'Overcoming the Corporate Veil Challenge'); S. Joseph, *Corporations and Transnational Human Rights Litigation* (Hart Publishing 2004); Gwynne Skinner

tional corporate law where the subsidiary company is incorporated as a distinct entity from the parent corporation. It creates a separate legal personality for the newly incorporated company, dividing it and its shareholder-owners into separate spheres and bestowing limited liability on the shareholders.[169] It is a device used to shield parent companies from liability for the debts of their subsidiaries and establish multiple layers of insulation from liability.[170]

However, this insulation is not absolute. Sometimes, despite the formal separation of the two entities, the conduct of the subsidiary can be attributed to the parent company.[171] The 'corporate veil' can be pierced to ascribe vicarious liability on the parent company for the conduct of the subsidiary. The circumstances in which it is pierced vary from state to state,[172] so there is no fixed legal formula for when and how the corporate veil is pierced, neither in tort/contract law nor in criminal law.[173]

The French criminal law provisions in force since 2005 (Article 121-2 of the criminal code) provide that corporations can be held criminally liable when perpetrators of crimes act *on the company's behalf*.[174] This does not exclude the criminal responsibility of the acting individuals. Instead, the clause 'on behalf of the corporations' forges a link between the individual and the corporation by means of employment. It has been interpreted to mean that a corporation can be held 'criminally liable for the acts of any of

and others, *Third Pillar: Access to Judicial Remedies for Human Rights Violations by Transnational Business* (ICAR, CORE, ECCJ, 2013); Simon Baughen, *Human Rights and Corporate Wrongs: Closing the Governance Gap* (Edward Elgar 2015) 179–90; John Ruggie 'Report of the Special Representative of the Secretary-General on the Issue of Human Rights and Transnational Corporations and Other Business Enterprises' (UNOHCHR, 2011) UN Doc A/HRC/17/31.

169 Vastardis and Chambers, 'Overcoming the Corporate Veil Challenge (n 168) 394.

170 Phillip Blumberg, *The Multinational Challenge to Corporate Law: The Search for a New Corporate Personality* (Oxford University Press 1993) 139.

171 Desislava Stoichkova, *Towards Corporate Liability in International Criminal Law* (Intersentia 2010) 141 (hereinafter Stoichkova, *Towards Corporate Liability*); Sarah Joseph and Sarah Louise Joseph, *Corporations and Transnational Human Rights Litigation* (Vol 4, Hart Publishing 2004).

172 Jennifer Zerk, *Corporate Liability for Gross Human Rights Abuses: Towards a Fairer and More Effective System of Domestic Law Remedies* (UNOHCHR 2012) 66.

173 Stoichkova, *Towards Corporate Liability* (n 171) 141.

174 Article 121-2 of the French Criminal Code: *Personnes morales* (legal entities) with the exclusion of the State, are criminally responsible according to the distinctions in Articles 121-4 to 121-7 and in the instances provided for by law or regulation for offences committed on their behalf by their corporate bodies or by their officers. However, territorial authorities and their groupings are criminally responsible only for offences committed in the course of activities assignable by agreements in order to delegate public services. Criminal responsibility of *personnes morales* does not preclude criminal responsibility of the natural person perpetrators or accomplices for the same conduct.

its agents if an agent commits a crime within the scope of their employment and with intent to benefit the corporation'.[175]

Attribution of the conduct of individuals acting on behalf of the subsidiary company to the parent company, however, is further removed and requires multiple intermediary steps. Factors such as stock ownership, economic integration, administrative, financial, and employee interdependence, and a common public persona determine attribution in a subsidiary–parent context.[176] For the parent company to bear direct responsibility, the most relevant element in such structures is the strictly construed element of 'control'.[177] It has been argued that corporate relations are determined not just by ownership but also by 'authority relations' that arise wherever the economic dependence of one party upon the other effectively requires compliance with the dominant party's wishes.[178]

Therefore, in this case, it is the conduct of Lafarge Cements Syria and its employees which is attributed to the executives of Lafarge SA in France based on the argument that the former were acting on behalf of the latter. Several factors make it a particularly strong case regarding attribution of conduct of the subsidiary to the parent company. Firstly, control: at the time of commission of the crimes in question, Lafarge SA owned almost 99% of Lafarge Syria.[179] Secondly, economic dependence: evidence suggests that even if the funds paid to IS did originate from Lafarge SA's accounts, Lafarge Cements Syria at the time was being financially sustained through loans from the parent company.[180] Thirdly, decision-making authority: according to evidence in public access, the Operational Deputy Director in Paris had agreed in an email to authorize an intermediary to make payments to the armed groups from July 2012 onwards (although at the time he and the Lafarge Cement

175 Celia Wells, *Corporations and Criminal Responsibility* (Oxford University Press 1993) 118 (hereinafter Wells, *Criminal Responsibility*); for a more detailed analysis of the 'the benefit of corporation', see Harmen van der Wilt, 'Corporate Criminal Responsibility for International Crimes: Exploring the Possibilities' (2013) 12 Chinese Journal of International Law 1, 43–77 (hereinafter Van der Wilt, 'Corporate Criminal Responsibility for International Crimes').

176 See Phillip Blumberg and others, *The Law of Corporate Groups: Jurisdiction, Practice, and Procedure* (Wolters Kluwer 2007); Phillip Blumberg, 'The Transformation of Modern Corporation Law: The Law of Corporate Groups' (2004) 37 Connecticut Law Review, 605.

177 Stoitchkova, Towards Corporate Liability (n 171) 150–156.

178 Steven Ratner, 'Corporations and Human Rights: A Theory of Legal Responsibility' (2001) 105 Yale Law Journal 443,519 (hereinafter Ratner, 'Corporations and Human Rights'); Hugh Collins, 'Ascription of Legal Responsibility to Groups in Complex Patterns of Economic Integration' (1990) 53 Mod. Law Review 731.

179 Case Dossier (Sherpa, Nov 2018) <https://www.asso-sherpa.org/french-company-lafarge-sued-forfinancing-isis-and-complicity-in-war-crimes-and-crimes-against-humanity-in-syria> accessed 24 February 2022.

180 Tixeire and others, 'Updates in the Lafarge Case (Part I)' (n 113).

Syria Director believed this was going to be a one-off arrangement).[181] Fourthly, the power to intervene: the plant's first security manager explained the payment of funds as a result of a joint strategy between the executives of the two corporate entities, as he reportedly said, 'the dynamic between the CEO and myself was to always find solutions to make the business work. And I think we pushed it a little too far'.[182] Finally, knowledge: there is evidence to suggest that in September 2012, a meeting was organized in Turkey between the plant Security Manager, the Lafarge Head of Security, and some of the Syrian opposition armed groups. The minutes of regular security committee meetings reflect that the relevant actors were aware of ongoing transactions with armed groups and of the increasing danger of the situation for its employees.[183]

These strong pieces of evidence suggest that the subsidiary was acting on behalf of the parent corporation, and despite being separate legal personalities, they were acting as a single undertaking. More generally, such extension of responsibility has the propensity to encourage meaningful changes in the supervision, control, and culture in complex transnational corporate structures.[184]

3. *The Mental Element of Shared Purpose versus Knowledge*

In November 2019, the Investigation Chamber of French Court of Appeals dismissed the charge of complicity in crimes against humanity on the ground that Lafarge and its executives lacked a shared intent to commit the crimes in question.[185] But the French Supreme Court, in September 2021, held that one can be an accomplice in crimes against humanity even if one does not share the intent with those committing the crimes: it is necessary and sufficient to have had the knowledge of the preparation or commission of such acts and that aid or assistance facilitated them; it is not necessary to belong to the criminal organization nor to subscribe to the conception or execution of the criminal plan.[186]

181 Ibid.

182 Belhoste and Nivet, 'The Organization of Short-sightedness' (n 132) 1596.

183 Ibid 1590.

184 Ratner, 'Corporations and Human Rights' (n 178) 473–75.

185 Claire Tixeire, Cannelle Lavite, Marie-Laure Guislain, 'Holding Transnational Corporations Accountable for International Crimes in Syria: Update on the Developments in the Lafarge Case (Part II)' (Opinio Juris, 27 July 2020) <http://opiniojuris.org/2020/07/27/holding-transnational-corporations-accountable-for-international-crimes-in-syria-update-on-the-developments-in-the-lafarge-case-part-ii/> accessed 24 February 2022 (hereinafter Tixeire and others 'Updates in the Lafarge Case (Part II)').

186 Cour de cassation (7 septembre 2021) Pourvoi n° 19-87.367 (excerpt is an unofficial translation).

In the case of contribution through fungible multipurpose goods, such as cash payments, the *mens rea* threshold is usually heightened as a finding of guilt requires special knowledge of where the money will be put to use.[187] This would be in contrast to support made in the form of weapons and arms, for instance, where their use is largely pre-determined as opposed to money which can be used for several different purposes.

With the heightened threshold, the key issue is whether it is sufficient to argue that the company had the knowledge of the crimes (or the way in which the money was going to be used by the group) or whether the accused persons need to share the intent with those of the direct perpetrators.

In this case, there are ample internal and external sources confirming that the different layers of management in the company were generally well informed, from the subsidiary to the headquarters. Nevertheless, shutting down the plant was not considered as a feasible option, as is demonstrated by the following extracts from the company's internal communications:

> A complete shutdown of the activity would be conducive to possible looting or sabotage. (Sept/Oct 2012)

It is becoming increasingly difficult to operate without having to negotiate directly or indirectly with these networks classified as terrorists by international organizations and the United States. (August/September 2013)[188]

Their consistent objective was to continue operations, first to keep selling cement and make profits, and then to protect assets and avoid losses on investment.[189] It becomes difficult to draw the line between business activity and criminal complicity when operating in an armed conflict. Continuing business in an armed conflict does not per se warrant criminal responsibility. It is a legitimate objective, the *raison d'être* of any business activity. Instead, blameworthiness does arise when the business activity disregards its harmful effect on third parties and in doing so gives an acquiescence to human rights abuses for the sake of profit.[190]

187 Van der Wilt, 'Corporate Criminal Responsibility for International Crimes' (n 175) 43–77.

188 Belhoste and Nivet, 'The organization of short-sightedness' (n 132) 1591.

189 During a hearing on 8 June before the Court of Cassation, Patrice Spinosi, a Lafarge lawyer, stressed that the firm's only intention was 'to continue the activity of the cement plant'. See Ismaël Halissat 'Affaire Lafarge : une note prouve que l'Etat était informé des versements d'argent à Daech' (Liberation, 13 July 2021) <https://www.liberation.fr/societe/police-justice/affaire-lafarge-une-note-prouve-que-letat-etait-informe-des-versements-dargent-a-daesh-20210713_VFOB4UF6N5EGTJRBYTQZMEMVIA/> accessed 24 February 2022.

190 UN Special Representative on Human Rights and Transnational Corporations UN DoC. A/HRC/8/16, 15 May 2008.

The security staff testified in the investigation that bombings near the plant were not considered to be as a risk for the employees or the factory.[191] When two months later, in 2014, the IS attacked the plant, and the employees reported that there were no precautionary measures in place to ensure their security. As most employees used buses to come to the factory, the absence of an evacuation bus left them stranded at the plant.[192] They barely managed to flee, packed in small private cars. One explained:

> If I had run away one hour later, I would not be able to play with my daughter today. Daesh would have cut our heads. ... I cannot believe that I worked six years for Lafarge, and they could not give us cars to leave the plant.[193]

Various employees reported that not only the evacuation plan was kept to a bare minimum but they were also encouraged to stay there in order to protect the plant.[194] Some staff were evacuated by bus, but there were not enough buses; about 30 employees had to flee by their own means and 4 were taken as hostages. As one employee present on the day of the attack revealed, 'we tried to make personal arrangements to stay safe, but nothing was done by the Lafarge's management to protect us. The evacuation was done individually as ordinary people, on our own'.[195]

If the judges determining culpability of the accused perpetrators adopt a high threshold of *mens rea* for complicity, i.e. shared intent or common purpose, it might be difficult to argue that the Lafarge SA shared the intent of committing crimes against humanity with the armed groups while paying them in cash in order to continue their operations. The French Court of Appeals favoured this interpretation when striking down the charge of complicity in crimes against humanity.

The two organizations, Sherpa and ECCHR, submitted before the Court that the requisite *mens rea* threshold in this case was mere knowledge. A knowledge-based threshold in accomplice liability is supported not only by

191 Tixeire, 'Can Lafarge Case be a Gamechanger' (n 116); Soren Seelow, 'Ce que révèle l'enquête judiciaire sur les agissements du cimentier Lafarge en Syrie' (Le Monde, 20 September 2017) (quoting an employee *'Pour moi, l'attentat à 10 kilomètres n'existe pas. [...] Maintenant, c'est peut-être un type qui s'est fait sauter. En aucun cas, il n'y avait un risque pour les employés et l'usine.'*)

192 Tixeire, 'Can Lafarge Case be a Gamechanger' (n 116).

193 Paul Waldie, 'How a Desmarais investment got entangled in an alleged terror-financing scheme in Syria' (The Globe and Mail, 23 June 2018) <https://www.theglobeandmail.com/business/article-how-a-desmarais-investment-got-entangled-in-an-alleged-terror/> accessed 24 February 2022.

194 Tixeire, 'Can Lafarge Case be a Gamechanger' (n 116).

195 ECCHR case report on Lafarge case <https://www.ecchr.eu/fileadmin/Fallbeschreibungen/Case_Report_Lafarge_Syria_ECCHR.pdf> accessed 24 February 2022.

French case law but also by international and comparative legal standards. This view was also supported by the *Avocat Général* to the Supreme Court in his submission to Court in this case.[196]

As for French law, there are only two cases where a similar question has been discussed. In the *Touvier* case of 1992, the French Supreme Court convicted the perpetrator for aiding crimes against humanity as he knew about and shared the intent of furthering the Nazi interests.[197] In the second case, the *Papon* case of 1997, the French Supreme Court's judgment established that complicity in crimes against humanity does not require supporting the ideology of the principal perpetrators, nor is it necessary for the accomplice to know the specific crime was being planned and actually perpetrated.[198] Therefore, purely on the basis of domestic law, it would not be an anomaly, but rather an extension to the existing jurisprudence to suggest that Article 121-7 of the French Criminal Code requires the accomplice to only know of the perpetrator's intent to commit a crime, not for the accomplice to share the intent of the direct perpetrator.[199]

To strengthen their arguments, the two organizations also relied comprehensively on doctrinal interpretations of Article 25(3)(c) in light of Article 30 of the ICC Statute. They made a case that a stricter interpretation of *mens rea* where the accomplice is required to share the intent for the principal offence would lead to systematic impunity for actors who provide assistance to the commission of crimes knowingly and consistently,[200] and that the stricter interpretation runs counter to the common sense reality of how atrocity crimes are committed. In the limited international and comparative jurisprudence on this question, the only cases where corporate executives have been held guilty for being complicit in crimes under international law are when the courts have adopted the lower 'knowledge' threshold for *mens rea*.[201]

196 Opinion available at <https://www.courdecassation.fr/getattacheddoc/6137092ff585960512dfe633/f9b7e19516e0bf90e13d8a9c81815c9a> accessed 25 February 2022.

197 *Touvier* [1992] French Court of Cassation, 100 ILR 350, 352; see Michael Tigar and others, 'Paul Touvier and the Crime Against Humanity' (1995) 30 Texas International Law Journal 285.

198 *Papon* [1997] French Court of Cassation, JCP No. 22812.

199 Ibid.

200 Elies van Sliedregt and A Popova, 'Interpreting "for the purpose of facilitating' in Article 25(3)(c)?', (James G Stewart Blog, 22 December 2014) <http://jamesgstewart.com/author/elies-and-alex/> accessed 5 March 2022; Brief of D.J. Scheffer, Director of the Center for International Human Rights, as amicus curiae in *The Presbyterian Church Of Sudan, et al. v. Talisman Energy, Inc.* (No. 09-1262) para 17 <www.justsecurity.org/wp-content/uploads/2016/09/Amicus-brief-David-Scheffer-aiding-and-abetting-Rome-Statute.pdf> accessed 24 February 2022.

201 See for instance, *USA v. Carl Krauch et al.* [1948] US Military Tribunal, Nuremberg; *USA v. Ernst von Weizsaecker, et al.* [1949] US Military Tribunal, Nuremberg; *re Tesch & Others*

The French Supreme Court appeared to agree with the reasoning above, as it stated:

> [a] different interpretation ..., which would require that the accomplice to a crime against humanity participate in the design or execution of a concerted plan, would result in many acts of aiding and abetting going unpunished, whereas it is the multiplication of such acts that makes the crime against humanity possible.[202]

This decision by the French Supreme Court may very well be construed as a judicial acknowledgement of the underlying economic structures that sustain and fuel large-scale human rights violations.

4. *Lafarge's Response to Criminal Liability*

Interestingly, Lafarge has already taken the French government within the fold of these proceedings. The judicial enquiry on the relationship between Lafarge and IS had already secured confessions from the executives that they knew about the transactions. In the court, Lafarge has tried to use its status of 'strategic economic importance for France' to also implicate the French government. Christian Herrault, former Lafarge Deputy Director-General of Operations, reportedly stated that the French Ministry of Foreign Affairs had encouraged Lafarge to remain active as it was a matter of the 'French flag' for them to continue operations.[203] One day before the Supreme Court decision in September 2021, another leak revealed that there were multiple meetings between Lafarge and the French domestic, foreign, and military intelligence services during the time period in question.[204]

Not only did Lafarge claim that France was informed of its activities in Syria, but also that the government encouraged it to continue operating in Syria, particularly because ending cement production and reopening it again

---

[1946] British Military Court, 1 UN War Crimes Commission, Law Reports of Trials of War Criminals 93 (Zyklon B case); *Franz Van Anraat* [2005] Case No. 09/751003-04 (The Netherlands)

202 Cour de cassation (7 September 2021) Pourvoi n° 19-87.367, para 70.

203 Soren Seelow, 'Ce que révèle l'enquête judiciaire sur les agissements du cimentier Lafarge en Syrie' (Le Monde, 20 September 2017) <https://www.liberation.fr/societe/police-justice/affaire-lafarge-une-note-prouve-que-letat-etait-informe-des-versements-dargent-a-daesh-20210713_VFOB4UF6N5EGTJRBYTQZMEMVIA/> accessed 24 February 2022.

204 'Anadolu Agency Accesses Documents Showing French Intelligence Aware of Lafarge Financing Daesh/ISIS' (Andalou Agency, 7 September 2019) <https://www.aa.com.tr/en/world/anadolu-agency-accesses-documents-showing-french-intelligence-aware-of-lafarge-financing-daesh-isis/2357992> accessed 24 February 2022.

would have been very costly.[205] In return, the government also sought protection of the plant from the US forces present on the territory.[206] At Sherpa and ECCHR's request, former French diplomats, including the former Minister of Foreign Affairs, have been heard in the first stage of the case.[207]

Furthermore, classic delay tactics are also being used. The case is currently on appeal before the Supreme Court against a judgment that enforced a previous Supreme Court order.[208] However, given that active involvement of former employees and non-governmental organizations is highly significant to these proceedings, the long delays in the proceedings are expected to weigh in on the continued perseverance of these parties. The company refused to hand over their computers, scrubbed them before the investigative raid, and challenged every step of the proceedings in appeals.

The imbalance of resources between the two non-profit organizations and Lafarge that is visible at the court hearings is a telling story of the asymmetry between the two sides. On the one hand, the corporate group is being represented by one of the most expensive law firms in France that hosts dozens of high-profile lawyers. At the Supreme Court, one of the most popular lawyers is representing them. On the other hand, the plaintiffs are being represented mainly by two teams of two lawyers each in Sherpa and ECCHR, supported by a few cooperating local lawyers, most of whom are young with the exception of an accomplished lawyer who represents them at the Supreme Court. [209]

In October 2022, in a separate US proceeding, Lafarge SA and LCS pleaded guilty before a federal court to conspiring to provide material support to foreign terrorist organizations and agreed to pay US$778 million in fines and forfeiture.[210] It remains to be seen the implications, if any, this payout will have for the criminal proceedings against the company in France.

205 See UN Working Group on Mercenaries, 'Relationship Between Private Military and Security Companies and the Extractive Industry from a Human Rights Perspective' (29 July 2019) A/HRC/42/42.

206 Emmanuel Jarry, 'Exclusive: France asked U.S. not to bomb Lafarge factory in Syria in 2014 – emails' (Reuters, 25 April 2018) <https://www.reuters.com/article/us-lafargeholcim-syria-france-exclusive-idUSKBN1HW2DE> accessed 24 February 2022.

207 Tixeire, 'Can Lafarge Case be a Gamechanger? (n 116).

208 Cossart, 'Insights into the French Court Decisions' (n 167).

209 Interview with Claire Tixeire, Senior Legal Advisor (online, 31 August 2021).

210 US Department of Justice, 'Lafarge Pleads Guilty to Conspiring to Provide Material Support to Foreign Terrorist Organizations', 18 October 2022 <https://www.justice.gov/opa/pr/lafarge-pleads-guilty-conspiring-provide-material-support-foreign-terrorist-organizations> accessed 16 March 2023.

V. Conclusion

In many ways, it seems premature to draw conclusions on strategic litigation practice seeking corporate accountability in Europe as the organizations are young, often still led by their original founders. Will their practice turn into sustainable methods of legal interventions on pressing political questions, or will they be read as episodic game-changers? The few relevant promising cases against corporations are, in fact, all pending before the courts at various stages. However, this nascent stage offers a different kind of practice, in comparison to the other two case studies, that is worth analysing within the framework of TWAI(C)L. Therefore, the following observations on the (potential of the) practice merit acknowledgement with an eye on future developments.

Relative Application of Universal Norms

Extraterritorial prosecutions against corporations for their complicity in crimes under international law have become another potential avenue to seek accountability that addresses complex structural issues. While these domestic courts offer new sites to make claims based on international criminal law, they are mainly taking place in Western Europe, therefore keeping the 'Eurocentric' character of international law intact. These cases underlined by the moral claims of global justice, even though taking place before domestic courts, strengthen the universalist claims of international criminal law. Arguably, universal jurisdiction proceedings can also be construed as an extension of Mutua's 'savage, victim, saviour' narrative: where these states acting on behalf of the international community are pursuing cases against the 'evil perpetrators' who somehow landed on their territory, on the pretext that these countries cannot be 'safe havens' for those accused of such violations.

Without discounting the validity of this claim, it must be acknowledged that this narrative reproduces the idea of a 'helpless and powerless' victim who lacks any agency. In many cases of extraterritorial prosecutions, as exhibited from the discussion on Syria above, the victim communities are heavily lobbying for these proceedings and stand to benefit from an additional avenue for accountability. At the same time, if strategic litigation actors – who work with an awareness and understanding of the geopolitical factors that inform the use of tools such as universal jurisdiction – are also involved in these processes, the possibility of making counter-hegemonic interventions in these settings becomes more real.

These contradictions are inherent in the universal jurisdiction practice that is unfolding at this stage and must be simultaneously considered. In its present form, it is marked by three characteristic features: one, enhanced democratization and accessibility; two, politically cautious selection of defendants; and three, transnational complementary collaborations to enforce international criminal law before domestic courts. With a steadily expanding practice of universal jurisdiction in Europe, the states and their institutions are getting accustomed in dealing with large-scale crimes committed in complex socio-political contexts. But some of the limitations in the process are glaring, such as the unaccustomed procedural standards, its dependence on the will of the states, and physical and/or cognitive distance from the survivors and their communities.

Despite these limitations, cases such as Lafarge highlight the possibility of pursuing a different conception of justice where communities most affected by the crimes are directly involved as legitimate stakeholders. In this conception, the victims and their representatives are contesting the inadequacies of universalist international criminal law, i.e. the lack of corporate accountability. Also, these local sites challenge the spatial boundaries in which international criminal law is elaborated and practiced (see the discussion on 'open' universality in Section III.2 of Chapter 1).

Transnational Non-state Actors Practicing International Criminal Law

A related yet distinct element of this practice is that these proceedings, either triggered by non-state actors or involving their substantial contribution, challenge the notion that implementation of international criminal law is a prerogative of the state. Their contributions are impacting the development of law and legal norms.

An important feature of their work is the 'transnational' element: the multiplicity of jurisdictions and their arduous requirements in terms of technical expertise ensures that there is no one actor who can independently bring complex litigations in the European context without relying on collaborations with partners. Transnational organizations working with similar mandates are employing international criminal law to respond to their own unique jurisdictional challenges. This chapter discussed only one of them in greater detail, the ECCHR that challenge impunity enjoyed by the economically and militarily powerful actors and highlight the double standards of the states as well as the law in the implementation of a universally applicable regime. They indeed engage with international criminal law in a manner that would qualify as strategic (see Chapter 2). While making tactical legal interventions in national, regional, and international courts, they are informed by the far-sighted aim of exposing the biases of the structures that sustain an inegalitarian world order. Their practice, with each successive victory and loss, in that sense, writes resistance into the mainstream international legal order.

The transnational collaborations they pursue are not only with other actors in the neighbouring European countries but also attempts are being made to connect with the victimized communities and movements in the 'Third World'. These interventions against European actors appear to be based on partnership with the stakeholders across the North–South divide. It was beyond the scope of this study to analyse the terms and conditions of these partnerships and the concerns regarding the reproduction of similar structures of domination and subordinations within this relationship, but they are certainly present and need to be addressed.

Nevertheless, these collaborations result in a novel model of hybridity and transnational solidarity distinct from horizontal and vertical models based on national sovereignty. Such practice is contributing to international criminal law, on the one hand, by filling its loopholes and to domestic law, by bringing international criminal law home to several European domestic jurisdictions. In that sense, despite imperfections, their practice does manage to de-privilege the status of the nation-state in the development and implementation of international law (see Section III.2 of Chapter 1).

Challenging the Role of European Corporations in Conflicts Outside

The criminal complaints against Lafarge and its employees reflect an advancement in the practice of international criminal law on several grounds: one, domestic enforcement of international criminal law against corporate conduct for crimes committed abroad; two, criminal investigations and charges against a parent corporation as an entity for conduct of its subsidiary; and three, an upgraded placement of victims in proceedings carried out to enforce international criminal law.

Holding the multinational parent company responsible for the actions of its subsidiary that it controls financially and operationally is a huge leap in balancing the unequal relationship between the 'Global North' and 'Global South' (see Section III.4 of Chapter 1). As evidenced by the French Supreme Court judgment from September 2021, it is a litigation that targets the economic structures that aid and assist the violence. At the same time, it provides a strong counter to the narrative that violence is a problem indigenous to the 'Third World' and foregrounds the role of European actors who are seemingly far from the location of violence but stand to profit from it.

Moreover, the case illustrates that the debate between individual accountability and corporate responsibility, as sophisticated as it may be, is somewhat dated in the context of international criminal justice. This investigation against Lafarge and its employees exhibits how individual complicity and corporate responsibility can coexist. Attributing responsibility to Lafarge as the parent company does not imply that the factory managers and the executives who took the decisions will be absolved of their guilt. At the same time, insisting on corporate accountability *in addition to* individual liability is to underline the instrumental context of profit maximization for which the individual perpetrators take culpable decisions in the first place.[211] Criminal conviction of an entity symbolizes that it is not just the individual defendants, but also the structure of the company that forms an integral part of the criminal machinery.[212]

Foregrounding Crimes against Humanity over Financing of Terrorism

Admittedly, this is an exceptional case on several grounds, including irrefutable incriminatory evidence in public access, the reputation and the scale of violations committed by the armed group in question, and significantly, the terrorist attack by the same group carried out in the country of the parent corporation. All these factors make it a precedent-setting case. For the purposes of this study, it is noteworthy that if it were not for the strategic interventions of the two organizations involved, the precedent would have only been in the counter-terrorism paradigm. The restrictive counter-terrorism framework prioritizes the security of the state over human rights and civil liberties, at times even resulting in their total disregard. A strengthened counter-terrorism paradigm further targets marginalized groups as collateral damage.

Thus, it was crucial that strategic legal interventions were made in this case that at the same time critiqued the framework and its limitations but also capitalized on it to centre the vocabulary of human rights and international criminal law (see discussion on reform-oriented critique in Section III.1 of Chapter 1).

References

Aboueldahab S and Langmack FJ, 'The End of the Al-Khatib Trial: A Historic Verdict and a Trial of Missed Opportunities' (Völkerrechtsblog, 7 February 2022) <10.17176/20220207-120946-0> accessed 23 February 2022

Akande D, 'The Jurisdiction of the International Criminal Court Over Nationals of Non-Parties: Legal Basis and Limits' (2003) 1 Journal of International Criminal Justice 618

Al-Abdallah M, 'Syrian Civil Society: Strategic Litigation with No Strategy' (5 November 2020) <https://www.aljumhuriya.net/en/content/syrian-civil-society-%E2%80%9Cstrategic-litigation%E2%80%9D-no-strategy> accessed 23 February 2022

211 See Van der Wilt, 'Corporate Criminal Responsibility for International Crimes' (n 175) 43–77 (argues that the famous dictum of the Nuremberg Tribunal is in need of partial revision. Crimes against international law can be committed by abstract legal entities, provided that they act in tandem with [natural persons]).

212 Interview with Claire Tixeire, Senior Legal Advisor (online, 31 August 2021).

Amnesty International, 'Shell: A Criminal Enterprise?' (18 May 2020) <https://www.amnesty.org.uk/shell-criminal-enterprise> accessed 21 February 2022

Aparac J, 'Business and Armed Non-State Groups: Challenging the Landscape of Corporate (Un) accountability in Armed Conflicts' (2020) 5 Business and Human Rights Journal 2

Bakker C, 'Universal Jurisdiction of Spanish Courts over Genocide in Tibet: Can it Work?' (2006) 4 Journal of International Criminal Justice 3, 595–601

Baughen S, *Human Rights and Corporate Wrongs: Closing the Governance Gap* (Edward Elgar 2015)

Belhoste N and Nivet B, 'The Organization of Shortsightedness: The Implications of Remaining in Conflict Zones. The Case of Lafarge During Syria's Civil War' (2021) 60 Business & Society 7, 1573–1605

Ben-Ari, 'Universal Jurisdiction: Chronicle of a Death Foretold?' (2014–2015) 43 Denver Journal of International Law and Policy 165

Blumberg P, *The Multinational Challenge to Corporate Law: The Search for a New Corporate Personality* (Oxford University Press 1993)

Blumberg P, 'The Transformation of Modern Corporation Law: The Law of Corporate Groups' (2004) 37 Connecticut Law Review 605

Blumberg P and others, *The Law of Corporate Groups: Jurisdiction, Practice, and Procedure* (Wolters Kluwer 2007)

Brody R, *Victims Bring a Dictator to Justice: The Case of Hissène Habré* (Bread for the World 2017)

Brownlie I, *Principles of Public International Law* (5th edn, Oxford University Press 1998)

Burbidge P, 'Waking the Dead of the Spanish Civil War: Judge Baltasar Garzon and the Spanish Law of Historical Memory' (2011) 9 Journal of International Criminal Justice 3, 753–781

Caroline Fehl, 'The Partial Return of Universal Jurisdiction: Syrian Torturers on Trial in Germany' (Global Policy Journal, 12 May 2020) <https://www.globalpolicyjournal.com/blog/12/05/2020/partial-return-universal-jurisdiction-syrian-torturers-trial-germany> accessed 22 February 2022

Cassese A, 'Is the Bell Tolling for Universality? A Plea for a Sensible Notion of Universal Jurisdiction' (2003) 1 Journal of International Criminal Justice 589

De la Rasilla Moral I, 'The Swan Song of Universal Jurisdiction in Spain' (2009) 9 International Criminal Law Review 777

De Vos D, 'Corporate Accountability: Dutch Court Convicts Former "Timber Baron" of War Crimes in Liberia' (14 April 2017) <https://me.eui.eu/dieneke-de-vos/blog/corporate-accountability-dutch-courtconvicts-former-timber-baron-of-war-crimes-in-liberia/> accessed 21 February 2022

Dorfman A, *Exorcising Terror: The Incredible Unending Trial of General Augusto Pinochet* (Seven Stories Press 2011)

Dorothée Myriam Kellou and others, 'Syrie: les troubles arrangements de Lafarge avec l'Etat islamique' (Le Monde, 9 June 2016) <https://www.lemonde.fr/syrie/article/2016/06/21/syrie-les-troubles-arrangements-de-lafarge-avec-l-etat-islamique_4955023_1618247.html> accessed 23 February 2022

Dünkelsbühler A, Suttor A and Borger L, 'Universal jurisdiction without universal outreach?: The Al Khatib trial in Koblenz and the limits of domestic criminal procedure in the adjudication of international crimes' (Völkerrechtsblog, 13 January 2021) <10.17176/20210113-181614-0> accessed 23 February 2022

'ECCHR, European Responsibility for War Crimes in Yemen' (2019) <https://www.ecchr.eu/en/case/european-responsibility-for-war-crimes-in-yemen/> accessed 21 February 2022

Fox JR, *Dictionary of International and Comparative Law* (3rd edn, Oceana Publications 2003)

Gallagher K, 'Universal jurisdiction in practice: Efforts to hold Donald Rumsfeld and other high-level United States officials accountable for torture' (2009) 7 Journal of International Criminal Justice 5, 1087–1116

Geneuss J, 'Fostering a Better Understanding of Universal Jurisdiction: A Comment on the AU–EU Expert Report on the Principle of Universal Jurisdiction' (2009) 7 Journal of International Criminal Justice 5

Grunwald H, *Courtroom to Revolutionary Stage: Performance and Ideology in Weimar Political Trials* (Oxford University Press 2012)

Hansia F, 'French Tribunal Investigates Qosmos Over Surveillance Software Use in Syria' (Corpwatch, 21 July 2015) <https://www.corpwatch.org/article/french-tribunal-investigates-qosmos-over-surveillance-software-use-syria> accessed 21 February 2022

Hodgson J, 'The Police, the Prosecutor and the Juge d'instruction: Judicial Supervision in France, Theory and Practice' (2001) 41 British Journal of Criminology 2, 342–361

Hogson J, 'Suspects, Defendants and Victims in the French Criminal Process: The Context of Recent Reform' (2002) 51 International and Comparative Law Quarterly 4, 781

Huisman W, Van Baar A and Gorsira M, 'Corporations and Transnational Crime' in GJN Bruinsma (ed), *Histories of Transnational Crime* (Springer 2015) 147–170

Human Rights Watch, 'Long Arm of Justice: Lessons from Specialized War Crimes Units in France, Germany, and the Netherlands' <https://www.hrw.org/report/2014/09/16/long-arm-justice/lessons-specialized-war-crimes-units-france-germany-and#_ftnref1> accessed 22 February 2022

Jeßberger F, 'Corporate Involvement in Slavery and Criminal Responsibility under International Law' (2016) 14 Journal of International Criminal Justice 2, 327–341

Jeßberger F, 'International v. National Prosecution of International Crimes' in A Cassese and others (eds), *Oxford Companion to International Criminal Law* (Oxford University Press 2009) 208–215

Jeßberger F, 'Towards a "Complementary Preparedness" Approach to Universal Jurisdiction – Recent Trends and Best Practices in the European Union' in *European Parliament, Universal Jurisdiction and International Crimes: Constraints and Best Practices* (2018) 46 <http://www.legal-tools.org/doc/fb2d88/> accessed 22 February 2022

Jeßberger F, Kaleck W and Schueller A, 'Concurring Criminal Jurisdictions Under International Law' in M Bersmo (ed), *Complimentarity and the Exercise of Universal Jurisdiction for Core International Crimes* (TOAEP 2010) 233–246

Joseph S, *Corporations and Transnational Human Rights Litigation* (Hart Publishing 2004)

Joseph S and Joseph SL, *Corporations and Transnational Human Rights Litigation* (Vol. 4, Hart Publishing 2004)

Kaleck W, 'From Pinochet to Rumsfeld: Universal Jurisdiction in Europe 1998–2008' (2008) 30 Michigan Journal of International Law 927

Kaleck W, *Double Standards: International Criminal Law and the West* (TOAEP 2015)

Kaleck W, *Law versus Power* (OR Books 2019)

Kaleck W and Kroker P, 'Syrian Torture Investigations in Germany and Beyond: Breathing New Life into Universal Jurisdiction in Europe?' (2018) 16 Journal of International Criminal Justice 1, 165–191

Kaleck W and Saage-Maaß M, 'Corporate Accountability for Human Rights Violations Amounting to International Crimes' (2010) 6 Journal of International Criminal Justice 699

Kather AL, '"Water Finds Its Way"? Universal Jurisdiction as an Avenue for Justice in Syria' (Lieber Institute, 28 July 2021) <https://lieber.westpoint.edu/water-finds-way-universal-jurisdiction-justice-syria/> accessed 23 February 2022

Koskenniemi M, *From Apology to Utopia: The Structure of the International Legal Argument* (Cambridge University Press 2005)

Kyriakakis J, 'Corporations before International Criminal Courts: Implications for the International Criminal Justice Project' (2017) 30 Leiden Journal of International Law 22

Langer M, 'The Archipelago and the Wheel — The Universal Jurisdiction and the International Criminal Court Regimes' in Minow, True-Frost and Whiting (eds), *The First Global Prosecutor: Promise and Constraints* (University of Michigan Press 2015)

Langer M, 'Universal Jurisdiction is Not Disappearing: The Shift from "Global Enforcer" to "No Safe Haven" Universal Jurisdiction' (2015) 13 Journal of International Criminal Justice 2, 245

Langer M and Eason M, 'The Quiet Expansion of Universal Jurisdiction' (2019) 30 European Journal of International Law 3

Lapie OP, 'The Partie Civile in the Criminal Law of France' (1928) 10 Journal of Comparative Legislation and International Law 33–45

Mégret F, '"Do Not Do Abroad What You Would Not Do at Home?": An Exploration of the Rationales for Extraterritorial Criminal Jurisdiction over a State's Nationals' (2020) 57 Canadian Yearbook of International Law/Annuaire canadien de droit international 1

Mehta K, 'Hanan v. Germany (Eur. Ct. HR)' (2022) 61 International Legal Materials 1, 61–123

Morris D, *Legal Sabotage: Ernst Fraenkel in Hitler's Germany* (Cambridge University Press 2020)

O'Brien M, 'Prosecutorial Discretion as an Obstacle to Prosecution of United Nations Peacekeepers by the International Criminal Court: The Big Fish/Small Fish Debate and the Gravity Threshold' (2012) 10 Journal of International Criminal Justice 3, 525–545

O'Sullivan A, *Universal Jurisdiction in International Criminal Law: The Debate and the Battle for Hegemony* (Routledge 2017)

Onate S and others, 'Lessons Learned: Chemicals Trader Convicted of War Crimes' (2007) 2 Hague Justice Journal 1

Pearson Z, 'Non-Governmental Organizations and the International Criminal Court: Changing Landscapes of International Law' (2006) 39 Cornell International Law Journal 243

Ratner S, 'Corporations and Human Rights: A Theory of Legal Responsibility' (2001) 105 Yale Law Journal 443, 519

Reydams L, 'The Rise and Fall of Universal Jurisdiction' in William Schabas and Nadia Bernaz (eds) *Routledge Handbook of International Criminal Law* (Routledge 2012) 337–354

Richards I, *Neoliberalism and Neo-Jihadism* (Manchester University Press 2020)

Roht-Arriaza N, 'The Pinochet Precedent and Universal Jurisdiction' (2000) 35 New England Law Review 311

Rothenberg D and Garzón B, 'Let Justice Judge: An Interview with Judge Baltasar Garzón and Analysis of His Ideas' (2002) 24 Human Rights Quarterly 4, 924–973

Ruggie J, 'Report of the Special Representative of the Secretary-General on the Issue of Human Rights and Transnational Corporations and Other Business Enterprises' (UNOHCHR 2011) UN Doc A/HRC/17/31

Ryngaert C, *Jurisdiction in International Law* (Oxford University Press 2015)

Saage-Maaß M, Zumbansen P, Bader M and Shahab P (eds), *Transnational Legal Activism in Global Value Chains: The Ali Enterprises Factory Fire and the Struggle for Justice* (Springer 2021)

SAJC Trial Monitoring Report <https://syriaaccountability.org/library/inside-the-raslan-trial-the-al-gharib-verdict-in-detail/> accessed 6 March 2022

Skinner G and others, *Third Pillar: Access to Judicial Remedies for Human Rights Violations by Transnational Business* (ICAR, CORE, ECCJ 2013)

Slaughter AM and Burke-White W, 'The Future of International Law Is Domestic (or, the European Way of Law)' (2006) 47 Harvard International Law Journal 327

Stahn C, 'Daedalus or Icarus? Footprints of International Criminal Justice Over a Quarter of a Century' Footprints of International Criminal Justice Over a Quarter of a Century (September 27, 2016)

Stoichkova D, *Towards Corporate Liability in International Criminal Law* (Intersentia 2010)

Stokke E and Wiebelhaus-Brahm E, 'Syrian Diaspora Mobilization for Prospective Transitional Justice in the Absence of Transition' (2022) 214, Journal of Human Rights 1–17

Sweden Authorises Indictment of Lundin Oil Executives Over Alleged Complicity in War Crimes in So. Sudan; co. denies allegation' (BHRRC, 18 October 2018) <https://www.business-humanrights.org/en/latest-news/sweden-authorises-indictment-of-lundin-oil-executives-over-alleged-complicity-in-war-crimes-in-so-sudan-co-denies-allegations/> accessed 21 February 2022

Thamil Ananthavinayagan, 'A Tale of German Global Criminal Justice: A TWAIL Perspective on the Syrian Torture Trial' (Just Security, 30 June 2020) <https://www.justsecurity.org/70986/a-tale-of-german-global-criminal-justice-a-twail-perspective-on-the-syrian-torture-trial/> accessed 23 February 2022

Theurer K and Kaleck W (eds), *Dekoloniale Rechtskritik und Rechtspraxis* (Nomos Verlag 2020)

Tigar M and others, 'Paul Touvier and the Crime Against Humanity' (1995) 30 Texas International Law Journal 285

Tixeire C, 'Can the Lafarge Case be a Game Changer? French Multinational Company Indicted for International Crimes in Syria' (BHRRC, 31 August 2018) <https://www.business-humanrights.org/en/blog/can-the-lafarge-case-be-a-game-changer

-french-multinational-company-indicted-for-international-crimes-in-syria/> accessed 24 February 2022

Tixeire C, Lavite C and Guislain ML, 'Holding Transnational Corporations Accountable for International Crimes in Syria: Update on the Developments in the Lafarge Case (Part I)' (Opinio Juris, 27 February 2020) <https://opiniojuris.org/2020/07/27/holding-transnational-corporations-accountable-for-international-crimes-in-syria-update-on-the-developments-in-the-lafarge-case-part-i/> accessed 24 February 2022

Tixeire C, Lavite C and Guislain ML, 'Holding Transnational Corporations Accountable for International Crimes in Syria: Update on the Developments in the Lafarge Case (Part II)' (Opinio Juris, 27 July 2020) <http://opiniojuris.org/2020/07/27/holding-transnational-corporations-accountable-for-international-crimes-in-syria-update-on-the-developments-in-the-lafarge-case-part-ii/> accessed 24 February 2022

Tofan A, 'The Lafarge Affair: A First Step Towards Corporate Criminal Liability for Complicity in Crimes against Humanity' (Doing Business Right, 2 October 2018)

TRIAL International, Universal Jurisdiction Annual Review (UJAR) 2020 <https://trialinternational.org/latest-post/universal-jurisdiction-annual-review-2020-atrocities-must-be-prosecuted-soundly-and-rigorously/> accessed 22 February 2022

UN Working Group on Mercenaries, 'Relationship Between Private Military and Security Companies and the Extractive Industry from a Human Rights Perspective' (29 July 2019) A/HRC/42/42

Van der Wilt H, 'Corporate Criminal Responsibility for International Crimes: Exploring the Possibilities' (2013) 12 Chinese Journal of International Law 1, 43–77

Van der Wilt H, '"Sadder but Wiser"? NGOs and Universal Jurisdiction for International Crimes' (2015) 13 Journal of International Criminal Justice 237

Van Schaak B, 'National Courts Step Up: Syrian Cases Proceeding in Domestic Courts' in *Imagining Justice for Syria*, Lieber Studies Series (Online edn, Oxford Academic 2020).

Van Sliedregt E and Popova A, 'Interpreting "for the Purpose of Facilitating" in Article 25(3)(c)?' (James G Stewart Blog, 22 December 2014) <http://jamesgstewart.com/author/elies-and-alex/> accessed 5 March 2022

Vastardis AY and Chambers R, 'Overcoming the Corporate Veil Challenge: Could Investment Law Inspire the Proposed Business and Human Rights Treaty?' (2017) 67 International and Comparative Law Quarterly 389–423

Verhaeghe M, 'The Political Funeral Procession for the Belgium UJ Statute', in W Kaleck and others (eds), *International Prosecution of Human Rights Crimes* (Springer 2007)

Ward K, *Networks of Empire: Forced Migration in the Dutch East India Company* (Cambridge University Press 2009)

Wells C, *Corporations and Criminal Responsibility* (Oxford University Press 1993)

Zappalà S, 'The German Federal Prosecutor's Decision Not to Prosecute a Former Uzbek Minister: Missed Opportunity or Prosecutorial Wisdom?' (2006) 4 Journal of International Criminal Justice 602

Zerk J, *Corporate Liability for Gross Human Rights Abuses: Towards a Fairer and More Effective System of Domestic Law Remedies* (UNOHCHR 2012)

Fischer-Lescano A, 'Torture in Abu Ghraib: The Complaint Against Donald Rumsfeld Under the German Code of Crimes Against International Law' (2005) 6 German Law Journal 689–724

Ratner M, *The Trial of Donald Rumsfeld: A Prosecution by Book* (The New Press 2008)

Part III

Conclusions

Chapter 7

Terms and Conditions of Corporate Accountability

A Strategic Practice of International Criminal Law

Power shaped the foundations of international criminal law. Its practice, even as it moves to the domestic courts, continues to be married to international politics. The ICC has been repeatedly indicted with the charges of double standards and selectivity that challenge its legitimacy. Existing scholarship has placed remarkable emphasis on the limitations of the ICC. International criminal law continues to bear substantive blind spots and the international criminal justice system at large has also been subject to challenge, inter alia, on account of its Eurocentricity as well as its coloniality.

This book, while stemming from and grounded in the aforementioned critiques of international criminal law, moved a step further. It engaged with two competing claims made with respect to the engagement of those affected by atrocity crimes with international criminal justice as a system: its hegemonic tendencies and counter-hegemonic practice. Recognizing the claim that international law has and continues to serve the interests of select Western states, the book foregrounded a practice that uses international law in ways that could potentially address the concerns of Third World peoples. In an attempt to further nuance the critical discourse on international criminal law, the book analyses the practice of strategic litigation organizations within the framework of TWAIL.

It weighs in on the eternal dilemma of reform or resistance: resist or reject the structures that are unfair; or engage with them to challenge its inadequacies and seek its reform. The book has hopefully substantiated the claim that an outright resistance of the international criminal law system, despite the structural flaws, deprives those affected by systemic violence of an important additional avenue of contestation. As evident through many ongoing situations of conflict, international criminal law has become an integral part of the language within which claims of justice and accountability are made by stakeholders, including states, international organizations, and civil society. To disengage with this framework because of its inherent biases and coloniality would imply losing a significant platform to articulate some of the worst violence that peoples from the Third World experience either at the hands of powerful international political and economic actors or at times their own

DOI: 10.4324/9781003405047-11

state. On the contrary, a critical and informed engagement with international criminal law that uses it as a tool to limit or challenge this power allows contestation of its claims of universality and neutrality.

Against that backdrop, the book introduced and conceptualized novel actors that are engaging with international criminal law, at least with an intent to challenge such power structures: strategic litigation organizations. The book highlights strategic litigation practice by drilling deep into the workings of these transnational legal interventions initiated by non-state organizations which choose to employ international criminal law as a means of resistance, and critique its inadequacies and selective implementation. It demonstrates that the practice of strategic litigation which resorts to the vocabulary of international criminal law in and outside the courtrooms mirrors the potential of the law to respond to the needs and concerns of Third World peoples.

The key argument is that such invocation of international criminal law by strategic litigation organizations challenging its hegemonic tendencies explores the emancipatory potential of the international criminal justice system and in doing that, it impacts its practice and implementation as well. This practice interjects the broader legal order with counter-hegemonic claims. Taking this practice into account could potentially challenge the exclusive prerogative of (a select few) states to make and implement the law.

In the book, strategic litigation has been conceptualized from the vantage point of the aforementioned critiques in order to analyse its implications for international criminal justice. First of all, this conceptualization challenges the use of the label of 'strategic litigation' as a buzzword in the practice of international human rights and international criminal law. It is inherently a political characterization (see Chapter 2). The unreflective use of the label not only diverts the attention from truly strategic legal interventions but also poses bigger questions on the legitimacy of the actors involved. The book relies on Rob Knox's article to emphasize the understanding of the term strategy as distinguished from tactics. The term 'strategy' refers to the plan to win a *long-term war* that relies on tactical methods used to win *individual immediate* battles. Tactics are employed with a view to having long-term strategic consequences and objectives. Logically, the term 'strategic' indicates that there are two essential underlying elements necessary for such a classification: long-term (temporal aspect) and strategic objective (structural aspect). The book draws on this semantic distinction, to determine that for a legal practitioner's engagement with the law to qualify as strategic, their interventions must be far-sighted and made with a strategic objective.

In that case, the key question is what kind of interventions qualify as aiming at strategic objectives, if any? Every resort to international law to make an emancipatory claim runs the risk of whitewashing the oppression of the system, reinforcing the structural biases, and legitimizing the status quo. In most such cases, there are little to no chances of a court victory and even if these legal interventions manage to secure a stand-alone court victory, that success may serve to downsize the impact of the structural critiques. By that logic, any legal intervention from a critical perspective could be viewed either as tactical in case it highlights the oppression of the structures or as enabling in case it ends up perpetuating the existing structures of domination and exploitation. One would conclude that there would be no winning the long-term war against the domination and hegemony embedded within the international legal order.

As argued before, given the importance of international criminal law in international politics and the absence of alternative spaces where emancipatory claims can be made, abandoning the law – a 'true revolution' – is not an option. Despite its limitations, strategic litigation must leverage the vocabulary of international criminal law to challenge and constrain concentration of power. In that context, the indeterminacy of law can be usefully employed to tap into its counter-hegemonic potential.

This book suggests that strategic legal interventions may be informed by two primary objectives, ideally in combination: to highlight the critiques of the legal system *and* to work towards countering its structural biases within and outside the courtroom. In that sense, a strategic practice of the law is not disjointed from the theoretical critiques of the legal framework, but instead informed by it. Each legal intervention is far-sighted and speaks to or about the biases of the structures that sustain the existing international legal order. Thus, a strategic legal intervention would resort to international criminal law for the purposes of supporting, defending, and protecting those who seek to challenge the patterns of exploitation and subordination. A strategic litigation organization uses the international criminal justice system to bridge the gap between the lawmakers and those most affected by it. The practice of strategic litigation uses tactics that contribute to building a long-term sustainable movement where the Third World peoples can define the terms in which the law is being enforced and practised. For strategic litigation, a complaint, an arrest warrant, a trial, or a conviction are mere tactics that serve to achieve these strategic objectives. Therefore, in its essence, strategic litigation is a tactical approach to use international law in furtherance of a strategic objective, for instance, as seen in this book, challenging the economic structures that fuel large-scale violence.

The book relied on a multiple-case-study method with three distinct cases to analyse how transnational civil society organizations engage in strategic litigation and leverage the potential of international criminal law in different domestic jurisdictions. The three strategic litigation subjects of the case studies were *Centro de Estudios Legales y Sociales*, Argentina (CELS) (see Chapter 4); Center for Constitutional Rights, US (CCR) (see Chapter 5); and European Center for Constitutional Rights, Germany (ECCHR) (see Chapter 6).

The three organizations illustrate the discussion on strategic objectives above. CELS worked inside and outside the courtroom over several decades to unpack the systematic nature of corporate involvement in crimes committed by the last military dictatorship in Argentina (1976–1983). Their legal interventions highlighted how corporate accountability remains an elusive element of international criminal law as applicable in a transitional justice framework. Where the political or military powerholders remain the main subjects of attention, the corporations 'transition' through the conflict rather unscathed and more resourceful than before. Similarly, CCR's strategic practice is evident from their interventions that seek to highlight the misuse of executive power by the United States and particularly the impact of these actions on individuals who are not US citizens. In the third case, ECCHR's strategic legal interventions are intended to highlight the double standards and selective implementation of international criminal law by the Western states. In that, it also seeks to reform the legal system by bringing to the fore the complex politico-economic structures in which European actors contribute to armed conflicts outside Europe.

The book presents two broad components to determine whether a given practice qualifies as strategic: a combination of the legal and the extra-legal; and the choice of reform over repair.

On combining the legal and extra-legal: As outlined above, strategic litigation consciously uses the vocabulary of international criminal law to highlight or address structural problems of the legal order. Especially when the odds of legal victory are minimal, and the stand-alone impact of judgment is negligible, strategic litigation cannot be insulated within the four walls of a courtroom. Embedded within a broader social or political movement, such litigation or series of legal interventions lend weight to political action and mobilization outside the courtroom. An essential element of strategic litigation is that the social, the political, and the legal complement each other. The permeation of law and politics could work both ways. As demonstrated through the case studies, at times the lawyer may seek the social movement, for instance, CCR's engagement with the broader anti-invasion of Iraq and anti-privatization of war movements, or CELS' collaboration with the Grandmothers of the Plaza de Mayo. On other occasions, the communities may choose to invoke the law, for instance, the former employees of Lafarge Syria reaching out to strategic litigation organizations to participate in the trial proceedings against Lafarge in France. In both cases, legal reform is not the end goal in and of itself, but instead a significant starting point to inspire political action.

On choosing reform over repair: A strategic engagement with law begs a rephrasing of the eternal dilemma from 'revolt versus reform' to 'repair versus reform'. The idea of reform in this context is different from the usual understanding of making the legal system 'better'. A repair-focused approach takes unjust outcomes to be a product of the international legal system performing incorrectly, and thus would attempt to 'fix the machinery' so that all parts of it would perform as they are supposed to. A reform-based approach, by contrast, recognizes that, at least sometimes, unjust outcomes are precisely the product of the international legal system performing as it is supposed to, and would thus aim to change the way the machinery is set up in the first place. Thus, when the strategic practitioner acknowledges that the system subsists on unjust structures, any exercise that seeks to improve the system is merely an act of repairing the system without necessarily reconfiguring it. Therefore, a practice of strategic litigation, at every step, makes a choice of reforming the system rather than fixing it. When bringing interventions, international legal practitioners are always making an active choice in deciding who to bring the case against, on whose behalf, on what charges or claims, or before which courts. In all these cases, the strategic legal practitioners are intentional about how to challenge and reconstruct the social relations of domination and subordination. The practice of CELS in the last four decades is a good illustration of this account. While working in the limited confines of the Argentinian legal framework, the victims and survivors were consistently an important voice in the movement for 'memory, truth, and justice'. They used the Inter-American Commission of Human Rights and other international human rights organizations to champion the right to truth which, for instance, did not just work to 'repair' the system but challenged its flaws while at the same time laying a strong foundation for the ensuing reforms.

Admittedly, the preconditions of extra-legal interventions and prioritization of reform over repair significantly narrow down the scope of strategic litigation. Many lawyers and organizations claiming the label of strategic litigators may fail to meet these criteria. Nevertheless, these benchmarks are intended to serve as a classifying measure when the practice of global civil society is to be accounted to determine implementation of international criminal law. Additionally, if they are to be seen as democratizing agents within the international criminal justice system, these qualifying conditions could also serve as a credibility and accountability framework.

Given the plurality of jurisdictions, contexts, and legal frameworks involved, a comprehensive comparative analysis of the practice of these organizations was neither feasible nor desirable for this book. However, some patterns and commonalities do emerge from the practice of three strategic litigation organizations discussed in the case studies which further clarify the characteristics of strategic litigation. They are discussed hereunder:

1. *Use of Law as a Means to Critique:* The three organizations in their mission statements reflect an explicit consciousness of the limitations of the legal framework and the politics that surround it. CCR, CELS, and ECCHR share a somewhat similar origin story: lawyers, equipped with the skills of the trade (and in the case of CELS impacted directly by the injustices of the state and the legal order), started using the law to support broader social and political movements in their respective

domestic contexts. All three of them use law and litigation not as an end in and of itself but as a means to achieve a broader political strategic objective. Litigation is perceived as a platform that highlights the illegalities of American imperialism for CCR; a means to document and seek acknowledgement/justice for the systematic and large-scale crimes committed by the military dictatorship in Argentina for CELS; and a platform to highlight the double standards of the European states for ECCHR.

2. *Challenging Impunity:* A common thread that runs through the theme of their practice is to challenge those who are not being held accountable otherwise for reasons such as their economic, military, or political power. The choice of jurisdictions, defendants, and even victims is reflective of their positionality as organizations and lawyers. Their choice of defendants – corporations in the context of this book – is not a result of technical expertise or an act of supporting the legal system, or even of victims requesting these organizations to represent them (even in the case of ECCHR and Sherpa, both have had long practice and reputation for challenging corporations before the Lafarge case). In all three cases, the organizations choose defendants who hold strategic importance and exploit their privileged position to seek impunity for their misconduct. In some ways, these defendants represent the violent structures that perpetuate domination and subordination within and outside the national borders: be it the case of pointing at few corporate executives to highlight the deep nexus of the military and corporations in carrying out systematic crimes in Argentina, or war crimes committed by the private military security companies which make profits from illegal conduct and escape responsibility, or bringing criminal complaints against European corporations knowingly exporting weapons and offering support to regimes and armed groups committing war crimes and crimes against humanity in armed conflicts outside of Europe.

3. *Bringing International Law Home:* Rules around corporate responsibility for their involvement in egregious violations in domestic jurisdictions fall short of recognizing the complex nature of atrocity crimes and attribute commensurate liability. In absence of any international avenue to bring these litigations, the organizations have tried to incorporate international legal norms in domestic law to support the need and possibility of corporate accountability for their involvement in crimes under international law. For instance, CCR used international criminal law to capture the co-perpetration of war crimes by private military security companies in the Iraq war, in a civil liability tort law framework, thereby opening up a new avenue to highlight the gravity of the misconduct and the important role played by CACI in that process. CELS relied on international criminal legal vocabulary and classification of historical violations as crimes against humanity to seek accountability which would

have otherwise not been addressed in the domestic courts for reasons of statute of limitations. As a result, the domestic courts in Argentina are prosecuting crimes against humanity that took place between 1978 and 1983, up until 2023. ECCHR's practice over almost two decades in itself reflects increasing familiarity of the German legal system with international criminal law and its domestic practice. A consistent and explicit reliance on international criminal law and associated capacity-building activities have significantly contributed to an enhanced familiarity and application of international criminal law in their respective jurisdictions.

4. *Far-sightedness:* For all three organizations, the choice of legal battles is informed by a forward-looking political understanding of society. Every small, even short-term, action is brought in the context of broader national and international politics. CELS started documenting the violations in the later 1970s at the peak of Argentinian military rule, in the absence of any possible avenue to seek justice. This documentation served as the basis for trials that followed decades after the violations took place. CELS' interventions proved to be ground-breaking in the 'memory, truth, and justice' movement, at the time when the legal and political setup in the country was hostile and unfavourable. For instance, both truth trials and anti-amnesty litigation proceedings were conceived at the time when the current legal order was not addressing accountability for such violations. At the same time, ECCHR and CCR have also consistently taken up cases with slim chances of a court victory and possibly no immediately visible impact. Those cases and complaints (and their failures in court) are rather envisioned as a part of a series of actions that seek to drive home a strong critique of the inadequacies of the system.
5. *Action Outside the Courtroom:* The three organizations have had litigation as their primary professional mandate, but perceived the courtroom as complementary to other sites of protest and advocacy. International institutions, media, universities, and museums are all spaces which are an integral part of the litigations carried out by the three organizations. Any legal intervention is combined with a carefully crafted communications and publicity strategy. As shown in the case studies, be it representation of Guantanamo detainees, truth trials, or universal jurisdiction complaints against Rumsfeld in Germany, the law and its theatre are employed to trigger social and political mobilization by all three organizations. Such extra-legal mobilization further undermines the importance of a courtroom victory and in some cases, even allows winning through losing.
6. *Innovative Use of Law:* Innovative use of the existing legal system becomes inevitable for organizations that seek to practice strategic litigation. In posing a challenge, they have time and again read between the lines of the 'black letter law'. In the case of CCR, it was reviving

an eighteenth-century law that was meant to settle foreign claims and making it a potent tool to seek redressal for human rights violations abroad in the United States. On the other side of the American continent, CELS specialized in leveraging the loopholes of the legal system to their advantage. Invoking the victim's right to truth while amnesty laws that barred punishments were in force in order to lay down the scale and systematic nature of the crimes committed during military dictatorship was both ingenious and strategically consequential. When the circumstances permitted, the case seeking to repeal amnesty laws offers another example of innovative interventions. Similarly, ECCHR has also been resorting to clever use of law within and outside of the courtrooms. This has ranged from sharing dossiers of evidence against war criminals seeking diplomatic refuge in European states to using the law in limiting the world for the 'most responsible' high-ranking perpetrators enjoying impunity.

7. *Transnational Alliances:* Transnational collaborations form an integral part of the strategic litigation organizations that engage with international criminal law. These alliances not only include collaborations with the movements seeking similar goals for a given intervention but also with other organizations working with similar mandates. The collaborative nature of their work plays out in different forms. In cases where the legal proceedings are brought in the United States or European domestic jurisdictions, they are brought with an acute understanding of the manner in which these states, and the corporations based in these states, are outsourcing violence to the Third World peoples. Thus, the legal interventions tend to be built on a transnational partnership with those directly affected. The cases where the place of commission of crimes and the headquarters of the decision-making actors which led to such crimes are far removed from each other, transnational collaborations become inevitable.

   Beyond this, there are two more aspects of transnational collaborations discernible in this form of strategic litigation: expertise-based transnational collaborations and like-minded transnational collaborations. Particularly, in the case of European strategic litigation practice, most legal interventions tend to be initiated jointly by two or more organizations with a view to coordinate and combine their respective expertise and skill sets. These collaborations, arguably, are a response to peculiar technical legal challenges in different jurisdictions (see Section II of Chapter 6). The other form of transnational collaborations at play are the ones forged on the basis of similarity of goals. They may take the form of network meetings, filing supportive amicus submissions, sharing best practices, and serving as advisors and counsellors to each other. Such transnational collaborations appear to characterize strategic litigation in all the contexts discussed in the book.

These features, derived from the three case studies, form a general pattern in the current practice of strategic litigation. They are not meant to serve as universal defining criteria for strategic litigation but instead a reflection on commonalities that may be found in legal practice that seeks to achieve progressive social and political impact through their legal interventions.

To sum up, the book envisages strategic litigation as legal interventions that are informed by the critiques of international criminal law but are carried out to either highlight or counteract those critiques. These interventions are backed with action outside the courtroom and attempt to reform the underlying structures of the legal system. Creative and innovative use of law, transnational alliances, and political far-sightedness are some of the features that characterize strategic litigation.

Against that backdrop, this strategic practice was analysed in the thematic context of corporate complicity in crimes under international law. This book adopted a broad notion of accountability for such complicity. Substantively, the preliminary research was built on the emerging consensus that a general principle of international law already exists that corporations can be held liable for serious violations of international law. However, to mirror the current status of practice on corporate accountability for crimes under international law, the research included domestic legal interventions against corporations and their persons in-charge carried out in domestic criminal law framework *as well as* civil law framework. This expansive notion of accountability acknowledged and accommodated the diversity of approaches adopted by relevant actors in different national legal systems.

The book revisited the time in the lead up to the international trial before the International Military Tribunal, Nuremberg, post–World War II to highlight that economic aspects of atrocity crimes either in the form of individual criminal responsibility of corporate leaders or by also recognizing organizational accountability of corporations could have been an essential mandate of international economic criminal law. However, for various practical and political reasons, the Nuremberg Trials left a lamentable legacy on this account. The international trial excluded the economic case altogether, and the domestic trials preferred individual responsibility over capturing the collective criminality of corporate conduct. An international trial especially for the industrialists who contributed to the German war effort had been initially planned but was later skipped because of the haste and internal disagreements between the prosecutorial teams of the Allied powers. For the trials held by the United States, alternative theories to capture corporate criminality were proposed and discussed internally, but were rejected for they may have prevented a smooth establishment of the post-war order in Germany. As a result, the half-hearted conviction of some corporate leaders led the 'economic case' in international criminal law off to a rough start (see Chapter 2).

Currently, the ICC does not hold jurisdiction over legal persons. The French delegation had unsuccessfully proposed a comprehensive model of corporate responsibility to be included in the ICC Statute. The proposed model recognized the liability of corporations as legal persons in addition to holding the individuals responsible. But the proposal was not voted upon in Rome and was withdrawn for paucity of time and lack of consensus on the matter. Not addressing the economic structures that contribute towards and sustain atrocity crimes is a clear limitation of the international criminal legal framework.

However, even if the ICC Statute does not recognize the accountability of corporations, there is no explicit barrier to holding corporate leaders responsible for the acts carried out in the name of the corporation. Individuals can be held liable through one of the prescribed modes of liability. The three case studies in the book deal with business conduct that warrant responsibility under distinct modes of liability: for instance, common purpose liability in the case of CACI's involvement in torture and war crimes committed in the Abu Ghraib detention camp in Iraq; accomplice liability in the case of Lafarge for crimes committed in Syria; and principal liability in the case of Ford Motors and other companies involved in torture and kidnapping of their workers during the last military dictatorship in Argentina. As discussed in Part II, each of these modes of liability come with a distinct set of challenges in attributing responsibility arising from corporate conduct.

Given the contentious state of international law norms regarding corporate responsibility, it does seem somewhat counter-intuitive to invoke international criminal law before domestic courts to hold corporations accountable for egregious human rights violations. It is precisely this fact that made strategic litigation on the question of corporate accountability worthy of further examination and analysis. The three case studies demonstrated the use of the vocabulary of international criminal law in corporate complicity cases in three different ways. In each of the three cases, the attempt to incorporate international criminal law in domestic legal proceedings served a unique counter-hegemonic purpose. In the case of CCR, the models of liability derived from international law were introduced in a tort liability framework to capture the exact nature of the criminal plan that led to the torture and mistreatment of detainees in US-controlled prisons in Iraq. The vocabulary of international legal norms not only helped underline the gravity of the violations but also brought in other strategic advantages to further mobilization against privatization of war (see Chapter 5).

With respect to the Lafarge case, as argued by ECCHR and Sherpa, the narrative of international criminal law helped in bringing the case from a repressive counterterrorism paradigm to a more progressive human rights framework. Concerning Lafarge's economic support to armed groups in Syria, including the Islamic State, the case was essentially built to prosecute a harm done to the security of the French state. By attempting to incorporate crimes against humanity as an additional charge in the trial against Lafarge as well as its executive staff, ECCHR and Sherpa placed the victimization of

Syrian workers of the Lafarge's subsidiary in the foreground. As a result, this could become the first case where a parent company is held liable for complicity in crimes against humanity through its subsidiary. The proceedings track down the structure that enabled violations in Syria back to France that would have been easy to ignore in conventional counterterrorism proceedings (see Chapter 6).

CELS, however, fought a different battle while leveraging the benefits of a narrative built on international criminal law. The trials for historical violations in the domestic framework would not have been possible if it weren't for the incorporation of a crimes against humanity framework in the domestic law as well as domestic policy and public discourse.

Through distinct models of responsibility, adding claims based on violations of substantive law, then incorporating these claims into the public discourse, these organizations used international criminal law as a tool to seek accountability of multinational corporations involved in crimes under international law. In this process, they served as norm-entrepreneurs: by provoking interaction, by provoking interpretation, and consequently by provoking international legal norm-internalization through a judicial process.

With regard to corporate responsibility for their involvement in crimes under international law, there are two key normative questions that mark the debate in scholarship: one, individual accountability vis-à-vis corporate liability; two, civil remedies vis-à-vis criminal punishment. The practice, however, suggests there might not be as much of a space of conflict or the need to arrive at a universally agreed-upon solution as the scholarship emphasizes. Regarding the first question, the three cases analysed here approached corporate responsibility in three unique ways: CACI, as a corporation, is being sued for damages within a tort framework for having been complicit in torture and mistreatment; corporate managers of Ford Argentina were sentenced to imprisonment for their participation in the crimes committed by the military against the workers – however, with no direct sanction against the company; and finally, Lafarge France is being prosecuted as an entity through the culpability of its employees for crimes committed in the name of its subsidiary in Syria.

These diverse situations are not only reflective of the multiple forms that attribution of responsibility can take, but also mirrors that each comes with its respective legal challenges. Where the required culpability threshold may be slightly lower in a civil remedy framework, the criminal legal framework comes with the advantage of prosecutorial powers often essential to procure evidence establishing the internal hierarchy and decision-making structures of the corporations. Of the three systems discussed here, the French model does appear to be the most comprehensive framework for corporate accountability, with the corporation being held liable in addition to the individuals. Such a model mandates an economic guarantee to ensure reparations for victims in addition to criminal punishment for the most responsible individuals. The investigation against Lafarge and its employees exhibits how individual complicity and corporate responsibility can coexist and interact. Attributing blame on Lafarge as an entity does not imply that the factory managers and the executives who were the most responsible in the decision-making chain will be absolved of their guilt. At the same time, insisting on corporate accountability in addition to individual liability also serves to underline the critical context of profit maximization in the name of which individual perpetrators take these decisions in the first place.

In terms of practical challenges, the major impediment common to all these cases is the asymmetry of power between the defendants and those victimized. Stark contrast in resources devoted by those who initiate strategic litigation and those against whom such legal interventions are brought is inescapable. During the proceedings, the intimidating economic might of the corporate defendants, regardless of the political context and country, poses one of the greatest practical challenges in these litigations. As evidenced by the three case studies, disproportionate resources are employed by the corporate defendants to delay the case and file challenges on every possible ground at different instances. Of the three, the CACI case is a classic example of the use of 'delay' as a tactic as a result of which after over a decade the matter is still pending and has even gone up to the US Supreme Court for adjudication on an intermediary order rather than on merits. This seemingly innocuous tactic, in most cases, has the potential to prejudice the existence of the proceedings altogether. Delays test the perseverance of already vulnerable victims and further contributes to their precarity. Over a period of time, the relatively under-resourced organizations are compelled to take difficult decisions and shift priorities within projects. Particularly when cases involve historical violations, delaying may translate into stopping the motion of the entire proceedings until the ageing individual defendants are declared unfit for trial. This phenomenon is particularly visible in the ongoing cases regarding historical accountability in Argentina. In a transitional justice context, legal action against corporations for crimes committed during the dictatorship came as an afterthought to begin with and then, such stop motion tactics end up having significant implications for the accountability process as a whole.

To circle back to the accountability gap and critiques of international criminal law, the book analysed strategic litigation practice through critical legal scholarship arising from the broad rubric of TWAIL. This scholarship offered a largely coherent framework to articulate some of the main critiques against international criminal law. At the same time, the lack of rigid boundaries in TWAIL scholarship also provided a platform to examine a set of concrete practices that use international criminal law to constrain power with varying degrees of success.

Traditionally, TWAIL scholars have argued that international law is illegitimate because, inter alia, it has become the primary language of domination and subjugation of the Third World. The colonial and imperial origins of international law along with its continued operations being governed by 'the West' substantiate the TWAIL argument that international law is structurally biased against the interests of the Third World peoples and hence illegitimate. Given the decentralized nature of the TWAIL scholarly network, this fundamental critique has developed many different versions over decades. Under the broad umbrella, TWAIL accommodates varied critiques, diverse visions of the future, and commensurate paths to realize those visions.

In order to cull out an analytical framework from this multifaceted body of scholarship, it became imperative to identify some of the key concerns of TWAIL, particularly in so far as they apply to international criminal law, which the book has termed 'Third World Approaches to International (Criminal) Law – TWAI(C)L' (see Section III of Chapter 1). Although there is a real risk of oversimplification while fleshing out a few key TWAI(C)L concerns, such an exercise was important for this book in order to generally streamline TWAIL's engagement with international criminal law and to present an analytical framework for the practice of strategic litigation seeking corporate accountability for international crimes. The following is a brief discussion on each of these four central concerns and how they surfaced in the three case studies.

Reform-based Critique: One of TWAIL's primary occupations has been to revisit the history of the international legal order to understand, deconstruct, and unpack the ways in which its structures sustain and perpetuate domination. TWAIL scholars attend to varied histories with the purpose of reforming the future relationship of the 'Third World' with international law. Building on the realization that colonial and Eurocentric legacies influence current operations of international law, TWAIL offers ways to reconstruct an international legal order that is more just and equitable. Along the same lines, this research builds on the existing critique of international criminal law and its structural biases but foregrounds its counter-hegemonic capacities. The case studies speak about the lived experience of Third World peoples and about strategic litigation organizations which are employing the law in a manner that writes resistance into the international legal order. The three cases offer concrete examples of what a reform-based critique could look like. The legal interventions in all three situations discussed in the book aim to address the impunity enjoyed by giant corporations and at the same time critique the geopolitical structures that led to such corporate misconduct in the first place. While that is the broader critique of the international legal and political order, these legal interventions are also a critique of the inadequacies of the international criminal legal framework. By winning these cases, these actors may initiate a modest reconstruction of international criminal law that is more directly informed by the victims and survivors. And if they lose these cases in court, they would have at least lodged a challenge against the limitations of the system. Through the three case studies, this book has also hopefully responded to one of the criticisms of TWAIL scholarship, namely that it is limited to assertions and constructs without substantial empirical basis to support these claims.

Relativizing Universality: Classic TWAIL scholarship challenges the universalist claims of international law as a mere pretext for European subjectivity. It questions whether the universal can truly exist and instead places a crucial emphasis on pluralism. In the case of international criminal law, the claim of universal values takes centre stage as it ostensibly works on behalf of the 'international community' to protect the interests of 'humanity' and achieve 'global justice'. And yet, its origins, practice, and implementation continue to be determined by European interests and sensibilities. This book, through the three case studies, dealt with the paradox of the universal and the plural in the context of the domestic application of international criminal law. On the one hand, by highlighting the impunity enjoyed by economically and politically powerful actors, this discussion corroborates the challenge of the claims of 'universality' in international criminal law. On the other hand, the case studies serve a more constructive function as they track how Third World peoples have adopted this essentially subjective legal framework and they are interjecting its implementation and understanding while challenging its Eurocentricity. In the process, the case studies highlight the potential of relativizing the purportedly 'universal'. This is exemplified rather well by the situation in Argentina where the activists and practitioners insisted on framing atrocities committed during the dictatorship as 'crimes against humanity' to underscore the systematic and planned nature of the crimes. At the same time, once international law was incorporated into the domestic legal system, it was implemented at the behest of local actors, including courts, judges, lawyers, etc. Such close involvement of victims and/or their survivors as well as agency exercised by actors such as CELS helped execute a plural version of universal ideals. In cases involving CACI and Lafarge, one may argue that the countries of litigation, i.e. the United States and France, are still informing this practice as the cases are being initiated in Western legal frameworks. However, the involvement of victims from other countries, the nature of claims, and the kind of defendants in these cases are all elements that challenge the validity of universalist claims made by international criminal law.

De-privileging the State: According to TWAIL scholars, the privilege of states as the sole law-making actor must be problematized. This concern stems from the contestation not only between the Third World and the West, but also between the Third World states and the Third World peoples. As the post-colonial state increasingly tends to act against the interests of Third World peoples, TWAIL scholars place significant importance on the lived realities of Third World peoples as a legitimacy source for international law. In that vein, a customary international law that is primarily based on state practice would be an undemocratic source of law, according to scholars such as B.S. Chimni. TWAIL scholars have argued that decolonizing the configuration of *opinio juris* and by extension customary international law is possible by including the practice of global civil society to determine the customary nature of international law. With respect to international criminal law, the primacy of customary law and the exclusive dependence on states for law-making as well as law enforcement makes it impossible to disassociate from the interests of the states, particularly Western states. The practice of three non-state organizations has hopefully exemplified how non-state actors can influence the logics of law-making and implementation. All three organizations, CCR, ECCHR, and CELS, brought their legal interventions based on varied kinds of transnational alliances of organizations. In some ways, these alliances also transcend the boundaries between states based in the 'Global North' and the 'Global South' with the involvement of various actors and partners involved in bringing and supporting these legal interventions. However, because of the nature of how law is implemented, a decoupling from the state is not possible. Therefore, their interventions must be viewed as attempts at 'de-privileging' the exclusive status of the state. By not entirely relying on the will of the states to bring legal action against responsible individuals, these case studies exemplified ways to take into account the practice of non-state actors largely working on behalf of those most affected by these crimes.

Addressing Material Inequality: TWAIL's critique of international law has also highlighted the ways in which international legal doctrines contribute to the dominance of certain states by favouring their interests in maintaining an unjust international economic order. International law may not be the only factor advancing material inequality in the global order; nevertheless, it still offers the cloak for exploitative commercial expansion without proportionate consequences. Lack of international criminal law practice on corporate accountability strengthens the claim that 'economic structures' which sustain crimes under international law are being shielded. The principle of individual criminal responsibility not only narrows down the concept of justice, but also removes necessary context to any situation of large-scale violence. The creation and condemnation of one enemy often translate into the impunity of the criminal machinery which enabled and created the individual. The legal interventions discussed in the case studies highlight the ways in which international criminal law continues to shield such exploitative economic structures. This practice also confronts the predominant notion that large-scale violence is a particularly 'Global South' or 'Third World' problem. They foreground the many ways actors headquartered in the 'the West' are contributing to or profiting from such outsourced violence. At the same time, the case studies demonstrate how such complicity of the law can be challenged and criticized. It is clear that despite the absence of an explicitly recognized rule from the ICC Statute, it is possible to challenge these structures or at least to unpack their role and responsibility in large-scale violence.

With the above analysis, this book hopes to have laid out a blueprint for a reform-based critical practice of international criminal law. While the purpose of this book was to foreground strategic litigation organizations as novel actors and shed light on their workings, it should only be construed as a nudge for further scholarly discourse on these actors. More research and consideration are warranted on the precise questions of the legal, political, and social impact of such practice. Moreover, it must be noted that the omission of words such as 'victim-centred' and 'victim-oriented' in the whole book is not unintentional. In cases of strategic legal interventions, the immediate needs of the victims of large-scale systematic violence and the organizational objectives to counter the biases of the legal system do not always seem to align. While in some cases like that of Argentina and CELS, the synergy between the victims and the strategic litigation organizations was more obvious, other cases merit a more nuanced analysis as power dynamics within these relationships may not be very straightforward. There is a real risk that the workings of these transnational organizations may reproduce the same relations of domination and subordination that they seek to oppose, in the same way that such legal interventions run the risk of legitimizing the system they intend to dismantle. In some cases, the co-option of the social and political movements through law and legal means may also have a de-radicalizing effect on the cause. Finally, if their practice is to be taken into account while analysing the implementation of international criminal law, then the lack of accountability of these non-state actors is another important factor that must not be overlooked.

Strategic litigation is as much about politics as it is about law. Difficult choices mark the everyday practice of a strategic litigation. A realistic stance is warranted while situating them in the larger universe of actors practising the law as well as engaging in movement politics. Situated in this broader universe that needs further analysis, the book introduced these novel actors to the discourse on international criminal law who acknowledge its limitations and yet try to leverage its counter-hegemonic potential. Both in their successes and their failures, they can serve as signposts on the way forward.

Annexure

Case Mapping Table

The following table was used as a preliminary case mapping to select the three case studies discussed in Part II of the book. It is an inventory of cases initiated from 2001 to 2022 by non-governmental organizations or victim groups against corporations for their involvement in crimes under international law before domestic courts. The corporate defendants are listed in alphabetical order, with each case profile identifying the main actors involved, including victims/survivors and representative organization(s). The table also includes a concise summary of facts of each case and relevant context, the legal basis of the litigation, and the outcome or latest status of the legal action if it is still pending. The reference index that precedes the case profiles catalogues all the cases under four separate headings, i.e. on the basis of non-governmental organizations involved, the alleged crimes and misconduct attributed to the corporations, the countries where the legal actions have been filed, and the countries where the violations took place. The reference index is a befitting reflection of patterns emerging from this practice.

The table is mainly based on information gathered from the official websites of the organizations involved in the litigation, open-source databases such as the Business and Human Rights Resource Centre, International Crimes Database, Universal Jurisdiction Database by TRIAL International, and reports by other international human rights organizations such as Human Rights Watch, FIDH, etc. The list was last updated in March 2023.

Index

Organizations Involved	*Case Numbers*
CCR	5, 8, 9, 34, 35
CELS	15, 20, 21, 24
ECCHR	11, 12, 17, 18, 22, 24, 27, 31, 36
FIDH	2, 7, 10, 28, 30
International Rights Advocates	10, 13, 26
TRIAL Int.	4

Sherpa	6, 12, 18, 22
Other	1, 3, 14, 16, 19, 23, 25, 29, 32, 33, 37, 38

Alleged Crimes	*Case Numbers*
War crimes	1, 3, 4, 5, 6, 8, 9, 11, 12, 13, 23, 29, 31, 32, 36
Crimes against humanity	6, 7, 13, 15, 16, 18, 20, 21, 22, 24, 25, 29, 30, 32, 36, 38
Genocide	6, 7, 14, 18
Torture	2, 7, 8, 9, 10, 17, 19, 26, 27, 28, 30, 33, 34, 35, 37

Countries of Litigation	*Case Numbers*
Argentina	15, 20, 21
Belgium	38
Brazil	37
Canada	3, 25, 33
Colombia	10, 13
Democratic Republic of the Congo	11
France	1, 2, 7, 12, 18, 22, 28, 30, 32
Germany	6, 11, 17, 24, 36
Italy	31
Sweden	23
Switzerland	4, 27
The United Kingdom	17
The United States	5, 8, 9, 10, 13, 14, 16, 19, 24, 26, 29, 34, 35

Countries of Commission	*Case Numbers*
Argentina	15, 20, 21, 24
Bahrain	17
Brazil	37
China	18
Colombia	10, 13, 27, 29
Democratic Republic of the Congo	3, 4, 11
Egypt	28
Eritrea	25
France	32
Iraq	5, 8, 34
Israel	1
Libya	2
Mali	26
Myanmar	14, 35, 38
Palestine	9
Rwanda	6
South Africa	16
Sudan	7, 23, 33
Syria	22, 30, 36
Yemen	12, 31
The United States	19

No.	*Defendants, Year, Organizations/Complainants*	*Cause of Action*	*Legal Basis, Forum, and Charges/ Claims*	*Outcome/Current Status*
1.	**Alstom and Veolia Transport** 2007 By Association France Palestine Solidarité (AFPS) and the Palestinian Liberation Organization (PLO)	The two French corporate entities were allegedly involved in a consortium which contracted with the Israeli government in July 2005 for an illegal construction of a tram system in West Jerusalem. The plaintiffs' claimed that their involvement in the project aided and abetted Israel's occupation and commission of war crimes.	Sought injunction and cancellation of contract at the court of first instance in Nanterre, France, for violations of Articles 49 and 53 of the Fourth Geneva Convention, The Hague Convention, as well as the customary IHL.	Jurisdiction upheld by the French Supreme Court in 2011. On merits, the first instance and appeals court dismissed the case on the ground that 'international agreements create obligations between states and could not be used to hold the corporate entities liable' in 2013. Trams in operation.
2.	**Amesys** 2011 By FIDH and la Ligue des droits de l'Homme (LDH) On behalf of two Libyan human rights defenders	In 2007, Amesys signed a contract with the Libyan government headed by Gaddafi to provide sophisticated communication surveillance equipment which the government allegedly used to intercept private communications. The company allegedly contributed to targeting of dissidents, including disappearance and torture.	Complaint against the company and its executives for complicity in torture under the French Criminal Code (Art. 221-1 and 689 – 1, 2) on the basis of the principle of extraterritorial jurisdiction.	Investigation opened in May 2012. In November 2022, Paris Court of Appeal confirmed the indictment of Amesys and its executives. Ongoing.

No.	*Defendants, Year, Organizations/Complainants*	*Cause of Action*	*Legal Basis, Forum, and Charges/ Claims*	*Outcome/Current Status*
3.	**Anvil Mining** 2006 (in the DRC- military court) 2010 (in Canada and before the African Commission of Human & People's Rights) By Canadian Association Against Impunity in Canada and RAID, ACIDH, and IHRDA (before ACHPR) On behalf of survivors from Kilwa, DRC	In 2004, an armed conflict between the Congolese Armed Forces and a non-state armed group took place in Kilwa. An attack by the armed forces resulted in serious violations against civilians, including summary executions, arbitrary arrests, rape, and torture. Anvil operated a copper mine near the town and allegedly provided transportation (planes and vehicles) and financial support to the state armed forces during the attack.	Before Military Court in DRC: Three employees of Anvil were charged for complicity in war crimes. Class action suit was filed in Canada before the Superior Court of Quebec as the corporation had an establishment in Quebec Canada (Articles 307, 3135, 3136, 3137, and 3148 of the Civil Code of Québec). Communication was submitted to African Commission for violations of the African Charter.	DRC: The Court acquitted all Anvil employees and Anvil in 2007. Canada: In 2012, the Supreme Court dismissed the case for lack of jurisdiction. The African Commission held the DRC responsible and demanded that victims be awarded $2.5 million as compensation in 2017.
4.	**Argor-Heraeus SA** 2013 By TRIAL International (along with OSJI, and Conflict Awareness Project)	The Swiss company allegedly refined gold that had been pillaged by an armed group from the north-eastern region of the DRC. Thus, corporate conduct contributed to war crimes carried out by the armed group between 2004 and 2005.	Criminal complaint to the Office of Swiss Federal Prosecutor for abetment of war crimes and aggravated money-laundering.	In March 2015, the investigation and the case was closed for lack of sufficient evidence indicating that the company knew about the origins of the gold.

No.	*Defendants, Year, Organizations/Complainants*	*Cause of Action*	*Legal Basis, Forum, and Charges/ Claims*	*Outcome/Current Status*
5.	**Blackwater** 2007 By CCR On behalf of Iraqi nationals, victims/survivors of the Nisoor Square and Watahba Square incidents	On 9 September 2007, employees of Blackwater, a US private security contractor, reportedly opened fire on a crowd of Iraqi civilians in Al Watahba Square, killing three. On 16 September 2007, in a similar incident of opening fire at a crowded Baghdad traffic circle known as Nisoor Square, at least 17 Iraqi nationals were killed and dozens were injured. The company was serving as US military contractors in Iraq.	Federal lawsuit in the United States for war crimes under ATS, Racketeer Influenced and Corrupt Organizations (RICO) Act, and assault and battery, wrongful death, intentional and negligent infliction of emotional distress, and negligent hiring, training, and supervision, under state law. In 2008, criminal charges were pressed against five individuals for voluntary manslaughter and attempted manslaughter.	Confidential settlement was reached with the victims on 1 January 2010. Regarding the criminal case, four guards were found guilty by the jury rejecting the claim that they were acting in self-defence in October 2014. In 2020, the guards were pardoned by the Trump administration.
6.	**BNP Paribas** 2017 By Sherpa, Ibuka France, and the Collectif des Parties Civiles pour le Rwanda	The French bank was alleged to be complicit in the Rwandan genocide. The allegation was based on a 1.3 million USD transfer carried out by the bank (in violation of a United Nations arms embargo) made to an arms dealer to purchase weapons used for serious human rights violations.	Complaint under the French Criminal Code alleging complicity in crimes against humanity, war crimes, and genocide.	In 2017, judicial investigation was opened. Ongoing.

No.	*Defendants, Year, Organizations/Complainants*	*Cause of Action*	*Legal Basis, Forum, and Charges/ Claims*	*Outcome/Current Status*
7.	**BNP Paribas** 2019 By FIDH, Ligue des droits de l'Homme (France), Project Expedite Justice, the African Centre for Justice and Peace Studies (Sudan), and Sudan Human Rights Monitor On behalf of nine victims as plaintiffs	The French Bank and its Swiss subsidiary reportedly acted as the primary foreign bank of the Sudanese government between 2002 and 2008. The plaintiffs alleged that providing essential banking services made the bank complicit in violations committed by the Sudanese military, security forces, and Janjaweed militias.	Complaint filed under the French Criminal Code alleging complicity in torture, crimes against humanity, and genocide.	Judicial investigation opened in October 2020. Ongoing.
8.	**CACI International** 2008 By CCR On behalf of Al-Shimari and three other Iraqi detainees	The US military contractor was hired to provide translation services in interrogations conducted during the Iraq war. Detainees at the Abu Ghraib detention camp between 2003 and 2005 alleged that the corporation employees subjected them to torture, war crimes, assault and battery, and sexual assault.	Civil lawsuit in the United States on the basis of ATS alleging torture and war crimes.	Several motions to dismiss filed and appealed by the defendants, inter alia, on political questions doctrine, presumption of extraterritoriality. Supreme Court denied review of one such motion. Pending.
9.	**Caterpillar** 2005 CCR, Palestinian Center for Human Rights, etc. On behalf of an American HRD and other Palestinian civilians	US company Catterpillar's bulldozers were used in the demolition of the homes of Palestinian civilians by the Israel Defense Forces (IDF), resulting in killings and serious injuries. In an attempt to save these homes from being demolished, an American human rights defender was also killed.	Civil lawsuit before a US district court under ATS, Torture Victim Protection Act (TVPA), and Fourth Geneva Convention for aiding and abetting the war crimes committed by the IDF.	In 2009, the case was dismissed based on political question doctrine.

No.	*Defendants, Year, Organizations/Complainants*	*Cause of Action*	*Legal Basis, Forum, and Charges/ Claims*	*Outcome/Current Status*
10.	**Chiquita** 2007 and 2008 (in the United States) May 2017 (ICC) 2018 (in Colombia) By International Rights Advocates (in the United States) FIDH, CAJAR, and others (ICC) On behalf of victims who were both Colombian and US nationals	Between 1997 and 2004, Chiquita, a US company, admitted to making payments to non-state armed groups in Colombia in order to continue the company's operations in the Colombian banana-growing region (URABA). According to the complaints, Chiquita was complicit in extrajudicial killings, torture and forced disappearance, crimes against humanity, and war crimes committed by the armed groups. In 2007, when Chiquita admitted to having made illegal payments, it paid 25 million USD in fines to the US government.	The United States: Federal lawsuits ATS and Torture Victims Protection Act on behalf of Colombian victims. Separate suits were also filed on behalf of six US nationals who were killed by the paramilitary groups in Colombia. ICC: An Article 15 Communication to the OTP was filed seeking expansion of the ongoing investigation in the situation of Colombia to include 14 senior executives of Chiquita. Colombia: Criminal investigation against executive members of the company on the charge of aggravated conspiracy.	The United States: In September 2022, the Eleventh Circuit Court of Appeals ruled that there was enough evidence to connect the death of the plaintiffs' relatives to the AUC. The case is on jury trial. Regarding claims made by the US nationals, a settlement was reached in 2018. ICC: The OTP decided not to proceed with the situation in Colombia in October 2021. Colombia: In 2018, 13 executives were charged by Colombia's Attorney General. Pending.

No.	*Defendants, Year, Organizations/Complainants*	*Cause of Action*	*Legal Basis, Forum, and Charges/ Claims*	*Outcome/Current Status*
11.	**Danzer Group and SIFORCO** 2012 (DRC) 2013 (Germany) By ASF (in DRC) ECCHR, Global Witness (in Germany) On behalf of residents of the village Bongulu, DRC	In May 2011, a village in northern DRC was attacked by the police and state military. During the attack, several human rights violations took place, including rape and arbitrary arrests of villagers. Senior staff of Danzer Group, a Swiss and German timber manufacturer, allegedly aided and abetted these abuses by failing to prevent these crimes from being committed. Congolese security forces were also reported to have received financial and logistical help from Danzer's former subsidiary, SIFORCO (now part of Blattner).	DRC: Civil claim against the company and criminal complaint against the employees for complicity in crimes against humanity. Germany: Criminal complaint was filed against a senior manager of Danzer Group for complicity in human rights abuses based on the principle of duty to care.	DRC: In 2019, a military court sanctioned officers and imposed a fine on the government, but found the company not guilty. Germany: The prosecutor discontinued the investigations in 2015.

No.	*Defendants, Year, Organizations/Complainants*	*Cause of Action*	*Legal Basis, Forum, and Charges/ Claims*	*Outcome/Current Status*
12.	**Dassault, Thales, and MBDA** 2022 ECCHR, Sherpa, Mwatana for Human Rights, and Amnesty International	Despite the knowledge of indiscriminate attacks on Yemeni civilians by Saudi Arabia and UAE since 2015, France reportedly delivered more than 8 billion euros worth of war materials, ammunition, and maintenance services to SA and the UAE between 2015 and 2020. The documentation suggests that French-produced fighter jets, as well as missiles and guidance systems produced by Thales and MBDA France, are used in the conflict in Yemen.	Under French Criminal Code, criminal complaint requested initiation of an investigation against French companies that, while fuelling the conflict, are aiding and abetting war crimes and crimes against humanity allegedly perpetrated by Saudi Arabia and UAE.	Request pending.
13.	**Drummond** 2002 and 2013 (in the United States) 2018 (Colombia) By International Rights Advocates On behalf of 600 families of victims, Colombian nationals	Drummond, the US coal giant, allegedly financed Autodefensas Unidas de Colombia (AUC), an armed group designated as a terrorist group by the United States, and hired them to protect Drummond's Colombian mine operations in Cesar Province from civilians who lived in the area. The company is also alleged to have provided logistical support and other assistance to the AUC's operations, resulting in war crimes, from 1996 to 2006.	The United States: Civil lawsuits under ATS, Torture Victim Protection Act, and Alabama State laws for aiding and abetting extrajudicial killings and war crimes committed by AUC. Colombia: In 2018, the Colombian Specialized Criminal Prosecutor's Office reopened investigation against six current and former Drummond officials over allegations of financing the armed group's activities amounting to crimes against humanity.	The United States: Cases dismissed. Colombia: In 2020, the Specialized Prosecutor's Office indicted the current President, José Miguel Linares, and the former President, Augusto Jiménez, for complicity in crimes against humanity.

No.	*Defendants, Year, Organizations/Complainants*	*Cause of Action*	*Legal Basis, Forum, and Charges/ Claims*	*Outcome/Current Status*
14.	**Facebook (Meta)** 2021 By Rohingya refugees in the United States	In 2017, the Myanmar military launched a violent crackdown against Rohingyas, razing villages, raping, torturing, and perpetrating large-scale violence that killed thousands of Rohingya men, women, and children. Over 750,000 Rohingya fled to neighbouring Bangladesh. In 2018, Meta accepted the role it played in the genocide against the Rohingyas: 'The ethnic violence in Myanmar is horrific and we have been too slow to prevent misinformation and hate on Facebook'.	Class action suit for complicity in genocide by failing to prevent circulation of calls for incitement.	Pending.
15.	**Ford Motors** (Argentina) October 2002 By direct victims assisted by CELS lawyers	The company was alleged to have collaborated with the 1976–1983 military dictatorship. The executives directly assisted the military regime in political repression of workers, enforced disappearance, and mistreatment of workers, and provided logistical support. The litigation in Argentina is a part of a series of similar interventions arising from an investigative report by CELS against over two dozen corporations (see La Fronterita, Ledesma below)	In Argentina, crimes against humanity incorporated in domestic laws. Until 2005, amnesty laws prevailed which were later struck down by the Supreme Court. No limitation law. Three executives were charged for complicity in crimes against humanity.	In December 2018, two of them (one accused died during the proceedings) were convicted and sentenced to 10 and 12 years of imprisonment.

No.	*Defendants, Year, Organizations/Complainants*	*Cause of Action*	*Legal Basis, Forum, and Charges/ Claims*	*Outcome/Current Status*
16.	**Ford, IBM, and others** (Apartheid reparations lawsuits) 2002 and 2003 By Khulamani Support Group On behalf of a group of victims/survivors, South African nationals	Over 20 banks and corporations, including Daimler, Ford, IBM, General Motors, Rheinmetall Group, who were conducting business in South Africa during apartheid were alleged to have encouraged and contributed towards abuses against black Africans during that time. The plaintiffs, victims of extrajudicial killings, torture, and rape, alleged that the defendants through their corporate activities in South Africa provided essential assistance to the apartheid state.	Federal lawsuits in the United States based on jurisdiction derived from ATS. South African government initially opposed the jurisdiction of US courts as interference on sovereignty and 'judicial imperialism' but later in 2013 retracted their opposition and agreed that US courts were the appropriate forum for these cases.	In 2009, the claims were narrowed to only against Daimler, Ford, General Motors, IBM, and Rheinmetall for sufficient direct connections. Cases were dismissed after Kiobel ruling and the courts held that the conduct of the corporations didn't satisfy the touch and concern test. Final order in 2016. In 2012, an out of court settlement was reached with General Motors
17.	**Gamma International** 2013 By Bahrain Center for Human Rights (BCHR), Bahrain Watch, ECCHR, Privacy International, and Reporters Without Borders	In 2011, British–German surveillance technology provider Gamma International sold its surveillance technology products such as 'state trojan' FinFisher that allegedly contributed to arrests, imprisonments, and torture of opposition members, journalists, and dissidents in Bahrain.	Complaints filed before the British and German OECD – National Contact Point (NCP) alleging failure of due diligence processes.	In 2013, Germany NCP rejected the complaint. In 2015, the UK NCP in the final assessment of the complaint confirmed violations of human rights obligations.

No.	*Defendants, Year, Organizations/Complainants*	*Cause of Action*	*Legal Basis, Forum, and Charges/ Claims*	*Outcome/Current Status*
18.	**Inditex, Uniqlo, SMCP, Skechers** 2021 By Sherpa, ECCHR, and others On behalf of Uyghur victims	Since at least 2019, journalists and researchers have highlighted the existence of systematized forced labour in the Xinjiang Uyghur Autonomous Region by the Chinese government, where nearly 20% of the world's cotton is produced. Reportedly, these textile giants have continued using the cotton in their manufacturing despite knowing the crimes committed against the Uyghurs in the region.	Complaint filed under provisions of French Criminal Code alleging concealment of the crime of aggravated bondage, crime of human trafficking in an organized gang, crime of genocide, and crime against humanity.	Investigation was opened in July 2021. Ongoing.
19.	**Jeppesen** 2007 By ACLU On behalf of five victims of CIA's rendition program	According to the plaintiffs, Jeppesen Dataplan, a subsidiary of Boeing, assisted CIA in abducting and transferring the victims by airplane to secret locations where they were subjected to torture and cruel treatment through the US Government's 'extraordinary rendition' programme. Since 2001, Jeppesen provided the US Central Intelligence Agency with flight plans and logistical support for the aircraft used in the extraordinary rendition flights.	Federal lawsuit in the United States under ATS for complicity in abduction and torture.	US government intervened claiming that the case is subject to state secrets privilege. The case was dismissed in 2010 for national security concerns.

No.	*Defendants, Year, Organizations/Complainants*	*Cause of Action*	*Legal Basis, Forum, and Charges/ Claims*	*Outcome/Current Status*
20.	**La Fronterita** 2015 By CELS On behalf of victims and former workers of the company	CELS report on business involvement in military dictatorship (1976–1983) revealed systematic involvement and direct support of the sugar company in crimes committed by the military in Argentina. The company held an on-site detention centre for the military dictatorship.	Crimes against humanity incorporated in Argentinian Constitution. Until 2005, amnesty laws prevailed which were later struck down by the Supreme Court. No limitation law.	In 2017, six executives were called in for questioning by the prosecutor. Ongoing.
21.	**Ledesma Sugar Company** 2011 By CELS and partners On behalf of victims and former workers of the company	Allegations of complicity in crimes of the military dictatorship in Argentina (1976–1983). Provided transportation to the military for abduction/torture of 400 former employees which led to the disappearance of 55 trade unionists.	In Argentina, crimes against humanity incorporated in domestic laws. Until 2005, the Supreme Court struck down the amnesty laws. No limitation law.	In 2012, two executives were summoned for questioning and indicted. In 2015, appeals court reversed the indictment. Ongoing.
22.	**Lafarge** 2016 By ECCHR and Sherpa On behalf of Syrian employees	Allegations against Lafarge SA (now LafargeHolcim) about financing terrorism, complicity in crimes against humanity committed by the Islamic State in Syria (ISIS), and deliberate endangerment of people's lives. The company admitted having paid millions of euros to the armed group to continue their factory's operations in Syria.	France amended its law in 2004 allowing the prosecution of companies for all crimes entailed in its Criminal Code – including for their activities abroad. The condition is that a physical representative of the company must have committed the crime (in the present case, Eric Olsen and other executives) in order to prosecute the corporation as a person.	In 2018, Lafarge as a company and its executives were indicted In May 2022, the French Court of Appeals enforced the judgment of the Supreme Court charging Lafarge for complicity in crimes against humanity. Pending.

No.	*Defendants, Year, Organizations/Complainants*	*Cause of Action*	*Legal Basis, Forum, and Charges/ Claims*	*Outcome/Current Status*
23.	**Lundin Oil** 2018 Swedish Prosecutor took cognizance based on a report by UNPAIDDebt and Pax	In the context of a non-international armed conflict in Sudan from 1983 to 2005 between the government and Sudan People's Liberation Army, Lundin formed a consortium in 1997 which carried out oil exploration in (now) South Sudan. Company's business operations allegedly contributed to further violence leading to thousands of deaths and forced displacement of local population.	The crimes will be prosecuted on the basis of universal jurisdiction as provided for in Chapter 2, Section 3(6) of the Swedish Penal Code.	In 2018, Swedish government authorized the Prosecutor to continue investigations (procedural condition required for exercising extraterritorial jurisdiction). In November 2021, the Swedish public prosecutor formally charged the CEO of Lundin Energy, Alex Schneiter, and the chairman of the Board. Swedish Supreme Court confirmed its jurisdiction to hear the charges in November 2022 against Schneiter, a Swiss citizen. Ongoing.

No.	*Defendants, Year, Organizations/Complainants*	*Cause of Action*	*Legal Basis, Forum, and Charges/ Claims*	*Outcome/Current Status*
24.	**Mercedes Benz** 2004 (the United States) 1998 (Germany) By CELS, ECCHR, and German Institute of Human Rights On behalf of former workers and victims in Argentina	Allegations of complicity in crimes of the military dictatorship in Argentina (1976–1983). At least 20 Mercedes Benz workers were the victims of crimes against humanity. Of those, 15 remain missing to this day.	Germany: Criminal complaint against executives for assisting in torture and allowing murders of the workers. The United States: Federal lawsuit under ATS. Argentina: Criminal proceedings after amnesty was lifted.	Germany: Investigation was discontinued by the Prosecutor in Nuremberg for lack of sufficient evidence. The United States: In 2014, US Supreme Court decided the United States does not have jurisdiction. Argentina: Proceedings ongoing.
25.	**Nevsun Resources** 2014 By three Eritrean nationals	The Canadian company was alleged to be complicit in the use of forced labour by its local sub-contractor, Segen Construction (owned by Eritrea's ruling party), at the Bisha mine in Eritrea The plaintiffs alleged they were subjected to cruel, inhuman, and degrading treatment.	Civil claim in Canada, one of the first lawsuits in Canada where claims are based directly on violations of international law, for complicity in crimes under international law and forced labour.	In 2020, the Canadian Supreme Court rejected the defendant's appeal to dismiss. Later that year, the company settled the lawsuit with the plaintiffs.

No.	*Defendants, Year, Organizations/Complainants*	*Cause of Action*	*Legal Basis, Forum, and Charges/ Claims*	*Outcome/Current Status*
26.	**Nestlé and Cargill** 2005 By International Rights Advocates On behalf of six victims from Mali	Plaintiffs alleged that they had been trafficked from Mali as child slaves and forced to work in harvesting/ cultivating cocoa beans on farms in Cote d'Ivoire. Working included long hours without pay and being kept in locked rooms combined with physical abuse. Alleged aiding and abetment in torture, forced labour, and arbitrary detention	Federal lawsuit in the United States based on ATS and Torture Victim Protection for violation of rules of customary international law.	In 2021, the US Supreme Court decided the case in favour of corporations as the conduct in question did not rebut the presumption of extraterritoriality.
27.	**Nestlé** 2012 (Switzerland) 2015 (before ECtHR) By ECCHR On behalf of Sinaltrainal and Romero's widow, a Colombian national	In 2005, members of a paramilitary group in Valledupar (Colombia) abducted, tortured, and killed trade union leader, human rights activist, and former Nestlé Cicolac worker Luciano Romero. The assassination was preceded by many death threats in the context of a long-standing labour dispute between the Colombian Sinaltrainal union and the Nestlé subsidiary Cicolac. The complaint accused Nestlé managers of being in breach of their obligations by failing to prevent crimes of the Colombian paramilitary groups and failing to adequately protect trade unionists from these crimes.	Criminal complaint with the prosecutor of the Swiss canton of Zug against Nestlé executives and the company as such. ECtHR: Claimed violations of right to life and procedural right to an effective investigation.	Case transferred to Vaud, dismissed in May 2013. The case was declared inadmissible by the ECtHR.

No.	*Defendants, Year, Organizations/Complainants*	*Cause of Action*	*Legal Basis, Forum, and Charges/ Claims*	*Outcome/Current Status*
28.	**Nexa Technologies** 2017 By FIDH and LDH, Cairo Institute for Human Rights Studies	Nexa Technologies (previously Amesys) allegedly participated in repressive operations carried out by Egyptian authorities, through the sale of surveillance equipment. Alleged complicity in torture and enforced disappearance, as the company sold, in March 2014, 'a listening system at 10 million euros to fight – officially – against the Muslim Brotherhood', the Islamist opposition in Egypt.	Complaints as *partie civilie* under the French Criminal Code alleging complicity in torture and enforced disappearance.	Executives indicted in June 2021 by the investigating judges of the Paris Judicial Court.
29.	**Occidental Petroleum** April 2003 By Center for International Human Rights, Northwestern University, International Labour Rights Forum, etc. On behalf of residents of Santo Domingo, Colombia	In 1998, the Colombian Air Force (CAF), in an operation carried out against guerrilla groups, dropped a cluster bomb in the centre of the village of Santo Domingo, killing and injuring civilians and destroying homes and property. The village was near the Occidental Oil pipeline which had been a target of the guerrilla groups of the region. The complaint alleged that Occidental and Airscan (its security contractor) helped the CAF by providing key strategic information, as well as ground and air support to the CAF and were complicit in extrajudicial killings, torture, crimes against humanity, and war crimes.	In the United States, the corporation was sued for reparations under Alien Tort Statute; Torture Victim Protection Act 1991 for complicity in crimes against humanity and war crimes.	November 2014 (after Kiobel) the appeals court dismissed the case, finding that the case had insufficient ties to the United States. In 2015, the Supreme Court also declined to hear the victims' appeal to reinstate the lawsuit. In 2012, the IACtHR held in *Santo Domingo Massacre v. Colombia* that the attack was in violation of the right to life.

No.	*Defendants, Year, Organizations/Complainants*	*Cause of Action*	*Legal Basis, Forum, and Charges/ Claims*	*Outcome/Current Status*
30.	**Qosmos** 2012 By FIDH and LDH	Complainants argued that the French company, Qosmos, installed a large-scale electronic communication surveillance system for Assad's regime in Syria which was used to track, torture, and execute its opponents since 2011.	Criminal complaint as *partie civile* alleging complicity in torture and other violations under French Criminal Code.	In 2020, the case was dismissed for lack of evidence to establish a causal link between the surveillance equipment and the acts of torture and crimes against humanity perpetrated by the Syrian regime.
31.	**RWM Italia** (subsidiary of German arms manufacturer Rheinmetall) 2018 By Mwatana Organization for Human Rights, ECCHR, and Rete Italiana Pace e Disarmo	In October 2016, an airstrike by the Saudi-led military coalition struck the village of Deir Al-Hajari in Northwest Yemen. The airstrike killed a family of six, including a pregnant mother and her four children. Complaints allege that CEO of RWM Italia and officials of Italy's National Authority for the Export of Armament (UAMA) contributed to war crimes by selling at least parts of the deadly weapons used in the strike to Saudi Arabia or another member state of the Saudi-led military coalition.	Criminal complaint in Italy for complicity in war crimes taking place in Yemen through gross negligence under Italian Criminal Code. The NGOs also filed an Article 15 communication to the ICC detailing allegations of 26 such strikes also against Airbus Defence and Space, BAE Systems, Dassault Aviation, and Leonardo.	Judge for Preliminary Investigations in Rome dismissed the case and found that public officials had complied with the formal procedures of the arms export authorization process.

No.	*Defendants, Year, Organizations/Complainants*	*Cause of Action*	*Legal Basis, Forum, and Charges/ Claims*	*Outcome/Current Status*
32.	**SNCF** 2000, 2005, 2015 (the United States) 2001 (France) By Holocaust survivors and their descendants	During World War II, Société Nationale des Chemins de Fer Français (SNCF), the French national railroad company, transported 76,000 civilians to Nazi death camps. Holocaust survivors filed lawsuits against SNCF in the United States and France alleging that SNCF committed war crimes and crimes against humanity, by knowingly transporting French and other European civilians to Nazi death camps. At the time, the French company was a private company with the French Government as a shareholder.	Three different lawsuits in the United States seeking compensation. In France, a civil claim was filed before the Administrative Court of Toulouse, France.	The United States: The first two cases were dismissed. France: In 2007, the suit was dismissed but in 2014, the French Government agreed to compensate Holocaust victims for SNCF's role in transporting victims to Nazi camps.
33.	**Talisman Energy** 2001 By Earth Rights International and others	Complaints alleged that the Canadian oil and gas producer, Talisman, was complicit in violations committed by the government of Sudan against non-Muslim Sudanese living in the area of Talisman's oil concession in southern Sudan and that these abuses amounted to war crimes, crimes against humanity, and genocide.	Federal lawsuit in the US courts under ATS for massive civilian displacement, extrajudicial killings, torture, rape, and the burning of villages, churches, and crops.	Dismissed in 2009 on the grounds of insufficient evidence to prove that the company intended its acts of assistance to contribute to international crimes.

No.	*Defendants, Year, Organizations/Complainants*	*Cause of Action*	*Legal Basis, Forum, and Charges/ Claims*	*Outcome/Current Status*
34.	**Titan Corporation (L-3, Engility)** 2004 and 2008 By CCR On behalf of 250 Iraqi detainees and later 72 Iraqi civilian detainees	Titan is a private military contractor hired by the United States during the Iraq war. Complaint alleged participation in a torture conspiracy, along with US government personnel, that led to rape and other acts of torture, assault, and killing of Iraqi detainees.	Two separate federal lawsuits were filed in the United States under ATS for torture and other serious violations of international law seeking compensation and punitive damages. One also attributed responsibility to Adel Nakhla, a former employee, as a co-conspirator for his role in instigating, directing, and participating in torture and other abusive conduct.	Case dismissed in 2009 by the Court of Appeals on political question doctrine. In 2011, the US SC denied the Plaintiff's petition for certiorari, thus closing the case. In Nakhla, an out of court confidential settlement was reached in 2012.
35.	**Unocal** 2002 By CCR and others On behalf of residents of southern Burma	UNOCAL, a US oil and gas corporation, was alleged to have supported the Myanmar military's human rights abuses against the local villagers in Myanmar during the construction of an oil pipeline in Myanmar.	Federal lawsuit before US district court under ATS for corporate complicity in forced labour, rape, torture, and murder by the military.	District Court dismissed the claims in summary judgment. In 2002, the Appeals Court reversed the judgment – violations needn't occur through state action. In 2005, Unocal offered to pay compensation.

No.	*Defendants, Year, Organizations/Complainants*	*Cause of Action*	*Legal Basis, Forum, and Charges/ Claims*	*Outcome/Current Status*
36.	**Utimaco** 2018 By ECCHR On behalf of victims from Syria, living in Germany	According to the complainants, high-ranking employees from Syrian Telecom and members of the military intelligence service passed secretly collected information to repressive Syrian regime. The regime apparatus used the information to carry out intimidation, abuse, torture, and killings of human rights activists and dissidents. The employees relied on software from German firm Utimaco.	A criminal complaint to the German Federal Public Prosecutor (Generalbundesanwalt, GBA) in Karlsruhe against high-ranking employees of the Syrian military intelligence service, Syrian Telecom as well as Utimaco. The crimes alleged: aiding and abetting crimes against humanity and war crimes.	The Federal Public Prosecutor did not take up investigations against Utimaco but added the information from the criminal complaint to the structural investigation underway, on the basis of the German Code of Crimes under International Law, into crimes committed in Syria.
37.	**Volkswagen** 2015 By Rose Cardoso (lawyer) On behalf of former employees	Allegedly, the German company collaborated with the military dictatorship that governed Brazil from 1964 to 1985, and some of its former employees were blacklisted and tortured.	Civil lawsuit seeking compensation in Brazil.	Out of court settlement (around 5 million pounds in compensation) in September 2020.
38.	**Total** 2002 By four Burmese refugees in Belgium	In the course of the construction and operation of the Yadana Gas Pipeline in Myanmar, of which Total owns the largest stake, the company contributed to military repression directed at civilians. The complaint was filed against TotalFinaElf (now Total), Thierry Desmarest (chairman of Total), and Hervé Madeo (the former director of Total's Myanmar operations).	Universal jurisdiction case in Belgium alleging complicity in crimes against humanity by providing moral and financial support to the Myanmar military government	The case was dropped in 2005, after the domestic provisions allowing universal jurisdiction were amended.

Index